The British Labour Party

The British Labour Party
A Short History

Carl F. Brand

Stanford University Press, Stanford, California   1964

Preface

This book was designed for the general reader as a short narrative history of the British Labour party, but one that would also show some results of research. To keep it within these limits has necessitated condensation, with all the attendant problems of generalization and simplification. The story of the party's origin and early years, so well treated in a number of recent studies mentioned in the Bibliographical Note, may appear slighted as compared with the fuller account of the years since the War of 1914, when Labour became a major party. Emphasis is naturally upon policies and programs accepted by the majority and the leadership, but attention is given to minority views as well. In the interest of brevity extensive quotation and elaborate documentation are avoided, but sufficient citations are given to show the path that has been followed, to indicate the chief primary sources and secondary materials used, and to provide some guidance for further study.

Some of the material has been utilized before in the author's *British Labour's Rise to Power: Eight Studies* (Stanford, 1941), and in a number of articles published in the *American Historical Review,* the *Journal of Modern History,* the *Pacific Historical Review,* and the *South Atlantic Quarterly*. The generosity of the periodicals in granting permission to use this material is gratefully acknowledged. I would also like to acknowledge the work of a number of graduate students; it has been a pleasure to delve with them into the collection of British labor materials assembled in the Hoover Institution on War, Revolution, and Peace at Stanford University. Grateful thanks are also extended to the willing and helpful staff of the Hoover Institution.

C. F. B.

Stanford University
May 19, 1964

Contents

The British Labour Party

1. The Rise of Political Labour

In recent British elections certain regions have shown consistent loyalty to the Labour party. The mining and industrial areas of South
Wales, the Midlands, south Lancashire, the West Riding of Yorkshire and a strip south to Nottingham and Derby, Durham and Tyneside, and central Scotland—along with working-class London and the
lower Thames—have returned a majority of Labour M.P.'s. By contrast, rural England and Scotland, the well-to-do suburbs, and the
fashionable seaside resorts have been as faithfully Conservative. The
correlation between political affiliation and economic interest is
marked. Yet it is not absolute. No social class votes as a unit. Labour
has supporters in Conservative-dominated areas and among the well-
to-do, just as Conservatives have supporters in Labour strongholds.
The trade unions are Labour bulwarks, but about three-eighths of
their members contract out of the political levy which is its main
source of income, and about one-fourth apparently vote Conservative
or Liberal.

The Labour party does not seek to divide the country along sectional or class lines. Its objective is the classless society, and its methods are those of peaceful parliamentary democracy. Hugh Gaitskell,
then its leader, said at its 1961 annual conference that he would
build the classless society "not by class war but by a party drawn from
all classes, as ours is."[1] Such words point to a fundamental difference of outlook between most Labourites and the Marxists. The Labour party is a party of change, but it is deeply concerned with the
preservation of what is good; it is idealistic in its approach to both
domestic and foreign affairs, but it is eminently practical and pragmatic in its methods; it stresses internationalism without being anti-

national; it is a party of the middle way in spite of an extremist wing; it is socialist, but it does not forget the individual.

But the significance of those election returns cannot be overlooked, and the large solid patches of Labour's red on an election map call for explanation. As well-defined areas they are a century older than the Labour party because they resulted from the Industrial Revolution, during which miners' villages spread over once green valleys and great factory towns arose with their squalid slums. There were gains: it was better for the operative to work and sleep in different rooms. The new towns, however, were ugly, crowded, filthy, and demoralizing. The conditions of life and labor there left memories that long influenced the working-class outlook, even after a century of piecemeal reform.

Social legislation ameliorated the hard lot of the masses. An aroused national conscience led to factory acts that cut working hours and struck at some of the most obvious abuses. Reform was accomplished in spite of bitter opposition from vested interests that said it should not be done, some dismal economic theory that said it could not be done, and a quietism that preached the virtue of contentment with things as they were in this world and of hope of reward in the next. Nevertheless, the lot of the working class was made much happier when reformers began to use the state as their agency. In the latter half of the nineteenth century real wages doubled. Political gains were registered, too, when in 1867 and in 1884 property qualifications for voting were lowered to the point where five-sixths of the adult males were enfranchised; the remainder were admitted to the suffrage in 1918 and women in 1918 and 1927.

The working class itself contributed much to the solution of its problems. An age that applauded thrift and self-help blessed its efforts to found social clubs, friendly societies, building societies, and libraries. In 1844 a little group of workingmen in Rochdale, Lancashire, founded the cooperative society from which the modern movement sprang; it now has 13,000,000 members enrolled in Britain alone. The workers created the trade-union movement, now so great and powerful.

The legalization of unions in 1824 was followed by a time of trial during which an effort at one big all-inclusive union collapsed miserably in 1834 in the face of employer and government hostility. A turning point came in 1850, when the engineers solved the problem of organization by federalism, whereby central direction of policy was combined with autonomy in branch affairs. In 1859 the formation of trades councils began, which enabled local unions to cooperate. National organization followed with the establishment of the Trades Union Congress (T.U.C.), which in 1868 and thereafter provided an annual parliament for the whole movement. The number of affiliated trade unionists rose from 125,000 in 1868 to about 8,300,000 in 1960, and the importance of the T.U.C. in British affairs increased correspondingly.

Finally, the workers took an active interest in politics. Disappointed in the Great Reform Bill of 1832, which gave power to the middle classes but for themselves was more of a disfranchising measure, they began the prolonged and fruitless struggle for the People's Charter, which was designed to give Parliament a truly democratic basis. They had better success in the agitation of 1867, which gave the urban worker the vote. A few workingmen ventured to stand for the House of Commons; in 1874 two, both miners, were elected as Liberals. Yet whatever the portent of their presence, the workingmen of the seventies were still content to vote for men of the existing parties, especially Liberals, who were wealthy enough to perform this unpaid service. The very few workingmen elected as Liberals, known as Lib-Labs, were not regarded as the nucleus of a Labour party.

The last two decades of the century, however, witnessed a movement that at its end saw the formation of a Labour party. Thanks to the spread of education, the urban workers were now literate and thinking men. Some turned away from the Liberals and listened to reformers who complained that alongside wealth and luxury were slums and abject poverty, the extent of which was soon fully documented by Charles Booth's great pioneer survey of the *Life and Labour of the People of London* and Seebohm Rowntree's sociological study of York. Socialist thought revived and was now linked with political action, something foreign to the thought of Robert Owen, that pioneer of British socialism who ignored the possibility of utilizing the state as the agency to realize his aims.

Owen had been generally contemptuous of politics. He devoted his life and fortune to the formation of voluntary societies for production and exchange. It was these non-political Owenites who first used the word "socialism" to describe their ideal society. For a brief time in the thirties Owen attempted to refashion the new trade unions into the tool he sought; he hoped to transform them into national guilds to carry on production under a system of workers' control. His schemes failed, but it was Owenite workingmen who at Rochdale founded the consumers' cooperative movement.

For a few years after 1848 a Christian Socialist movement, in which F. D. Maurice and Charles Kingsley were prominent, preached social reform. In 1877 Stewart Headlam revived this tradition in the Guild of St. Matthew, and in 1889 Scott Holland did the same in the Christian Social Union, but both societies were very small. It was left to a well-to-do middle-class man, Henry Mayers Hyndman, to found the first socialist political party in Great Britain.

Hyndman, who became a socialist as a result of reading Karl Marx, was a businessman whose socialism never caused him to discard his top hat and frock coat. He wrote *England for All* (1881), for which he drew heavily upon Marx without giving him credit or mentioning him by name, something Marx never forgave. In this book Hyndman argued that since power was rooted in ownership, the private capitalist should be replaced by the state and the latter controlled by the proletariat. In 1881 he organized the Democratic Federation, an advanced radical body with a program covering a wide range of subjects from Ireland to labor. Soon the labor theme dominated. In 1884, to indicate an increased socialist emphasis, the name was changed to the Social Democratic Federation (S.D.F.), a title like those of the new continental socialist parties. In 1882 the word "nationalization" was first heard. Hyndman used it in connection with the land problem, which was much discussed after Henry George's visit to England. S.D.F. programs called for the collectivizing of the land, banks, and basic industries like railways, but soon the idea was extended to cover all the means of production, distribution, and exchange.

The Federation remained disappointingly small; for years its membership was in the hundreds, and by 1900 it had reached only ten thousand. It was mainly middle class. The radical workingmen's clubs refused to join, while a manifesto to the trade unions was so critical that it alienated them. Hyndman did win a valuable recruit in H. H. Champion, a former artillery officer, who became secretary to the Federation and the first editor of its weekly organ, *Justice*; later he disagreed with the autocratic Hyndman and was expelled.

Another associate was William Morris, author, artist, and craftsman, who like Carlyle and Ruskin found the physical and social landscapes of industrialism equally depressing. Morris accepted some aspects of Marxism, such as its theory of history and the class struggle, but had no interest in parliamentary action and statism. His writings, such as *News from Nowhere*, envisaged a society in which the state was replaced by small voluntary cooperative units where artist-craftsmen would revive the beauties of the pre-industrial age. Neither his views nor his personality was compatible with Hyndman's, so he and his followers withdrew to found their own Socialist League. It, too, was small, torn by dissension, and short-lived. When Morris died in 1896, it did not survive him.

None of the socialist organizations gained numerical strength. When in 1885 three S.D.F. men stood for Parliament, they received pathetic polls of 27, 32, and 598. Some S.D.F. demonstrations led to clashes with the police and unfavorable publicity. A number of later Labour leaders had their political apprenticeship in these groups, however, and their persistence kept the problem of poverty before the public. Charles Booth set out to refute their charge that a quarter of the working classes earned too little to provide a decent living, only to discover through his famous study of London life and labor that the proportion was actually one-third. Such works as Morris's *News from Nowhere* (1891) also reached a far wider audience than did the street-corner speakers.

The Fabian Society, founded in January 1884, had a greater and more lasting influence upon British thought and politics than did the S.D.F. This famous organization was the outgrowth of a small ethical society, the Fellowship of the New Life. Among founders or early members were G. B. Shaw, as yet little known, Hubert Bland, at first its most prominent member, Mrs. Annie Besant, already known as a radical agitator, Sydney Olivier and Sidney Webb, clerks at the colonial office, and, later, Beatrice Potter, whose marriage to Webb began a famous partnership. Although the Society at its period of greatest influence enrolled only about four thousand members, its intellectual activity and output were enormous. They wrote, lectured, and debated. The *Fabian Essays on Socialism* (1889) provided a basis for later British socialist thought.

Although in its early days some members such as Shaw were influenced by Marx, the Fabians owed more to Bentham, Mill, and other early Radicals. As constitutionalists they disbelieved in the necessity of revolution in Britain. Adapting Darwinian biology to politics, they thought in terms of evolution and continual adjustment. They did not advocate a separate political party, although on this point Hubert Bland dissented from his colleagues. Instead, the Fabians preached a policy of permeation; they would infiltrate, educate, and utilize any party or organization suitable for their purpose. Because of progress in national-welfare legislation and Joseph Chamberlain's municipal activity at Birmingham, they believed the process of socialization was already under way; peaceful pressure could accelerate it. They were confident that the growth of joint-stock corporations, managed by salaried officers, had created a situation in which the now function-less stockholders could be expropriated by the community with no more dislocation of industry than was caused by the daily transactions on the stock exchange.

The Fabians envisaged a society that was neither strictly egalitarian nor monotonously uniform. They would guarantee a necessary minimum to every member but provide extra reward for exceptional effort and talent. They would utilize all public authorities, each in its appropriate area. The nation should own the railways, mines, and harbors, as it already did the postal system, but it was local authorities, so close to the people, that particularly attracted the Fabians. Birmingham had shown how efficiently these authorities could manage their utilities; they might do equally well with small industries. Sidney Webb saw there an outlet for the competitive instinct; let communities enter into honorable and productive rivalry with one another for excellence in supplying drainage, water, lighting, housing, and medical services. They would thereby provide a salutary check against overcentralization and a super-state.

The Fabians did not forget the individual; in the new society there would be a place for private enterprise and ownership. In the *Essays* (1899), Graham Wallas wrote that since the pleasures chosen by the majority were by many not recognized as pleasures at all, private property and private industry should exist along with public property and public industry. Private homes and furniture might be economically wasteful but, if wanted, were necessary for personal independence and happiness. The Fabian policy report of 1896 stated the importance of individual enterprise in a socialist state:

The Fabian Society does not suggest that the State should monopolise industry as against private enterprise or individual initiative further than may be necessary to make the livelihood of the people and their access to the sources of production completely independent of both. The freedom of individuals to test the social value of new inventions; to initiate improved methods of production; to anticipate and lead public enterprise in catering for new social wants; to practice all arts, crafts, and professions independently; in short, to complete the social organization by adding the resources of private activity and judgment to those of public routine is, subject to the above conditions, as highly valued by the Fabian Society as Freedom of Speech, Freedom of the Press or any other article in the charter of popular liberties.[2]

Cooperative societies and trade unions, likewise, found places in the Fabian vision. Beatrice Potter's *Co-operative Movement in Great*

Britain (1891) was followed by the Webbs's *History of Trade Union-ism* (1894) and later by their *Industrial Democracy* (1898), all of which emphasized the possibilities of vocational organization. Within an all-embracing collectivism, accordingly, the Fabians envisaged opportunity for individual enterprise, a great diversity of organization, and a diffusion of power. These concepts, along with their constitutionalism, were passed on to the Labour party, while among socialists of many lands they stimulated a revision of Marxist ideas.

When the advocates of socialism failed to win wide popular support, some of their number urged a more broadly based political labor movement. In England H. H. Champion left the S.D.F. and in 1887 founded a monthly, *Common Sense,* to express his views. To reach the workingmen, most of them voters since the act of 1884, he would emphasize ordinary trade-union aims more than socialism; an independent labor party was his objective. In the Labour Electoral Committee, set up in 1886 by the T.U.C., he saw the means; if used to elect not Lib-Labs but independent labor men, it would put a labor party in the Commons. Champion persistently advocated such a party, but in practice was able to do no more than use the threat of it to force concessions from major party candidates.

It was a young Scottish miner who more than any other man diverted trade union discontent into independent political action. In the Mid-Lanark by-election of 1888 Keir Hardie, supported by the miners, sought the Liberal nomination, only to be turned down in favor of a well-to-do Londoner. Resentful at the Liberal rejection of a workingman and at the importation from the South, Hardie stood as an independent "Labour and Home Rule" candidate. Although supported by Champion and by Cunninghame Graham, a socialist Scottish laird, he lost by a wide margin. From the incident, however, some drew the lesson that if the older parties continued to be so inhospitable to able candidates from the working class, the latter would have to rely on its own efforts. Hardie and Graham proceeded immediately to organize the Scottish Labour party on the basis of a program of such practical reforms as the eight-hour day. Although socialists were prominent, it was a labor party without a definite socialist commitment.

The nineties appeared more favorable to the advocates of independent labor politics. Between 1885 and 1890 the trade unions affiliated with the T.U.C. experienced a revival that trebled their numbers to nearly 1,600,000. Even unskilled labor began to organize. London was amazed when the match girls and the gasworkers won strikes, but it was in the Great Dock Strike of 1889 that the dockers, led by Ben Tillett and John Burns, proved conclusively that even casual workers, if organized, could exert power. A great extension of organization followed among those hitherto considered incapable of it.

There was a spread of socialist thinking among the trade unionists, due in part to Champion's assistance during the strike. Burns and Tom Mann also were socialists. When in the same year a socialist congress met in Paris, British adherents participated in the foundation of the Second International. London was made aware of this new interest on the part of labor when on May Day, 1890, socialists and trade unionists joined in a popular demonstration on the scale of those earlier ones, impressive and still remembered, on behalf of the Reform Bills and the People's Charter.

Renewed labor and socialist activity appeared in the North of England. In Manchester Robert Blatchford, a former soldier who had become a journalist, turned to socialism when he was shocked by the sight of slum conditions, which he exposed in the *Sunday Chronicle*. In 1891 he founded the *Clarion,* a weekly journal with a vivacious style and popular appeal that contributed far more to the spread of the socialist gospel in England than the writings of Marx ever did. Clarion vans carried speakers and literature throughout the North, while Clarion cycling clubs contributed a sense of fellowship and solidarity to those in the movement.

In Bradford Joseph Burgess pioneered the idea of independent labor representation. Conditions were readied for him when the American tariff of 1890 brought distress to the Yorkshire woolen area. He organized the Bradford Labour Union with a policy of strictly independent political action; Fred Jowett soon became one of its leading spirits. In 1892 at Manchester Blatchford followed his example. Soon a number of local parties were in existence, but there was no central organization; so in the general election of 1892 labor candidates had mainly local support. Nevertheless, three were elected to the House of Commons: Hardie for South West Ham, John Burns for Battersea, and J. Havelock Wilson for Middlesbrough. Hardie chanced to arrive at his first session of the House of Commons clad in workmen's clothes and a deerstalker cap; it was widely interpreted as the symbol of a new militancy.

The need of a national organization with local branches everywhere was patent. It was pushed energetically by Joseph Burgess, who in the weekly *Workman's Times* had a good medium for his views. The outcome was a convention at Bradford, January 13–14, 1893, which was attended by about 120 delegates under the chairmanship of Keir Hardie. Old socialists like Dr. Edward Aveling, Blatchford, and Shaw were there, but noteworthy was the number of trade unionists, especially from the North and Scotland. The South was almost unrepresented. Some Fabians came, but the London S.D.F. stood aloof.

The choice of a name for the new organization symbolized the problem of socialist–trade-union cooperation. A proposal to include the word "socialist" in the title was rejected as a possible handicap; they would have to appeal to an electorate, especially the trade unionists, that was little concerned with theory but approachable on a basis of practical reform. The new organization, accordingly, was christened the Independent Labour Party (I.L.P.). In the program the socialists secured the inclusion of their ultimate objective of the collective ownership of the means of production, distribution, and exchange. For wider appeal there was a list of immediate aims including the eight-hour day and the abolition of overtime, piecework, and child labor; it called for a further extension of the suffrage, free and non-sectarian education, heavy taxation of unearned incomes, and public aid to the aged, infirm, widows, and orphans.

Some delegates wished to cut all bonds with other parties. Blatchford strongly backed a proposal that all I.L.P. members pledge themselves never to vote for a candidate of any other party, but it was defeated because it would disfranchise members in constituencies where the I.L.P. had no candidate. In opposition to Blatchford's view, Shaw maintained that Fabian permeation might usefully complement the work of the new party; he himself had taken the trouble to get on the executive of a Liberal Association and intended to stay in order to push labor interests there. Fabians therefore remained in the I.L.P. as individuals and many served on its council, but the Society continued its separate existence. The S.D.F. remained aloof because of the rejection of the socialist name and competed for members with the new party.[3]

The I.L.P. was energetic. Keir Hardie spoke in the Commons, especially in behalf of the unemployed, and reached his public through his weekly *Labour Leader*. Enthusiastic speakers carried the message throughout the land. Among the new recruits were James Ramsay MacDonald and Philip Snowden. Women were attracted to the cause; the "new women" of the nineties, still denied the vote, could find an outlet in party work. New branches were formed, especially in the North and in Scotland, but only a slight impression was made in London and none at all in the rural areas. In the election of 1895 a few of the 28 candidates polled respectable totals, but there were no victories; even Keir Hardie lost his seat, and Burns and Havelock Wilson had become Lib-Labs.

After 1895 the I.L.P. outlook was discouraging. It had no M.P., and in the country there was decline instead of growth. A number of branches ceased to exist. In the effort to escape from the stagnation, some suggested fusion with the socialist societies; it became a perennial topic of debate, but Hardie looked to the trade unions, which, now that the economic crisis of the early nineties was passing, were enjoying a steady growth. If they could be won for independent political action, he would have the material for a powerful alliance of labor forces.

The efforts of the political activists to bore from within were hampered by a T.U.C. rule adopted in 1894 which excluded as delegates all who were neither working trade unionists nor trade-union officials. It affected Hardie himself. There were, however, factors making for change. Some trades, such as the printers, engineers, and boot and shoe makers, sensed the threat from technical change and mechanization. The development of employers' federations roused fears of giant combines and trusts with policies hostile to labor. New court decisions apparently threatened the right to strike and picket. In 1898 the alarmed T.U.C. registered a change of outlook by accepting a resolution recommending that trade unionists support the working-class socialist parties.

By this time Hardie had clearly in mind his ideal of a grand labor alliance, which he announced in the *Labour Leader*. He believed that the trade unions, the socialist societies, and the cooperators—the three forms of the working-class movement—should each sponsor their own candidates for Parliament, but accept a common program and jointly bear the expense of a campaign. He got the I.L.P. council to approach the T.U.C. and the Scottish T.U.C. with a view to securing this united action. The Scots were quickly won. In April 1899 the Scottish T.U.C. acted, and on January 6, 1900, a conference met at Edinburgh with delegates from trade unions, trades councils, the I.L.P., the S.D.F., and some cooperators. It accepted the idea of independent working-class representation.[4] The British T.U.C. of 1899 followed the Scottish example. It instructed its committee that "with a view to securing a better representation of the interests of labour in the House of Commons," it should invite the cooperative, socialist, trade-union, and other working-class organizations to join in convening a special conference "to devise ways and means for securing the return of an increased number of labour members to the next Parliament."[5] Some still objected to embroilment in politics or expressed doubts about its utility, but the resolution was carried by a vote of 546,000 to 434,000. It was a decisive moment in the history of British trade unionism.

The inclusive conference thus authorized met, barely noticed by the press, on February 27, 1900, in the Congregationalist Memorial Hall, Farringdon Street, London. There was no intentional religious association, but in view of the long connection between religious nonconformity and political radicalism in Great Britain it was appropriate. There were 129 delegates; 7 came from the I.L.P., and the names of Hardie, Snowden, Burgess, Jowett, and MacDonald indicated their prominence; 4 were from the S.D.F. and one from the Fabian Society; the others came from 65 trade unions, which meant that less than half the workers affiliated with the T.U.C. were represented. Among them were Ben Tillett, J. R. Clynes, James Sexton, and G. J. Wardle, all of whom were members of the I.L.P. as well, which enhanced the importance of that body. While the trade-union delegates spoke for nearly half a million constituents, the other organizations had but a few thousand each.

Moderates set the tone and searched for the broadest possible agreement. At the outset some urged the narrow concept of a strictly working-class body, but it was opposed, especially by John Burns, who upon this occasion made his scornful remark about his weariness of hearing of "working-class boots, working-class trains, working-class houses, and working-class margarine."[6] It was finally agreed with only three dissentients that labor views could be voiced by sympathetic members of any class. An S.D.F. effort to link the conference with socialism and the class war failed. Hardie's resolution then carried; it proposed a labor group in Parliament, independent of other parties yet ready to cooperate in a common cause. It called for

establishing a distinct Labour Group in Parliament, who shall have their own whips and agree upon their policy, which must embrace a readiness to cooperate with any party which for the time being may be engaged in promoting legislation in the direct interest of labour, and be equally ready to associate themselves with any party in opposing measures having an opposite tendency.[7]

The conference set up an executive committee, the Labour Representation Committee (L.R.C.), consisting of two members each from the I.L.P. and S.D.F., one from the Fabian Society, and seven trade unionists. The last, accordingly, had a majority, but should two of them also be members of the other societies, a socialist majority might be had. For the post of secretary, important but unpaid, James Ramsay MacDonald was chosen; his marriage to a grandniece of Lord Kelvin made it financially possible for him to accept. Labour candidates would be financed by the sponsoring unions or societies. A successful parliamentary group with its own whips would be a new party regardless of whether it was given the name.

Accordingly, the closing year of the nineteenth century witnessed the conclusion of an alliance between socialism and trade unionism. It was done in characteristically British fashion; with scant regard for theory, the best tool possible under the circumstances was fashioned. In spite of the fact that for two decades the drive had come from the socialists, they did not insist upon their name or program. It was a triumph to win the T.U.C. to the idea of independent action; it meant that the unions had come a long way from the "no politics" of the mid-century. Unintentionally, the Liberals helped in the process; although the Newcastle program of 1891 made concessions to working-class needs, their persistent rejection of able working-class candidates turned the latter toward the socialists and prepared the way for their own decline. Yet the trade unionists who accepted the L.R.C. were in the main at heart still Liberal, not socialist, and hostile to the class war of the S.D.F. The Fabians, still advocates of permeation, were dubious of the work of the conference, although I.L.P. members who had imbibed their views were active in it. What was achieved in 1900 was the maximum possible, the federal alliance for an immediate objective. It might become something more. The *Clarion* staff member who attended put it cautiously: "At last there is a United Labour Party, or perhaps it would be safer to say, a little cloud no bigger than a man's hand which may grow into a United Labour Party."[8]

2. A Labour Party in Parliament

At the Memorial Hall meeting the advocates of independent labor politics finally effected the desired union of organized trades and socialist societies, but the immediate results were disappointing. The period between the conference of 1900 and the outbreak of war in 1914 was one of uncertainty and discouragement, but it did see Labour established as a third party in the House of Commons, where it finally registered sufficient success to prove the value of political action.

The L.R.C., with Frederick Rogers of the Vellum Book Binders as chairman and MacDonald as secretary, ran on the proverbial shoestring. Its first headquarters consisted of one room in MacDonald's flat at 3 Lincoln's Inn Fields. In the hope of enticing funds from the trade unions the affiliation fee was placed at the low figure of ten shillings per thousand members, and a circular in March 1900 invited them to join. They came in slowly, first the Steel Smelters, the Railway Servants, and the Gasworkers, but those unions that had to hold a members' ballot delayed. Not all had affirmative results. The Lancashire and Cheshire Miners Confederation, the only coal miners' organization represented at the conference, now decided against affiliation, and the Engineers at first did likewise.

The small proportion of members who troubled to vote revealed the general apathy; in the case of the Engineers it was but slightly over four per cent and in that of the Boot and Shoe Operatives about six and one-half. The votes exemplified the rank-and-file inertia against which trade-union activists have often struggled. Accordingly, the first anniversary of the Memorial Hall conference saw only 350,-000 unionists affiliated, which was less than the number represented there. Trades councils were slow to come in, too, until the affiliation fee was reduced from five pounds to one.[1]

When some cooperative societies in Scotland and a few south of the border showed signs of interest, Rogers went to Cardiff to put the case before the annual meeting of the great Cooperative Union. He found resistance unexpectedly strong. George Jacob Holyoake, though an old Chartist, opposed entry into politics. Their organization was neutral, he said, and this proposal was too explosive and revolutionary to be placed before an assembly pledged by its constitution to neutrality in politics and religion. The cooperators of 1900, still in the frame of mind of those earlier trade unionists who said "no politics," rejected the invitation to join the labor alliance.

The general situation was highly unfavorable to the L.R.C. It was launched at the height of the Boer War, so with British troops in action popular attention was centered on South Africa. Feeling ran high during the initial defeats and then during the march to Pretoria. The Memorial Hall meeting could not compete for space in the press with the news of General Cronje's surrender.

Some individual socialists, like ex-soldier Blatchford of the *Clarion*, supported the war, but some constituent elements of the L.R.C. were so openly antiwar that they became highly unpopular. The I.L.P. and the S.D.F. overlooked any oppressive features of Boer rule or obstinacy on the part of President Kruger, and interpreted the war as a case of capitalist exploitation backed by aggressive imperialism and emotional jingoism. They joined with a section of the Liberals in open opposition and in efforts to bring it to an end.

Feeling in the T.U.C. was divided, but an antiwar resolution passed by a small majority. The Fabians disagreed among themselves. Shaw and the Webbs, to whom it was not essentially a socialist problem, would have preferred that the Society take no stand on it. Personally they thought it would be an economic gain to those concerned and to the world at large if small backward agricultural states could be brought into larger units. Olivier, Wallas, and MacDonald, however, stood with the I.L.P. in outright denunciation. Their insistence upon an official statement led to a postal poll of the membership. When the majority opposed such a pronouncement by a vote of 259 to 217, fifteen members, including MacDonald, resigned.

However, the Society did attempt a constructive statement on imperialism; the burden of Shaw's *Fabianism and the Empire* (1900) was that such territory should be governed in the interest of the world at large. It was the antiwar attitude of the L.R.C. majority, however, that attracted attention. The championing of an unpopular cause and the support of peace moves in wartime proved a serious handicap to the effort to win the electorate to the new and struggling L.R.C.[2]

Under these circumstances, L.R.C. candidates made a poor showing in the "khaki" election of October 1900. The Unionist government called the election shortly after the occupation of Pretoria and the apparently successful conclusion of the war. The L.R.C. entered fifteen candidates, of whom eight were sponsored by the I.L.P., four by trade unions, one by the S.D.F., one jointly by the I.L.P. and S.D.F., while one, though mistakenly, assumed he had trades council support. The number of I.L.P. candidates indicated the activity of that small organization, which then affiliated 13,000 but actually had under 5,000 dues-paying members. True to the federal idea there was no program; each candidate stood for the principles of his own organization.

Thanks in part to the absence of Liberal opposition in eight instances, the fifteen candidates polled a total of 62,698 votes. Two were elected, Keir Hardie at Merthyr Tydfil and Richard Bell, general secretary of the Railway Servants, at Derby. Fred Jowett came within 42 votes of success in Bradford, while MacDonald in Leicester, Will Thorne in South West Ham, and George Lansbury in Bow and Bromley polled well. The presence in the Commons of two members, however, was not a success that fulfilled the hopes of the L.R.C. founders.[3]

The prospects of the L.R.C. improved unexpectedly as the result of a judicial decision in the famous Taff Vale Railway case. This case originated in a dispute in South Wales, where the railway employees felt aggrieved over low wages and lack of union recognition. A strike led to picketing, a right that had been endangered by a previous decision. The company brought suit and won a judgment which put in jeopardy the union's accumulated funds, including those for benefits; they could be taken to compensate shareholders for losses due to any tortious act committed in connection with a strike. If picketing, even peaceful, was illegal, the gains in the legislation of 1871 and 1875 were lost. The union appealed and secured a reversal, but when in July 1901 the company carried the case to the highest court, the House of Lords, the five law lords unanimously reaffirmed the first decision. The union was assessed £23,000 for damages and costs and, in addition, had to pay its own costs. Two weeks later in a boycotting case the court took the same position.

Meanwhile, employers were active; a National Free Labour Association and an Employers Parliamentary Council were formed. In the influential *Times* of London a series of articles placed the blame for Britain's trade difficulties upon union restrictions. In the face of defeat and hostility it seemed obvious to labor that it should organize in its own defense.[4]

Labor responded to the challenge. Although South Africa still held the center of interest, the working class was stirred sufficiently to give a considerable impetus to the L.R.C. On August 1, 1901, in the Commons, when Hardie asked if the government intended legislation to remedy the ill effects of the recent decision and to protect union funds, he was met with a flat negative. On the same day MacDonald circularized the unions on the necessity of a labor party in Parliament. Affiliations came in more rapidly, so that the number of workers represented increased from 383,773 in July 1900 to 847,315 in February 1903. A by-election at Clitheroe, Lancashire, returned David Shackleton unopposed to make a third L.R.C. representative in the Commons, though Shackleton was still a Liberal.

This success of 1902 was followed the next year in by-elections at Woolwich and Barnard Castle, so that Will Crooks and Arthur Henderson joined the growing group. When the latter came over from Liberalism, the movement gained an organizing genius who was to leave a mark on the Labour party greater than that of any other man.

Outside the fold, however, were still about 1,100,000 trade unionists, and against the gains was registered one loss. In August 1901, the S.D.F. seceded when its demand for a socialist test on all L.R.C. candidates was rejected. The association had been an uneasy one, because the I.L.P. and trade-union leaders had no liking for the Marxism of the S.D.F. Class war, even as a means to socialism and the classless society, had no place in the minds of men who stressed the brotherhood of man. In 1905 MacDonald wrote, "Socialism marks the growth of society, not the uprising of a class."[5]

Most of these early leaders took their gospel from the Bible and their nonconformist churches. It would have been impossible for Arthur Henderson to serve as a Methodist lay preacher on Sundays and preach hatred during the week; he was but one of many active in the churches and temperance movement. To such men moral, social, and political reform were phases of one movement to improve the lot of all human beings.

In a House of Commons of 670 members, two or even five labor men could make no great impression. Owing to increasing state activity, the government was taking over a greater proportion of the House's time; it prepared the legislative program, and there was little opportunity for members' bills. Private members were in the main reduced to asking questions. The L.R.C. representatives, accordingly, utilized question time to ventilate the grievances of soldiers and workers. Hardie raised the question of the unemployed so often that he became known as "Member for the Unemployed." They spoke against the South African war. They urged school meals for children of the destitute. They sought unsuccessfully to secure action that would, in effect, nullify the Taff Vale decision. They opposed Joseph Chamberlain's proposed return to protection.[6]

Hardie hoped for good relations with the Lib-Labs with the aim of winning them to his own group, but, instead, lost his colleague Richard Bell to the Liberals, whose views he had never really abandoned, and Bell's supporting Derby Trades Council withdrew from the L.R.C. Henderson, Shackleton, and Crooks often took courses very similar to that of the Lib-Labs, and even appeared on a free-trade platform in support of a Liberal. Hardie found himself so isolated that it was difficult to maintain the ideal of independence. Both he and MacDonald considered the possibilities of alliance with other radical and progressive elements. They were even ready to make a deal with the Liberals for the sake of mutual electoral advantage.

The practical matter at hand was preparation for the next general election. In February 1903, the Newcastle conference of the L.R.C. resolved that each affiliated society should pay annually into a general fund a sum equal to a penny a member. It would result in a considerable war chest with which the L.R.C. could fight a number of constituencies and pay £200 a year to enable a successful candidate to accept the unsalaried position of an M.P. The creation of this fund was a most important step. It greatly strengthened the L.R.C., because candidates looked more to the L.R.C. than to a local organization, and a Labour member would represent the entire movement rather than a particular trade or society. It also provided the wherewithal to bargain with the Liberals.

These developments in the L.R.C. did not go unnoticed at Liberal headquarters. Although local associations had been loath to accept working-class nominees, the leadership sympathized with the idea of more working-class men in the Commons. Campbell-Bannerman and Herbert Gladstone, Liberal chief whip, both favored it. Moreover, the Liberals were feeling financially poor, because the secession of the Liberal Unionists following Joseph Chamberlain had carried so many of the wealthy over to the Conservative side. The new L.R.C. fund excited interest; should a certain number of seats be left to the L.R.C., the Liberals could make better use of their own resources elsewhere and, further, secure labor support in the far larger number of constituencies that the L.R.C. could not contest. It would bring the desired working-class element into the Commons. An agreement might halt the Conservative (officially Unionist) inroads into the large towns.

On the L.R.C. side Hardie and MacDonald were friendly to a deal. Both possessed a good measure of opportunism, but an open alliance would have horrified their followers, who were now steeped in distrust of Lib-Labs. The negotiations, extending over about a year, were accordingly carried on in secret. MacDonald, later a critic of "secret diplomacy" in the international sphere, showed himself opportunistic and astute in the exchanges with Gladstone, while at the same time both he and Hardie untruthfully denied the existence of any pact. He knew, however, what a fighting fund of possibly £100,-000 would mean to the Liberals, and therefore proposed a list of fourteen single-member constituencies in which the Liberals would abstain and a list of eleven two-member seats in which one would be left to the L.R.C.

Gladstone approved the scheme and easily won Campbell-Bannerman's support. The Liberals were so anxious to conclude the bargain that their emissary sought MacDonald while the latter was still ill in a Leicester hospital. There the informal pact was confirmed; in the next election the L.R.C. would receive a free hand in certain constituencies.

A secret memorandum of Gladstone written March 13, 1903, set down after this consultation with MacDonald, listed 23 seats that could be turned over to the L.R.C. without difficulty, 5 that were adjustable, 5 that might be difficult, and 6 available alternatives. The agreement covered England and Wales alone, because the Scottish Liberal Association was an independent body. It was a bargain that brought the Liberal party a short-term gain but long-term loss; it assured victory in the coming election, but it also furthered the rise of a rival that ultimately replaced it as a major party.[7]

The pact was observed by its members. Because of its secrecy, MacDonald sometimes found it difficult to impose upon energetic local parties. In Leeds West it required all his finesse to persuade enthusiasts not to oppose Gladstone. Gladstone had his problems, too. In Lancashire, where the Liberals were weak, L.R.C. candidates had a free field, but in Scotland and Yorkshire, where they were strong, the local associations were unwilling to yield. Generally, however, the pact operated successfully. Of the 50 L.R.C. candidates, 32 had straight fights, or in two-member constituencies had only one Liberal opponent. Where there was no L.R.C. candidate, its adherents were free to support the Liberal or Lib-Lab candidate.

Meanwhile, the L.R.C. leaders strengthened their organization and prepared their program. In 1904 the contribution to the parliamentary fund, hitherto voluntary, was made compulsory. The L.R.C. began to extend to constituencies where no affiliated trade council existed, so that by 1906 there were 76 local parties; a national organization was in the making. These constituency parties had some success in local government elections. At the same time there were steps toward a program. Each constituent element of the L.R.C. had its own socialist or trade-union objectives, but in order to develop a common policy on current issues, MacDonald arranged conferences of parliamentary candidates.

Accordingly, for the election of January 1906 the L.R.C. had ready a manifesto that ignored socialist theory and dealt with practical problems. It demanded a greater place in Parliament for labor; it dealt with the problems of housing, underfed school children, and unemployment; it denounced the recent war in South Africa and the use of Chinese labor in the Transvaal mines; it labeled protection a red herring.

In the campaign the social issues were featured less than Taff Vale and free trade. The Education Act of 1902, surprisingly omitted from the manifesto of a party whose membership was so heavily nonconformist and resentful of clauses favoring the Church of England, was also featured. Emotion disproportionate to the importance of the problem was lavished on "Chinese slavery," the term applied to the use of indentured coolies in the Rand mines. To British humanitarians it was a moral issue; to Lord Milner, high commissioner in South Africa, it appeared the only ready means of increasing the output of gold necessary to speed the recovery of the war-stricken land.

The election gave the Liberals a resounding victory, while their Unionist, or Conservative, opponents were reduced to less than a quarter of the House of Commons. Significant for the future was the return of 29 L.R.C. members and a poll of 323,195 votes. In addition, 13 miners and 11 other Lib-Labs were elected, but one of the miners announced in advance that, if successful, he would join the L.R.C. group. The miners, alarmed by wage reductions and by legal decisions as costly to them as Taff Vale had been for the railwaymen, had been jolted out of their attachment to the Liberals, and, not yet ready for the L.R.C., had put up candidates of their own. Altogether there were 53 labor men in the House.

The area of greatest L.R.C. success was Lancashire, where twelve out of thirteen candidates were victorious; among them were J. R.

Clynes at Manchester and Philip Snowden at Blackburn. Yorkshire returned three; Fred Jowett won on a minority vote over two opponents at Bradford. The London area elected only two, because London workers were still Liberal. Scotland and Wales likewise remained Liberal strongholds; from Scotland only two L.R.C. men were returned, and from Wales only Hardie at Merthyr. MacDonald was elected at Leicester. Henderson and Crooks kept their seats. No socialist sponsored independently of the L.R.C. was elected; seven S.D.F. candidates all met defeat. Eighteen of the new L.R.C. group were I.L.P. members. In Hardie, MacDonald, and Snowden, labor would have able spokesmen in the Commons.[8]

In the House of Commons the L.R.C. group chose Hardie as its chairman and organized with its own officials and whips. It took the name of Labour party; at last the labor alliance had become formally a political party. The nucleus of 29 was enlarged when in 1909 the affiliation of the Miners Federation added their members and two by-elections resulted in Labour victories. Although socialists were influential in the party, it was still not socialist but opportunist. It was united in agreement upon certain immediate objectives, which were determined at the opening of each session of Parliament by a joint meeting of the party's national executive and M.P.'s. It supported the Liberal government wherever possible, but did not hesitate to oppose it when necessary. The parliamentary Labour party, though dependent upon the Liberals for the legislation it desired, emphasized its independence by sitting on the Opposition benches.[9]

During the first year of the Campbell-Bannerman government the new party won some striking successes. Its foremost objective was to nullify the effects of the Taff Vale decision. When a Labour member had good luck in the ballot for private members' bills, the party promptly introduced a measure to legalize peaceful picketing, limit liability to violations of the criminal code, and protect union funds. The government introduced its own measure, similar except weaker on the protection of funds, but when Liberal backbenchers, committed by election pledges, arose to support the Labour bill, the government yielded. In spite of Conservative gibes, it modified its own measure so that, when passed, it was essentially the Labour bill. The Trades Disputes Act of 1906, accordingly, was widely heralded as a triumph for the new party and an example of the value to labor of political action.[10]

There were other successes. The party introduced a bill, the Education (Provision of Meals) Act, to provide meals for needy school children, large numbers of whom were so ill-fed that they were unable to do their work properly. Jowett, who had pioneered this idea at Bradford, now had the satisfaction of speaking for it in the Commons. As finally passed, the bill was permissive only and in other respects disappointing, but the acceptance of the principle was welcomed. The attendant publicity led to a Medical Board circular permitting local authorities to arrange for medical inspection and treatment of school children. Labour also influenced the form of the Workmen's Compensation Act. Whereas the government bill provided a low scale of payments, excluded certain classes of workers, and included an initial seven-day period of nonpayment, Labour amendments resulted in a bill more satisfactory on these points. A Labour bill to forbid the importation of foreign workmen under contract to replace striking British workers passed the Commons but was thrown out by the Lords. Otherwise, the first year was one of achievement and satisfaction for Labour.[11]

The following years were less fruitful as Liberal zeal faded, controversies arose, and the struggle with the Lords loomed ahead. Labour failed in its attempts to improve the act for school meals, to establish the eight-hour day in the coal mines, and to deal with sweated industries. In 1908 interest centered on the Old Age Pensions Act. It dealt with another prime objective of Labour, but it criticized the age limit set at 70 instead of 65, the limitation upon income, and the disqualification of recipients of poor relief. Labour could secure only the elimination of this last feature. It had no success at all with MacDonald's Unemployed Workmen Bill, a "Right to Work" bill intended to secure work for every able-bodied man who desired it.

The party accepted the labor exchanges authorized in 1909, which were agencies to register the unemployed and job possibilities in the hope of bringing the two together, but criticized them as not dealing with the fundamental cause of the problem. Likewise it welcomed the Trades Board Act, the answer to prolonged agitation, which set up boards to fix minimum wages in four sweated industries; again it was acceptance of the principle that seemed important. The party's positive contribution in this period, however, was less than in the first year of the Liberal government, and its disappointments were many.[12]

Meanwhile, intense socialist propaganda was being carried on by dedicated enthusiasts who devoted their weekends and holidays to the cause. Recruits flowed into the socialist societies. Although Blatchford, fearful of compromising his principles, stood aside from the

L.R.C., the Clarion Fellowship, Vanners, Scouts, Cycling Clubs, and Glee Clubs deepened the fraternal aspect of the movement. Hardie's *Labour Leader,* however, was surpassing the *Clarion* as its outstanding organ, while other influential I.L.P. weeklies were the *Forward* at Glasgow and those entitled *Pioneer* at Bradford, Leicester, and Merthyr.

The plays and novels of two Fabians, G. B. Shaw and H. G. Wells, were read everywhere. The social-security proposals in the Minority Report on the Poor Laws, the work of Beatrice and Sidney Webb, made a deep impression. Women were playing an increasingly important part; in 1906 the Women's Labour League was formed. In 1908 the party joined the International Socialist Bureau, with which the I.L.P. and the S.D.F. were already separately affiliated, although except for the latter the British bodies had scant interest in the International's doctrine of the class war.[13] The S.D.F. continued to be active outside the Labour party, although through trades councils or trade unions individual members found their way into its annual conferences. The S.D.F., meanwhile, had suffered dissension and splits out of which came the even smaller Socialist Labour party in Scotland and the Socialist party of Great Britain, both Marxian opponents of moderation.

Many socialists, especially after the glow of 1906 began to pale, became fearful of prolonged association with the Liberals. Independence could be compromised away. Leaders might be lost to the movement as were Thomas Burt, the miner elected to Parliament in 1874, who now sat on the Liberal benches, and John Burns, who was now in the Liberal Cabinet. MacDonald, some thought, was steering the party off course. Particularly in the I.L.P. there arose a demand for a more socialist policy, which in 1907 flared up in the candidacy of Victor Grayson in Colne Valley, an old Liberal stronghold. When the I.L.P.'s national council refused to sponsor this youthful rebel, the local branch adopted him; as a "Socialist Labour" candidate he won over both Conservative and Liberal opposition.

This startling success made him the central figure of dissent until his defeat in 1910. The discontented sought to carry the I.L.P. out of the Labour party, but in its conference of 1909 they lost overwhelmingly by 378 to 8 votes. The latter figure was not a true index to the measure of dissatisfaction, however; a better one would be the minority of 136 against 244 on the issue of the I.L.P.'s right to put up its own candidates even though the Labour party disapproved.[14]

The Fabian Society likewise suffered stress and strain. H. G. Wells and S. G. Hobson led a movement to convert it into a political party in the belief that, in cooperation with the I.L.P., socialists could exert greater political influence. They failed, whereupon both resigned, leaving the "old gang," as Shaw, the Webbs, and their associates were called, in control, but as late as 1913 there were moves to disaffiliate the Society from the Labour party.[15] Other Fabians, weary of palliatives, began to question both the value of political action and the old concept of the replacement of the capitalist by the state. Hobson and G. D. H. Cole wrote for the *New Age,* founded in 1907 and edited by A. R. Orage, where they expounded the new doctrine of guild socialism. The guild socialists proposed to compromise the interests of consumers, which they assumed the state to represent, with those of producers, to be organized by industries into democratic national guilds; ownership of industrial assets would be vested in the state, which for actual operation would lease them to the appropriate guilds. Guildsmen thereby would abolish capitalism and the wages system, which would be replaced by industrial democracy, not by a bureaucratic super-state, which they feared would be the end product of a socialist regime.[16]

The Labour majority was concerned with domestic matters rather than foreign policy. Few understood the drift of the powers into two armed camps, although there was resentment at the cost of dreadnoughts that absorbed funds otherwise available for social reform. It was the socialists who displayed active interest in foreign affairs. To the I.L.P. it appeared that the Asquith-Grey-Haldane administration did no more than continue the Tory imperialist foreign policy. Jowett was one of the first to voice a suspicion of secret agreements in connection with the Anglo-French entente. To most Labourites Russia appeared the most objectionable power, autocratic and tyrannical. They raised funds for the victims of the 1905 uprising and urged the right of asylum for Russian political refugees. The I.L.P. denounced the Convention of 1907 as a sanctioning of infamous tyranny. The next year Hardie and MacDonald both criticized in strong language King Edward's visit to the Tsar. Blatchford and Hyndman, on the contrary, saw Germany as the great and immediate threat to Britain. In the *Clarion* Blatchford strove to rouse the country to the danger of a German invasion, while Hyndman urged the old S.D.F. solution of a citizen army to repel it.

Hardie and MacDonald sought peace; they would cooperate with their German friends in keeping it. MacDonald took part in goodwill tours of Germany, on one of which he addressed the Reichstag members at a luncheon gathering. He advocated cultural exchanges. During the Moroccan crisis of 1911, he helped organize peace demonstrations. From 1909 onward annual Labour party conferences dealt with resolutions on the questions of armaments, secret diplomacy, and the need for good Anglo-German relations. Most socialists had confidence that their International, with its millions of members in the continental countries, would in some way be able to exert pressure on their respective governments and keep them from plunging into war.[17]

On the national scene the year 1910 was noted for its two elections of January and December. The first was precipitated by the question of Lloyd George's budget containing taxation proposals then deemed revolutionary, and the second was over the issue of the House of Lords, which had rejected several measures on the Liberal program. On the eve of the first election the labor world was upset by a court decision in the Osborne case that had implications as serious as those of the Taff Vale verdict. To W. V. Osborne, a railwayman, it was a matter of principle that he, a Liberal, should not be compelled to contribute to a political fund for a party of which he was not an adherent. An appeal to the House of Lords was decided in his favor and against the union. The verdict, announced in the middle of the campaign, was a blow to the Labour party; at once it was deprived of the chief source of the political fund, without which fully half of its M.P.'s would be unable to serve. The action was widely ascribed to partisan prejudice on the part of the judges. Once more Labour had an immediate cause of first importance to fight for.[18]

In the campaigns it was evident that, at least in spirit, the Liberal-Labour pact still held. In the January election, in which Labour had 78 candidates, there was no Liberal opponent in 40 of the 65 single seats contested, while in 12 two-member constituencies only one Liberal stood. Where there was no Labour candidate, the party urged a vote for the Liberal. In the end the Liberals lost their abnormal majority of 1906 and came back with 275 seats to 273 Conservatives. Labour candidates polled 505,690 votes and won 40 seats, which meant a net loss of five, while the Irish party won 82. The support of these two parties was obviously necessary if the Liberals were to remain in office. The second campaign resembled the first, and the parties returned almost unchanged. Only 56 Labour candidates stood, so the total poll dropped to 370,802, but 42 M.P.'s were elected. Since the constitutional issue dominated the campaign, the voters were in no mood to turn to a third party.

Labour's position in the new House of Commons was symbolized by its presence neither on the government nor on the Opposition sides of the chamber but on the benches below the gangway. In order to keep out the Conservatives they were sometimes compelled to support the Liberals under circumstances hardly consistent with the theory of independence, which brought criticism from the socialist wing. The party was now led by MacDonald, the ablest of its parliamentarians. Hardie, troubled by ill health, was less in the foreground, but there were others, mostly I.L.P. men, who could hold their own in debate. Philip Snowden, although vitriolic in attack, could be logical and lucid, whereas MacDonald's chief fault was, on occasion, to be obscure. Arthur Henderson, who for two years had served as chairman of the parliamentary party, was happy to support MacDonald in the House while he devoted increasing attention to party organization. These four men were the dominant figures. The large contingent of Miners' representatives, now seventeen in number, furnished votes rather than leadership; then, as later, the Miners' Federation tended to make its safe seats in Parliament a reward for service to the union rather than a means for placing proven ability or promising youth in the Commons.

The party naturally supported the Parliament Act of 1911, which limited the veto power of the House of Lords. In the same year the government brought in a bill to provide a system of national insurance for health and unemployment; it would be compulsory on all employees between the ages of sixteen and seventy whose wages did not exceed £160, which would be about one-sixth of the total number employed; the scheme would be financed in part by weekly contributions from employer and employee and in part by the state; benefits would be at the rate of seven shillings a week. MacDonald and the parliamentary Labour majority accepted the measure and hoped to improve it, but most of their amendments failed. Nevertheless, they voted for it as a great gain in principle and because it would soften blows that otherwise might fall with crushing force on the individual. The more thoroughgoing socialists like Lansbury, Jowett, and Snowden, however, objected to the contributory principle; it placed the burden unduly, they claimed, on the victims of the social system, so they voted against the bill.

Outside Parliament the Fabians took the same position. The Webbs's *Prevention of Destitution* (1911) supported the view that such palliatives served only to postpone effective preventive measures. This opinion dominated the Labour party conference of 1912, where the delegates censured the parliamentary party for its compliance by a vote of 241 to 39. The National Insurance Act of 1911, nevertheless, provided a foundation for the later structure, so that MacDonald's confidence in step-by-step reform was vindicated.[19]

Legislation also largely, though not completely, nullified the Osborne decision. In 1911 a measure was passed to provide payment for members of the House of Commons, so that after three-quarters of a century another old Chartist demand was won and a man without independent means could afford to serve. The Trade Union Act of 1913 permitted unions, if a majority voted approval, to collect a special political fund to be kept separate from other funds, but it also allowed individual members to contract out of the obligation. This act did not leave the unions quite so free as before the Osborne decision, but it did enable them to finance political activity. It also necessitated a ballot of the membership on the question of continuing to maintain a political party. The vote was favorable by 605,433 to 363,-223, but the size of the minority indicated the number who were either discontented with the results of political action or still considered themselves Liberals or Conservatives.[20]

Although in retrospect the Liberal governments of Campbell-Bannerman and Asquith appear outstanding in accomplishment, at the time they seemed relatively barren to the working classes. The conditions described by Booth and Rowntree were scarcely touched. About a third of the city populations still lived crowded and destitute; a large proportion had wages so low that life was a struggle for bare necessities; they had no home they could call their own beyond the end of the week and no possessions except a few pieces of old furniture. Britain was wealthy, but to the many in poverty the pace of parliamentary action was appallingly slow. A Labour majority seemed remote. Fourteen by-elections between the second general election of 1910 and the outbreak of war in 1914 showed no gains, and, instead, three losses; the Labour party was apparently losing ground. MacDonald dallied with the possibilities of a Liberal alliance; during the constitutional crisis of 1910 he was even ready to accept a place in a possible coalition, but was prevented from considering it by Henderson. Fortunately for the future independence of the party, MacDonald, whose distinguished appearance and oratory made him such a good "front" man, deferred to the honesty, integrity, and sound judgment of the less colorful Henderson, who was content to remain the loyal second.

In the widespread disillusion with the meager results of political action, many workers turned to methods that promised more rapid returns. Some fell under new influences from abroad. From the United States came the ideas of Daniel De Leon and of the Industrial Workers of the World (I.W.W.); both believed that modern industrial organization rendered craft unions obsolete and necessitated union by industry, and the I.W.W. was also antipolitical and syndicalist. These views influenced the Socialist Labour party that in Scotland split from the S.D.F. French syndicalism found its chief exponent in Tom Mann, one of the most effective orators in the labor movement. The syndicalists, like the guild socialists, denounced nationalization, the familiar socialist tool, as nothing but a change of masters; wage slavery would end only when the workers themselves, organized by industries, owned and administered them. Unlike the guild socialists, however, the syndicalists now called for an active waging of the class struggle. They would utilize Parliament only as a sounding board for revolutionary ideas, and outside it they would wage the class war by direct action, including sabotage and the general strike. The *Daily Herald,* founded in 1911 as a strike sheet, survived to furnish an outlet for syndicalist views, class-war ideas, the encouragement of suffragette violence, and left-wing propaganda of all kinds, including attacks on the Labour party itself.[21]

In an atmosphere so unfavorable for the Labour party, the workers attempted shortcuts to their objectives. The year 1911 was one of great strikes. The newly formed National Transport Workers' Federation, led by Mann and Ben Tillett, and the railwaymen called strikes that ended in victories; workers felt a sense of participation in something that gave quick and tangible results. For the moment the new leaders outshone the politicians. In 1912, however, the miners' effort for a minimum wage failed and the London dockers lost a strike. When in 1913 the Irish Transport Workers struck, James Larkin strove to rouse the British workers to sympathetic action. There were widespread unauthorized stoppages in which the rank and file disregarded their cautious and responsible leaders. At the 1913 T.U.C., Robert Smillie raised the threat of a general strike; the formation of the Triple Alliance of Miners, Railwaymen, and Transport Workers with a combined membership of one and a quarter million made it a formidable possibility. The threat of civil war in Ireland and the tactics of the militant suffragists in England added to the tension. Those who have lived amid the stresses and strains of the "cold war" are apt to recall the years preceding 1914 as an era of peace, but the atmosphere of some of them was actually highly charged.[22]

In such a situation a spread of Marxism might have been expected, but it did not occur. The Labour leadership was unaffected. Hardie denounced the class war, and MacDonald reaffirmed his evolutionary faith. Henderson remained essentially the practical reformer. Snowden openly condemned as irresponsible the resort to crippling strikes. There was no flocking of the radicals into the S.D.F., which in 1908 had changed its name to the Social Democratic party in order to indicate its relation to the continental parties. In 1911, together with a left fringe of the I.L.P. and other dissident elements, it reorganized as the British Socialist party (B.S.P.). It applied for membership in the Labour party and in 1917 was accepted.

The end of this period, accordingly, found the Labour party dependent upon the Liberals, dissatisfied with its achievement, unsure of its aims, and apparently in decline. The war that broke out in August 1914 radically affected its fortunes. It created a situation in which Labour could assert its independence, chart its course ahead, and grow rapidly from a minority party to a major one.

3. The Impact of a World War

In August 1914 the pacific internationalism of the British Labour party was rudely shattered by the impact of a great war, generally but inaccurately called the First World War. No member took the antinational stand that the enemy was in the right; hardly a voice was raised in an unequivocal "stop the war" campaign, and no effort was made to turn the struggle into the Marxian social revolution. As in labor and socialist groups everywhere, however, serious differences appeared. The moderate center of trade unionists constituting the bulk of the membership accepted the official view of the war, opposed a premature peace, and hoped through victory to achieve a just settlement. Most of the Fabians, convinced of danger to the world inherent in German policy, believed in the righteousness of the Allied cause. Some Labourites, including old socialists like Blatchford and Hyndman, became belligerently nationalist. On the opposite wing were elements, chiefly socialist, that from the outset were suspicious of accepted explanations of the war, distrustful of a treaty extorted by force, and interested primarily in a negotiated peace.

Had Labour been a unified and disciplined party, such divisions might have wrecked it, but its loose federal organization and the absence of a dogmatic creed permitted the toleration of wide differences of opinion. Accordingly, unlike every continental socialist party, it emerged from this ordeal not with serious splits or losses but with significant gains. The hitherto small third party came out of the war solidly based in the country and in a position to influence the course of national and even international events. It was to the tolerance, patience, and ability of Arthur Henderson, more than any other individual, that Labour owed this fortunate outcome.

Down to the very moment of Britain's entry into the war, the sole aim of the Labour party was the preservation of peace. As an affiliate of the Second International, it was nominally committed to a resolution adopted in 1907 at Stuttgart by which the constituent organizations were bound in threat of war to exert every effort to avert it, and in the event of actual hostilities to utilize the crisis to hasten the social revolution. However, only the first clause of this pledge received consideration. In response to a call from the International Socialist Bureau, issued upon receipt of the alarming news of the Austrian declaration against Serbia, Hardie for the Labour party, J. Bruce Glasier for the I.L.P., and Dan Irving for the British Socialist party went to Brussels to plead eloquently for peace on the same platform with comrades from whom they were to be separated for over four years.

On July 31, 1914, after their return from Brussels, a manifesto voiced Labour's old distrust of Tsarist Russia rather than Germany and called resolutely for peace. It was followed by a series of demonstrations climaxed by one on August 2 at Trafalgar Square to demand that Britain confine its efforts to the restoration of peace. In the House of Commons the parliamentary party urged neutrality. Events moved so rapidly, however, that the same weekly journals that published the manifestoes and recounted the meetings simultaneously reported the march of armies and the first engagements. The men who so recently had stood together were now separated by censorship and martial law; on both sides of the battle line militant patriotism triumphed over pacifist internationalism.[1]

In Great Britain the invocation of the second clause of the Stuttgart resolution was never a possibility. The British party had never shown interest in the Marxist idea of converting an international war into the social revolution. Although there had been opposition to the foreign policy of Sir Edward Grey, especially from the I.L.P., the violation of Belgian neutrality inflamed opinion and more than any other event solidified it in support of the war; however disagreeable it might be, the only way out was through. Thus the effectiveness of internationalism was for the moment limited to a resolution by the party executive on August 5, the day after Britain's entry, that Labour's present duty was "to secure peace at the earliest possible moment on such conditions as will provide the best opportunities for the re-establishment of amicable feelings between the workers of Europe."[2] A rift appeared on the same day, however, when a majority of the parliamentary party opposed the proposal of MacDonald, its

chairman, to read that resolution in the House of Commons. Mac-
Donald thereupon resigned and was succeeded by Arthur Henderson.

Labour settled down to the task of the successful prosecution of
the war. The party entered into an electoral truce with the Liberals
and the Unionists under which no by-elections were to be contested
and each seat falling vacant would be retained by the party to which
the late member belonged, a provision under which Labour kept two
seats without a contest. It lent its machinery for recruiting campaigns.
On the industrial side the T.U.C. suspended the strike weapon. This
industrial truce, at first unilateral, was made formal on March 17,
1915, when at a Treasury Conference with Lloyd George the unions
agreed to relinquish for the duration of the war all practices and restrictions that might hamper the national effort.

Further conferences led to the acceptance of compulsory arbitration and to the admission of unskilled labor and women to do work
hitherto the preserve of the trade unionist, a practice that became
known as the "dilution" of labor. Henderson became chairman of a
National Labour Advisory Committee appointed by the government
to advise it on the execution of these agreements. Labour set up a
War Emergency Workers' National Committee to deal with industrial problems and to relieve the distress that would inevitably result
from the war. As all sections of the party were represented, the common effort helped to preserve unity in spite of rifts that appeared in
the movement.

On the left of the party were dissidents who, although they did not
believe the enemy right or guiltless, viewed the war as a tragic blun-
der for which responsibility was widely diffused; they found its causes
in balance-of-power policies, the system of alliances, secret diplomacy,
economic rivalries, and the chauvinist militarism that afflicted all
Europe. Militant patriots labeled them "pro-German," but the term
was an epithet and never accurately descriptive. The majority of the
British Socialist party and a large section of the I.L.P. assumed an
antiwar position. Their devotion to internationalism did not waver.
"Out of the darkness and the depth," ran the manifesto of the I.L.P.,
"we hail our working-class comrades of every land. Across the roar of
guns, we send sympathy and greeting to the German Socialists. . . .
They are no enemies of ours but faithful friends."[3]

When the German Social Democrats voted war credits, casualty
lists came in, and emotion heightened, this small minority heard many
embittered remarks about the conduct of those "faithful friends."
Hardie and MacDonald shared this popular odium, though they

attempted to follow a middle road by which they could cooperate in the war effort but at the same time strive for a just peace that would not have to wait upon victory or exhaustion. A right wing of the I.L.P., including two of its parliamentary group, J. R. Clynes and James Parker, dissociated themselves from its manifesto and unreservedly supported the war effort.

With internationalism in eclipse, Allied socialist and labor groups sought agreement on war aims. Camille Huysmans, secretary of the International, from its headquarters now at The Hague, attempted to mend the broken threads but found little support except among neutrals and small minorities such as the British far left. The Labour party leaders, however, together with Émile Vandervelde, president of the International but also a member of the Belgian government, arranged for an inter-Allied conference at London. Accordingly, on February 14, 1915, some forty delegates from the parties in France, Belgium, Russia, and Great Britain met under the presidency of Hardie to make a pronouncement on the war.

The outcome was a compromise between the views of the militants and the left. The invasion of France and Belgium was condemned, but it was emphasized that the Allied socialists were at war only with the governments and not with the peoples of the Central Powers. They protested against oppression whether German or Russian. They stood for the liberation of Belgium and Poland and for the right of all peoples forcibly annexed from Alsace-Lorraine to the Balkans freely to dispose of themselves. A resolve to fight for victory over Germany, which was characterized as the worst enemy of freedom, was coupled with a determination that the defensive war should not be transformed into one of conquest. Its conclusion must see the peaceful federation of Europe and of the world.

These resolutions stated fairly the views of British Labour as they were early in 1915. It supported the war, but desired a more concrete expression of aims than was to be found in the vague pronouncements of Allied statesmen. The document anticipated the language of Woodrow Wilson and the peace programs of the last year of the war. The British right, like the French and Belgians, would have preferred a more outspoken condemnation of German aggression and "barbarism"; the left would have omitted all direct references that might hamper German and Austrian participation in a later conference. Hardie did not long survive this conference; heartbroken over the war, he died later in the same year.[4]

There was no doubt either of the willingness of labor's cooperation in the war effort or of its importance. The government recognized that the war would have to be won in the workshop as well as on the battlefront. Its dealings with labor were facilitated by labor's organization. It was a situation that put labor in a new position of cooperation with government. Labor leaders were consulted; they made agreements on a national scale. Organized labor became part of the war machinery. It was a status that gave a new dignity to the leadership, which was soon reflected in the composition of the Cabinet.

In May 1915, a Cabinet crisis and reconstruction occurred. The Parliament elected in December 1910 and the Liberal Cabinet of Asquith were still the government; legally the term of Parliament ended in 1915, but by common consent the election had been postponed from year to year. The outcry over a reported shortage of munitions and the Gallipoli failure was so great, however, that the Prime Minister announced a reconstruction of his government by the inclusion of the leaders of other parties. As it was universally recognized that Labour should have a place in any "national" government, on May 19 Asquith invited participation and offered Henderson a Cabinet post.

Although it was emphasized that the connection was for war purposes only, it confronted the Labour executive committee with a problem. The committee was mindful of the fate of small third parties that found coalition only a step toward absorption; for this reason a provision against joining any "capitalist" government had been inserted in the party constitution. Members of the executive had contributed to the making of this rigid provision, but admittedly they had contemplated no such crisis. The committee, accordingly, followed the example of their French and Belgian comrades and decided for acceptance. But the parliamentary party, by a majority of one, came to a contrary decision; among the opponents of coalition were MacDonald, Snowden, Clynes, and Jowett.

The deadlock was broken by a joint session of the two bodies, which gave a majority for acceptance; so Henderson entered the Cabinet as President of the Board of Education. His office was largely nominal; his most valuable service would be given as labor adviser to the Cabinet, which put a seal on labor's new relation to government. He retained the party secretaryship. In addition to the Cabinet post, two lesser places were awarded to Labour: William Brace became Under-Secretary for Home Affairs and G. H. Roberts a Junior Lord of the Treasury. In the Commons the presence of Liberals, Unionists, and

Labourites on the Treasury Bench symbolized the national unity. The little knot of I.L.P. socialists indicated their disapproval by joining some irreconcilable radicals in the old seats of the Opposition.[5]

These I.L.P. leaders, however, considered their action a highly responsible one. The British system, they maintained, demanded an Opposition to furnish responsible criticism, which the fusion might eliminate. As Snowden wrote with his usual clarity:

The whole Labour movement will be united on one point—namely, that it is the duty of the movement to help the nation in its present difficulties. But the point of difference is that some members think that the Labour party can be much more useful outside the government than inside it. The acceptance of office in the Coalition government will take away the freedom of independent criticism, which at a time like this may often be the most valuable service a small party can render to the nation.[6]

The irreconcilables of the I.L.P. and the Marxists of the British Socialist party, however, regarded the move as the disarmament of Labour with Henderson and his colleagues held as hostages. They gloomily predicted that the end of the war would find Labour captive and tied and, like John Burns earlier, unable or unwilling to resume independence.[7]

The industrial truce suffered interruptions. In July 1915, the Treasury Agreement was written into statute as the Munitions of War Act with provision for compulsory arbitration and dilution of labor. It aroused discontent when inequalities became evident. Although labor was closely controlled, there was no effective limitation of profits, so that many were doing very well financially out of the war. During the first twelve months prices increased by about one-third without a comparable wage rise. Negotiated increases were difficult so long as the strike weapon was in abeyance, while dilutees were available and women worked for less than the men they replaced, and while a system of leaving certificates virtually gave the employer control over the worker's movements and bound him to the job.

In the eyes of many workers the dilutees from the Labour Exchanges and the corps of Munitions Volunteers who could be moved from place to place resembled too closely the "blacklegs" of peacetime. When local grievances arose, it was difficult to express them through union officials who were bound by national agreements. On the spot and easily available, however, were shop stewards. Their duties had been entirely local, but when discontented workers turned to them, they began to replace the regular union officials as spokesmen.

Some extensive strikes resulted from this situation, especially along the Clyde and in South Wales. In the former area the shop stewards were often militant, aggressive, and imbued with syndicalist ideas. They were apt to belong to the Socialist Labour party, the British Socialist party, or the I.L.P. left. In February 1915, contrary to the advice of union officials, the Clyde-side engineers went on strike. It was conducted by the shop stewards, who organized a Central Withdrawal of Labour Committee, which remained in being after the end of the strike. Further stoppages led to a visit of Lloyd George and Henderson to Glasgow on Christmas Day; the former was greeted with boos and denied a hearing. Again in March 1916, shop stewards conducted an unofficial strike at the Parkhead works. Sentences followed, and William Gallacher and others were imprisoned or deported from the area. In July 1915, 200,000 South Wales miners went on strike; although strikes were unlawful, such was the need for steam coal that most of the miners' demands were granted.[8]

The army's need for men and Lord Kitchener's call for them led to a crisis over conscription. Labourites were opposed to compulsory military service. They shared the deep-seated antipathy to it long prevalent in Britain, and they associated it with the Prussianism they were striving to destroy. The proposal was unaccompanied by a corresponding conscription of wealth, and it was feared especially as a possible entering wedge for industrial conscription. Labour sought to save the voluntary system and in August 1915 launched a recruiting campaign of its own. When the government finally introduced a conscription bill, the argument for it was strong enough to convince Henderson, but sentiment was so hostile that a conference of labor organizations, industrial and political, was summoned for January 6, 1916, to consider the issue.

The leadership of both the party and the T.U.C. proposed that the Labour M.P.'s be left free to vote for or against the bill, but by a majority of nearly two to one the conference recommended opposition. The Labour executive and the parliamentary party thereupon took the serious step of withdrawal from the Coalition, and the three Labour ministers, though in personal disagreement with this decision, felt obliged to comply. They were alive to the importance of their action because, as Henderson pointed out to the conference, the Liberal Sir John Simon could resign on the issue as an individual, but a withdrawal of the Labour representatives took out of the Coalition one of its constituent elements.[9]

The Prime Minister, loath to lose the support of Labour, exerted his influence to secure reconsideration, and although the three ministers disappeared from the Treasury Bench, Henderson was invited to continue attending Cabinet sessions in order to keep the party informed. When the Prime Minister gave assurance that conscription would not be allowed to become an entering wedge for industrial compulsion and promised safeguards, the Labour men agreed to remain in the Coalition until the matter could be laid before the forthcoming party conference at Bristol.

This conference of January 26–28, 1916, the first regular one since the outbreak of the war, provided the first accurate index of opinion on many issues. Its tone was patriotic. Except for the I.L.P., the votes were almost unanimous in supporting the war effort, the political truce, and the recruiting campaigns. The Military Service Bill was disapproved, but, now that conscription was a fact, a move for a repeal agitation was defeated. Participation in the Coalition was approved decisively by a vote of 1,622,000 to 495,000; the opinion prevailed that it furnished emphatic proof to all the world that Britain was unitedly determined to see the war through, whereas withdrawal would be susceptible to misinterpretation by Allies and enemies alike. Although trade-union block votes sometimes concealed substantial minorities, which in the case of the miners amounted to one-third, the vote was generally accepted as a faithful reflection of Labour opinion.[10]

The minorities continued to wage their own campaigns for present and future peace. The Union of Democratic Control (U.D.C.) was an early and important effort. On the day after Britain's entry into the war, C. P. Trevelyan took the first step toward its formation; he was soon joined by MacDonald, Norman Angell, E. D. Morel, and Arthur Ponsonby. This group, shocked by the revelation of secret commitments that had been persistently denied, hoped to prevent future wars by securing open diplomacy and a democratic control of foreign policy. Of the original five only MacDonald was Labour, but he was quickly followed by I.L.P. leaders, including Philip and Ethel Snowden, W. C. Anderson, and H. N. Brailsford, and by outstanding trade unionists such as Henderson, J. H. Thomas, Ben Turner, and Robert Smillie.

As early as September 1914, the U.D.C. issued a statement of four principles that must govern the peace treaty if it was not to contain the seeds of future wars, namely: no territorial transfers without the consent of the populations, the democratic control of foreign policy, an organization of Europe to replace the system of alliances and balance of power, and the reduction of armaments together with control of their manufacture. The I.L.P. weeklies, such as the *Labour Leader,* opened their columns to the U.D.C. For the later history of the Labour party this wartime cooperation with Liberals in the U.D.C. proved most important, because it provided a bridge over which many, including some with little interest in socialism, passed from Liberalism to Labour, where they strengthened the party's moderate wing.[11]

The left-fringe socialists continued in opposition. George Lansbury, editor of the *Herald,* first a daily then a weekly, took a prominent part in it along with the I.L.P. majority. The increasing pacifism of the B.S.P. led to an outright split. Hyndman and the prowar minority carried with them the weekly organ *Justice* and founded a new National Socialist party. The antiwar majority replaced *Justice* with *The Call.* These leftists were so vocal that, though but small minorities, they were often mistakenly assumed to be the voice of Labour. Actually, their views were highly unpopular with the Labour majority. When peace moves were made at the 1915 T.U.C. conference, John Hodge was loudly cheered when he denounced as traitors men who under the circumstances talked of peace. The conference almost unanimously carried a resolution justifying Allied policy and pledging support for the successful prosecution of the war.[12]

In order to counteract the pacifism of the far left, some of the more enthusiastic supporters of the war, including Hodge, Victor Fisher, Tillett, G. H. Roberts, Wells, and Blatchford, founded the Socialist National Defence Committee. After 1916 this body expanded as the British Workers' National League, which was ardently nationalist and advocated war for victory, a punitive peace, and economic reprisals after the war.[13]

The task of repairing the broken International was undertaken by the Italian Socialist party. When it discovered that the International Socialist Bureau was dominated by the belligerent outlook of the Belgian and French sections, which interpreted every peace move as a German maneuver, it turned to the pacifist minorities and the neutrals. Some, including the British far left, were sympathetic, so a meeting was arranged in neutral Switzerland. The I.L.P. named Jowett, its chairman, and Glasier, editor of the *Socialist Review,* as its delegates, and the British Socialist party selected E. C. Fairchild. Their hopes of attending, however, were promptly dashed by the government's refusal to give them passports, so the British were limited to a telegram of greeting.

On September 5–8, 1915, in the village of Zimmerwald, near Berne, about forty antiwar socialists met in a conference that became historic. The majority, pacifist and not revolutionary, passed antiwar resolutions and drew up a manifesto containing the peace formula of no annexations, no indemnities, and the right of nations to dispose of themselves. These Zimmerwaldians conceived of their function as a "ginger group" within the International to sponsor a world-wide campaign for peace, and therefore set up a permanent commission with headquarters at Berne. A small minority following Lenin would have preferred a revolutionary manifesto, a new international, and a policy of converting the "imperialist war" into the social revolution. They signed the majority appeal, but alongside the Berne commission set up a bureau of the Zimmerwald left, which contained the germ of the Third International.[14]

Some months later, on April 24–30, 1916, while attention was centered on the titanic struggle at Verdun, the Zimmerwaldians met again at the little Swiss village of Kienthal. Once more the British parties were absent because they could not obtain passports. This conference showed a decided trend to the left. Although Lenin did not get his full program adopted, his hand was apparent in the statement of principles. The demand for a peace without annexations or indemnities was renewed. The policies of the war socialists, who were styled "social nationalists" or "social chauvinists," and of bourgeois pacifists alike were denounced. Such proposed guarantees of peace as compulsory arbitration, limitation of armaments, and the democratization of foreign policy were ridiculed on the ground that peace and capitalism were incompatible. The only way to end war, accordingly, was for the workers to cease all collaboration with governments, resume the class war, and seize power for themselves. A large section now opposed the existing International as a prisoner of the Allies.[15]

In Britain the I.L.P. approved an organized drive for peace, but objected to the Zimmerwaldians' condemnation of other socialists and reiterated its loyalty to the existing International. The smaller B.S.P., which had shed its Hyndman right wing on the eve of Kienthal, was more sympathetic, but it was still hopeful of action from the Bureau at The Hague. The Labour party generally viewed the activity of these minorities with indifference or dislike. Its annual conferences of 1916 and 1917 revealed no change in the determination to prosecute the war vigorously.

Distrust of the German socialists was now so great that the T.U.C. conference of September 1916 rejected by a two-to-one vote an American Federation of Labor proposal for a labor conference contemporary with the peace congress. During the debate feeling ran high; not even after the end of hostilities would British workers sit down with German Social Democrats. The Labour party conference of the following January likewise opposed an international socialist conference to be called to influence the peace. To put French and Germans or Serbs and Bulgarians together, said Clynes, would produce a "frightful bear garden." The majority as yet saw no road to peace except through war.[16]

In Parliament and in the country the Labour party continued to support the Coalition, and until the beginning of December 1916, when the Asquith–Lloyd George dispute over the proposed smaller War Cabinet came to a head, there was no need to reconsider the position. In the early stages of that dispute Labour had no part. In spite of rumors even its leaders had little accurate knowledge of the situation and were taken by surprise at the sudden upheaval.

Whatever Asquith's faults, no alternative Prime Minister appeared more attractive. On December 1 Henderson referred to him as "the indispensable man" to lead Great Britain successfully to the end of the war.[17] On December 5 the party's acting chairman, G. J. Wardle, issued a strong pronouncement in his favor, but later on that very day Asquith resigned and the King sent for Bonar Law, the Unionist leader. Bonar Law failed to secure the support of Labour and the Asquithians, however, so the next day Lloyd George received the opportunity he coveted. This sequence was so rapid that by the time the Labour executive and the parliamentary party could meet jointly it was too late to express a preference for the retention of the Asquith government. They found themselves confronted by an accomplished fact with Lloyd George ready and anxious to make overtures for their support.

Although it was unanimously against the methods by which Lloyd George and the Northcliffe press had brought down the Coalition, the party was uncertain about what to do. It had high personal regard for Asquith but distrusted Lloyd George as an intriguer who had gained his ends by "as vile a conspiracy as ever disgraced English political life."[18] The parliamentary committee of the T.U.C. condemned those responsible for their failure to observe the loyalty and self-sacrifice they had so repeatedly urged upon the working classes. Others pointed out how sinister was the action of an influential section of the press, which in a national crisis had deliberately destroyed a government.

Although in the interest of efficiency many welcomed the innovation of a small War Cabinet, the majority feared it as potentially dangerous; it would be virtually a triumvirate of the Prime Minister, Milner, and Curzon, which might end in dictatorship. Leftist proponents of a negotiated peace predicted the supremacy of a reckless fight-to-a-finish group. The only Labour element that rejoiced in the fall of Asquith was the small rightist British Workers' National League, which was vehement in its attack on him and welcomed any step in the concentration of authority that might help to win the war.[19]

Early on December 7 the Labour executive and the parliamentary party met jointly to consider the situation. Through Henderson they heard Lloyd George's invitation to join the new Coalition, whereupon they decided to seek a personal and fuller explanation. The meeting took place that noon at the War Office. Much depended upon the outcome, because the official Liberals had decided to stay out, and Labour's attitude might very well determine Lloyd George's fate. He was ready to bid high for Labour support. He admitted the justice of Labour's claim to a greater share in the responsibilities of office and agreed that it should have a place on the War Cabinet together with the Pensions Ministry, the new Ministry of Labour, and several lesser posts. He foreshadowed strong action with respect to food production, control of coal mines and shipping, and mobilization of labor. Furthermore, he made a promise, not disclosed till the end of the war, that Labour should have direct representation at the peace congress.

His auditors raised a number of questions, especially on the possibility of industrial conscription. Lloyd George explained that a volunteer scheme was contemplated; if that failed, mobilization of labor might follow. The question was left open, because the Labour members preferred to await the definite plan. On the question of civil liberties and the right of propaganda, Lloyd George reminded his hearers that he himself had once been unpopular as an opponent of the Boer War and would now be no party to a policy of repression and persecution. The Labour men then withdrew to debate and make a decision which all knew to be crucial.

In the Labour meeting held later in the day, the discussion did not always run smoothly. Again it was apparent how little sympathy there was for the methods by which the break-up of the old government had been secured; but, since it was gone beyond recall, the party looked to the future. Henderson, seconded by several trade-union representatives, strongly urged that they throw in their lot with Lloyd

George. Clynes, who had opposed the first Coalition, was now converted. MacDonald, Snowden, and the left-wingers remained irreconcilable, but the idea prevailed that by joining they might influence
the government's policy; tenure of office, moreover, would afford
valuable experience that some day might stand them in good stead.
Acceptance was coupled with a resolution hoping that the new government would strive to settle the question of Ireland, which was
then in the bitter aftermath of the 1916 rebellion.[20]

The accession of Labour was a great victory for Lloyd George. It
created a profound impression and ensured his success. When the
ministerial list appeared, it contained six Labour names. Henderson
went to the War Cabinet of five. Hodge and G. N. Barnes were both
in the Cabinet, the former in charge of the first Ministry of Labour
and the latter of the newly created Pensions Ministry. In the ministry William Brace continued as Under-Secretary for Home Affairs,
G. H. Roberts became Parliamentary Secretary to the Board of Trade,
and James Parker a Junior Lord of the Treasury. Later, in 1917,
Stephen Walsh became Parliamentary Secretary for National Service
and in July 1918 Clynes became Food Controller. In the House of
Commons the party under the leadership of Wardle was now ranged
behind ministers, but the unreconciled group of the I.L.P. took seats
with the Asquithian Liberals on the Opposition benches. In the country the masses hearkened to the plea that the new government must
be given its opportunity, but the dissident minority left no doubt
of its contempt for the "bargain" with Lloyd George.[21]

The party's annual conference of January 23–26, 1917, at Manchester afforded a test of the strength of the two opinions. In the
debate on the Coalition, which came at the outset, Henderson stated
the position of the executive committee and parliamentary party,
saying that in the national emergency Labour should be more concerned with what it could give than with what it could get. He frankly
recognized the criticism of the methods by which the change of government was accomplished, but preferred to pass over that question
and attend to the main issue. He was ably seconded by Thomas and
Clynes, both recent converts to the need for coalition. The opposition
was voiced chiefly by Snowden of the I.L.P. and Fairchild of the
B.S.P. Snowden attacked the plea of expediency with the passionate
scorn and bitter irony of which he was master.

The debate changed few votes, however, because most delegates
came instructed. The Coalition was endorsed by a vote of 1,849,000
to 307,000, a majority even more decisive than that of the previous

year at Bristol. It should be noted, however, that all but about 40,000 of the opposition were from non-socialist groups and that minorities were concealed in the block votes. It was observed, too, that some leaders of the left were personally respected and popular, for Mac-Donald and Snowden had received spontaneous ovations. While the six-to-one majority testified eloquently to Labour's interest in the vigorous prosecution of the war, the presence of an opposition was evidence of an alertness to the importance of the party's indepen-dence.[22]

Labour's accession to the Coalition symbolized to the world British unity and determination to carry on the war to a successful conclu-sion. To the country it was a comforting assurance of continued co-operation from the men in the mines, in the factories, and on the land, without which the national effort could not be sustained. For the parliamentary party it actually marked a step toward the estab-lishment of independence. Whereas in the past it had been com-pelled to work in such close association with the Liberals that it was in danger of being regarded as a wing of that party, in the second Coalition it was on terms of partnership with the Unionists and the Lloyd George group, while the official Liberals were in Opposition. Labour, thenceforth, pursued a more independent course.

4. For Peace and Socialism

The last two years of the war witnessed changes of profound importance for the policies and prospects of the Labour party. Until 1917
the party with few exceptions accepted the official statements of war
aims and the necessity of peace through victory. That year, however,
saw a significant shift to the opinion that, although the military effort
should be continued unabated, alternative roads to peace should be
explored simultaneously. Doubts arose, too, about the vaguely stated
official aims, which led to an active search for the basis of a sound
and just peace that would not contain the seeds of future wars. It
meant that the moderate center, mainly trade unionist, was moving
toward the position hitherto occupied by the socialist left. One result
was the development of an independent foreign policy. In 1918 a
new constitution provided a better organization and for the first time
stated a socialist aim. A policy statement, *Labour and the New Social
Order,* outlined a program for a better Britain. By the end of the
war the national situation was such that many were ready to heed the
Labour appeal. The result was a rapid expansion of the small third
party into a major one.

In 1917 several factors combined to alter Labour opinion. People
were weary of the long war; the apparent stalemate on the Western
Front made victory seem remote, while the long casualty lists from
the Somme and Flanders brought home the cost. High prices and
food shortages led to discontent. There was resentment over conscription, and suspicion that trade-union conditions, once surren-
dered, might not be restored. The inadequacy of official war aims and
the failure to make much of the German peace offer of December
1916 added to distrust of the government, which was increased by

the exposure of its secret agreements with Italy and Russia. Above all, the Russian Revolution, with its direct appeal to the peoples of all the belligerents for a peace without annexations or indemnities, profoundly influenced Labour, while the speeches and diplomacy of President Wilson rallied the party enthusiastically behind his leadership.

The shift of opinion did not carry the party to the extremist anti-war position, but did bring it closer to that of the more moderate critics such as MacDonald. MacDonald was never a non-resister or a peace-at-any-price man. He opposed a premature peace that settled nothing. From a serious study of history, however, he drew a lesson that the fruits of sacrifice in war had too often been destroyed by the makers of the peace; so if a better world was to emerge from the present conflict, work on the provisions of a just settlement could not begin too soon. At the very outset of the war he wrote, "It is just as essential for national honor and safety that this preparation should now be made as that men should be trained in arms and hurried to the front." Otherwise the old mistakes would be repeated: "Our sacrifices will have been made in vain, and our children will have to tramp over the same battlefields and repeat the price we ourselves are now paying for the short-sighted follies which have been our inheritance."[1] The war should be fought for a policy and not for victory, but the policy should be thoroughly prepared. The diplomatic weapon should not wait on the military one, but should be employed simultaneously, so as to achieve a cessation of bloodshed as soon as the policy was attainable. The views of Hardie, Snowden, and Jowett were similar. It was a stand that required courage, because at the time all of them were rewarded with charges of pacifism, defeatism, or worse. In 1917–18, however, MacDonald saw his party approach his own position. It prepared the way for his postwar resumption of the leadership.

News of the tremendous event in Russia thrilled all sections of the Labour movement. The idealistic slogan of no annexations or indemnities appealed to majority and minority alike. The new order in Russia, together with the entrance of the United States as a belligerent, fitted into the concept of a war of democracies against despotisms, while the slogan of no annexations or indemnities would recall the Allies to their asserted purity of war aims. The majority welcomed the appointment of two of their number, Will Thorne and James O'Grady, as an official mission to Petrograd to discourage pacifism there and to maintain enthusiasm for the war for democracy.

The Labour left promptly identified the point of view of the new Russia with its own. A settlement on the Russian formula might halt imperialist ambitions and enable a league of nations to be founded that, in turn, might help to solve the vexing questions of national minorities in Europe and of the more backward peoples elsewhere. On May 16, 1917, in the House of Commons, Snowden moved to welcome the Russian lead and to join with the Allies in a restatement of peace aims in harmony with the Russian formula. The government maintained that "no annexations" did not exclude the emancipation of submerged nationalities, the reunion of artificially separated peoples, or the acquisition of strategic points necessary for defense; no practical differences, therefore, existed between Russia and its allies. On this question the Labour majority agreed with the government rather than with the I.L.P.–U.D.C. group, so Snowden's motion was lost by a vote of 238 to 32.[2]

The left, nevertheless, persisted in an effort to seize the initiative. The I.L.P. and the B.S.P. formed a United Socialist Council, which, aided by Lansbury and the *Herald,* called a conference that met on June 3 at Leeds. Some 1,115 delegates were there, but rightists came only to oppose the sponsors and the left sent numbers excessively disproportionate to its strength. Neither the Labour party nor the T.U.C. would have anything to do with the conference; so since the I.L.P. sent 294 delegates and the B.S.P. 88, the resolutions adopted reflected the left point of view.

Snowden proposed the motion for peace on the Russian formula and defined "no annexations" as no transfer of territory without the consent of the populations involved; and, mentioning Ireland and Egypt along with Alsace-Lorraine, Poland, and the Balkans, he indicated that the right of a people to control its own destinies should be observed on both sides. In order to implement the conference program it was agreed that councils of soldiers and workmen should be set up in Britain, but this revolutionary gesture remained a dead letter.[3]

A Women's Peace Crusade was launched at about the same time, and on its platforms Mrs. Philip Snowden, Mrs. Bruce Glasier, and Miss Margaret Bondfield, all members of the I.L.P., were frequent speakers. It bears testimony to British tolerance that in the darker days of the war their opinions could be voiced from Land's End to John o' Groat's with minimum interference from censorship and with but minor disturbances resulting.[4]

The news from Russia also stirred the International to action. A neutral Dutch-Scandinavian committee, joined later by the Petrograd Soviet, called for a socialist and labor conference at Stockholm to formulate a possible basis for peace. The Zimmerwald left, following Lenin, refused to cooperate because "social patriots" were invited; it planned instead to hold its own conference on the eve of and at the same place as the general one.

The Labour party, concerned with keeping Russia in the war for democracy, was averse to a meeting where socialists from enemy countries would be present. It reverted to the alternative of another inter-Allied conference, but before steps were taken news arrived that the Petrograd Soviet favored the Stockholm proposal. Because the relation of Russia to the war was as important as it was uncertain, the Labour executive suspended its preparations and determined that a deputation representative of all sections of the movement should go to Petrograd to secure information. It seemed logical that it should stop at Stockholm, too, where the organizing committee was receiving similar groups from many lands. The majority delegates, G. H. Roberts, W. Carter and W. C. Robinson, agreed to go on the understanding that they would consult only with the president of the committee, Hjalmar Branting of Sweden, and not participate in any congress.

For the I.L.P. MacDonald and Jowett were appointed, but were halted at the port of embarkation by the Seamen, who refused to carry them. It was a case of retaliation against alleged pacifists by a union, now on the extreme Labour right, that was embittered by what it regarded as German inhumanity in sea warfare. This feud with the left lasted throughout the war. The majority delegates would not go on without the I.L.P. men. The Labour executive decided that, before proceeding further, they would await the return from Petrograd of Henderson, who a few weeks earlier had gone there upon an official mission.[5]

Henderson went to Russia opposed to a meeting of the International. There he joined with Émile Vandervelde and Albert Thomas, who were on missions from the Belgian and French governments, respectively, in an attempt to dissuade the Petrograd Soviet from the project. When the latter persisted, Henderson changed his opinion; since a conference appeared inevitable, the sensible course would be to join and seek to guide it; the alternative was either to leave the Russians exposed to German influence unchecked or to meet in a left-wing congress such as Lenin was advocating. Stockholm might even offer positive advantages. Useful contact might be made with the growing German Socialist minority now opposing its government and the Allied position clarified for them. If limited to an exchange of views, much good might come out of the proposed conference.

On July 24 Henderson returned to London in company with four delegates from the Petrograd Soviet. He prevailed upon the Labour executive to call a special party conference and recommend the acceptance of the Stockholm proposal, provided that it was only consultative, to reach agreement with the French party, and to hold a preliminary inter-Allied conference. Henderson, MacDonald, Wardle, and the Russians thereupon went to Paris to discuss the terms upon which Stockholm should be recommended to the French and British parties. The Labour executive set August 10 as the date for its special conference.[6]

Stockholm became the topic of the day. To Labour it offered a means of breaking the military stalemate and of saving the Russian Revolution. Some Liberals shared this view, but Conservatives were violently hostile to it as a German trap. There were rounds of abuse for Henderson and demands for his resignation in which the Labour extreme right, including the British Workers' League and Hyndman's National Socialist party, was as vehement as the Conservatives. The Cabinet was uneasy. Lloyd George wavered. In May he had favored Stockholm. In June he first refused, then granted, passports to the delegation to Petrograd. He was impressed by the need to conciliate organized labor. The French and Italian governments, however, had consistently opposed Stockholm, and the Prime Minister finally fell into line. On August 7 a legal opinion was obtained that the common law forbade intercourse with enemy aliens without license. It was not made public, though, because the government, not sure of the extent of the Labour swing to the left, thought the party might reject the proposal.

The Labour conference of August 10 held the spotlight, because to the public the resurgence of internationalism was as startling as it was unexpected. Attention centered on Henderson, who read a carefully prepared speech explaining why he, who had gone to Russia as a member of the government, had come back convinced as a Labour official that his party ought to go to Stockholm. He told of his impressions of Russia, of his anxiety lest the Allies be misunderstood there, and of his desire that the German workers receive first-hand knowledge of the British Labour attitude. He concluded that the time had come to use the political weapon to supplement the military in order to secure an honorable and democratic peace. Such phrases hitherto had been uttered by MacDonald, the spokesman of the left, rather than by the leader of the trade-union center. It was one of those rare speeches that determine votes; the Stockholm resolution was carried by a vote of 1,846,000 to 550,000.

For Henderson it was a remarkable personal triumph. Largely on the basis of his own observation, judgment, and reliability, the party reversed its position on Stockholm. The executive then recommended a delegation of 24, of which the executive, the parliamentary committee of the T.U.C., and the present special conference would appoint 8 each. The Miners, intending to prevent separate socialist representation, offered an amendment that no additions be made to the list. This maneuver was inconsistent with the terms of the invitation to Stockholm, because the socialist societies were independently affiliated to the International even before the Labour party joined it. The conference adjourned until August 21 to consider this and other problems.[7]

To the country the decisive ballot came as a surprise. The warlike press raged. In the House of Commons Labour was denounced as unfit both mentally and by tradition to deal with such questions as would come under discussion at Stockholm. The Cabinet now announced its decision to refuse passports. On the very night of the London conference, Lloyd George and Henderson had an interview that led to the latter's resignation.[8]

Some very unpleasant features were connected with Henderson's withdrawal from the War Cabinet. In the press and in the Commons, the Prime Minister charged that Henderson had deceived his colleagues about his intentions and misled the party conference on the attitude of the Russian government. Yet even before Henderson left Russia he had announced his support of the proposal, and after his return to England he had devoted every day openly to preparations for it. His version of the Russian attitude was correct and within a week was confirmed by Kerensky. As Labour resented his expulsion and the manner of it, the affair contributed to the party's resumption of independence and to its determination to have a share in shaping the peace. It would, in the meantime, get on with the war, so Barnes took Henderson's place in the War Cabinet and Hodge became Minister of Pensions. Roberts succeeded Hodge as Minister of Labour, and Wardle entered the ministry as Parliamentary Secretary to the Board of Trade.[9]

On August 21 the Labour executive committee submitted to the adjourned conference its Stockholm resolution, admitting separate socialist representation as heretofore. In these terms it was carried by the narrowest of majorities, 1,234,000 to 1,231,000. The opposition hailed the vote as a virtual defeat for Stockholm; and many were the editorials on the supposed landslide from internationalism and compliments to Labour on its soundness and good sense. With few exceptions it was overlooked that the shift in the vote was chiefly upon a condition and not upon the principle of the conference. The issue at the moment was whether there should be a single united delegation or separate socialist representation as well. When the I.L.P. and the B.S.P. made it clear that they intended to voice minority views at Stockholm, several large unions, including the Miners with a block vote of 600,000, refused to accept the motion in its existing form. When immediately afterward a resolution on the composition of the delegation incorporating a Miners' amendment denying separate socialist representation was offered, it was carried overwhelmingly by 2,124,000 to 175,000. Clearly, the Labour majority was convinced of the desirability of exploring this road to peace.[10]

Henderson, relieved of his Cabinet post, was now free to head the movement for a statement of war aims, which made him the central figure in the labor movement. He won the approval of the T.U.C. That great organization had relinquished politics to the Labour party and was not affiliated with the International, but the factors that produced the leftward shift in the party now drew the T.U.C. actively into the political scene. The executives of the two sides of the labor movement then began a close collaboration that in 1921 became formal in the National Joint Council of Labour, which was known a decade later as the National Council of Labour. One of its first fruits was a draft memorandum on war aims, which was essentially the work of three men, Henderson, MacDonald, and Sidney Webb. The last two had differed widely on the war, but under the moderating influence of Henderson they agreed on a pronouncement. The draft was circulated and discussed throughout the party and generally approved. The Labour executive next sought the support of the socialist and labor parties of the Allied Powers.

On August 28–29 under the presidency of Henderson, the inter-Allied Socialist conference met at London to deal with the problems of Stockholm and war aims. It was doomed to failure, however, when the Belgians and the prowar section of the now divided French party refused to accept anything as binding unless adopted unanimously. That most sections of Allied labor had moved leftward was indicated by the censure of governments for refusal of passports to international conferences and by the defeat of Hyndman's motion against any consultation with Germans so long as their armies occupied Allied soil. Agreement on war aims proved unattainable, however, which effectively nullified the possibility of Stockholm; while the Allies were at odds among themselves, it was useless to meet the socialists of the enemy powers.[11]

The National Joint Council, although disappointed in its hope of speedy success, proceeded with its intention of producing a statement of war aims that might become the basis of Allied and, finally, of international agreement. As the year wore on the atmosphere appeared slightly more favorable. Peace talk was in the air. The peace note of Pope Benedict XV and Lord Lansdowne's plea for a revision and restatement of peace terms, the latter published in the *Daily Telegraph*, made deep impressions. Of utmost importance were events in Russia, where the Bolsheviks carried through the November revolution, entered into an armistice with the Central Powers, and appealed for a general peace. They also published the texts of secret treaties by which the Allies in their desperate need had bound themselves to objectives so often at variance with their professed aims.[12] Doubts and suspicions increased and were not clarified by governments, which strengthened Labour's determination to press the issue. The party and T.U.C. executives thereupon joined in calling a conference representative of all bodies connected with either side of the labor movement. It was, accordingly, an unusually large assembly that on December 28–29, 1917, met in London to consider the statement on war aims.

The conference fully revealed the shift of opinion in the labor movement. There were no hot debates and few emotional demonstrations, because delegates came convinced or instructed. A reply from the Prime Minister to a request of the National Joint Council asserted that Britain's objectives were the same as when it entered the war; a year earlier it would have brought a cheer, but it was now heard in complete silence. Henderson's presentation of the memorandum drew prolonged applause that foretold the result. The conference listened with deepest sympathy to Havelock Wilson of the Seamen, because the reasons for his right-wing position were well understood, but his motion to reject the memorandum and to make no peace until the Germans were humbled secured hardly a dozen votes. An attack from the B.S.P. on the other extreme was equally futile. When the chairman finally put the question, dissent was negligible.[13]

Labour's statement of war aims reaffirmed the fundamental aim of a world safe for democracy and an end to war as an instrument of policy. As a means to these ends it relied upon the democratization of all governments, limitation of armaments, abolition of private arms manufacture, and, especially, the establishment of a league of nations with an international court and legislature, conciliation machinery, and provision for common cause against recalcitrant members—essentially the same plan for a league developed two years earlier by the Fabians.[14]

Territorial problems filled half the memorandum. Belgian independence should be restored and reparations paid by Germany. It opposed imperialist expansion. It suggested that disputed areas such as Alsace-Lorraine, the Italian borderlands, and Poland be settled on the basis of self-determination. It supported Zionist aspirations in Palestine. For the non-Turkish provinces of the Ottoman Empire and the conquered German colonies, the statement avoided both extremes of annexation and return to old regimes by suggesting a middle course that furthered the idea of the responsible mandate. Constantinople and the Straits should be neutralized and administered by a commission under the proposed league. European possessions in tropical Africa should be erected into a single independent state to be administered by the league primarily for the benefit of native populations. Labour, hostile to some current talk of an economic war after the peace, urged freer trade, the development of natural resources for universal benefit, and international action to improve social and economic conditions everywhere.

The concrete idealism of this program won the favor of many British Liberals and attracted widespread attention. It brought some immediate results. On the very evening of its adoption an interview was arranged with Lloyd George. The moment was opportune, because the need to fill gaps on the Western Front was impelling the government to win the consent of organized labor for release from earlier promises regarding the replacement of skilled trade unionists by women and unskilled workers.

Accordingly, the Prime Minister yielded to the deputation's request, and on January 5, 1918, before a special trade-union conference, he delivered the first official pronouncement of war aims that went beyond generalities. He won approval by his moderation and apparent agreement with Labour's concrete proposals. He said nothing about a "knockout blow" and disavowed imperialist aims. He denied an intention to disrupt Germany or destroy Austria-Hungary, except for the irredentist areas of the latter, and expressed a willingness to leave the disposition of the German colonies to a peace conference; these statements were interpreted as an acceptance of the "no annexations" principle. His proposals to leave the Turkish homeland untouched and to admit the claims of nationalism elsewhere in that empire were assumed to nullify the secret treaties. It was noted that some statements were obscure and that Russia was dismissed with a declaration that it must be saved by its own people, but such was the glow of satisfaction at this prompt response that the tendency was to place the most favorable interpretation upon his words.[15]

The rising tide of labor opinion that compelled a response from Lloyd George also contributed to the timing of President Wilson's Fourteen Points. Labour received them gladly and lauded the President as its own spokesman. The protagonists of a league perceived there the means to a better world. On Russia he appeared in favorable contrast to Lloyd George, for he paid tribute to its idealism and insisted that it should not be deserted. On subject nationalities the President's points closely coincided with Labour's own statement. His methods were applauded: he was neglecting neither the sword nor the pen; without abating the military effort he simultaneously employed the diplomatic weapon. The Seamen objected to some implications of the reference to the freedom of the seas, and on the opposite wing the I.L.P. regretted the absence of mention of such recently acquired Allied possessions as Egypt and Tripoli.

From this moment, however, Wilson's leadership was most hopefully regarded by the Labour party. His prestige was enhanced when on February 11 his reply to Count Hertling, the German Chancellor, and Count Czernin, the Austro-Hungarian Foreign Minister, laid down four principles of a territorial settlement. His insistence that provinces must not be the subject of barter and that territorial readjustments must be for the benefit of the people concerned brought him even closer to the heart of Labour. If any statesman could secure a peace of justice and reconciliation, it seemed it would be Wilson.[16]

Wilson's championship of a league was particularly welcome, for by this time the Labour party was its chief proponent in Great Britain. While most Conservatives were hesitant and Liberals gave limited support, Labourites devoted much attention to the consideration of details. They were agreed that the League must not be a continuation of the wartime alliance or based upon governments, but universal and democratically based upon parliaments. They wanted an organization that would function continually and not only during crises; it might remove a primary cause of war by ensuring to each nation an equitable share in the world supply of essential food and raw materials. Machinery for conciliation, judicial settlement, and arbitration in international disputes would provide a substitute for war. The I.L.P., however, was not reconciled to the concept of a league that would exercise military force to keep "peace."[17]

In order to further the union of Allied socialism and labor on a peace program, the National Joint Council called a third conference for February 20–23, 1918, in London. The American Federation of Labor was invited, but declined to consider any move toward an international conference that would include the enemy, while the Russians would have no part in one that did not. The absence of these two extremes, together with a preliminary understanding with the French party, facilitated agreement.

The British party's war aims, somewhat amended, emerged as the program of inter-Allied labor and socialism. Most additions were intended to stiffen the league: constituent members would pledge themselves not only to submit every threatening issue to arbitration but also to make common cause against an aggressor, which was defined as a state that declined to submit to arbitration. A provision for the retrocession of Alsace-Lorraine to France before a plebiscite placated the French right. Czecho-Slovak and Jugoslav claims now received sympathetic attention, although the same paragraph disavowed any desire to dismember Austria-Hungary and suggested the alternative of Danubian federation. On central Africa the proposed independent state under international control disappeared in favor of administration by separate nations under league supervision, one source of the mandate system. A committee of three—Henderson, Albert Thomas of France, and Émile Vandervelde of Belgium—was set up to prepare for a meeting of the labor and socialist parties of all the belligerents and to convene a conference to be held simultaneously with the official peace congress.[18]

The success of this inter-Allied conference, due mainly to the energy and tact of Henderson, raised hopes, but censorship and circumstances made it difficult to ascertain the views of the parties of the Central Powers. When after long delays the replies were received, some, including that of the German minority, were favorable. The attitude of the German majority, however, was not; with the Central Powers victorious on the Eastern Front and on the offensive in the West, it was evident that a peace-by-negotiations movement would not flourish there. The British party continued to debate it, but with decreasing hopefulness. There was a fourth inter-Allied labor and

socialist conference in London, September 17–20, 1918, held partly
to bring American labor into line, but Samuel Gompers and his colleagues still held to views that in Britain survived only on the right
wing of Havelock Wilson and the British Workers' League. The
Americans opposed any meeting with enemy groups not in open revolt against their government, but they approved the demand for
authorized labor representation on each peace delegation and for the
concurrent labor convention. Gompers was added to the committee
of three to prepare for the convention.[19]

Henderson, meanwhile, turned to the task of reconstructing his
party and giving it a more definite goal and program. He secured the
cooperation of Sidney Webb and MacDonald, and, thanks to his tact,
the intellectual Fabian and the courageous but emotional parliamentarian worked in harmony. Henderson was well aware that the old labor alliance was insufficient for the needs of a modern political party.
There were a few local Labour Representation Committees and other
local affiliates, but ordinarily there was no way for a nonunion recruit
to enter the party except through one of the socialist societies; in
many constituencies there was no organization at all to sponsor a
Labour candidate. Henderson wanted a sound national basis. He
kept aspects of the old federalism, for the trade unions were too
strong and too necessary financially to be cast aside and the socialist
societies had a unique place in the movement, but he supplemented
them by a great extension of the system of local Labour parties.

The resulting structure lacked uniformity, but it has worked and
is still, with some changes, the Labour party of today. As accepted by
the party conference of February 1918, it had an executive of 23 members elected by the party conference of whom 13 would be nominees
of the affiliated trade unions and socialist societies, 5 those of local
Labour parties, and 4 women members; the other would be the party
treasurer separately elected. The I.L.P., its power reduced to that of
nomination, was naturally unhappy over the loss of direct representation, but the trade unions, still resentful of separate socialist representation at international conferences, would have none of it; indeed,
there were moves afoot for a trade-union party without the socialists.
Henderson's plan, however, saved this important source of strength.

The establishment of local Labour parties proceeded so rapidly
that within a year the number increased from 85 to 292, but the socialist societies continued to fare well. When in 1919 the first elections to the executive under the new constitution were held, I.L.P.
members secured the treasurer's office, two places for the affiliated so-

cieties, two for the women's section, and one local Labour party place. The zeal and prominence of the leaders of the 75,000 socialists could still win places in spite of the numerical preponderance of the trade unionists and the expansion of the constituency parties.

For the first time there was a definition of objective which went beyond that of the organization and maintenance of a political party. Section "d" under "party objects" read: "To secure for the producers by hand or by brain the full fruits of their industry, and the most equitable distribution thereof that may be possible, upon the basis of the common ownership of the means of production and the best obtainable system of popular administration and control of each industry and service."[20]

Although the word "socialism" was avoided, the Labour party thereby became a socialist party. Actual use of the word might have alienated the Miners and other recent recruits. In 1918, the term "common ownership" was not taken literally to mean the elimination of all other forms of ownership, but it became a symbol and the standard under which the party fought, so that forty-one years later, when an attempt was made to revise and define "Clause 4," resentment at tampering with it was such that the move had to be abandoned. The final phrase about the best obtainable system of administration and control was a "straddling plank" inserted to avoid conflict between the advocates of state socialism and those of some form of "workers' control," guild socialism, or industrial democracy, about which there was much discussion at the time.

The annual conference would direct and control the work of the party. It would decide general policy, but prior to each general election the national executive and the parliamentary Labour party would determine measures necessary to give effect to the party program. Here the language of the constitution gave rise to later disagreement over the extent to which the parliamentary leadership was bound by conference decisions, as in the conflict over unilateral nuclear disarmament, in which the leadership insisted upon greater independence.

Henderson suffered one failure. He desired an arrangement with the cooperators, who, irritated at proposals to tax their savings and convinced that they had been slighted in the allocation of food supplies, were considering entry into politics with a party of their own. The overlap of membership with Labour was great, and a few societies were affiliated with local Labour parties, but the Cooperative Union leadership was still shy of any formal arrangement.

A fuller statement of Labour policy, *Labour and the New Social Order,* issued in June 1918, was debated, revised in accordance with twenty-six resolutions, and accepted at a special party conference. This document was mainly the work of Sidney Webb. His "House of Tomorrow" would rest upon four strong pillars, which he described as (a) the universal enforcement of the national minimum, (b) the democratic control of industry, (c) the revolution in national finance, and (d) the surplus wealth for the common good. By the first pillar the state would guarantee a minimum standard of living to every citizen. It would provide employment or maintenance; it would develop the existing machinery of factory acts, public health, housing, and education, and in times of depression it would utilize public works to keep up the level of employment. The conference added a demand for a maximum working week of forty-eight hours.

By democratic control of industry Webb meant state socialism and democratic parliamentary control, not "workers' control." This section and the supplementary resolutions contained some nationalization proposals; they named the railways, mines, electric power, industrial insurance, alcoholic drink, land, and communications. No proliferation of government departments was envisaged, however. One resolution, intended specifically to avoid "the evils of centralization and the drawbacks of bureaucracy," dealt with the wide range of services that local authorities, cooperators, friendly societies, and other bodies could perform.[21] The concept was Fabian—direction by the national government, emphasis upon efficiency, a mixed economy, and a plurality of agencies. Here, rather than literally in "Clause 4," the party conference revealed its vision of the future socialist society.

The revolution in national finance and the devotion of the surplus to the common good would make for greater equality of opportunity and a fairer sharing of the national product. A capital levy to reduce the war debt, the continuation of the excess-profits tax, a steeply graduated income tax, and heavy death duties would prevent the accumulation of over-large fortunes and the perpetuation of inequality. The sums so raised could be used to public advantage. The development of the nation's resources for the common good, instead of for private profit, would make possible a fuller participation by all in the amenities of civilization.[22]

Labour and the New Social Order was a significant document. Its socialist objective clearly distinguished the new party from its older rivals whose palliatives, it seemed to Labour, left virtually unchanged a system that placed a perpetual private mortgage on the national product. At the same time it eschewed extreme theories and methods that served to repel rather than attract. The Fabian gradualism of the program and the reliance upon parliamentary democracy enabled Labour to win support where its new Communist competitor failed dismally. It outlined the policies to which Labour has consistently adhered.

When in the summer of 1918 the end of the long war finally appeared in sight, the Labour rank and file became increasingly restless over the political truce, so disadvantageous to a small but growing party. During the unrest of 1917 feeling had found vent in the appearance of unofficial candidates at by-elections, all of whom were unsuccessful, though some polls were significantly large. The sentiment for independence grew so strong that the conference of June 1918 ended the electoral truce. By the time of the Armistice it was clear that the Prime Minister was preparing for a general election, so a special party conference was called for November 14 to decide on the future relations with the Lloyd George government.

The Labour ministers wanted to stay in the Coalition until the peace treaty was signed, and Clynes put the case for remaining in order to influence the course of events. The counter-argument that it could be done more effectively from without was well stated by J. H. Thomas and, especially, by Bernard Shaw, whose speech on this occasion was long remembered. The conference then voted, 2,117,000 to 810,000, to withdraw from the Coalition.[23] Clynes, Brace, Hodge, and Walsh soon heeded, but the other ministers clung to their posts as individuals. Barnes and Wardle stayed until after the Treaty of Versailles was signed. Parker and Roberts remained until 1922, when the last vestiges of the Coalition disappeared.

Membership in the Coalition enabled the party to make its maximum contribution to the war effort. Withdrawal freed it from the necessity of compromise and the danger of absorption. Independence made possible continued growth, power, and application of its own remedies for Britain's needs.

The atmosphere of the general election of December 1918 was highly unfavorable to Labour. Lloyd George started with a promise to make Britain a land fit for heroes, but an upsurge of popular feeling turned the slogan to "Hang the Kaiser and make Germany pay." Due to the campaign's brevity and its highly emotional character, the Labour program had scant opportunity for rational consideration. The party made its mightiest effort yet, however, and entered candidates in 363 constituencies, over half those in the United Kingdom. They polled 2,244,000 votes as compared with the 370,802 of the second election of 1910, though the increase was due partly to the increased number of candidates and partly to the fact that for the first time married women over thirty could vote.

But the heavy gain was not reflected in the House of Commons, because the system of territorial constituencies distorted the result to Labour's disadvantage; Labour's 24 per cent of the total elected less than 9 per cent of the House of Commons. It polled over two-fifths as many votes as did the Conservatives, but elected 57 as compared with the latter's 338. Labour's number, increased to 60 by the adherence of two unendorsed Labour candidates and one Cooperator, made it the largest single Opposition party, but with 34 Asquithian Liberals, 7 Irish Nationalists, and a few independents (since the Sinn Feiners refused to take their seats), they were left to face the overwhelming forces of the Coalition.

The successful Labourites came almost entirely from the manufacturing and mining areas of the North, Midlands, central Scotland, and South Wales. There were only four from Greater London. The party made little impression on the South or rural Britain. The Miners had the greatest success in the election of 25 of their 51 candidates. By contrast, only 3 out of 50 I.L.P. men were elected.[24]

Labour's best-known leaders, especially those popularly stigmatized as pacifist, were among the losers. MacDonald and Snowden were both defeated by members of the new right-wing National Democratic and Labour party, which came out of the British Workers' League. So was Henderson. The parliamentary Labour party, accordingly, was left extremely weak in leadership. Clynes, Hodge, Brace, Thomas, and Tillett, led by William Adamson, a Scottish miner, constituted an ineffective Opposition team. Henderson came back next year in a by-election, but continued to be absorbed in organization work.

Labour's showing in the country was, nevertheless, highly significant. In spite of the popular temper the returns recorded a great growth. Its independence and steadfastness gave promise of a better future when an atmosphere more normal than that of a "khaki election" should be restored. In the long view the advance scored by Labour seems more important than Lloyd George's momentary triumph.

5. The Development of Foreign Policy

The war ended whatever sense of detachment from world affairs existed in the Labour party, while the postwar disorganization of Europe brought home the relation between conditions abroad and welfare in Britain. The idea was taken seriously that this war, so costly in every respect, must be the last. There followed a prolonged examination of causes and a search for remedies, including disarmament, a democratic control of foreign policy, and the utilization of the League as an agency for conciliation. Labour's interest in the affairs of other peoples was rooted partly in a generous humanitarianism and partly in the knowledge that in helping others they might help themselves. This outlook and the search for a coherent foreign policy brought a stream of recruits from the badly divided Liberals, who, in turn, intensified the interest in foreign affairs.

The postwar party was in a position to be well informed on foreign affairs. In 1918 it set up an Advisory Committee on International Questions with Sidney Webb as the first president and Leonard S. Woolf, who served for many years, as its secretary. Among those who had long membership were C. R. and Noel Buxton, Arthur Ponsonby, Philip Noel-Baker, H. N. Brailsford, Arthur Greenwood, and Hugh Dalton, while outside experts often lent assistance. The Committee's reports covered a wide range of subjects; in one year there were eighteen on topics ranging from reparations in Europe to taxation in Tanganyika. Such reports provided the material for speeches and policy statements. In 1922 the Committee was attached to a Joint International Department set up by the Labour party and the T.U.C., with W. Gillies, a Glasgow Fabian, as its secretary, to carry on the international work of the labor movement.[1]

Thanks to this Advisory Committee, the Labour party had better knowledge of world problems. No other party had anything like it. Its findings were helpful in the development of a Labour foreign policy grounded more on solid study than on emotional attitudes. It contributed to the considerable success that the MacDonald governments had in foreign affairs. Also in these same years the political leaders had direct acquaintance with foreign lands. MacDonald traveled widely, while at international conferences Labourites met the chiefs of the continental parties, many of whom in postwar Europe were in positions of power. Thanks to the Workers' Travel Association, founded in 1922, a small but increasing number of the rank and file learned something of the Continent. This study of and interest in foreign affairs built up a public opinion of which any British government would have to take account.

After the election of 1918, immediate interest centered on the forthcoming peace conference at Paris. Labour had conceived a high regard for President Wilson, whose appearance in England called forth a welcome that indicated how fully and completely it had accepted him as its spokesman. Its hopes for a just settlement and a new international order rested on his ability to achieve them. Doubts appeared, however, when "open diplomacy," the first of the Fourteen Points, was interpreted less literally than Labourites expected. The continued blockade of Germany, denounced by Labour as "barbarous," and intervention in Russia likewise appeared out of harmony with other points in the program. The preliminary draft Covenant of the League, published on February 14, 1919, brought more criticism than praise because the concentration of authority in the proposed Council, dominated by five great victorious Powers, seemed like an effort of the wartime alliance to perpetuate itself.[2]

On May 8 the Labour party executive issued a manifesto on the draft treaty, which had been published on the preceding day. It revealed that the first impression of the executive, which was dominated by moderate trade unionists, was that the treaty, unacceptable in part, might be adapted by the League in accordance with Labour ideals to the changing needs of Europe.[3] The Labour left, however, loudly voiced opposition. The *Daily Herald* led off with a double-column editorial captioned: "Where There Is No Peace."[4] The I.L.P. executive denounced it as "a capitalist, militarist, and imperialist imposition" that violated every public statement of Allied war aims.[5] The pacifist Liberals, such as Arthur Ponsonby, E. D. Morel, and C. P. Trevelyan, now coming over to Labour, spoke in the same terms.

The points most criticized were the alleged violations of the principles of nationality, the Saar settlement, the Polish frontiers and corridor, the cession of the German colonies, the punitive economic and impossible financial provisions, the one-sided disarmament, the omission of Germany from the League, and the League's undemocratic basis.

The treaty with Austria was likewise denounced by Labour as out of accord with Wilsonian principles: blocks of Germans were assigned to Italy and the succession states; the financial obligations were impossible; and the truncated Austria could not survive. Often the worst of motives were attributed to the treaty makers. In a statement of May 19 on the Treaty of Versailles the U.D.C. executive said:

That purpose is obvious. It is to reduce the new democratic Germany to the position of a vassal state, to render her commercial recovery impossible; to drive her out of international life; to crush the spirit of her people. Their exclusion from the League of Nations; their disarmament alone among the Powers of Europe; the imposition upon them of enormous and indefinite financial burdens, combined with numberless handicaps to their commercial and industrial rehabilitation, display this purpose in the clearest light.[6]

These left points of view quickly permeated the Labour center. Many who at first overlooked points of disagreement in their enthusiasm for the League and the righting of some national wrongs became disquieted. "The treaty as a whole is not defensible," said the *New Statesman* on second thought, and "as one rereads it the hope of founding a real League of Nations on the basis of such a peace fades into a very far-off future."[7] Henderson, as secretary of the party, issued a statement that neither the policy of President Wilson nor that of British Labour had yet triumphed. The executive reconsidered its first hasty manifesto and on June 1 united with the parliamentary party to condemn the settlement as fundamentally bad in that it was based upon the very principles which had produced the war. Later in the month the party's annual conference agreed with this view. Its resolution, put by MacDonald and Clynes, urged the completion of the League by the prompt admission of Germany and the utilization of that agency to modify the harsh terms of the treaty.[8]

In the disappointment of the moment there was little effort to comprehend the outlook of the French, the Belgians, and the Italians, and of the necessity of compromise in order to get a treaty. The better features and positive gains, such as the League, the release of subject nationalities, the provision for plebiscites, the safeguards for minorities, and the mandate system were ignored in the concentration upon points open to criticism. In retrospect, many Labourites thought that in 1919 they had exaggerated the case against the treaties.[9] For some years after 1919, however, demands for their revision regularly featured Labour party conferences.

The League of Nations was long a subject of controversy in the labor movement. During the war it had been a cherished aim and a factor in rallying the party to the Wilson standard. In the constitution of 1918 one object was stated to be "to assist in organizing a Federation of Nations for the maintenance of Freedom and Peace," which would provide an agency for conciliation and arbitration and even "for such International Legislation as may be practicable."[10] Yet when the idea became a reality Labourites took a second look, were disconcerted, and felt uncertain of some features.

The I.L.P.–U.D.C. wing vigorously denounced the League as defective and dangerous in its present form. In the *Socialist Review, Forward,* and the *Labour Leader* MacDonald voiced his deep distrust: the League was a bulwark of capitalism and imperialism; it was based undemocratically on governments, instead of directly on parliaments with representation from both majority and minority parties. He opposed the concept of peace enforced by armed might. Snowden spoke in the same terms. His chairman's address at the 1920 I.L.P. conference described the League as "an instrument for the exaction of the terms of the treaties."[11] Yet MacDonald and the I.L.P. advocated not withdrawal but revision. The 1923 conference suggested separation from the Treaty of Versailles, a more democratic basis, and the inclusion of ex-enemy states to make it universal. E. D. Morel's *Foreign Affairs* voiced similar views. All of these critics were distrustful of France; they regarded the League as a means of keeping Germany down and Russia isolated.

Clynes and Henderson expressed the views of those who were more hopeful. In July 1919, Clynes welcomed the League as a means to deal with "blemishes" in the Treaty and to keep the peace; he thought economic sanctions alone would suffice. At first Henderson was less content; in November 1919, he referred to it as a coalition of victorious powers, and four years later he was still saying it was too much an instrument of Allied policy. Yet he thought it should be accepted and that, when revised, it might become the most effective instrument for permanent peace. In 1922 he proposed for its reconstruction: (1) it should be made universal; (2) the Assembly should be the sovereign authority and the Council its executive organ; (3) in certain classes of disputes arbitration should be compulsory and decisions binding;

(4) in case of aggression all members should come to the assistance of the one against which the warlike act was committed. Here Henderson implied sanctions, but stopped short of the word "military." He wanted further to see the League gradually strengthened by utilizing it in such activities as making investigations and reports, protecting minorities, aiding backward peoples, and enforcing labor standards.[12]

The T.U.C. and Labour majorities regularly endorsed the League and the International Labor Organization at their annual conferences. Clynes could preface the resolution on it at the 1921 T.U.C. conference with the statement: "This is not a gathering where anything need be said at length to convert anyone to the principle of a real League of Nations," and Tom Shaw, in seconding it, said, "In my opinion there is no chance of universal peace except through the League of Nations."[13]

In 1922 the Labour party election manifesto, *Labour's Call to the People,* which was signed by Webb, MacDonald, and Henderson, approved an all-inclusive League with power to deal with international disputes by arbitration and conciliation, and for arms limitation with general disarmament as the goal.[14] It reflected the fact that hopes were really pinned upon the conciliation and disarmament possibilities of the League, while few were willing to face military sanctions and a need for preparedness. Many thought the latter could be disregarded; the fact that modern war was so costly that it permitted no real victors should in itself be a sufficient deterrent. Further, if the League were universal, no one country would be so mad as to attack fifty; if it did, economic sanctions alone would suffice. Many, accordingly, could simultaneously support the League and complete disarmament. Confidence in moral force was high. In these years the conviction that total war had taught mankind a lesson caused Labourites to cherish some illusions.

Labour considered armament limitation a practical policy. Because of the defeat of "German militarism," it seemed that the nations might now agree to disburden themselves of this ruinous and irrational expenditure. Christian and pacifist idealists united in No More War demonstrations. Socialists would deny armaments to capitalist governments. Some stressed rival armaments as a cause of war and would break the vicious circle at that point.

Some pacifists urged unilateral disarmament and called on the parliamentary party to vote against the estimates for the armed forces, but the leadership refused. Henderson labeled unilateralism absurd and foolish. MacDonald and Snowden, though bent on limitation, agreed. MacDonald said, "No responsible statesman will ever persuade the people of this country to disarm in a world armed to the teeth."[15] A Labour party–T.U.C. statement looked forward to universal disarmament coupled with the institution of an international police force, but said that in the meantime "The suggestion that Labour could leave the Empire defenseless in the face of potential enemies . . . is idle and false."[16]

The American move for naval reduction brought immediate approval. On the eve of the Washington conference of 1921 the National Joint Council issued a statement in favor of drastic naval reduction and limitation, but added that general action was contingent upon the existence of machinery for the equitable settlement of disputes. Unlike the unilateralists, the Joint Council held that a satisfactory means for the solution of problems would have to precede disarmament.[17]

The democratic control of foreign policy was much discussed, because in the current analyses of the causes of the war the secret commitments bulked large. Labour objected to the aristocratic nature of the foreign service, which was still monopolized by a small circle of families with old school ties. It would make entry more competitive and open to all classes. Popularly there was much condemnation of "secret diplomacy." This was a misnomer, however, because in the popular mind it meant usually a secret foreign policy. The Labour position was that covenants should be open, but that in the steps leading to them the Foreign Secretary had discretion. The Labour leadership was fully aware that delicate negotiations could not be carried on in the public view; it insisted, however, that Parliament should be kept informed of their existence and objectives, and that commitments, to be binding, required Parliament's approval.[18]

Labour devoted much attention to the defeated enemy. The British conscience and sense of fair play were touched by reports of German suffering due not only to war losses but also to the continuation of the Allied blockade for five months after the Armistice. The stories of hardship and hunger were successfully propagandized. Everyone heard of the word from General Plumer that he could not prevent his soldiers in the occupied Rhineland from sharing their food with starving German children. What was not well known was that the German government had rejected a very reasonable Allied offer of January 1919 to let Germany use some of its gold reserve and shipping to buy and transport food, and also that, when in March the German government yielded on this point and food was on hand, the

German High Command for its own purposes induced it to hold up the distribution of fats until the Treaty of Versailles was signed and there was no chance of a renewal of the war.

Meanwhile, soldiers and journalists played upon humanitarian sentiment with stories of hunger and consequent disease and moral decline. All sections of the labor movement loudly disapproved a statecraft that allegedly used blockade and starvation as an instrument of policy. The party conference of 1919 protested, "The Labour party has put the simple, decent, humane aspect of this thing first, before any political consideration whatsoever. It refuses to sanction the starvation of children, old men and women, the weak and ill, as an 'instrument of policy.' "[19] Labour demanded the end of the blockade, the provision of immediate relief, and the restoration of German productivity. Apart from simple humanitarianism, there was self-interest in that continued distress might become a cause of war and fear lest low standards abroad be reflected on those at home.

Attention centered increasingly on the economic provisions of the treaty, especially from 1920 onward, when the full force of the postwar depression struck Britain and the difficulties of a country that depended so largely upon manufacturing and trade stood fully revealed in dwindling export figures and lengthening lines of unemployed. There was great activity in Labour circles with special conferences, joint commissions, speeches in the Commons, and a flood of reports from the Advisory Committee and the Labour Research Department. In all of it the impact of J. M. Keynes's *Economic Consequences of the Peace* (1919) was manifest.

The theme was that in this interdependent world the economic ruin of one nation was the ruin of all. As to the depression, a report of 1920 stated, "One [country] cannot climb out of the pit while another, even though its enemy, remains there."[20] The territorial settlement was criticized because of its economic as well as its politicial implications. The deprivation of the Saar, Upper Silesia, and other areas meant a loss not only of German nationals but also of the means of economic recovery.

Labour agreed that Germany should pay reparations but that the amount should be reasonable, clearly defined, and distributed according to need. Right and left alike thought that the devastated areas of Belgium and France should be restored by means of German materials and German labor. A distinction should be made between these claims and those for pensions and allowances; the latter should be dropped, and, as they constituted a larger proportion of the British bill, Labour was thereby proposing to yield to France, whose need was admittedly the greater. Occupation forces should be withdrawn, so that their cost could be devoted to restoration. Impediments to trade should be removed; here Labour saw the means of Britain's revival, but Labour would apply the Open Door principle to Britain's nonself-governing colonies as well as to those of other nations. Labour favored a cancellation of inter-Allied war debts whether the United States joined in it or not; here Labour was offering to give, because on balance Britain was a creditor.

By the time of the Genoa conference of 1922, Labour was urging that Britain renounce all reparations as well as war debts. Again economics re-enforced idealism. British coal areas were in deep distress because surplus reparations coal was being sold cheaply by Belgium, France, and Italy. Coal exports during the first eleven months of 1921 were down by 19½ million tons as compared with a like period in 1913, but according to the Spa agreement Germany would continue to supply 22 million tons annually in reparations. Likewise shipyards along the Clyde and the Tyne were idled when German ships were taken as reparations. The economic dangers of receiving huge gifts were starkly revealed. For more than one reason, accordingly, attention centered on the economic problems of the peace.[21]

Labour was less sympathetic toward France than toward Germany, for the postwar Anglo-French rift that on the official level was so disastrous in international relations affected the labor movement as well. The British were concerned with the return of normal trade relations so necessary to their livelihood, while the French feared a restored Germany as a security threat. The French insistence upon security found scant support in Britain. Labour refused to believe in the reality of the need; it was convinced that French policy was aggressive, expansionist, and dangerous to peace. With the North Sea wider than the Rhine and the German fleet at the bottom of it, Britons felt less reason for fear from a revived Germany.

Such opinions, widely held in the Labour movement, were sometimes brutally expressed: "I find myself wholly uninterested in France," wrote Beatrice Webb in 1919. Later, in reflections upon the food shortages and famines, she said that she would save the family of a German professor or Austrian official, but "I am not certain that I would deny myself to save a Frenchman." During the 1923 election she wrote, "With Germany slowly drowning and those damned French knocking her on the head whenever she tries to save herself, what does it matter who wins this election—it is too late for Great Britain to save Europe from chaos and another war."[22]

Morel and the U.D.C. group portrayed France, especially under Poincaré, as ravenous and militant and Germany as the humiliated and suffering victim. Later, especially after the advent of the Nazis, there were admissions of too great tenderness toward Germany and too little understanding of France. As one Labourite wrote, "Most of us, alas, shed tears over the sufferings of Germany, while remaining blandly indifferent to the far greater sufferings of France . . . it would, at any time, have been far easier to rouse a popular audience against France than against Germany."[23]

The distrust of France was such that the suggestion of an Anglo-French defensive alliance brought immediate Labour disapproval. The party conference of 1921 went on record against it; the mover of the resolution denounced France as the "truculent military bully of Europe" with "Napoleonic dreams of European ambition."[24] The National Joint Council, through which the Labour party, the T.U.C., and the parliamentary party now often acted, issued a pronouncement against the proposed alliance and in favor of working through an inclusive League of Nations. Exchanges of visits with the French and Belgian parties led to statements in 1922 that revealed a greater appreciation of the French position and need for security, but still a preference for utilizing the League rather than an alliance. The conference of that year referred to the League as the most hopeful machinery for the preservation of peace and security, and rejected an alliance as incompatible with it.[25] Poincaré's threat to occupy the Ruhr, the industrial heart of Germany, in order to enforce reparations, increased Labour's tendency to rely on the League as the sole means of averting it.

The actual occupation of the Ruhr by the French, the Belgians, and a "token" Italian force on January 11, 1923, stirred all labor organizations. The National Joint Council immediately registered its disapproval, and on January 25 the T.U.C. general council and the Labour executive, in a more detailed statement, denounced the occupation as politically dangerous and economically disastrous. They proposed League action under Article 11, presumably on the theory that investigation and publicity would be sufficient without invoking sanctions; it was also true that, in addition to compunction at the use of force, there was the practical fact of its futility in view of the three Powers involved and the limited membership of the League. In March a Labour delegation went to the Ruhr to observe and report.[26]

Labour protests continued. The 1923 party conference condemned the invasion as aggression. The parliamentary party, which had been more than doubled by the election of 1922, proposed a meeting of representatives of all the political parties in the Parliaments of France, Belgium, and Britain; it was hard to believe that men of good will, given possession of the facts, could not reach an acceptable compromise. When the government showed no interest, it organized a meeting in Paris of parliamentary representatives of the Labour and Socialist parties of Britain, France, Belgium, and Italy. The conference urged the admission of Germany to the League and the use of the League's conciliation machinery. Another Labour proposal was for a special session of the League to set reparations at a reasonable figure and for concurrent negotiations by Allied and Associated governments to deal with their problem of debts. At the same time the Internationals, both the Trade Union and the Labour and Socialist, were continuously active with meetings and suggestions. In all the discussions the British delegates noted the bearing of the Continental situation on their own economic distress, though it was by no means their sole motivation.[27]

The causes and course of the war brought Central Europe and the Balkans to Labour attention. The party saw the conflict between the claims of nationalism and the realities of economics. It dreaded a Balkanization of the area with unrestricted protectionism and the danger of the numerous local wars to the general peace. MacDonald, a traveler there and a first-hand witness, held typical Labour views; he believed that small nationalities had a cultural contribution to make and should be protected, but that their erection into sovereign states of doubtful viability was a mistake and a menace to peace. Furthermore, the intermingling of peoples often made a satisfactory demarcation impossible.[28]

The broken unity of the Danube valley was the settlement most frequently criticized. Labour now complained that Austria was left a non-viable remnant, cut off from the sea and the raw materials vital for its industry, and denied the right of union with Germany, although Lloyd George's statement to the special trade-union conference had averred that he was not fighting to destroy Austria-Hungary. The cession of South Tyrol to Italy was condemned as an unnecessary violation of national rights. Hungary, likewise reduced and landlocked, shared this sympathy. The Rumanian invasion that stripped the country roused feeling, though there was no liking for the Soviet republic of Bela Kun. Reports of the White Terror under Admiral Horthy brought protests from the I.L.P. and the Labour party. The latter sent a delegation of five, including Colonel Josiah Wedgwood and F. W. Jowett, to investigate; it reported that the White Terror was even worse than the Red Terror that had preceded it.[29] There were similar protests against the White Terror in Finland, where Dr. Marion Phillips reported it had claimed thousands of victims.

On the Balkans Labour charged Lloyd George with being unduly and dangerously pro-Greek. It urged the restoration of an Aegean port to Bulgaria. It denounced the treatment of Turkey as likely to produce repercussions throughout the Muslim world. It thought Lloyd George had agreed too readily to support the Greek venture into Smyrna and Asia Minor. Labour's positive proposal was to neutralize the Straits under an international commission, demilitarize Thrace, and put the Near East minorities under League of Nations protection.[30] When the Turkish armies, having taken Smyrna, approached the Straits at Chanak and an Anglo-Turkish war seemed imminent, Labour antagonism to the Prime Minister flared high. The Joint Council denounced his communiqué of September 16, 1922, which implied the possibility of war, as "the crowning item of a dangerous policy."

The Council went on to protest the failure to summon Parliament so that the representatives of the people had no opportunity to secure information or influence policy; should the government fail to heed this protest, "We shall summon a conference of representatives of the whole of our affiliated organizations, and do all in our power to avert the national calamity of another war."[31] In the temper of 1922 this language implied a threat of direct action, but Labour was intent upon preventing a war. It did not praise the ephemeral triumph of Lloyd George, who, deserted by his allies, supported only by Winston Churchill and a few others in the Cabinet, and with but a small force at Chanak, nevertheless stopped the armies of Mustapha Kemal in the full flush of victory.

Labour watched the rise of fascism in Italy with disgust and without the excuses that led so many Conservatives to condone it. Naturally the raids and the destruction of trade-union and socialist centers roused sympathy for the victims. The bombardment of Corfu in 1923 and Greece's appeal to the League brought one of Labour's strongest expressions of support for that organization. The T.U.C., meeting shortly after the event, urged the League to take action to the extent of boycotting the offending country.[32]

Revolutionary Russia was central in Labour thought on foreign affairs. The Tsarist empire was detested as the worst prewar regime; the new Russia became the symbol of future promise, even though few liked the Bolsheviks or their methods. The enthusiastic reception given the fugitive Kerensky at the June 1918 party conference, where Henderson dramatically staged the whole performance, showed where Labour's preference lay; the Soviet state, nevertheless, apparently promised the miracle of socialism brought down from the realm of theory to reality. Russia seemed a fact and an achievement; if not yet a workers' utopia, it had, supposedly, a workers' government. As a prime object of capitalist attack, the very name became a slogan and a rallying point. No matter how seriously British socialists differed from Russian Communists, to the former it was axiomatic that there must be no interference with the Russian experiment.

This interpretation of Russia was not shared by British Conservatives, who resented the separate peace made in 1918, confiscation of British property, and propaganda aimed at disruption of the Empire. Many preferred to see the Soviet regime boycotted, weakened, and ultimately destroyed. Their policy was that of the sanitary cordon and assistance to counterrevolution. Even after 1920 when this policy was abandoned, the differences over Russia remained the chief issue in foreign affairs dividing these two parties.

In accordance with the policy of allowing the Russian experiment to proceed under favorable circumstances, Labour strove to secure the end of the blockade and the evacuation of the Allied troops from the North and the Far East. It argued that, if permitted to go their own way in peace, the Russians would be too busy to make trouble for others—a comforting theory that reappeared in the closing days of the Second World War. A pamphlet by the party's Advisory Committee on International Questions stated,

The Soviet Government have a vast constructive domestic policy which must absorb all their attention and energy for many years to come: there is at least a very good chance that, if we cease to attack them and offer them a real and honest peace, they will have too much to do in connection with their domestic program and internal difficulties to think of military adventures and external aggression.[33]

Sentiment against intervention was so strong that at the party conference of June 1919, direct action was suggested; Labour's demands should be enforced "by the unreserved use of their political and industrial power." Robert Smillie, the Miners' president, favored it, and Herbert Morrison, now well known for his work as an organizer in the London area, made his first speech at an annual conference in support. Henderson, Clynes, and the executive warned against the use of the strike weapon for political purposes, but such was the temper of the conference that they lost.[34] In July the Triple Alliance threatened to invoke its power if the occupying forces were not withdrawn. Within a few days the government announced that by the end of the summer all British troops would be out of North Russia and that no more would be sent to any part of that country. In September they were evacuated.

The agitation continued, nevertheless, because of support, including subsidies, to the White counterrevolutionaries Kolchak, Denikin, Yudenich, and, later, Wrangel. In November a Hands Off Russia Committee was formed. On December 9–10 the T.U.C., in this critical period almost as active politically as the party, devoted attention to Russian relations. Disturbed by Clemenceau's references to the use of the border states as a sanitary cordon, the T.U.C. expressed fear that it implied the mounting of an attack on Russia. It sent a deputation to Lloyd George in behalf of peace and in conjunction with the Labour party sent a delegation to Moscow. When Russian trade unionists, attempting a return visit, were denied entry into the United Kingdom, the incident deepened distrust of the government.

The delegation to Russia, which included moderates such as Ben Turner, chairman, Tom Shaw, Margaret Bondfield, and Ethel Snowden of the I.L.P., and left extremists such as A. A. Purcell and Robert Williams, was sympathetic toward the Russians in their struggle against famine and the Whites and in the determination to make "their kind of socialism" succeed. The members interviewed Lenin, who was very frank about the dictatorial nature of his government and the ruthlessness of his policy. They noted, however, the unwillingness of people to speak freely, and most agreed that the Bolshevist way was not for democratic Britain. The delegation, nevertheless, sent home an interim report attributing the worst aspects of the regime to the Allied blockade and intervention.[35]

A contemporary and spectacular private visit to Russia was made by George Lansbury, editor of the *Daily Herald*. This Christian socialist, known as a devout Anglican and affectionately regarded for his work for the London poor, was dazzled by Russia from the moment he first saw the red flag flying at the border. Although he disliked the dictatorship, he saw almost everything else in rosiest hues. He met Lenin, whom he interpreted as a pure-hearted man whose religion consisted in doing good. His glowing accounts were telegraphed to the *Daily Herald*, and upon his return he addressed an overflow meeting in the Albert Hall.

For a time Lansbury held a unique position in the movement, and

Labour's only daily was used in an attempt to swing it to the Third International. When the *Daily Herald* was in financial distress, the Russians offered aid, and Francis Meynell, a director, on his own authority and unknown to Lansbury, brought out a gift from Russia in the form of jewels reportedly £75,000 in value. When the transaction became known, the opposition was such and the clamor in the British press so great that the proffered aid was rejected, Meynell resigned his directorship, and the *Herald* attempted to solve its problem by raising its price. Lansbury's personal repute was such that his influence was not seriously damaged.[36]

When early in 1920 the Poles, backed by France, prepared to invade Russia, twenty-two prominent labor leaders signed a manifesto asserting their determination to oppose British participation even though it might necessitate direct action. The Poles launched their attack and on May 8 captured Kiev. In Britain tension was so high that on May 10 the dockers refused to coal the *Jolly George*, a vessel laden with munitions for Poland. A few days later their union, led by Ernest Bevin, who now became a national figure, banned the loading of military supplies destined for use against Russia.

Later in the summer a change in the fortunes of war brought a new crisis to Labour. The Russians rallied and drove the Poles back almost to Warsaw. The Poles appealed for aid, which France was prepared to give, but British Labour was determined not to be drawn in. On August 4 Henderson called for demonstrations. On August 9 the three executives of the party, the parliamentary party, and the T.U.C. combined to warn the government that the industrial power of organized labor would be used to defeat any move to involve Britain, to call upon affiliated organizations to be ready to "down tools," to set up a Council of Action, and to appoint a delegation to interview Lloyd George. That meeting occurred the next day, when Bevin spoke for labor but found Lloyd George unyielding. The agitation redoubled; some 350 local Councils of Action were formed, and demonstrations were held throughout the country.

Among the 27 members of the Council of Action were a few from the extreme left, such as Robert Williams and A. A. Purcell, but the majority were moderates. Even moderates such as Clynes and new recruits from Liberalism such as Wedgwood were now stirred so deeply that they accepted the possibility of industrial action for a political end. It was eloquent of the desire to save revolutionary Russia.

On August 13, on three days' notice, the Council assembled a conference of 1,044 delegates from trade unions and local Labour parties that Snowden later pronounced the most impressive of his long career. In an atmosphere of unanimity, the Council of Action was instructed to remain in being until it had secured an absolute guarantee that British armed forces would not be used in support of Poland or any other military or naval effort against the Soviet government; it was authorized to call for any and every form of withdrawal of labor necessary to make this policy effective.[37]

It was evidence of the depth of feeling that the moderates should now accept direct action. J. H. Thomas, who presided, stated that it was a challenge to the constitution justifiable only by the urgent necessity of averting war, but most spokesmen defended it as not revolutionary because limited in scope and specific in purpose. Whatever the theory, however, there was no mistaking the temper. When the question was carried, wrote Snowden, there was "a scene the like of which I have never witnessed in any Labour conference . . . a hurricane of cheering," followed by a period of absolute silence to register determination to abide by the decision.[38]

In more positive peace moves the Council approached the Soviet delegation and the Polish legation in London. It urged the former to clarify its position on Polish independence, and in return received copies of official pronouncements deemed satisfactory. Fortunately, no occasion for direct action arose; a Polish counterattack threw the Red Army back from Warsaw, and by October the fighting was over. Thereafter British policy changed, which convinced Labour that it had won a notable victory. The party executive asserted flatly that Labour's action had prevented open war with Russia.

Whether British support of Poland would have extended to military intervention is very doubtful, but whatever the might-have-beens, the events of 1920 revealed the measure of Labour's sympathy for Russia. They also colored its outlook for the next two decades. It remained highly sensitive to any suggestion of interference in Soviet internal affairs. It became an obsession that militant Toryism might use British power to crush collectivism, so that Labour hesitated to entrust a Conservative administration with powerful national armaments. Not until Nazi Germany became an immediate and obvious danger did Labour thinking change and the party shift its position on national rearmament.

Labour welcomed the trade agreement of 1921, which followed the cessation of the intervention policy. It was convinced of the vast potential of the Russian market, which might go far toward a solution of the unemployment problem. The party pressed, accordingly, for the restoration of normal diplomatic relations, aid to the famine-stricken areas, and the extension of trade credits. Credits, admittedly, were risky, but they might in the long run provide the cheapest means of British unemployment relief.

Although Labour showed such concern for the Soviet experiment, it was fully aware of its undemocratic and aggressive character. It disliked the dictatorship and the police state. It resented the harsh treatment accorded the Social Revolutionaries for acts of 1917–18 in resisting the Bolsheviks. Bevin, for example, although so prominent in the Council of Action, at a Berlin meeting felt disgusted to hear Karl Radek justify the whole repressive policy. The overthrow of a Social Democratic republic in Georgia was viewed by Labour, especially by the I.L.P., as an attack upon its own kind. The 1922 party conference asked for a mixed commission from Socialist and Communist parties to discover the wishes of the Georgian people through a free vote, which the Russians rejected.[39] The Communists were always a thorny problem in Britain. The responsible Labour leadership well knew the lack of tolerance on the part of those for whom they sought tolerance.

Labour was ready to apply to the Empire the principle of self-determination wherever peoples were capable of self-rule. It urged that India be given the same status as Canada. Egypt should be evacuated; there were suggestions that the Suez Canal, as an international waterway, be placed under League control. Since a special position in Persia might provoke war with Russia, withdrawal was advocated.[40] Mandates should not become a disguised annexation, nor should the system be confined to ex-enemy possessions, but extended to all those which for the time being were incapable of standing alone.

The affairs of Ireland, closer to home, compelled attention as the irregular civil war dragged on with the daily story of outrage and reprisal. Ambushes and murders by the Irish Republican Army received less attention than the raids and reprisals by the Royal Irish Constabulary, known as the Black and Tans. This difference was due to Labour's long sympathy with Home Rule, to the greater publicity given to Black and Tan acts, and to the opinion that British policy should not sink to the level of such reprisals, whatever the justification. Labourites seldom stated the Ulstermen's point of view that they were a separate people, were determined to resist reduction under Home Rule to a perpetual minority status governed by a Catholic agrarian majority, and were devoted to the Union with Britain.

In the House of Commons Henderson called for an investigation of the situation in Ireland, and when it was rejected, Labour sent its own commission. Its report detailed acts of Black and Tan lawlessness and terror. It urged the withdrawal of British forces and the convocation of an Irish constituent assembly to draw up a constitution without limitations except that it should afford protection for minorities and provide that Ireland become no naval or military menace to Great Britain. A special party conference endorsed this report, which was printed and widely read. It contributed to the atmosphere in which it was possible for the government to change its policy and make the treaty that led to the setting up of the Irish Free State.

The postwar years, accordingly, witnessed a developing Labour foreign policy. It included restoration and reconciliation in Europe, a peace policy based upon the democratic control of foreign policy, agreed disarmament, and the use of the conciliation machinery of the League. It accepted the principle of self-determination for states economically viable and, as in the case of Russia, opposed intervention based on dislike of a system of government. It believed national prosperity could not exist in isolation; it urged an economic liberalism that would permit fair access to raw materials and freer trade. It would apply its principles to the British Empire. Nothing in this policy was peculiarly socialist. The principles were shared by most Liberals; they facilitated the flow of Liberal recruits now coming over to Labour, and they made possible official Liberal support to a Labour government.

6. The Constitutional Road

The end of the war was followed by a short-lived economic boom, which was succeeded late in 1920 by a slump that deepened into a serious depression. Such were the resulting unemployment and distress that, in view of the slowness of parliamentary methods, some in the labor movement sought speedier solutions. Many advocated resort to the strike weapon, and some thought communism offered an alternative to Labour's moderate socialism, but the party kept to the middle road of parliamentary democracy. Its confidence was rewarded in the next election by a doubled popular vote and a much strengthened parliamentary party.

As the economic situation deteriorated, the working class bore the brunt of it. Wages declined faster than the cost of living. The lot of the employed worker was difficult, but for the unemployed it was far worse. Unemployment, with fluctuating numbers, confronted Britain with a problem it was to face for the next two decades. In December 1920 the figure stood at 5.8 per cent of those covered by unemployment insurance; by June 1921 the number was 2,171,288, or 17.8 per cent; it fell to 12.2 per cent by December 1922, with 1,431,929 unemployed. The industries particularly affected, with from one-fifth to more than one-third workless, were shipbuilding, iron and steel, engineering, and building. The areas hardest hit were Belfast, Glasgow, the Midlands, and the Northeast. Parades of the unemployed appeared daily in London streets, and out-of-work veterans played street organs and passed tin cups for pennies at every theater queue. Demonstrations were held in London and all major cities. There were protest marches to the capital from as far away as Glasgow. George Lansbury and 29 Poplar councillors went to jail for six weeks as a demonstration. Since the unemployment-insurance fund could not meet the need, it was supplemented by extra relief known as "the dole," but even so measures always lagged behind need.[1]

In the heated postwar atmosphere trade unionists were tempted to resort to "direct action" rather than wait upon slower parliamentary solutions. By 1920 there were 8,334,000 trade unionists, of whom 6,418,000 were affiliated with the T.U.C. New leaders such as Bevin and Robert Williams, who were less conservative than the older trio of Henderson, Clynes, and Thomas, were becoming prominent. A wave of strikes resulted. In 1913, a year of industrial conflict, the total days lost in stoppages amounted to 9,804,000, but in 1919 the number was 34,969,000; the next year it was 26,568,000, and in 1921 it rose to 85,872,000. In 1919 there was a serious strike by the Railwaymen and even one by the London police. In the same year a general strike was narrowly averted when the Miners, backed by the Railwaymen and the Transport Workers in the newly formed Triple Alliance, threatened to strike if the nationalization of the mines was not carried out. Lloyd George stalled off the strike. The Sankey Commission, appointed to make recommendations for the coal industry, had a majority of one in favor of nationalization, but because the members could agree on no single report, Lloyd George refused to adopt that solution. A special T.U.C. meeting in December decided against a strike and in favor of a "Mines for the Nation" campaign, which ended in talk without action.

In 1921 the Miners were again central in a general strike threat, one precipitated by wage reductions that in South Wales would have ranged from 40 to 49 per cent, though less elsewhere. Again the Triple Alliance was invoked, and the government prepared for a showdown. When the Miners insisted on keeping negotiations in their own hands until the Railwaymen and the Transport Workers were actually out, however, the latter unions refused to follow, so that on the very eve of the date for "down tools," the Triple Alliance collapsed. The Miners called it "Black Friday" and a betrayal, though the fault was mainly theirs in excluding their allies from the negotiations while expecting them to assume responsibility for the consequences.[2]

On three occasions during the postwar years, labor forces considered "direct action" for political objectives. In April 1919, it was suggested as the means to pry Allied troops out of Russia. In July 1920, it was used to protest official policy in Ireland. In August, it was seriously threatened when Labour tried to prevent British intervention on the Polish side in the Russo-Polish war. These protests and threats, although manifestations of the widespread unrest, were not really revolutionary in intent; they were not beginnings of the revolutions of Marx and Lenin in Britain. They were for limited and specific objectives. No preparations, significantly, were made for anything more than industrial action. It was pressure politics, though of a dangerous kind, as the older leadership recognized and frequently stated. Henderson, Clynes, and Thomas warned of the unwise and undemocratic character of extraconstitutional action, which might rebound by becoming a precedent for other classes to adopt. It required the threat of involvement in an unwanted Russo-Polish war to bring any of these men to the reluctant support of utilizing the strike weapon for a political objective.

Another challenge to the Labour party came from the Communists. Although the latter long continued to present a problem to Labour both in domestic politics and in foreign relations, it was in these early postwar years that the issues were defined and decisions taken to which Labour has consistently adhered. Whatever degree of sympathy Labour might have for the Communist ideal society, it rejected the politics of class against class, civil war, dictatorship, and rigid discipline in thought and action. It upheld the methods of parliamentary democracy and insisted upon maintaining the civil liberties with freedom of thought and expression.[3]

Although the entire British labor movement was profoundly affected by the events of 1917 in Russia, only a few extremists were ready to accept Bolshevist theory and leadership. The largest group was in the British Socialist party, which claimed about 8,000 members. In the Glasgow area was the even smaller Socialist Labour party, which stood for industrial unionism and direct action. In London's East End was the Workers' Socialist Federation, founded by Sylvia Pankhurst and composed largely of individuals who had a background of militancy in the suffragist movement and a lively hope of transforming society by revolutionary industrial action. This body was the first in Great Britain to assume the name of Communist. On the I.L.P. left were some who were impatient with MacDonald reformism as only a pale reflection of the light shining in Russia. In the factory centers the Shop Stewards and Workers' Committee movement, which was purely industrial in origin but had a political bent after the unrest of 1917, crystallized much of the discontent and precipitated strikes unsanctioned by official leadership.

The fusion of these elements into a united Communist party took three years. They attempted to draw the I.L.P. into the movement, and a minority there was ready to acquiesce. They held a joint conference, but it came to naught when, after hearing Arthur Mac-Manus present the Communist case, Snowden, the conference chairman, declared that to replace the ideal of evolutionary and democratic social change with the methods of Communism would involve the surrender of all the I.L.P. had cherished throughout its lifetime.[4]

The other groups reached agreement on the basis of acceptance of the soviet system, the dictatorship of the proletariat, and membership in the Third or Communist International, but not on political tactics or on affiliation with the Labour party. The Workers' Socialist Federation was contemptuous of political action and urged control of industry as the means for social change. Although the others conceded that political action was of only limited value, they upheld it as useful in stimulating the revolutionary fervor of the working class and believed that the House of Commons still afforded an excellent sounding board for propaganda.

On Communist affiliation with the Labour party the B.S.P. stood alone; it held that affiliation would enable the Communist party to forge links with the masses and prevent it from becoming a doctrinaire sect. The others, however, ridiculed the Labour party as "a bourgeois opportunist outfit" more interested in class collaboration than in class war. The majority agreed to submit these differences to a delegate conference, whose decision should be binding. The Workers' Socialist Federation dissented, stole a march on the others, and on June 19, 1920, with the aid of seven small local societies, formed the Communist party (British Section of the Third International) on the basis of complete abstention from parliamentary action.[5]

The other groups proceeded with their plans for amalgamation into a Communist party that would be "a party of action" and "wage the class war up to the point of revolution."[6] Their convention in London, July 31–August 1, 1920, was unanimous upon the replacement of parliamentary democracy by soviet communism and upon the necessity of a dictatorship of the proletariat to crush the inevitable capitalist opposition. By a vote of 186 to 19 it repudiated the view that the social revolution could be achieved by constitutional means. Parliaments and elections should be utilized for propaganda purposes, but a Communist elected to office would hold his mandate from, and be responsible to, the party, and in no sense be answerable to the constituency for which he happened to sit. The warmest debate was over relations with the Labour party. Affiliation was carried by the narrow margin of 100 to 85 on the argument that it would afford a great tactical advantage for combating the reactionary leaders and, like participation in Parliament, would provide a fine platform for propaganda. On this basis a second Communist party was founded.[7]

In closing the debate on the critical points still dividing the two Communist parties that now existed, the influence and advice of Lenin was decisive. In letters to Sylvia Pankhurst, Lenin expressed his opinion that the tactics of the Workers' Socialist Federation were a deviation from the correct party line. He followed in June 1920 with a pamphlet on *"Left Wing" Communism,* in which he dealt at length with the British situation.[8] He emphasized the necessity of establishing contact with the masses and the stupidity of tactics that abandoned politically backward workers to the unchecked influence of reactionary leaders. Parliaments might be obsolete in a developed communist state; but, in order to pave the way for future soviets, it was necessary to get inside and disrupt existing ones. Although the Labour party was hopelessly reactionary, the Hendersons and Snowdens, he said, should be helped to power so that the ensuing revelation of their worthlessness would facilitate their overthrow. "I want to support Henderson with my vote in the same way as a rope supports one who is hanged," was the simile by which Lenin instructed British Communists in their duties toward British Labour.[9]

The debate continued at the Second Congress of the Communist International at Moscow, where Sylvia Pankhurst and representatives of the Shop Stewards, including William Gallacher, spoke against joining the Labour party. Lenin himself put the case for affiliation. Although in his view the Labour party was controlled by "the worst bourgeois elements," he regarded it as unique in that its federal character enabled it to become the comprehensive organization of the British working class. Affiliation, therefore, was not only permissible but desirable. Instead of being a case of reprehensible class collaboration, the Communist role in it would be that of a vanguard leading the masses.[10] The Comintern executive thereupon ordered the British groups to meet within four months to compose their differences.

In accordance with these instructions 170 delegates met at Leeds on January 29–30, 1921, to complete their union. The I.L.P. left wing was not included as yet, because its members awaited the result of their efforts at the coming party conference to swing the entire organization into the movement. The Workers' Socialist Federation, although still unconvinced of the efficacy of political action, obeyed the Comintern's injunction, so that from this conference emerged the Communist Party of Great Britain.[11]

The Labour party became directly concerned with these developments when, shortly after the formation of a united Communist party in 1920, a request came for affiliation. This application of August 10, signed by Arthur MacManus and Albert Inkpin, chairman and secretary, respectively, was little more than a quotation of their convention's resolutions favoring soviets through dictatorship, repudiating reformist views of social change by parliamentary action, and deciding for affiliation with the Labour party.

The Labour executive promptly rejected the request with a brief note that the new party's objects did not appear to be in accord with the constitution, principles, and program of the Labour party.[12] This generalization brought a request for a more detailed explanation of the implied criticism of the Communists' aims and methods. Whereas the original application contained the resolutions stressing the differences between Communists and Labour, the second letter emphasized the degree of accord. Since admission was requested on the same footing as the I.L.P. and other socialist parties, it was argued that exclusion was not logically possible. The communication stated:

The Communist party, in deciding to make application for affiliation to the Labour party, did not suppose that the whole of its principles, methods, and policy would find acceptance on the part of those who at present constitute the executive of the Labour party. But it understood the Labour party to be so catholic in its composition and constitution that it could admit to its ranks all sections of the working-class movement that accept the broad principle of independent working-class political action, at the same time granting them freedom to propagate their own particular views as to the policy the Labour party should pursue and the tactics it should adopt.[13]

Henderson replied for the Labour executive that the differences between the two parties were neither temporary nor secondary, but fundamental and insuperable. He cited Communist utterances to support his charge that the Communists were less concerned with the Labour ideal of union for independent working-class action than with the desire to get within the party to effect its capture or disruption. A third Communist communication added nothing to previous statements and elicited in reply only the information that the matter would be reported in June 1921 to the next annual conference.

Although clear-thinking leaders like Henderson might from the very outset perceive the incompatibility of the two parties, there were factors that in 1920 might make it difficult for a Labour adherent to arrive easily at a decision on the question of Communist affiliation. As the Communists pointed out, the Labour party was originally conceived of by Keir Hardie and his colleagues as an all-embracing alliance of the labor movement. The federal organization had been specifically adopted for this objective, and, as conservative and moderate trade unionists were included along with outright socialists, Hardie's ideal had been largely achieved. The B.S.P. was admitted with its interpretation of Marxism so revolutionary that it facilitated the conversion of most of its members to communism. The party had never indulged in heresy hunts or purges, so that during the war, unpopular as were the pacifist and dissident elements, there had been no move for their expulsion. If the party still intended to become the complete political expression of the working-class movement, it was possible to argue a case for admission. At the moment thousands of disillusioned Liberals were flocking into the party. The welcome extended to these middle-class and even aristocratic recruits might appear in glaring contrast to the exclusion of bona fide workingmen, some of whom had to their credit a lifetime of devotion to the movement. To balance a strengthened right wing, it might be of advantage to maintain a revolutionary left. Communists, with their admitted enthusiasm and enterprise, might provide valuable "ginger" and leaven.

Finally, at the very moment (August 1920) when Labour was considering industrial action and even setting up Councils of Action to prevent Britain's entry into a Polish-Russian war, it might appear inconsistent to lay such heavy emphasis upon the sanctity of parliamentary methods. It is no wonder that such an outstanding democrat and pacifist as George Lansbury should reflect the puzzled and confused mind of many Labourites, so that upon his return from Moscow in 1920, emotionally moved by what he had seen, he welcomed the formation of a Communist party as an undoubted gain for the labor movement and urged his party to enter the Third International.[14]

At the same time the dogmatic and uncompromising attitude of the Bolshevists repelled most Labourites. When in March 1919 the Third International was established, it emphasized that it was out for a "fight without mercy" against the "social patriots" of the Second. When in May of the next year the Labour party–T.U.C. delegation interviewed Lenin in Moscow, he put his case in a letter to the British working class that was largely an attack upon their leaders. He was contemptuous of their loyalty to democracy, civil liberties, and peace. The more they piled up their pacifist resolutions, he stated, "the sooner they will share the fate of Kerensky, the Mensheviks, and social revolutionists in Russia." He added, "The freedom of the Press and assembly in a *bourgeois* democracy is tantamount to the freedom of the well-to-do to plot against the working people. It means freedom of bribing and buying up newspapers by the capitalists."[15]

Similarly, the Comintern executive replied to a detailed questionnaire from representatives of the I.L.P. who had traveled to Moscow with the Labour delegation. This response emphasized the sins of Henderson and his fellow reformists, insisted that parties joining the Third International must accept the whole of its program, and warned that victory in Britain could never be won by easy parliamentary methods but only "by heavy civil war."[16] That conformity to Bolshevik teaching and practice was demanded from constituent elements of the Third received further confirmation when in August that body laid down its twenty-one conditions for parties seeking affiliation.

If these views and statements were designed to win British Labour, they were failures; they had the opposite effect. The *New Statesman* said of Lenin's letter:

Regarded as an endeavor to influence working-class opinion in this country, this letter of his is an almost incredibly inept piece of work. Its crude violence, its tone of contemptuous condescension, its doctrinaire shibboleths, its wholesale condemnation of British labor leaders as corrupt traitors to their class, the utter absence of any constructive spirit or any touch of idealism, the ignorance and gross credulity displayed in its references to conditions in this country, in short, nearly every one of its features, might have been expressly designed by some subtle enemy to discredit its writer.[17]

The replies helped waverers to make up their minds and to seal the British movement against permeation. They prevented the reading of too much constitutionalism into Lenin's admission that the course of the social revolution would not be identical in all countries. While minor differences in tactics, such as affiliation to the Labour party, might be permitted, on all fundamentals it was clear that a British section of the Third International would have to accept the latter's creed and discipline.

Although in the correspondence relative to affiliation the Communist party stressed the normality of its procedure, its conduct followed the Moscow line. Its journals, such as the *Labour Monthly* and the *Communist Review,* regularly developed the Marx-Lenin theses, including the inevitability of violence and the dictatorship of the proletariat. It attempted to permeate labor organizations, to get its members in strategic positions in the Labour party and in the unions, and to carry on a campaign against the leadership. In some union and party branches where individual Communists were personally liked, they obtained positions of trust. Sometimes countermeasures were taken against them, as when the London Labour party, in which Herbert Morrison was the leading spirit, set an example by refusing to affiliate any branch of the Communist party.

The drive against the Labour leadership reached a climax in March 1921 in the East Woolwich by-election, in which the Labour executive sought the return of MacDonald in order to strengthen the weak parliamentary party. MacDonald, however, as an outstanding champion of constitutionalism, had long been to Communists a marked man. The Communist party now seized the opportunity not to enter a candidate but simply to discredit him. Its manifesto stigmatized Mac-Donald and his party as "forces of capitalism"; the Conservative and Labour candidates were bracketed as "two of a kind." Arthur Mac-Manus led a corps of speakers into the constituency. Afterward the Communists boasted that MacDonald's defeat by the narrow margin of 683 votes in an unusually heavy poll of 27,000 was due to this intervention.[18]

When the Labour party met in annual conference at Brighton, June 21–24, 1921, such theory and tactics made the defeat of the Communist application a certainty. Their request had some support from local Labour parties and trades councils, and, particularly, from mining sections where Communists had rendered aid during a recent prolonged lockout. Debate offered an opportunity for a restatement of views, but nothing new appeared in the way of argument. Supporters stressed the advantages of enlisting the zeal and enthusiasm of Communists in their cause and the value of their votes in doubtful constituencies. Opponents emphasized the incompatibility in aims and methods, the impossibility of cooperation with a party disciplined from Moscow, and the demoralizing effects of the onslaught against Labour's leaders. In summing up for the executive, Henderson asserted that there was no particle of evidence to prove the Communist party was ready to abide by Labour's constitution, but a vast amount to the contrary. By a decisive vote of 4,115,000 to 224,000, the conference rejected the Communist application. By a five to one vote, the I.L.P. likewise defeated the move to capture that party for the Third International.[19]

After this repulse the Communists redoubled their attacks upon Labour leaders. Men like Henderson and Clynes were denounced as reactionaries and traitors, but Thomas, because of his part in calling off the strike on "Black Friday," was the particular object of venomous attack. It was so libelous that, when he brought suit, he was awarded £2,000 in damages. When in a by-election in Caerphilly in the South Wales coalfields the Communists entered their first parliamentary candidate, they directed their campaign against the Labourite as much as against the Conservative. The Communist finished a weak third. Within ten days of their rebuff at the Labour party conference, however, the Communists were again knocking at the door. The Labour executive promptly denied the appeal for entry.

The end of the year found the persistent Communists back once more. The reason for this renewed effort was in the international situation. The institution of the New Economic Policy in Russia, with the consequent need for financial aid from the capitalist world, caused a retreat from the tactics of immediate world revolution in favor of an effort to enlist moderate labor in its support. Accordingly, the policy of direct attack and disruption gave way to promise of cooperation. This shift, which became evident in the summer of 1921, was announced to the world on December 18 at the Third Congress of the Communist International as the "United Working-Class Front."

In line with this switch in policy the British Communists asked for a conference with Labour to discuss the obstacles to affiliation. A meeting on December 29 followed between Jowett, Henderson, R. J. Davies, Lansbury, and Webb for Labour, and William Gallacher, F. H. Peet, MacManus, J. Hodgson, and Thomas Bell for the Communists. Henderson promptly raised the issue of parliamentary democracy in order to emphasize the incompatibility of outlook. In the course of the discussion it was suggested, in order to clarify the differences, that the Labour executive draft and submit to the Communist party conference a questionnaire so that the latter could respond with a reasoned and accurate definition of its position.

The Labour questionnaire called for statements upon four fundamental issues. First, it contrasted its own objective of "the political, social, and economic emancipation of the people by means of Parliamentary Democracy" with the Communist support of the soviet system and the Third International, the theses and regulations of which were inconsistent with the aims and ideals of British Labour. It inquired if, since the avowal of these differences in the original application, there had been any shifts in the Communist party's constitution and objective toward conformity with those of Labour. Second, since the Labour party confined its operations to lawful means, it asked if the Communist position were consistent with it. Third, the Labour constitution and practice precluded the idea of placing members of Parliament under pledges that might conflict with undertakings given publicly, and likewise, if elected as Labour candidates, to resign when called upon by any other party. In view of specific instructions of the Third International on these points, a statement of the present position was requested. Finally, because of the repeated assertions that hostilities against the Labour party could best be waged from within and the open admission that the object of affiliation was to effect its disruption, Labour asked if the Communist party really intended to become a loyal constituent body, conform to the constitution, and work for Labour objectives.

The Communist party protested that such an "inquisition" before affiliation was unprecedented, and that under Labour's own constitution it could not honestly deny the application. On the first question, the Communist party complained that the key phrase "by means of Parliamentary Democracy" could not be found in the constitution. This was literally true but to Labour hardly worthy of consideration because that idea underlay the document, governed the entire party program, and was confirmed by years of preaching and practice. The reply went on to admit a preference for soviets but said that the Communists proposed to utilize the parliamentary system for advancing the struggle toward the common ownership of the means of production, an affirmation hardly consistent with the heretofore persistent denunciation of parliamentary action as valueless except as a means of propaganda.

With respect to violence the reply argued that the Labour constitution contained no statement that never under any circumstances would extra-legal action be contemplated, and, as the Communist party normally kept within the law, the implication was that the two positions were fundamentally the same. This assertion was unconvincing. While Labour would have upheld the ultimate right of revolution, it accepted peaceful means as the normal, desirable, and eminently practical method of social change. Even the proposed industrial action in the Polish-Russian crisis of 1920 contemplated only peaceful tactics.

Concerning the position of a Communist in Parliament, the reply admitted that he would be essentially a delegate responsible to his party executive and would have to sign a pledge to this effect. An analogy to the status of the I.L.P. was attempted on this point, but the degree of independence claimed by the Communists and the greater divergence of their program vitiated the logic of the comparison.

The Communist answer evaded an unqualified promise to become a loyal constituent element in the Labour party, because its definite refusal to alter its own program and tactics and the saving clause of "without prejudice to its right of criticism" called to mind its thousand-times-repeated intention to unmask the Labour leaders, disrupt the party, and capture the command of the Labour movement.

The Labour executive responded that, since the reply made it clear there had been no change in the Communist position, it warranted no reversal of its own decisions. The executive then went before the annual conference at Edinburgh, June 27–30, 1922, to define the party's relation to Communist organizations. It laid the correspondence before the delegates and fortified its statements by extracts from the theses of the Third International. The temper of the conference was shown when with only six dissentients a resolution was passed condemning the treatment of the Social Revolutionary prisoners in Moscow and the conduct of their trials as a scandal. When the question of affiliation came up, the debate was brief and the outcome obvious. Harry Pollitt of the Boilermakers based the Communist case on the usual ground that, as part of the working-class movement and a necessary leaven in it, they ought to be inside the Labour party. Speakers for the executive reminded the conference of the Communist disruptive tactics and the wide gap between their own constitution and the theses of communism. The rejection of the Communist request was upheld by a vote of 3,086,000 to 261,000.

The conference not only excluded the Communist party but also sought to scotch the activity of individuals in their midst. Two rules designed to prevent Communists from serving as Labour candidates or as delegates to national or local party conferences were passed: first, that every nominee should individually accept the party constitution and principles; and, second, that every person was declared ineligible as a delegate who belonged to any organization having as one of its objects the return to Parliament or to any local government body of a candidate not endorsed by the Labour party or approved as running in association with it. Because of objections to anything resembling a heresy hunt, these proposals evoked less unanimity than the affiliation issue. They were, nevertheless, carried by a vote of more than two to one.[20]

To the great majority of the Labour party the decisions at Edinburgh were final. The positions of the two parties had been carefully explored, and the Communists had been given a fair opportunity to state their case. The fundamental differences were clarified. The disposition of the Labour party thereafter was to tighten the lines against the Communists rather than to dally with the possibility of cooperation.

The Communists, less convinced, renewed their application. Almost in a routine manner its rejection by the Labour executive was confirmed, 2,880,000 to 366,000, by the next party conference in June 1923. By a similar majority the conference endorsed the action of the parliamentary party in refusing the whip to J. T. Walton Newbold, the sole Communist in the Commons. At the same time Webb's presidential address, keyed to "the inevitability of gradualness," emphasized the party's attachment to its evolutionary faith and its rejection of the Communist thesis. In one respect, however, there was a slight modification of the Edinburgh position. Certain powerful trade unions, resenting the second rule regarding delegates as an infringement of their autonomy, refused to disqualify any member who fulfilled his obligations to his own union. After the clause in question was rescinded, accordingly, there existed a situation, unwillingly tolerated by the leadership, in which an individual Communist in the guise of a trade unionist might find his way into a party conference or even be elected to a position of trust.[21]

Meanwhile, the Labour party waged its conflict with the Communists on a wider front. It sought to reactivate the Second International, shattered by the war, only to find a new rift created by the impact of Bolshevism and the emergence of a rival organization. Some four years were devoted to rallying wavering elements and the Second was finally revived, although the Third or Communist International remained to divide the world movement.[22]

Due largely to the persistence of the British Labour party a conference of labor and socialist parties met, February 2–9, 1919, in Berne with the twofold hope of influencing the decisions being made at the Paris peace conference and of reviving their own organization. The Berne conference was united on resolutions for the creation of an effective league of nations, for a just territorial settlement, and for an international labor charter, the last of which contributed to the establishment of the International Labor Organization (I.L.O.). The debate on "Democracy versus Dictatorship," however, revealed deep differences that boded ill for the prospect of a unified International. As the committee on this problem failed to agree, two resolutions were submitted to the conference.

The British delegation defended the majority report, which maintained that the socialist movement must support the principles of democracy, liberty, and free institutions and oppose dictatorship; on its behalf MacDonald made an eloquent speech that won an ovation. The minority resolution, sponsored by Friedrich Adler of Austria and Jean Longuet of France, leaders of a conciliatory middle group, objected to the implied condemnation of Russia, warned that such action would alienate many parties, and insisted upon a single International with a base broad enough to include the more revolutionary elements. Since no agreement could be reached, both resolutions were placed on record and a commission of inquiry to go to Russia authorized to secure facts upon which to base a later decision. An executive committee consisting of Henderson, Camille Huysmans, the Belgian secretary of the International Socialist Bureau, and Hjalmar Branting, leader of the Swedish Social Democrats, assisted by a permanent commission, was named to further reconstruction of the International.

The permanent commission found the outlook gloomy. The delegation of inquiry was unable to go to Russia because it was refused passports. In March 1919 the Russians formed their rival Third International, which denounced the Second as weakly reformist and called for a merciless fight against its leaders. The Italian and Norwegian parties went over to the Third, while the French, Austrians, Swiss, and the German Independents withdrew from the Second and entered into negotiations with the Third. In Britain the Communist party joined it. The I.L.P. divided into three factions. The right, led by MacDonald and Snowden, never departed from its old position, but on the left were some ready to go to Moscow. The center wavered. At the Glasgow conference in April 1920, the I.L.P. decided by a vote of 529 to 144 to leave the Second International, but by 427 to 206 the center policy of a consultative conference won over the proponents of immediate adherence to the Third. It decided to explore the Third's position before further action, so R. C. Wallhead, its chairman, and Clifford Allen, an exponent of total pacifism, went to Moscow. There they were repelled by the insistence upon the necessity for violence and dictatorship, a candid avowal of aims and tactics that ended any possibility of immediate affiliation. The I.L.P., accordingly, broke direct relations with the Second International, but, because of its membership in the Labour party, it continued to be indirectly affiliated.

As the only large parties left to the Second International were the British and the German majority, the rebuilding was an uphill task. To further it a meeting was held in Geneva, July 31–August 5, 1920. The British delegation of twenty-five, the largest of all, met with representatives from Germany, the Low Countries, Denmark, Sweden, and a few others. The emptiness of the hall, which at a prewar con-

ference would have been crowded with eight or nine hundred delegates, emphasized the losses. Nevertheless, the conference proceeded
with its program and organization. The resolution on socialism called
for the gradual, legal, and compensated substitution of the community for the capitalist and for production in the interests of society, a
Fabian outlook that was not surprising in view of the presence of
Webb on the committee that presented it. The moderation of Mac-
Donald and Mrs. Webb was likewise manifest in the report repudiating violence and dictatorship and upholding parliamentary democracy. At every point the influence of the Labour party was evident.
It was entrusted with the task of negotiating with the absent organizations, and the secretariat was moved from Brussels to London. Of
the new executive of nine, Henderson, its president, Thomas, its treasurer, and MacDonald were British.[23]

While the Second International gathered these remnants at Geneva, the jubilant forces of the Third assembled in Moscow. They
reiterated the assertion of the inadequacy of parliamentary methods
and violently assailed the leaders of the Second; Lenin singled out
MacDonald for especial attack. Moscow and London were clearly
poles apart.

This polarization caused the center parties to meet in Vienna in
February 1921 to form an organization of their own, the International Working Union of Socialist Parties, commonly called the Vienna Union and facetiously styled by its opponents the Two-and-
a-half International. It was envisaged by its founders not as another
International but as an agency to bring a united one into existence.
It granted that democracy afforded a favorable position for the workers in the class war, but stated that the proletariat must be restricted
neither to the democracy of the Second nor to the mechanical imita-
tion of Russia. The Southport conference of the I.L.P. voted, 529 to
97, to adhere to the Vienna Union, whereupon its left minority went
over to the Communist party.[24]

The Labour party, entrusted with the task of negotiating reunion
by the Second, made approaches to the Vienna Union but without
success. The Vienna Union kept insisting upon Communist participation, but Labour saw no hope of compromise from the side of
Moscow. There was another impasse, but toward the end of 1921 the
Soviet shift to its New Economic Policy and its promulgation of the
United Working-Class Front possibly created a more favorable situation. Although Labour strongly suspected that the United Front
very thinly masked dangers to those who joined, it felt obliged to

explore its possibilities. When the Vienna Union agreed, on April 2, 1922, there was a meeting of the executives of the three Internationals in the Reichstag building in Berlin. The British delegates present were MacDonald, Thomas Shaw, and H. Gosling attending for the Second, and Richard Wallhead of the I.L.P. for the Vienna Union. MacManus and William Gallacher, Communists, were refused visas.

Adler of the Vienna Union, who presided, opened with an appeal for unity. Klara Zetkin, fiery orator of the German Communist party, doubted the possibility of organic unity but hoped for a world front against capital. Vandervelde frankly voiced the Second's mistrust based upon the Communist tactic of cell-building in trade unions, the overthrow of a Socialist government in Georgia, and the imprisonment of Socialists in Russia; all of these questions would have to be satisfactorily settled before the Second would consider any measure of cooperation with the Third. On these issues the Vienna Union supported the Second. Days of acrid charge and countercharge settled nothing, though the Third agreed to allow representatives of the Second to defend the accused Social Revolutionaries in a public trial and to assist in the collection of evidence concerning Georgia.

The conference left further negotiations to a committee of nine consisting of three from each executive. That committee met on May 23 in Berlin, but in the interval the abuse of Vandervelde and the commission that had gone to Moscow to aid the accused Socialists, the continued repression in Georgia, and the persistence of cell-building made failure inevitable. The meeting served only to emphasize the impossibility of an agreement not only on basic issues but even of a limited one on current problems. The only hopeful sign was seen in the many points upon which the London and Vienna groups were in accord.[25]

The pressure of events soon brought the right and center Socialists together. As the Moscow trials of the Social Revolutionaries progressed, the evidence of political motives so alienated the Vienna executive that it publicly stigmatized Russian justice as transparent vengeance. In Germany the schism between the Social Democratic parties was healed. The victory of fascism in Italy, the strengthened position of the dictatorship in Hungary, and the French invasion of the Ruhr were interpreted by many Socialists as ominous advances of world capital. The Vienna executive concluded that it could no longer wait upon the Communists. The outcome was a joint conference on May 21–23, 1923, at Hamburg, with the Second International, which easily brought about the desired reunion. British initiative had been important throughout. The secretariat continued at London with Tom Shaw as joint secretary with Adler of Austria. H. Gosling was treasurer. Henderson was elected chairman of the executive, of which MacDonald and Thomas were also members.[26] The Communists charged that the Labour party had split the world movement,[27] but the British delegates returned from Hamburg to report a long and difficult task completed. On the international front the party's stand had been vindicated.

In domestic politics, meanwhile, Labour improved its position. The local government elections of 1919 were an early indication of a trend toward Labour. Whereas before the war the party had held only a few seats, in 1919 it actually won control of Bradford and twelve London boroughs and elected a considerable number of councillors in Birmingham, Manchester, and other industrial centers in the North and Scotland. It controlled county councils in Durham, Glamorgan, and Monmouth, all coal mining areas. Not all gains were held consistently, but the party thenceforth remained a factor in local politics, especially in the metropolis and the mining and manufacturing centers.

On the national level Labour party gains were the chief feature of the general election of 1922. Conservative discontent with Lloyd George led to the famous Carlton Club meeting of October 1922, and his replacement by Andrew Bonar Law and a purely Conservative government. When Bonar Law immediately called for a general election for November 15, Labour was ready. It contested 414 seats, two-thirds of the total in Great Britain, secured a popular vote of 4,236,733, and elected 142 members. It was a striking increase from the 2,224,945 votes and 57 elected in 1918. The parliamentary party was now without question His Majesty's Opposition. The successful Conservatives' poll was 5,383,896, about one-quarter greater than Labour's, but they elected 347 members with a majority of 88 over all others. The National Liberals following Lloyd George polled 1,678,088 and the Independent Liberals of Asquith 2,507,204. The Communists elected J. T. Walton Newbold for Motherwell.

Of the Labour members 85 were trade unionists, as compared with 42 in 1918. The socialist societies sent 34, of whom 32 were of the I.L.P. One, Webb, came from the Fabian Society and the other from the Social Democratic Federation, the old name resumed by the loyal right wing of the British Socialist party. Divisional Labour parties elected 19 and the Cooperative party 4. Territorially, the bulk of the Labour members came from London, South Wales, Yorkshire, Lancashire, Durham and Tyneside, and Central Scotland, with a scattering from elsewhere. Back in the Commons once more were the so-called "pacifists" eliminated in 1918, including MacDonald, Snowden, Lansbury, and Jowett. New names that would be heard later were those of Clement Attlee, Arthur Greenwood, and A. V. Alexander. Ex-Liberals were Charles P. Trevelyan and H. B. Lees-Smith. From the Clyde, mainly I.L.P. members, were David Kirkwood, James Maxton, John Wheatley, Emanuel Shinwell, and Thomas Johnston; it was their votes that elevated MacDonald to the party leadership in the belief that he would be a more active advocate of socialism than Clynes. Clynes loyally accepted the position of deputy leader.[28]

Labour's success was due both to its improved organization and to its program and methods. Henderson saw the results of his work, although he himself lost his seat and had to find his way back in a by-election. There were now local Labour parties, or organizations of some sort, in all but three constituencies in Great Britain. Labour paid attention to the women voters. The Women's Labour League, headed by Dr. Marion Phillips, had no parallel in other parties. It was now organized as women's sections of the local parties. The I.L.P. was active, too, and its membership, averaging about 30,000 in these years, brought it to the height of its influence.

Finally, Labour's program and methods won much approval. Its foreign policy attracted the discontented Liberals. Its constitutionalism, maintained in the face of temptation to direct action and the example of Russia, won recruits who otherwise would have been repelled. Its battle on two fronts with the Communists emphasized its confidence in parliamentary democracy. Its insistence upon remaining British and not becoming Bolshevist made it seem worthy of trust.

7. The First Labour Government

The general election of 1922 installed a Conservative government with a majority that apparently ensured a full five-year term. Yet just a year later another election gave Labour its first tenure of office, an experiment in minority government during which some useful things were accomplished, but which came to an early and inglorious end.

Bonar Law retired in May 1923 on grounds of ill health and was succeeded by Stanley Baldwin. Baldwin had come to the conclusion that the only cure for Britain's economic ills, especially the mounting unemployment, lay in the reintroduction of protection. He felt honor bound, however, by Bonar Law's pledge that there would be no changes in the fiscal system without first submitting them for electoral approval. To the general surprise, accordingly, he made his announcement, and on November 16 Parliament was dissolved with December 6 set for polling day.

The Conservative campaign centered on the proposal for a tariff on manufactured goods coupled with preferences for the Dominions. There was some effort to associate Labour with communism, pacifism, and direct action. The Liberals joyfully accepted the challenge to fight on their historic battleground of free trade. It enabled the warring factions of Asquith and Lloyd George to effect a reunion to which the latter brought a full "war chest." The Liberals devoted their major assault against the proposed tariff; they also suggested public works at home, while abroad they would strive for the economic recovery of Europe and the restoration of relations with Russia.

Labour welcomed the trial of strength. Like the Liberals it regarded tariffs as unwise and insufficient; most Labour leaders were convinced free traders. Labour, too, proposed public works as a palliative for unemployment; its slogan was "Work or Maintenance." On foreign affairs its election manifesto called for an enlarged and strengthened League of Nations, the settlement of disputes by conciliation and arbitration, an international conference to revise the Treaty of Versailles and deal with reparations and debts, the restoration of economic and diplomatic relations with Russia, and disarmament. Distinctive features not on the Liberal program were proposals for the nationalization of the mines, railways, and electric power stations, and for a capital levy to reduce the debt.[1]

The campaign was a three-way contest. There were few local pacts, because the reunited Liberals sought to recapture their lost position and Labour was bent upon victory. Labour put up 434 candidates. It had the unwanted and unwelcome support of the Communists, who in pursuit of their current united-front tactic opposed no Labour candidate. Only two stood as Communists, though because individual Communists could still enter local Labour organizations, six others succeeded in getting Labour nominations. The Communist theorists, such as R. P. Dutt and Thomas Bell, explained that their struggle to unmask the reformist Labour leaders must not be allowed to interfere with the fight against the common enemy.[2]

The popular vote showed little change from the vote of 1922. The three parties were almost in equilibrium. The Conservatives lost 115,-485 votes and were down to 5,483,277 in spite of 64 additional candidates. The Liberals were up by 186,109 to 4,299,121. Labour gained 121,310 for a total of 4,356,767, which rejoiced those who liked to think in terms of a steady march toward inevitable victory. The two Communists were defeated, as was S. Saklatvala, who had been elected in 1922 from North Battersea as a Labour man.

In this three-party situation, however, greater changes were reflected in the House of Commons. The Conservatives dropped from 346 at the dissolution to 259, which left them the largest party but short of a majority. The Liberals rose from 117 to 159 and Labour from 144 to 191. The latter had net gains at the expense of both rivals, taking 37 from the Conservatives and 10 from the Liberals. All its leaders were back except Henderson, who was the victim of a local anti-Labour pact. Again he had to find his way back in a by-election— another example of the usefulness of that British method of providing continuity in public life for able men. Labour's chief gains were in Greater London, where it acquired 37 M.P.'s as compared with the previous 16, but it also added to its strength in the Midlands, the Eastern counties, Lancashire and Cheshire, and Scotland. It suffered a slight loss in the Northeast. In Northern Ireland it was not a factor, and in rural areas it was still very weak.

The parliamentary party was now less dominated by the trade-union element. Successful trade unionists numbered 98 as compared to 85 previously; 44 of them were Miners. Divisional parties, however, elected 35, as compared with 19 in 1922, and the socialist societies 52 instead of 34. Among the latter the 46 I.L.P. members bore witness to the energy of that small party.[3]

Although the election had been fought on the Liberals' favorite issue, Labour successfully withstood their attempt to recover their lost position. On balance they lost seats to Labour, though in the English counties and in Manchester they registered gains at the expense of the Conservatives. The Asquith wing of the reunited party fared better than the Lloyd George wing, which lost half its seats, with Labour the chief beneficiary.

The situation frightened some timid Tories, who feared for the monarchy and the constitution, and even some saner ones who expected a popular budget, an appeal to the people, and then five years of socialist experiment. Most Britons, however, viewed the prospect of a Labour government with equanimity, or even with satisfaction; a taste of responsibility might be good for those who had flourished on criticism. One thing was clear: protection had been rejected by an eight to five majority, so Baldwin would have to resign. There were suggestions of a coalition to keep Labour out, but the Liberals could hardly join the proponents of the policy just rejected and they well knew that coalition would lead to weakening or, possibly, absorption. Asquith himself ended such speculation when, speaking to the Liberal parliamentary party on December 18, he said that Baldwin would have to go and that he assumed a Labour government would follow. He envisaged a Labour government, but one so dependent upon the Liberals that the latter would effectively control the situation.

The Labourites debated their course. Under the circumstances not all were anxious to take office. Some thought that a Liberal-Conservative coalition might help to resolve the three-party situation into one of clear distinction between a capitalist alliance and their own party. Clydeside I.L.P. members suggested the introduction of a socialist program, sure to be defeated, and an immediate appeal to the country on the issue of socialism, but this tactic had slight appeal. Everyone foresaw the difficulties of a minority government.

Henderson, however, was always anxious to take office, gain practical experience in the working of government departments, and possibly enact some useful legislation. On December 11 there was a dinner at the Webbs's with MacDonald, Henderson, Clynes, Thomas, and Snowden present to discuss the problems of office and policy. All except Henderson displayed some fear at the thought of responsibility without power, but agreed that they ought not to refuse.[4] The Labour party executive and the T.U.C. general council urged that office, if offered, should be accepted. After these moves there was no doubt about Labour's position. On January 8, 1924, the rank and file showed their enthusiasm at a rousing rally in the Albert Hall. No one suggested the alternative of coalition with the Liberals; Labour was more interested in the demise of that party than in its preservation.

In the manner of the early nineteenth century, Baldwin awaited defeat in the House of Commons before resigning. When Clynes offered an amendment to the Address, Asquith made it clear that the Liberals would stand with Labour. On January 21, 138 Liberals joined 188 Labourites and 2 Independents to turn the Conservatives out. The next day Baldwin resigned, and King George V sent for MacDonald to receive the commission to form a government.

After that December dinner at the Webbs's, MacDonald went to Lossiemouth, his Scottish birthplace, to fashion his Cabinet. Thanks to Sidney Webb, he had the customary free hand of a Prime Minister in the choice of colleagues and was not compelled to deal with party committees and conferences, which some had urged as more befitting a democratic Labour premier. However, individuals and sections had claims that could not be ignored. Accordingly, the trade unions were represented by seven names, though that was hardly in proportion to their strength. Clynes became Lord Privy Seal and Deputy Leader of the House, Henderson Home Secretary, Thomas Colonial Secretary, Stephen Walsh Secretary for War, William Adamson Secretary of State for Scotland, Thomas Shaw Minister of Labour, and Vernon Hartshorn Postmaster-General.

From the I.L.P. Snowden was Chancellor of the Exchequer, John Wheatley Minister of Health, and Jowett First Commissioner of Works. Of the Fabians Sidney Webb went to the Board of Trade and Sydney Olivier, as Lord Olivier, to the India Office. Recruits from the Liberals were Lord Haldane as Lord Chancellor, Wedgwood as Chancellor of the Duchy of Lancaster, and C. P. Trevelyan as President of the Board of Trade. General C. B. Thomson, now Lord Thomson, a recent Labour convert, became Secretary for Air, Lord

Parmoor, an ex-Conservative, Lord President of the Council, and Lord Chelmsford, former Viceroy of India, First Lord of the Admiralty. MacDonald assumed the arduous dual role of being his own Foreign Secretary. Not in the Cabinet were some under-secretaries who later achieved prominence, including C. R. Attlee, A. V. Alexander, Margaret Bondfield, William Graham, Arthur Greenwood, and Emanuel Shinwell.

Some choices were obvious; others came as surprises. The government needed strengthening in the House of Lords, but few Labour men were willing to sit there—hence the new titles and the nomination of Lord Chelmsford, who consented to help carry on the King's government as a nonparty man; he might also get along better with the Sea Lords than a trade unionist or "socialist agitator." MacDonald was so anxious to enlist the experience of Lord Haldane that the latter was able to dictate his own terms. In the case of Henderson MacDonald's first list omitted his name entirely, which was inexcusable unless it was true that MacDonald foresaw a very brief tenure of office and felt that Henderson would be better employed in preparing the party for an early election. Even so, the omission was followed by the offer of a minor post which Henderson indignantly rejected. He finally took the Home Office. On the whole, however, the Cabinet was as good as could have been obtained, and the union of diverse elements to compose a government had plenty of precedent. It was certainly no body of revolutionaries. If any still feared it, their minds were surely more at ease after the new ministers, in spite of the discomfort of some in unaccustomed attire, consented to wear formal dress on ceremonial occasions, while the wives of the working-class members went to Beatrice Webb's Half-Circle Club as a place to meet others socially.[5]

Confronted by a strong antisocialist majority, the Labour government was unable even to consider such distinctive features of its election manifesto as a capital levy and measures of nationalization. It contented itself necessarily with acts of immediate welfare, which suited MacDonald's concept of "step-by-step" reform. In the fields of housing and education, by legislation or by administrative action, lasting contributions were made, and Snowden's freer trade budget was successful and popular. It was a modest but creditable record, and it did show that Labour could govern responsibly.[6]

The government made a major contribution toward the solution of the housing shortage, a success for which John Wheatley, a Clydesider who combined Catholicism with political radicalism, was mainly responsible. The problem was long-standing, but intensified by the recent growth and shift of populations, influx of refugees, wartime restrictions, and depletion of the building trades. Little had been accomplished by the postwar Coalition, although in 1923 during the Conservative government Neville Chamberlain had initiated a constructive policy that included a subsidy of £6 per year per house for twenty years. Its shortcoming was that it failed to provide houses at low rental, which was the greatest need, and private building by the well-to-do did not leave many empty houses for the less well off. It was to meet this need for cheap rentals that Wheatley turned to the building trades themselves.

A committee representative of employers and employees with a secretary from the Ministry of Labour made an analysis of the shortages. Based upon this report and proposals from the industry Wheatley introduced his Housing Bill, which provided for a state subsidy of £9 per year for forty years with £12 10s. per year in certain agricultural areas, to enable local authorities to build houses at low and controlled rentals. Conservatives opposed the bill on the ground of cost, but Wheatley and Arthur Greenwood, his under-secretary, successfully steered it through the House.

Meanwhile, Wheatley negotiated an agreement with the trade unions in the building industry to increase the labor force, even though it involved "dilution" by upgrading some unskilled labor and shortening apprenticeship from five years to four. This act was the government's most successful stroke in domestic legislation. The fact that 504,500 houses were built under it before the subsidy was abolished in 1933 was an example of what could be accomplished by such an approach involving the central government, local authorities, and trades concerned. The Ministry of Health became largely a ministry of housing.[7]

Efforts at rent control were less successful, as were those to deal with evictions for nonpayment of rent in areas plagued with heavy unemployment. The situation was critical, with rent strikes in Glasgow, London, and other large towns, where Communists made great capital of it. A Labour private member's bill failed, and the government met defeat on one of its own. All it could salvage was a minor measure to make evictions more difficult where landlords wanted possession for themselves. Failure to accomplish more brought down severe criticism on the government from its own left wing, but it never adopted the alternative of direct subsidy to the unemployed tenant.[8]

Under C. P. Trevelyan, Minister of Education, significant progress was made due to his initiative in administration. The ambitious Fisher Act of 1918 had been one of the chief victims of Coalition economy, so that instead of expansion in the educational system there were cuts in expenditure, reduction of services, and a standstill in school building. Trevelyan reversed the trend and restored vitality to the system in the interest of education for all children and not merely those whose parents could afford to pay for an expensive private one. He set forty as the maximum size of classes in elementary schools, encouraged local authorities to raise the leaving age from fourteen to fifteen, increased free places in secondary schools, restored scholarships to universities, and promoted school building and adult education. Under him the Board of Education became the patron of progressive local authorities rather than an agent of financial restriction.[9]

The unemployment problem baffled this government as it did all others of the interwar years. One palliative ended the gap of three weeks between periods of benefit and another increased the rates of benefits and children's allowances. The idea of public works to make jobs, which would have won Liberal support, came to nothing because the government was unprepared with a tangible program. There were proposals for a major development in electricity, with a "grid" covering the whole of Great Britain, town and country, such as the succeeding Conservative government implemented, and also for road and railway improvement. The gap between grandiose ideas and practical plans, however, was never bridged. Time was lacking. Ministers were still learning the work of their departments, and the government was out before anything crystallized that would have provided work for an appreciable proportion of the million jobless.

Wheatley was confronted with the problem of Poplar, an East End borough, where Lansbury and the Labour-controlled council insisted upon providing adequate unemployment relief regardless of the burden on the rates. The council's objective was not only to maintain the workless but also to secure a more equitable distribution of the burden whereby the West End boroughs with their great wealth and small unemployment would bear a fair share of it. For violating an order of Sir Alfred Mond, the Minister of Health in the Lloyd George Coalition, Lansbury and twenty-nine Poplar councillors had gone to prison for contempt of court. Wheatley now rescinded Mond's order, whereupon in Parliament Asquith promptly threatened to withdraw Liberal support from the government. The existence of the government was immediately at stake, but Wheatley saved it and discomfited the Liberals with a masterly reply demonstrating that all he had done was remove a discrimination against Poplar.[10]

A bill to establish a minimum wage for agricultural workers passed but fell short of the original intention. The Liberals proposed a definite figure of 30 shillings per week, but Labour preferred to leave the figure to a new Central Wages Board on the ground that wages should be tied to the cost of living, and, in view of changes in the price level, Labour feared that 30 shillings might become a maximum rather than a minimum. The Liberals weakened the measure, nevertheless, by an amendment that left the final word with local county committees, which effectively prevented the enforcement of a national minimum.

Snowden's "free trade" budget won the enthusiastic support of Liberals. He halved the duties on sugar, tea, cocoa, and coffee to provide a cheaper breakfast table and lowered the entertainment tax. He abolished the corporations' profits tax as a hindrance to investment, which brought acclaim from quarters usually hostile. He likewise repealed the McKenna duties, originally imposed in wartime to control luxury spending, but retained as protective measures for the motor car and other industries. This action brought predictions of disaster from the automobile industry, including interested trade unions, but it continued to flourish. No taxes were increased. It was a Gladstonian budget rather than a socialist one; there was no use of the tax power in the interest of greater equality. It won general approval. The other parties were relieved that the renowned socialist propagandist was essentially orthodox in finance, while such was Snowden's prestige in his own party that there was no serious opposition to him.[11]

The Labour government was confronted with the problems of strikes and lockouts, though there was no direct relation between its advent and their outbreak; most of them were already in the making. Their number was greater than in 1922 or 1923, but less than one-third of those in 1920 or 1921, and less than one-fourth of those of 1919. The stoppages of 1924 were due to the state of trade and employment rather than to the political complexion of the government.

Strikes under a Labour government naturally made the headlines. A walkout of the Locomotive Engineers and Firemen coincided with its accession, but the T.U.C. general council quickly and successfully exerted its influence, ended the walkout, and saved the new government from serious embarrassment. A few weeks later the dock workers were out. The Minister of Labour appointed a court of inquiry.

The workers' case was ably presented by Ernest Bevin, and they won their wage increase. In March there was a tram and bus strike in London. Weary Londoners walked to work, but Bevin, the powerful Transport and General Workers' secretary, scorned public opinion and threatened to call out the Underground men as well, for to the Bevin of these years the existence of a minority Labour government, in office but without power, was no reason to abandon the basic struggle for the workers' welfare.[12] The worried Cabinet invoked the Emergency Powers Act to set up a committee under Wedgwood to provide alternative transport, including lorries operated by the armed forces. Tension remained high until conferences, initiated by MacDonald, produced a compromise settlement that promised wage increases.

A local strike of Southampton shipyard workers, undertaken in defiance of their own executive and due in part to Communist inspiration, became a national lockout in April; negotiations were resumed, however, the lockout raised, and a settlement achieved. The coalmining industry was the center of another strike threat, but it was averted by the efforts of Emanuel Shinwell, the Secretary for Mines, who brought the two sides together for talks and set up a court of inquiry to investigate the question of wages. A higher minimum wage was the outcome.[13]

Labour's policy on defense owed much to Lord Haldane, whose desire to maintain it adequately was a major reason for his acceptance of office. The armed services were not starved. A pacifist amendment to reduce the army was overwhelmingly defeated. Under Lord Thomson the building up of the air force continued. Cruisers authorized by the Conservative government were the subject of controversy; construction was continued but the number reduced from eight to five. The decrease was a pacific gesture; the five were justified as replacement, not expansion, and as a contribution to the prevention of dockyard unemployment.

The I.L.P. conference reversed an earlier recommendation that the parliamentary party should vote against all defense estimates. The government changed policy, however, on the proposed Singapore naval base, which after the termination of the Anglo-Japanese alliance had been projected as the Gibraltar of the Far East. It was not an issue in the election of 1923, but on February 20, 1924, the government announced it would not proceed with the project. In spite of protests from Australia, New Zealand, and Newfoundland, MacDonald held to his course. He gave as his reasons the desire to eliminate suspicion and tension in the Far East and to encourage the settlement of disputes by conciliation and arbitration under the auspices of the League of Nations.[14] Haldane agreed, but more because of his conviction that the defense of Western Europe held priority than for any other reason.[15]

The Labour government made no significant contribution to the evolution of the Empire into the Commonwealth. In spite of a strong tradition of anti-imperialism, in office the party showed an awareness of the political and economic interdependence of the Empire. Colonial Secretary J. H. Thomas announced that there was no desire to detract from the greatness of the Empire, which was safe in the hands to which it had been entrusted; he desired to promote its welfare by drawing closer the ties that bound it together.[16]

The government did deal with a number of inherited imperial problems. One demanding immediate attention grew out of the Government of Ireland Act of 1920. This Act divided the island into two political units and stipulated that the boundary between the six counties of Northern Ireland and those of Southern Ireland (in 1922 the Irish Free State), be determined by a commission consisting of a representative from each with a chairman appointed by the British government; it would take into consideration economic and geographic factors and the wishes of the inhabitants. The Free State anticipated the transfer of large tracts, possibly including the whole counties of Fermanagh and Tyrone. Northern Ireland interpreted it as intending minor rectifications only, and therefore refused to appoint a commissioner. The Prime Minister called a conference, which failed completely. In spite of the exertions of MacDonald, Thomas, and Henderson, further efforts came to nothing because neither side would compromise. The government, left with no alternative, introduced legislation to enable it to appoint a commissioner for Northern Ireland, which passed with Liberal support. The commission then acted; its recommendation was to leave the six Ulster counties intact and the existing boundary unchanged.[17]

A far greater problem, the dimensions of which the party leaders well knew, was pending in India. MacDonald had first-hand knowledge of India and had written on it. The party was sympathetic toward nationalism and on record as favoring a solution based on self-determination with adequate safeguards for minorities.[18] The leadership, however, had no sympathy with the resort to violence, murder of officials, obstructive tactics in legislative councils, and boycotts. On the eve of taking office, in an open message to India, Mac-

Donald insisted upon constitutional methods: "No party in Great Britain will be cowed by threats of force or by policies designed to bring government to a standstill."[19]

The Secretary for India, Lord Olivier, as a Fabian, stressed peaceful evolution. He believed in self-government as the eventual goal but also in careful preparation for it; the best procedure for the moment was to make the Act of 1919 operate successfully as a step toward independence. This Act was a long step toward self-government. It provided for a two-house legislature for all British India, the upper partly and the lower mainly elective, while in the provinces a system known as dyarchy made the governor and the council responsible for certain matters, especially those of law and order. Other matters were transferred to Indian ministers responsible to mainly elective legislatures.

Lord Olivier believed that no quick and easy method of applying self-determination was feasible; no agreed solution of the problems of the bitterly antagonistic religious groups, the castes, and the princes seemed possible. On most of these points the cost of the final solution in the lives and dislocation of the multitudes, together with the incompleteness of the union, bore him out. At any rate, little could be done in ten months. Gandhi was released after serving only two years of a six-year sentence for sedition, and the Muddiman committee, consisting of three British and three Indians, was appointed to suggest remedies within the framework of the Act of 1919, but the government was out before it could report.

The Treaty of Lausanne with Turkey, ratified in April 1924, left for future negotiation the boundary of Iraq, a British mandate. The Turks claimed the vilayet of Mosul, which raised problems of oil fields, Kurdish areas, and a home for displaced Assyrian Christians. Negotiations failed to secure agreement, so the Labour government referred the matter to the League of Nations. When, in the meantime, Turkish bands raided Iraq, British forces were used to repel them, which led to a Turkish protest and a British justification by Lord Parmoor. A year later the League adjudged most of the disputed territory, including the oil wells, to Iraq. Elsewhere in Iraq the borders were harassed by tribal raiders. Again bombers were used and their use was defended by William Leach, Under-Secretary for Air—like Parmoor, with a pacifist record—as effective, economical, and relatively merciful. Police alone were inadequate and the use of ground forces costly in life to both sides, whereas the new method, with notice given in advance, was a punishment and a deterrent that took no lives. Opponents were vocal, but had no alternative to offer.[20]

Egypt presented an intractable problem. In 1922 it became independent, subject to reservations with respect to the security of the Suez Canal and imperial communications, defense, the protection of foreign interests and minorities, and the status of the Sudan. Before 1924 the Labour attitude was one of generous sympathy for nationalism and of condemnation of the occupation of Egypt as mainly in the interests of bondholders and imperialists. Its policy was that of self-determination with British action limited to that which a responsible national government of Egypt might freely accept.[21] In office, however, it was faced with Prime Minister Zaghlul Pasha's demand for complete independence and the evacuation of the Sudan and also by the terrorist methods of his Wafd followers. Confronted with Zaghlul's intransigence MacDonald took his stand on treaty rights, while in the upper house Parmoor stated that Britain would not abandon the Sudan in any sense whatever.

MacDonald tried direct negotiations and in September invited Zaghlul to London. The latter, as intolerant of Sudanese nationalism as he was insistent upon his own, would concede nothing. MacDonald was not prepared to yield on protection of the canal so vital to Britain. He recognized Egypt's interest in Nile waters, but emphasized Britain's moral obligation for the political and economic development of the Sudan. The negotiations were fruitless. In Egypt an epidemic of attacks on British persons and property followed. To Labour the inability to reach agreement with the uncompromising Egyptians was a disillusioning experience. The disorders culminated in the assassination of Sir Lee Stack, Commander-in-Chief of the Egyptian army and Governor-General of the Sudan, whereupon the Conservative government of Baldwin adopted a policy of firmness, the Wafd government fell, and a more moderate regime followed in Egypt.[22]

Toward the more backward dependencies Labour's intentions were benevolent, but its brevity of tenure allowed little opportunity to translate them into something tangible. For East Africa there was a commission appointed to report on measures of economic development and social amelioration, but the government resigned before it could report.

Official Labour, accordingly, was too preoccupied to do much more than preserve the imperial inheritance and apply a little Fabian gradualism in dealing with strident nationalism. It suffered attacks from its own I.L.P. leftists, who continued to relish the privilege of criticism. There were those, however, who thought more constructively. Dr. L. H. Haden-Guest formed a Labour Commonwealth Group to formulate a more positive policy, and Thomas Johnston, editor of the left-wing *Forward*, began to write that the Empire might be made "the greatest lever for human emancipation the world has ever known."[23] Some noted that the break-up of a great political organization had not always redounded to the betterment of mankind, and, as the Balkanization of Central Europe made manifest, nationalism had been no unmixed good.

In the field of foreign policy the Labour government enjoyed great success, although one slip was the immediate occasion of its fall. For the handling of both the successful and the inept, MacDonald himself was largely responsible. He attempted the impossible by doubling as Foreign Secretary; either office was a full-time one and the dual load broke his health. Any criticism of Labour's shortcomings in domestic accomplishment must take into consideration the leader's preoccupation with international affairs.

MacDonald had some good qualifications for the foreign office. He was possessed of fine personal appearance and charm and could be most gracious in manner. He was at his best in presiding over conferences and composing differences. Here the aloofness that hampered relations with his own followers was not apparent. His first-hand acquaintance with men and affairs abroad and the serious study that compensated for the lack of formal education provided him with an international outlook and knowledge not possessed by some of his predecessors. He hoped to bring a changed spirit into foreign policy and to eliminate some of the secrecy. It was announced that all treaties would be made available for discussion by both Houses of Parliament. He authorized the publication of documents relating to the origins of the War of 1914 without waiting for the customary lapse of fifty years, an act for which historians have been grateful. Ten months were not enough to solve all problems, but in the realm of international relations MacDonald left matters better than he found them.

MacDonald's first effort was toward ending the rift with France, which had been so disastrous for postwar Europe. It involved a reorientation of his party's outlook, which had regarded French political and economic schemes as the greatest danger to peace and recovery. The interchanges of 1922 with the French Socialist party had led to greater sympathy for the French desire for security, but the occupation of the Ruhr revived all the old suspicions. When Labour came into office, the French were still in the Ruhr, although disillusioned about the possibility of exacting reparations thereby, but an international commission under General Charles G. Dawes was at work attempting to determine how much Germany could pay and by what methods. The commission's plan, called after Dawes though really the work of Sir Josiah Stamp, set a first annual payment of 1,000 million gold marks rising in the fifth and subsequent years to 2,500 million; meanwhile there would be an international loan to Germany to aid its recovery. The total sum due was not fixed, but the amounts given were supposed to be within Germany's capacity to pay.

MacDonald's method was that of a personal approach to Poincaré. Although he was his own Foreign Minister, it was as the head of one government to another that he made his appeal—an exercise in what some thirty years later came to be known as "summitry." On January 26, 1924, a personal note to Poincaré, very friendly in tone, expressed his regret at the number of problems outstanding, but also his confidence that "by the strenuous action of good will" a solution could be found and the peace and security of Europe advanced. Poincaré's reply, equally gracious, encouraged MacDonald to raise more concrete issues. In a second letter of February 21, he stated frankly the British suspicion of French motives in the Ruhr; he contrasted France's concern for its own restoration and security with Britain's interest in a more general security and economic recovery, in which, of course, Britain's own welfare was involved. Again Poincaré's reply was friendly; he agreed with the analysis of the different points of view, but denied any intent to destroy Germany or annex territory.[24]

While this exchange of letters perceptibly improved Anglo-French relations, MacDonald turned to the Belgians, whose Premier and Foreign Minister came to Chequers for talks. In May he invited Poincaré, but a general election in France unexpectedly resulted in his defeat. In June Edouard Herriot, a Radical Socialist supported by the *cartel des gauches,* became premier, which provided MacDonald with an opportunity of which he made the most. He invited Herriot to Chequers, where on June 22–23 the two reached agreement on the desirability of a general conference to put the Dawes plan into effect. Some alarm was sounded in France and Belgium over possible renunciation of military occupation before the Dawes guarantees were effective, so MacDonald made a hurried visit to Paris to quiet fears that the Dawes plan would be used as a cover for a revision of the Treaty of Versailles, while at home Asquith voiced criticism of the "new diplomacy" which substituted personal talks for ambassadorial exchanges.

MacDonald proceeded with arrangements for a general conference held August 16 in London, where French, Belgian, Italian, Japanese, and, later, the German delegates joined the British, with Americans present as "observers." MacDonald presided with tact and skill, calmed the storms that arose, and impressed all with his capacity for incessant labor. The Dawes plan was finally accepted and a schedule set up for the evacuation of the Ruhr.[25] To have secured agreement on reparations surpassing that of the several previous conferences was an accomplishment in which MacDonald and his government could rejoice. There were rumblings about the reception of payments in kind and, from the left and the Communists, gloomy predictions of an enslaved German working class, but generally there was pride in the introduction of a better spirit into diplomacy and a solution of a phase of the reparations problem.[26] Once again there was some amity in the Entente and a better understanding between Germany and the Allies.

MacDonald improved relations with Italy. The Labour government inherited a problem dating from the wartime treaties of "proper compensation" in East Africa for Italy. A British offer of a cession of territory between Kenya and Somaliland had been countered with a demand for a larger slice. The matter became confused by being linked with a settlement of the Dodecanese Islands question in the Eastern Mediterranean. Fascism was highly unpopular in British Labour circles and Mussolini well hated, especially after the murder in June of Matteotti, a respected Socialist deputy, but MacDonald entered into direct negotiations with Mussolini and effected a settlement. The African issue was dissociated from that of the Dodecanese, and Jubaland, an area of approximately 33,000 square miles, was ceded to Italy. An advantage for the future was the union of the Somalis of that region with their brethren in Italian Somaliland.[27]

The League of Nations had a special place in Labour's policy, and the assignment of Parmoor, the Lord President of the Council, to deal with it indicated its importance. Yet on July 5 the Labour government rejected and, in effect, destroyed the Draft Treaty of Mutual Assistance, which was largely the work of Lord Robert Cecil and was an effort to reconcile French security with League principles. This proposal would have obligated all signatories to come to the assistance of any of their number against an aggressor. Aggression, however, was undefined, and its determination left to the League Council. Military obligations would be limited to powers on the continent where the aggression occurred. The plan was coupled with one for disarmament. The Labour government maintained, and the Dominions, too, that the proposed regional agreements could not be reconciled with the organization of the British Empire. In addition to its other objections to the plan, the government pointed out that aggression was not defined, and said that the League Council had been given too much power. Underlying this reasoning was the fact that most Labourites were still averse to the concept of a League war, and, although the Draft Treaty associated security and disarmament, it did not emphasize conciliation. Henderson was ready to strengthen the sanctions features of the Covenant, as his *Labour and Foreign Affairs* (1922) revealed, but the majority of the party, like MacDonald, were as yet unwilling to go beyond economic sanctions.

MacDonald and Herriot had already agreed to attend the September assembly of the League at Geneva to deal with the problem of security. It was the first occasion upon which heads of states dignified that body by their presence. MacDonald's opening-day speech won an ovation. He proposed to bring Germany and Russia into the League, to move for disarmament, and to make better provision for arbitration; he suggested that refusal to accept arbitration be made the test of an aggressor.[28] Herriot likewise linked arbitration with security and disarmament, but it was Edvard Benes, Czechoslovak Foreign Minister, who turned attention toward effective sanctions.

The two premiers departed, but a committee on which Henderson and Parmoor were active dealt with this question and produced the Geneva Protocol for the settlement of international disputes. Like the rejected Draft Treaty, it included a system of pooled security; the signatories would unite against an aggressor, defined in MacDonald's terms, which, however, had been heard for nearly twenty years in socialist circles. It tied security to disarmament; at Henderson's insistence the coming into force of sanctions was made dependent upon the prior meeting and success of a disarmament conference.[29] Another reservation kept control over the use of national forces with the government concerned; any use of the British navy would be subject to the decision of the government of the day. France, satisfied, signed at once and was followed by a number of other nations. Within a few days, however, the Labour government fell, and its Conservative successor rejected the Protocol.

What would have happened had Labour remained in office is, of course, speculative. Some have assumed that Labour would have accepted the Protocol; others have been skeptical.[30] Before leaving Geneva, MacDonald told Parmoor not to sign. His intentions were never clear. He spoke of an arrangement to prevent war, but disliked coercion even by economic sanctions. Ponsonby, the under-secretary, opposed the Protocol, but Henderson's advocacy was strong. Wedgwood, himself unwilling to guarantee imposed or unjust boundary settlements, said later that Henderson "nearly, but not quite" converted the Cabinet.[31] When MacDonald cautioned Parmoor against signing immediately, he may possibly have had in mind the desirability of still further reservations. He was soon saying, however, that if they tore up the Protocol they would lose credit in the eyes of the world and he preferred it to a limited pact such as the Conservatives were proposing.[32]

Party opinion was changing, too. By early 1925 the party and trade-union executives, and also the parliamentary party, were all endorsing the principles of the Protocol and denouncing the Conservative government for destroying it. Whether or not in 1924 reservations would have won sufficient Labour and Liberal votes to secure acceptance of the Protocol, the agitation over it hastened the conversion of the party to Henderson's concept of the place of the League in Labour's foreign policy.

Formal recognition of Soviet Russia was an avowed intention of the Labour government. Russia was a fact that could not be ignored. The regime had survived efforts at its destruction and was apparently stable. There were outstanding problems to be solved; it seemed logical to give *de jure* recognition in order to deal with them in the regular manner. Neither the method by which change in Russia had been effected in the past nor the irritation caused by Communists in Britain in the present seemed of as great consequence as the need to bring Russia back into the family of nations. To MacDonald the recognition of a Communist country seemed very much like the recognition of a Muslim state by a Christian one. On February 1, accordingly, unconditional recognition was formally extended. The Conservatives resented it; they still looked upon Soviet Russia as a pariah among nations. They believed that recognition, if accorded at all, should follow a settlement of problems. Labour was accused of putting the cart before the horse. Throughout the decade the parties continued to differ on this issue; Russian recognition became a political football.

The note of recognition suggested a conference in London to deal with such questions as outstanding claims of the government and nationals of each country and Russian propaganda in the British Empire. Such a conference opened in London on April 14 with Ponsonby and Rakovsky, Soviet chargé d'affaires, as principal negotiators. It was troubled, prolonged, and held in an atmosphere of increasing tension. The language of British opponents imputing moral obliquity to the Russians was more than equaled by Russian abuse of British Labour leaders. Anti-British propaganda in the Empire and the Far East continued unceasingly. British leftists, still optimistic and charitable wherever Russia was concerned, had visions of a great market there that would ease their own unemployment problem; they continually sought to exert pressure on the government. Throughout the negotiations the harassed Cabinet was preoccupied with such issues as reparations and Ireland.

The conference struggled for weeks over British claims for seizures of property, default upon bonds, and injury to individuals; Russian counterclaims for damages during the intervention; Anglo-Russian trade, which involved the extension of credits to Russia; and, later, a loan to Russia. There was little progress and by June a deadlock; the two sides looked with different eyes upon debts and compensation. On August 4 there was a fresh start, but soon there was a threatened collapse over the wording of a statement on compensation for former British property nationalized by the Russians. Complete breakdown was averted by a formula suggested by four leftist M.P.'s, an incident seized upon by the Opposition to charge that the government was coerced by its own radicals.[33]

Two treaties finally emerged from this prolonged negotiation. A commercial treaty gave Russia most-favored-nation treatment and extended export credits to it, together with diplomatic immunity for a limited number of members of the Russian trading mission in Britain. A general treaty was more notable for the matters it postponed than for those it settled. It conceded in principle the claims of Britons who had suffered loss because of Russia's seizure of property or default on bonds, but left details to later negotiation and commissions. A future treaty would embody their findings; after all those steps were completed—in the case of bondholders, for example, after a settlement to the satisfaction of the holders of at least half the value of the bonds in default—there would be a loan to Russia guaranteed by the British government. On August 8 these treaties were signed. That night MacDonald, aware of the resentment over them, especially over the proposed loan, wrote the King that he thought that an interval of calm reflection would prevent any crisis from coming to a head.[34]

Nevertheless, the storm over the treaties raged furiously. The material for partisan advantage was too good to lose. The treaties were criticized as meaningless, because of the many provisos attached, and at the same time as highly dangerous and made under coercion from extremists. Lloyd George used the word "fake," but in the upsurge of anti-Russian feeling saw an opportunity to oust the government, so he and his paper, the *Chronicle*, raised the hue and cry. His party needed an issue to halt the drift away to Labour. There were Liberals such as Commander Kenworthy, soon to go over to Labour, who supported the treaties, but on September 22 Asquith came out against them. His decision meant that the government could no longer command the support of the Liberals; from that moment its days were numbered. It had made a commendable effort to restore normal relations with Russia. The failure was due only in part to its own handling of it; the difficult Russians and the partisan Opposition shared the responsibility.[35]

Until mid-August the Labour government enjoyed a measure of approval that extended beyond the party. H. W. Massingham wrote that it had disproved Churchill's gibe about being unfit to govern.[36] J. L. Garvin, the independent Conservative critic, summed up:

Mr. MacDonald has largely succeeded in restoring confidence to Anglo-French relations; he has brought Germany into negotiation on an equality; he has helped to bring the Reparations question within sight of a genuine solution for the first time; by the Jubaland settlement he has cleared away a cause of friction with Italy, and he has followed recognition of the Russian Government by the treaty signed last week. Labour can claim that it has made a mark upon the foreign policy of the country.[37]

Whatever feelings of pride may have been roused by such compliments were quickly dashed by the badly managed Campbell case and the succeeding Red Letter election.

The Campbell case grew out of an article of July 25 in a Communist paper, the *Worker's Weekly*, which exhorted members of the armed forces that "neither in the class war nor in the military war" would they turn their guns on their fellow workers. Agitation against the use of the military in industrial disputes was nothing new, but reference to "the military war" could mean incitement to mutiny. The Attorney-General, Sir Patrick Hastings, announced that the editor would be prosecuted. When investigation revealed, however, that the article had been written by J. R. Campbell, a temporary editor only and a man who had volunteered for war service, had been decorated for exceptional gallantry, and had been wounded and permanently maimed, Sir Patrick concluded that there was no case upon which a jury would convict and dropped the prosecution.

It was a trivial incident, but one that in the atmosphere of the day could be blown up into a first-rate issue. The Conservatives seized upon it, and the Communists were not averse to assuming credit for exerting pressure. The Conservatives, charging that outside forces were deflecting the course of justice in England's courts, tabled a vote of censure. The Liberals offered an amendment calling for a committee of investigation. MacDonald, whose explanation of the affair served to confuse rather than clarify, said he would regard the amendment as a vote of censure. The Conservatives grasped their opportunity; they voted for the Liberal amendment, and this combination by 364 to 198 defeated the government. This time the defeat was a notice to quit.[38] On October 8 the government announced the dissolution of Parliament. It went to the country with a weak issue instead of awaiting a good one. But now that the Liberals had abandoned the government on the treaties question, MacDonald might never have had that freedom of choice.

Labour entered the contest in a confident mood. It had done well in by-elections. Spirits were high at the annual conference at London, October 7–10, where MacDonald's announcement that the fight was on was wildly cheered. Its manifesto, *Labour's Appeal to the People*, emphasized the supreme need for peace among nations and proudly listed its successes in foreign policy as contributions to it. It called for the nationalization of mines and minerals. No mention was made of the capital levy.[39]

The Liberals, struggling to maintain their independence, fought on two fronts. They attacked the Labour record, especially on the treaties, but, fearful of a clear Tory majority, pointed to possible dangers from tariffs, a restored House of Lords, and other reactionary measures. They entered fewer candidates than in 1923, partly because three elections in three years had depleted party funds. One result was far fewer three-way contests—17 instead of the 96 of 1923 —and some local Liberal-Conservative pacts.

The Conservatives said something on Labour's failure to cure unemployment, but made the Russian treaties a leading issue. They played up the perils of Bolshevism and linked them with the treaties and the Campbell case. They sought to identify socialism with communism. Official leaflets went so far as to assert that the home, the family, and religion were at stake. By no means all Conservatives became hysterical, but these myths were asserted in spite of Labour's fight against the Communists at home and in the International. They were repeated in spite of the recent party conference's decisions: the Communist party's application was again rejected overwhelmingly by a vote of 3,185,000 to 193,000 and, in the effort to plug the loop-holes of individual Communists' activity, by 2,456,000 to 654,000 it made them ineligible for endorsement as candidates for office either nationally or locally; by a narrow majority of 1,804,000 to 1,540,000 it made them ineligible even for individual membership.[40]

On Friday, October 24, just five days before the poll, the so-called Zinoviev letter was made public, the episode by which this election is most remembered. This letter directed British Communists not only to work for the ratification of the Anglo-Russian treaties, but also to prepare for military insurrection in working-class areas and to subvert the allegiance of the armed forces for this purpose. Among the signatures affixed were those of Zinoviev, president of the Com-munist International, and MacManus, a British member of the pre-sidium. No original of this letter has ever been produced, but pur-ported copies reached the Foreign Office and the *Daily Mail*. Foreign Office officials, assuming it to be genuine, sent it to MacDonald. The latter authorized publication, should examination prove it to be authentic, together with a strong note of protest to the Soviet chargé d'affaires. J. D. Gregory, a civil servant in the Foreign Office, there-upon gave both letter and protest to the press. In a campaign already heated, the temperature went sharply up. Tories shouted that it was proof Labour would hand the country over to Moscow. Labour can-didates were in a quandary; they looked to MacDonald for the lead that he failed to give. When the poll was only two days away he finally spoke, but handled the matter badly. Evidently he did not see the implications or the urgency, though others did; "We're bunk-ered," said Thomas to Snowden.[41] So this campaign ended in com-motion and confusion.

The authenticity of the Zinoviev letter has often been debated, but positive prooof or disproof is lacking. Its content was in harmony with the idea of world revolution. A number of details, however, threw the letter open to suspicion of forgery in whole or in part. Mac-Manus's signature, for example, habitually included his first name or initial, but here it was lacking; there were other discrepancies, such as those in connection with Zinoviev's title and the correct name of the Communist International.[42] It may be of significance, too, that in spite of the recent furor over Campbell the Baldwin government instituted no proceedings against MacManus.

On October 29, thanks to the excitement over the Russian issue and over the Red Letter, the voters turned out in such force that the total poll increased to 76.6 per cent from the 70.8 of the previous year. The Conservatives were the chief gainers. Their popular vote was up by over 2,000,000 to a total of 7,385,000, and with 415 seats they had another huge over-all majority and an assurance of a full term of office. The Liberals were the real losers. Their poll was down by over 1,250,000 and their seats to 42; even Asquith lost at Paisley. Differences between the antisocialist parties dwindled in the anxiety to turn Labour out; a vote for a Liberal might let the Labourite in. Possibility of a Liberal come-back, so bright in 1923, was all but ended; such was their reward for joining the Tories in the vote of censure and the ousting of Labour. The Communists entered seven candidates but elected only one.

In the popular vote Labour gained 1,130,882 for a total of 5,487,620, which would indicate that any panic due to the Red Letter was not universal and that many were impressed by Labour's record, though some of that increase was due merely to the fact that the party put up 514 candidates instead of the 434 of the previous year. Due mainly to the decrease of 120 in the number of three-cornered contests, however, those elected were down by 40 to 151. Losses were heavy in Greater London, the Eastern counties, Lancashire and Cheshire, and Scotland. The trade-union group suffered less than candidates sponsored by divisional Labour parties and the socialist societies.[43] The Miners' seats seemed particularly secure. The parliamentary leadership returned almost intact, though Jowett narrowly lost Bradford East, and, due in most cases to local Liberal-Conservative pacts, some junior ministers were out.

On November 4 MacDonald resigned, and the episode of the first Labour government came to an end. The manner of its going gave it no glory, but in spite of the inexperience of most of its members and the brevity of its term, it had to its credit a very considerable achievement both at home and abroad. It had improved relations with France, Italy, Germany, and Russia, and at home, although it made no advance toward socialism, it made important contributions in housing and education. Labour had proven its responsibility. It had supplanted the Liberals as the alternative government.

8. The General Strike and a Turn to the Right

The loss of the general election was followed by internal dissension. There were postmortems on the leadership. The trade unionists, ordinarily the more conservative element in the party, temporarily moved left and resorted to direct action. The I.L.P., impatient with "gradualness," called for "socialism now." Moderation reasserted itself, however. The general strike led not to revolution but to the Mond-Turner talks. Instead of *Socialism in Our Time* the cautious *Labour and the Nation* became the policy statement. Always the Communist solution was rejected. In 1929 the party again fought under the MacDonald banner.

Following the defeat of October 1924, there was widespread criticism of MacDonald's bungling in the Campbell case and on the Zinoviev letter; his general caution was condemned as calculated to allay middle-class fears at the expense of socialist advance. There were moves to shelve him. James Maxton of the I.L.P. proposed Lansbury for the leadership, but he refused. Some, including H. N. Brailsford, pressed Trevelyan to stand, but he, too, was unwilling. Snowden, Bevin, and the Clydesiders urged it upon Henderson, but he was as modest in ambition as he was loyal to MacDonald, whom he had always regarded as best suited for the role.[1] MacDonald, accordingly, was re-elected by the parliamentary party with only five dissenting votes. Among the rank and file his popularity was as great as ever, as the enthusiasm for him at the 1925 party conference revealed. Whatever resentment might linger among his late colleagues, he was still looked upon as the only possible leader.

There was some sentiment, too, that never again ought the party take office as a minority government. At the 1925 conference Bevin, who felt very keenly that this experiment should never be repeated, brought forward a resolution to that effect. MacDonald and Thomas opposed him on the ground that hands should not be tied in advance without knowledge of the circumstances. Bevin was overwhelmed by a vote of 2,587,000 to 512,000.[2]

The I.L.P. was a major center of criticism aimed mainly at the failure to launch a socialist program. Clifford Allen, its chairman, urged MacDonald to appoint a committee to blueprint a rapid advance toward socialism. When MacDonald failed to respond, Allen got his own party to assume the lead. Seven committees were appointed to plan for agriculture, finance, the Empire, India, industrial policy, the abolition of poverty and the realization of socialism, and the reform of Parliament. Interest centered on the work of the sixth commission, that on the abolition of poverty and the realization of socialism; its report became the subject of a long controversy. It was the work of J. A. Hobson, economist, Brailsford, editor of the *New Leader*, A. Creech Jones of the Transport Workers, and Frank Wise, who was mainly responsible for it.

Known as *Socialism in Our Time,* the report attempted to answer the question of how poverty and insecurity could be banished and socialism rapidly achieved without a catastrophic collapse of capitalism. It proposed an immediate program to provide for a more equitable distribution of the national income: health and social services should be expanded, and a minimum wage established and supplemented by children's allowances to provide for the varying sizes of families. Industries that could not pay the minimum wage would be subsidized by the state or, if redundant, closed or adapted to other purposes. Redistribution, however, was not enough; total national income would have to be increased, which would involve a planned economy with a national investment board to direct the flow of capital and control foreign trade. It would socialize banks and credit, land, coal, power, and transport.

This report stirred MacDonald to wrath; even before he read it, the sight of a headline, "Socialism in Our Time," the antithesis of his gradualism, upset him. He feared to frighten the electorate and those new recruits who were still more liberal than socialist. MacDonald believed that it was the duty of a Labour ministry to carry on the King's government and accomplish what it could; under the fiery James Maxton, the Clydesider elected chairman in 1926, the I.L.P. was concerned only with battling for socialism. The I.L.P. brought the report before the Labour party, but the latter referred it to its executive and that of the T.U.C. for inquiry. When the specific proposal for children's allowances was separately submitted to the 1926 party conference, it was defeated by a two-to-one vote, mainly because of trade-union fears that such allowances might be made the excuse for wage cuts. On this important feature of social security, the Labour party lagged behind the I.L.P.[3]

The radicalism of the new I.L.P. leadership and the adoption of a program in competition with that of the Labour party led to a breach with its former chiefs. The I.L.P. removed MacDonald from the editorship of the *Socialist Review* and ceased to name him as one of its delegates to Labour party conferences. MacDonald and Snowden, so long associated with the I.L.P., now took their departure from it. The I.L.P., steered by Maxton, embarked upon an independent course that ultimately carried it outside the Labour party.

Although the Labour party was not directly concerned with trade-union affairs, the overlap in membership and certain activities of the T.U.C. in these years were of great significance for it. In 1924–25 particularly the trade unions were affected by the tendencies of the time. Because of the assumption of office in 1924, Thomas, Clynes, and other moderates went off the general council and leftists appeared on it; among the latter were A. A. Purcell of the Furnishing Trades and a founder of the Communist party, George Hicks of the Bricklayers, and Alonzo Swales of the Engineers. The moderate Frank Hodges was replaced as secretary of the Miners' Federation by A. J. Cook, a man of personal integrity, devoted to his union, and an impassioned orator. He was a Communist and a leader of the Minority Movement, the innocuous title under which in 1923 the Communists and their sympathizers launched the British section of the Red International of Trade Unions.

The trade unions, previously concerned mainly with reviving trade with Russia, now exhibited renewed interest in Russia as a political experiment. When Michael Tomsky, chairman of the Russian Trade Union Central Council, later a purge victim, appeared at the 1924 T.U.C., he received a warm welcome. The T.U.C. responded with a delegation to Russia, which returned impressed by the evidences of stability and the possibility of trade. A deputation to Baldwin urged him to develop the Russian market with the usual plea for it as a remedy for unemployment, but he was unconvinced.[4]

The T.U.C. proceeded, however, to form an Anglo-Russian Joint Advisory Council to further mutual understanding and possibly to unite the rival trade-union Internationals, though meetings at Paris and Berlin produced mainly friction. At the 1925 T.U.C. conference leftist tendencies and pro-Russian feeling reached their peak. The mood was militant. Again Tomsky was there, while among the more than 700 delegates Harry Pollitt and nine other Communists constituted a well-organized "fraction." At the very time when the Labour party was insulating itself from Communist penetration, the T.U.C. was exploring the possibility of cooperation with the Russians.

This enthusiasm soon faded. In October 1925, a new T.U.C. secretary was chosen, the cautious Walter Citrine, later Sir Walter and after 1946 Baron Citrine, and the moderates were back on the general council. Bevin, already a powerful influence, was elected to it; for long these two men were dominant in the trade unions. The 1926 T.U.C. conference received a telegram from Tomsky, a combination of the criticism and abuse so commonly heard from Moscow, that roused deep resentment and such a demand for "Hands off the British Labour movement" that the next year this flirtation with the Russians came to an end. The presidential address of George Hicks in 1927 recognized "the crude arrogance of the Russians in telling us how to conduct our own affairs," but pleaded for an understanding of the men who had come through such a terrible school of exile, imprisonment, and death.

Citrine and Bevin, however, were determined to end the Anglo-Russian Council. Citrine emphasized the Russian failure to understand that others need not slavishly copy their methods. Bevin, too, forcefully put the point of inability to match minds with men of such different standards, and that one could not hammer out differences with those who substituted abuse for argument. If the general council were asked to meet the Russians on the Joint Council, how could amity be preserved? "How would we meet them? If you had been called a traitor, a twister, a liar, and everything else that can be thought of, and you had to meet the man who called you that, would you meet him as a friend or as an antagonist? That does not promote international unity; that is the wrong way to assemble for a conference."[5] By a vote of 2,551,000 to 620,000 the T.U.C. ended this essay at a joint council with the Russian trade unionists.

The general strike of 1926 occurred at a time when the leftward trend seemed to have halted and the moderates were again in control. It grew out of the bad situation in the coal industry, which slumped after the evacuation of the Ruhr was followed by the resumption of production there. The coal owners' solution featured longer hours and pay cuts, though the former would produce coal that could not be sold and the latter would reduce wages by 13 to 48 per cent. At the same time the margin of profit would be left untouched. The Miners rejected such an offer, and the T.U.C. prepared to support them. The government intervened, but it soothed no feelings when Baldwin observed that all workers in the country would have to take wage reductions to help restore British industry. A delegate conference of trade unionists stood by the Miners, and on Friday, July 31 the government backed down. It promised a subsidy to keep the mines going, while the Miners agreed to cooperate in an inquiry for improving their efficiency. It was a victory for the Miners in that the whole burden of an industry's loss through inefficiency was not thrust upon them. The *Daily Herald* called it "Red Friday" to distinguish it from the earlier collapse of "Black Friday."[6]

The government appointed a royal commission of inquiry headed by Sir Herbert Samuel; it contained an economist, a banker, and an industrialist, but no labor members. At the same time it took the precaution of forming an Organization for the Maintenance of Supplies to carry on vital services in case of a general strike. In order to prevent the Communists from taking advantage of any crisis, twelve of their leaders were brought to trial and sentenced to prison for terms of six months to a year, an incident which gave that party of 6,000 members an opportunity to advertise its views.[7] The labor movement made no serious preparations, though A. J. Cook spoke in violent terms and the miners in part nullified the effect of any strike by producing a record amount of coal before it began.

The commission's report of March 1926 recommended the nationalization of coal royalties and reorganization of the industry by consolidation into larger units; it asked for more amenities for the miners, such as better housing and holidays with pay, but also for an immediate reduction in wages. It pleased neither side. The owners were intent upon longer hours, lower wages, and district agreements, while they stubbornly resisted reorganization. The Miners insisted upon a minimum wage, a national scale, and reorganization. Baldwin sided with the owners on immediate wage cuts, but promised future legislation on reorganization. By April 30 lockouts were in effect at many mines, and on that date the government declared a state of emergency.

The negotiations committee of the general council continued its efforts, and a special conference of trade-union executives met in Memorial Hall. While the government planned and announced its preparations, the trade unionists were still undetermined on their course, although instructions were printed in case a strike should be called. On May 1 a test at Memorial Hall indicated that, if necessary, "coordinated action" would be approved. The time for it was set at 11:59 P.M. on May 3, but negotiations continued. The general council confidently expected a repetition of the success of the previous year, but within the Cabinet was a "war party" including Churchill, Joynson-Hicks, L. S. Amery, and Neville Chamberlain, who were bent upon a "show-down" with labor. Their opportunity came when printers of the *Daily Mail* refused to set up an editorial attacking the threatened strike. They seized upon this trivial incident as an excuse to break off negotiations. When the trade-union committee came to the Cabinet room, they found it dark; Baldwin had gone to bed. This incident compelled the general council reluctantly to go on with the strike. Immediate responsibility for the strike, accordingly, rested with the government; there was no war party anxious to force the issue in the general council as there was in the Cabinet.[8]

The great strike lasted for nine days. Actually it was not general, because only certain industries were affected, such as the workers in transport, chemicals, building, electricity, and gas. The printers were also called out, which gave an advantage to the government, who controlled the new radio. The response in the trades was all but unanimous. There were some local disturbances and in London some parade of force, but the atmosphere was on the whole surprisingly peaceful, and there were even some displays of good humor on both sides. It was, however, a situation that the responsible leaders did not relish. A "national strike," as the T.U.C. called it, on such a scale inevitably involved the government and raised a constitutional question.[9] It was easy to get into such a quandary; no one had considered how to get out of it. When Samuel offered his services as a negotiator and suggested some reforms of the mining industry, the general council gladly accepted them as a basis for negotiation. On May 12 the general council yielded, though the rank and file were still solid, and on May 13 more men were out than ever. It was an unconditional surrender. The men were soon back to work, except for the Miners, who held out obstinately for another six months, but in the end had to accept defeat, wage cuts, and a high rate of unemployment.[10]

The general council knew what it was doing when it yielded unconditionally. Tempers had been generally kept, but there were symptoms that a flare-up with serious consequences would have occurred had they been subjected to longer strain. The council saved the country from it at the loss of "face" for itself. The Labour party profited in the long run. The cost and failure of industrial action confirmed faith in political methods; it strengthened the hold of the political leaders who for the moment had been shunted aside by the advocates of strong action.

The Tory militants pressed their advantage to the utmost. In 1927 the government put through the Trades Disputes and Trade Union Act, which declared a sympathetic or general strike illegal, forbade civil servants to be members of unions affiliated with the T.U.C., and in the case of the political levy substituted "contracting in" for "contracting out." Much of the language was obscure and susceptible of prejudiced interpretation, e.g., what was a strike that "inflicted great hardship on the country"?

The provision on the political levy, however, was Labour's greatest grievance. The party contained few wealthy contributors and the divisional parties were poor; the main reliance was on the shilling a year (today from eight pence to four or five shillings) from the members of affiliated trade unions. Unwilling members had the privilege of contracting out of this obligation by filling out a prescribed form, which was easy to do. There had been no spate of protesting letters in the press, and Conservatives continued to encourage their trade-union followers, no inconsiderable number, to contract out by showing the ease with which it could be done.

The question at issue was the shillings of that middle group, which was not so antagonistic as to contract out but too careless or indifferent to contract in. In March 1925, a Tory backbencher had introduced a private member's bill to abolish the levy, but Baldwin then opposed it in a speech that ended, "Give peace in our time, O Lord."[11] In 1927, however, the right wing had its way; in this matter, so completely unconnected with the general strike, its members crudely admitted their objective of crippling Labour finances.[12] This vindictive act was a severe blow to the party. Although the total number of trade unionists decreased but slightly, those affiliated with the Labour party dropped from 3,388,000 in 1926 to 2,077,000 in 1928, a sharp decline due only in part to loss of the civil-service unions; it cost the party over one-fourth of its income. In the face of a hostile Liberal-Conservative majority the second Labor government was unable to effect a repeal, but such a measure was one of the first acts of the Attlee government.[13]

The Conservative right insisted further on reversing Labour's Russian policy. On May 12, 1927, the way was prepared by a police raid on the premises shared by the Russian Trade Delegation and by Arcos Ltd., a British company trading with Russia. Neither the document ostensibly the object of the search nor anything else of importance was discovered, but it served as an excuse to terminate the trade agreement and to break off diplomatic relations.

Labour had its own quarrel with the Communist party at home and at the moment was voicing indignation at political executions in Russia, but it did not share the hatred of that country which obsessed some Tories. In its press and annual conferences it protested the break. Much was made of the volume of trade, which in 1925 was reported as £67,060,000. In the Commons Snowden put the Labour view on propaganda and on isolating Russia. The way to defeat propaganda was by its exposure: "I am not at all afraid of the communist propaganda provided it is known. It is only when it is subterranean that it is effective." The surest way to modify the Russian system was to expose it to contact with the West: "The closer are the commercial relations between this country and Russia, the more the economic system of Russia will approximate to the economic and commercial conditions of the countries with which she is in relation."[14] With such optimistic views Labour was determined at the first opportunity to reverse the Conservative policy.

The Labour party, meanwhile, continued its efforts to protect itself from the Communists at home. The one avenue of entry still open to them was through affiliated bodies which were in turn federations based on organizations that did not exclude individual Communists. The executive, intent upon consistency, proceeded to block this road. With local Labour parties it was in a position to be mandatory, so at the 1925 conference it carried its proposal, by 2,870,000 to 321,000, to make Communists ineligible to any section of any affiliated local Labour party. With respect to the trade unions, jealous of their autonomy, the executive tactfully contented itself with an appeal to refrain from sending known Communists as delegates. The left wing complained that it was dictatorial, but the conference voted 2,692,-000 to 480,000 to support the executive.[15] Most of the Communists promptly disappeared from Labour conferences; but the next year, when the Boilermakers persisted in sending Harry Pollitt, the chairmen ruled that he had a right to speak on the ground that the executive could only recommend and could not dictate to the unions.

If British workers had been genuinely revolutionary, the general strike would have afforded the Communists an opportunity to divert the unrest to their own ends. Their utmost achievement was a slight increase in membership from 6,000 to 10,730, but after the collapse of the strike even this gain melted away. The publication of documents seized in the Arcos raid revealed clearly how Communist "nuclei" and "fractions" operated in Labour organizations. It followed that in succeeding party conferences the executive policy on the Communist issue was upheld almost without debate, and the few trades councils and constituency parties that defied the exclusion rule were disaffiliated and replaced by others more amenable. In 1928 at the Birmingham conference the executive took the decisive step of closing the trade-union route into the party councils and of excluding them from all Labour platforms. The slight opposition to the passage of the so-called "loyalty resolutions" by which this was accomplished indicated the rank-and-file unanimity on the Communist issue.[16]

While the executive was tightening control so that action within the Labour party became increasingly difficult and even impossible for Communists, there was a corresponding shift in the latter's strategy. Although conquest from within remained the objective, the failure of direct assault necessitated the development of more subtle weapons. The Communists resorted to the creation of new organizations or the utilization of existing ones, ostensibly independent and often non-political, as instruments for reaching large masses of workers. Great ingenuity was manifest in the number and kind that were built up. The Communist central committee became a sort of general staff while its disciplined followers officered these various bodies. Each loyal Communist, whether a member of a "cell" planted in a factory, or of a "nucleus" in another society, or of a "fraction" theoretically responsible to another constituency, was to have his assignment and, regardless of his position, be responsible solely to the party. By such maneuvers the Communists sought to frustrate Labour's policy of isolating them and, in spite of hostile leaders and unfavorable congresses, to establish contact with the masses.[17]

The most ambitious of these undertakings were efforts to organize the followers and sympathizers on the left fringes of the trade unions and the Labour party. The organization of the National Minority Movement in 1923 among the trade unionists has already been mentioned. It promoted unofficial strikes, captured offices, and prepared resolutions for others to place before the T.U.C. Every important conference, local or national, was preceded by a caucus. It was the Communist party's boast that the National Minority Movement was its biggest achievement. In 1925, following the anti-Communist stand of the Liverpool conference, the National Left Wing Movement was started to do the same for the Labour party. It formed committees inside constituency parties, packed meetings, and prepared resolutions for adoption by Labour affiliates as a means of getting Communist views before the annual conference.[18]

Other satellites, sometimes externally nonpartisan or beneficent, served the Communist purpose. The International Class War Prisoners Aid and the Workers International Relief were philanthropic and charitable in purpose; but of the former it was a Communist boast that, although they composed but 12 per cent of the membership, they had 88 per cent of the management. The Friends of Soviet Russia and the League Against Imperialism were Communist sponsored. The National Unemployed Workers' Committee Movement for a time attracted the interest of the T.U.C. general council sufficiently to share its management, but this connection was broken in 1927 when Communist influence became dominant. About 1921 the Labour Research Department, originally sponsored by the Fabian Society, became largely Communist in personnel and accepted some large payments from Arcos "for work done." Many workers, ignorant of the Communist theory of "nuclei" and "fractions," were attracted by sympathy with their ostensible objects. Few read the lengthy reports of the Communist International, so most remained unaware of the fact that these societies were there treated as part of that movement.[19]

The net result of this manifold effort, however, was disappointing to the Communists. The volume of recruits was exceeded by that of losses. The Labour countermeasures effectively frustrated their efforts to convert it into the means of Communist success; the hold of the orthodox leaders remained unshaken. The failure led to another of those Communist abrupt changes of front; the new party line was to be one of independence and of open opposition to Labour. At first it was a minority headed by Pollitt and R. P. Dutt which decided that the Labour party was too hopelessly reformist to become the vehicle for communism; the Communist role should be to fight all forces of reaction and, in order to emphasize this new freedom, to contest the seats of prominent Labour members. Work inside the party should be limited to the unmasking of the "reactionaries," especially through the agency of the Left Wing Movement.

This difference within the British party was submitted to the executive of the Communist International at Moscow where, on February 18, 1928, the views of Pollitt and Dutt were upheld. This decision was accompanied by detailed instructions for electoral tactics, which included the adoption of a campaign platform, the entry of the largest possible number of candidates, especially against the best-known Labourites, and the utilization of disaffiliated branches of the Labour party. Under the Communist theory of "democratic centralism" a wide latitude of opinion was permitted in advance of a decision of the

Comintern executive; but, once that authoritative body had spoken, its word was final. Accordingly, the Moscow verdict was accepted by the whole British delegation and in April ratified by the party executive. Thenceforth, Pollitt and Dutt, under the direction of Stalin and the Comintern, guided the British Communist party. The passage of Labour's "loyalty resolutions" in the following October reconciled the opposition to the policy of complete independence from Labour, so with the slogans of "Class Against Class" and "A Revolutionary Workers' Government," Communist candidates appeared in local government elections and in parliamentary by-elections. It was clear that in the next general election the Communists would not be unwanted and unwelcome allies of Labour but open opponents.[20]

In the field of foreign affairs Labour looked with mixed feelings upon the Baldwin government's abandonment of the Geneva Protocol in favor of the regional agreement in the treaties of Locarno whereby Britain, France, Belgium, Italy, and Germany collectively guaranteed the western frontiers of Germany. Labour derived satisfaction from the restoration of Germany to a position of equality and its prospective entry into the League. It looked upon Locarno as a conciliatory move in which Britain had led, but it credited much of the friendly atmosphere, the "spirit of Locarno," to the work of the MacDonald government. It disapproved, nevertheless, the substitution of a policy of separate and limited alliances for that of universal solidarity; it was fatal to the basic concept of a threat to one being a threat to all. It criticized the pact as relying too little on arbitration and too much on force and for failing to include something specific on disarmament. Further, it neglected Middle and Eastern Europe, called the real danger spots; MacDonald referred to those areas as "a tremendous hinterland of war left untouched."[21] Such mingled feelings were revealed in the Commons debates. The parliamentary party finally agreed to support ratification, although 13 members broke discipline to vote against it.[22]

When contrasted with the limited guarantee of Locarno, the discarded Geneva Protocol now looked better to Labour. The Protocol, it was argued, would have provided security for fifty nations instead of five; under it partial pacts would have been unnecessary. In 1925 the executive committees of the party and the T.U.C. and the succeeding party conferences all went on record in support of the Protocol. The party urged the practical step of signing the Optional Clause to bring most classes of disputes under the jurisdiction of the Permanent Court of International Justice. Always it stressed conciliation and arbitration instead of resort to sanctions; pooled security should emphasize these tools of peace. In the 1927 conference even the I.L.P. representative defended the Protocol as the best instrument yet developed.[23]

In the hope of minimizing the danger of war the Labour party supported most moves for disarmament, though not always optimistically. Interest in this avenue toward peace was intense in a decade when studies of the causes of the War of 1914 placed so much emphasis on the role of competitive armaments. The parliamentary party, accordingly, resisted increases in estimates for the armed services. It opposed resumption of work on the Singapore base.[24] Labourites watched with deepening disappointment the prolonged and painful attempts of the League's Preparatory Commission to lay the basis for a general disarmament conference, and likewise the futile effort of Britain, the United States, and Japan to achieve naval reduction. So far as the American navy was concerned it did seem to many, like MacDonald, that in view of the generally good relations between the two countries there was little need to take it into account when calculating British requirements.[25]

Few Labourites had faith in dramatic gestures. The party regarded Litvinov's proposal for complete disarmament, made at the fourth session of the Preparatory Commission, as a manifesto rather than a plan. The National Joint Council formally welcomed it as it did any peace suggestion, but pointed out that arbitration and security were essential accompaniments; without them the "crude proposal" of Litvinov, as MacDonald called it, was empty. Nor did the party accept "disarmament by example"—the "unilateral disarmament" of a generation later—as feasible. When proposed by Ponsonby, the 1928 conference rejected it.[26]

The Kellogg-Briand pact for the renunciation of war, though in 1928 signed by fifteen nations, was likewise looked upon as a benevolent gesture that might contribute to better feeling; it might even have some practical value in that a signatory of one day might be less apt to threaten war the next. It was good, too, that the initiative came from the United States; it might make that country less aloof from Europe and the League.[27] Labour, accordingly, advocated signing this pact, but urged that it be made effective by improving the machinery for the pacific settlement of disputes.[28] The test of the pact would be the acceptance of drastic disarmament; it noted, regretfully, that it did not follow.

Words were not enough. Good intentions needed machinery by

which they could be implemented. During the long and serious debate on world peace and disarmament at the Birmingham conference MacDonald said realistically:

It was not enough to say 'peace'; it was not enough to outlaw war; they had at the same time to do something to settle those questions which in the past had inevitably resulted in war, and unless they could make an arrangement by which national disagreements could be settled, they could outlaw war until doomsday, but they would still have war.[29]

He added later that, with Labour in office, he would not wait till all the delegates at Geneva were socialist in order to implement disarmament; he would work with what he found there. First, however, he would strive to create the conditions necessary for success; that would take at least two years, after which a disarmament conference would be practicable. It was a foreshadowing of his policy in office.

The party, meanwhile, was engaged in providing a policy for peace. In 1927 it prepared a new program, *Labour and the Nation,* to supersede that of 1918. Written mainly by R. H. Tawney, it was debated and adopted at the 1928 conference. It outlined a program based squarely on the League; it announced unequivocally that a Labour government would use that machinery for settling pacifically all international disputes whatever the interests and powers involved. On this foundation it would erect six "Pillars of Peace." It would (1) renounce war as an instrument of national policy, (2) reduce armaments by international agreement to the minimum required for police purposes, and (3) sign the Optional Clause, thus accepting the jurisdiction of the Court of International Justice in most classes of disputes. These three points alone, it was believed, would provide a sense of security and end appeals to force.

The next pillar (4) advocated economic cooperation among nations and full use of the International Labor Organization, and (5) demanded publicity in foreign policy. The last pillar (6) on political cooperation was emphasized as of utmost importance; it involved the repudiation of military alliances as dangers to peace, and the substitution of general agreement for pooled security against an aggressor—the concept that an attack on one would be resisted by all. This section stated, further, that it implied a reversal of imperialist domination of the weaker by the stronger, such as was at the moment creating revolt in Asia against Europe and—prophetically—would eventually in Africa. It would make the League universal.[30]

The Birmingham conference accepted this important statement, which became the basis of the foreign policy of the second Labour government. The belief was that this machinery would provide the means for removing fear and for the peaceable settlement of all disputes, while the wanton aggressor would find the sixth pillar an insuperable obstacle. The acceptance of the program marked the triumph of Henderson's efforts; it was his concept of the role of the League. Labour's policy appeared to its makers far more realistic than the Kellogg-Briand approach to the problem of peace.

While the Labour party was developing this coherent program, the I.L.P. pursued a divergent course that put it increasingly out of touch with the party of MacDonald and Henderson. It had declined by a quarter in membership from its postwar peak of approximately 40,000, but not at all in fervor. Its 1926 conference stressed immediate disarmament and war resistance; any threat of war would be met by refusal to bear arms, produce armaments, or render material assistance. To the Labour conference of that year Fenner Brockway, a wartime conscientious objector, brought this I.L.P. proposal. After Ponsonby seconded, the resolution was accepted without debate.[31] To the I.L.P. pacifists it was a serious proposal; to the Labour delegates, with no conflict in sight, it was a safe protest against war, and only in a situation parallel to that of 1920, which called Councils of Action into being, would there have been a resort to industrial action.

The I.L.P. not only sponsored disarmament by example but became increasingly revolutionary in its program of war resistance. To its 1928 conference the Lancashire divisional council proposed that in case of a threat of war, the labor movement should assume complete economic and political control: the parliamentary Labour party would become a National Committee of Public Safety and take over the government; the T.U.C. general council would organize transport to halt movement of troops and munitions and direct food distribution; the Cooperative movement and acquiescent local authorities would organize food supplies; local trades and labor councils would become local committees of public safety. Presumably Maxton would be the Robespierre of this British revolution. It was opposed as committing the I.L.P. to a policy of civil war and a challenge to democracy; it was defeated, though narrowly, by 197 to 145.[32]

Yet early in 1929 the I.L.P. accepted the same revolutionary tactics, modified and more generalized, when brought forward by the same sponsor and opposed with the same objection; it proposed that the labor movement should build the necessary machinery to take control in the event of an actual or threatened declaration of war by the government of the day. At a time when the labor movement was in a rightward trend, the I.L.P. under Maxton was still living in the mood of the general strike. It proceeded to recommend a vote against all funds for the armed services. Among the minority opposing was Emanuel Shinwell, later a Minister of War.[33]

The labor movement continued to condemn imperialism and to give moral support to what it deemed good causes everywhere. In 1925 the T.U.C. forthrightly and all but unanimously denounced British imperialism, 3,082,000 to 79,000, after a debate in which Communists led the attack and J. H. Thomas futilely opposed; the latter ridiculed the idea that problems such as those of Palestine and Kenya could be dealt with on the basis of three-minute speeches.[34] The party conferences thought Britain was moving too slowly in Egypt. They discussed sympathetically the reported misfortunes of victims of the White Terror in Lithuania and of extremists on both sides in Bulgaria. There were references to the Sacco-Vanzetti trial in Massachusetts and to the independence of the Riff. At the 1927 T.U.C. conference Bevin, recently returned from the United States and impressed by the advantages of an extensive free-trade area, made a powerful speech in favor of the economic unification of Europe exclusive of Russia; a fragmented Europe could not prosper. The leftists attacked his proposal as a diversion from the battle against capitalism, but he carried the conference by 2,258,000 to 1,464,000.[35]

Greatest attention was paid, however, to China, which was rent by civil war and was the scene of attacks on British concessions at Hankow and Nanking and of danger to Shanghai. Labour conferences expressed sympathy for Chinese nationalism, registered protests against exploitation and conditions of labor, and demanded the abolition of extraterritoriality. They urged strict neutrality in the civil war and opposed the dispatch of warships to Chinese waters and troops to Shanghai, though there were voices like those of Thomas, who insisted on the right and duty to protect British lives. Early in 1927 the National Joint Council issued a manifesto expressing sympathy for Chinese independence and hope for a negotiated settlement. It thought the Nationalists at Canton now sufficiently established to deserve recognition. It sent a deputation to Austen Chamberlain to state its view and backed it up with an Albert Hall demonstration. In all this activity the I.L.P. attacked the Labour leadership as too moderate.[36]

In the realm of industrial relations the thoughtful on both sides were impressed by the cost and danger of a general strike, and therefore drew back from the abyss that had suddenly yawned before them. Responsible leaders, such as Sir Alfred Mond and Lord Weir on one side and Bevin and Citrine on the other, were prepared for an alternative. The outcome was a series of conferences that began early in 1927 between twenty leading industrialists, acting only as individuals, and the T.U.C. general council. They became known as the "Mond-Turner talks" after the prominent industrialist and Ben Turner, chairman of the general council. Bevin and Citrine were both empirical in their approach to problems: improvement of the lot of the working class could not and need not await the coming of socialism; they would use such tools as were available. They were fully aware of industry's need for "rationalization," the word of the day for large-scale organization and modernization. They favored it, provided that its gains were not at the expense of one class; provision would have to be made for the workers displaced by the process.[37]

In July 1928 an interim report was issued. It agreed that trade unions should be recognized as bargaining agencies and membership encouraged by employers. It advanced a plan for joint consultative machinery to be set up by the T.U.C., the Federation of British Industries, and the National Confederation of Employers; it hoped that the government would consult it before introducing legislation concerning industry. There were proposals to deal with unemployment. Tangible results were slight, however; negotiations continued into 1930 but ended in the bitterness of 1931 that accompanied the demise of the second Labour government. In the long view, nevertheless, the talks did much to lend dignity and status to the general council, and they helped to ease the tension that followed the great strike.

Some leftists objected strenuously to the Mond-Turner talks, the object of which they regarded as nothing less than a further move to "tame" labor. Arthur Cook, the Communist secretary of the Miners, and Maxton, chairman of the I.L.P., joined in a manifesto denouncing this "class collaboration" and calling for unceasing war against capitalism. The 1928 T.U.C. rejected the Cook-Maxton manifesto by a vote of nearly six to one. Dissension followed in the I.L.P., because Maxton signed the manifesto without consulting his colleagues on that body's executive. The latter finally upheld him by a one-vote margin, but resignations followed. Maxton's course increased the tension between the I.L.P. and the Labour party; the latter could not indefinitely endure this party within a party with a program in competition with its own.

As the Baldwin government approached its constitutional time limit, Labour prepared its program for the general election. The position of *Labour and the Nation* on foreign policy has already been noted. Otherwise it was a general statement of socialist objectives in the tradition of Webb gradualism. It was in harmony with Mac-Donald's concept that the party ought not be tied to a specific set of proposals that might later be embarrassing; its policy statement should underscore a point of view and a set of principles that might be applied to problems as they arose. It called for a minimum standard of living for every member of society, the conversion of industry from a sordid struggle for private gain into a cooperative undertaking for the service of the community, a rapid extension of the social services, the adjustment of taxation so that surpluses created by social effort would be applied to the good of all, and a foreign policy based upon disarmament, arbitration, and the League of Nations. It promised a National Economic Committee to act as a sort of economic general staff. It suggested land, coal, power, transport, communications, life insurance, and the Bank of England as candidates for nationalization "without haste, but without rest." It urged extensive municipal enterprise and said that the cooperative movement was an indispensable element in the socialist commonwealth.

To meet the demands for a short and specific program, MacDonald and the executive produced an election manifesto. It failed to mention socialism. A pledge to deal with unemployment held first place. It promised public works—housing, slum clearance, land reclamation, electrification, railway and transport reorganization, and afforestation, a program that owed much to Keynes and Lloyd George. It would endeavor to increase purchasing power among the workers at home and in the Empire. Most of the candidates for nationalization disappeared from the manifesto, but in case Labour achieved a clear majority it said it would nationalize the mines; it promised public control, not nationalization, of land. Committees of Inquiry would consider reorganization of the cotton and steel industries.

For the election Labour had the advantage of a better understanding with the Cooperative party, which in 1927 entered into an electoral agreement to arrange for joint candidatures and to avoid competitive ones. Local cooperative societies could affiliate with divisional Labour parties. The Royal Arsenal society with 20,000 members affiliated directly with the Labour party, but others did not follow that example immediately. Due to the agreement, however, the two parties campaigned in close association.

The campaign was undramatic. An element of uncertainty was the fact that women under thirty were voting for the first time; at last Britain had adult suffrage. There was no clear-cut issue to place before the electorate. The Conservatives went to the country less with a program than with the slogans of "Safety First" and "Trust Baldwin." The Liberals summed up years of inquiry and reports with *Britain's Industrial Future,* the famous "Yellow Book" with its program of public works that then seemed very bold.

The result of the ballot of May 30, like that of 1923, was indecisive. Labour polled 8,362,594 votes to win 287 seats; for the first time it was the largest parliamentary party, but it fell short of the desired majority. The Conservatives had the largest vote, 8,664,243, but secured only 261 seats. The Liberals had 5,300,947 votes but elected only 59 M.P.'s. The Communists, following the new party line, contested 25 seats against Labour, lost them all, and did so poorly that 21 forfeited their deposits for failing to secure one-eighth of the vote.[38]

Labour suffered only five casualties and made many gains, especially in Greater London, Lancashire-Cheshire, and Yorkshire. It even invaded the old Conservative (or Unionist) stronghold of Birmingham to win as many seats as did its rival. There were smaller gains in Scotland, Wales, and the Northeast. In the South, excluding London, it made 11 gains, but in this whole area it held only 13 out of 94 seats. In the parliamentary party there was a shift of relative strength among the component parts. The socialist societies were up from 33 to 37, trade-union–sponsored candidates from 88 to 114, and the Cooperative party from 4 to 9, but the divisional Labour party members jumped from 25 to 118. The prosperity of the divisional Labour parties was due in part to the satisfying growth in individual membership, in part to the fact that many trade unions, poorer after the Act of 1927, ran candidates under divisional party auspices, and in part to accessions from the I.L.P. MacDonald, Snowden, and Clement Attlee, for example, no longer stood as I.L.P.-sponsored candidates. Among trade-union–sponsored members the Miners led with 42; the Railwaymen with 8 were next.[39]

The count revealed that Labour had profited by adhering to constitutional methods and had not been diverted by the alternative of direct action. Its steady growth was unchecked. It still did not have the desired parliamentary majority, however. The 59 Liberals would determine whether Labour would hold office.

9. The Second Labour Government

Uncertainty about who would govern in the three-party situation was ended when on June 4, 1929, Baldwin resigned and the King sent for MacDonald. Once more Labour was in office but dependent upon Liberal support. As in 1924 something was accomplished, especially in foreign relations, but the end was even more humiliating and disastrous. An underlying factor was the great depression that followed the collapse of October 29, 1929, on the New York Stock Exchange and created a situation in which several governments fell, Labour among the first.

In personnel the second Labour Cabinet resembled the first, though there was some shuffling of offices. This time MacDonald did not attempt to carry a heavy dual burden, so the Foreign Office went to Henderson, who filled it with great credit. Thomas, who had cherished an ambition for that post, was made Lord Privy Seal, but would grapple with the compelling unemployment problem. Snowden, Parmoor, William Adamson, Lord Thomson, Noel Buxton, and Trevelyan were back at their old posts as Chancellor of the Exchequer, Lord President, Secretary for Scotland, for Air, for Agriculture, and for Education, respectively. Clynes became Home Secretary, Sidney Webb (now Lord Passfield) Dominions and Colonial Secretary, and Thomas Shaw Secretary for War.

Newcomers were Lord Sankey as Lord Chancellor, Wedgwood Benn Secretary for India, Arthur Greenwood Minister of Health, Margaret Bondfield Minister of Labour, William Graham President of the Board of Trade, A. V. Alexander First Lord of the Admiralty, and George Lansbury First Commissioner of Works. Among those in the ministry but not in the Cabinet were Herbert Morrison, Hugh

Dalton, and Sir Oswald Mosley. Dropped were John Wheatley, who died in 1930, and Jowett, both of the I.L.P., a development that signified an intention to pursue a moderate course. Lansbury was of the left, but was put into a position where he could occupy himself with small things.[1]

Henderson's conduct of Britain's foreign policy has been both lauded and belittled. Whereas Labour historians have praised his handling of foreign affairs, others have rated him "a failure" and "a well-meaning second-rate man," or as one so busy with party work at Transport House that driving force disappeared from the Foreign Office.[2] Actually, he won the respect of those with whom he worked both in Westminster and at Geneva. This ironfounder lacked utterly the glamorous exterior of MacDonald, but he possessed transparent honesty. He was without formal education, but his experience as a patient trade-union negotiator stood him in good stead in his new role. For technical aid he relied upon the excellent staff of the Foreign Office and he left much detail to his under-secretary, Dalton, but he thought through his own policies. MacDonald reserved Anglo-American relations for himself, but elsewhere Henderson set out to see what he could accomplish in the way of conciliation, arbitration, disarmament, and cooperation through the League of Nations. His measure of success did not always match his efforts, but it was by no means inconsiderable.

Henderson took the Foreign Office with conciliation with Germany as a major objective; by the time he left office the "economic blizzard" and the rise of the Nazis combined to make conciliation impossible. That he failed was due to no fault of his.

Henderson sought first to end the military occupation of the Rhineland, the visible reminder of the war and the absence of peace. On July 5, 1929, in the House of Commons he announced this aim, which in August he would put before a reparations conference at The Hague. Since withdrawal of British troops alone would have resulted simply in replacement by more French and Belgians, Henderson desired the cooperation of those countries in a complete evacuation.

At The Hague an unexpected obstacle appeared in the attitude of Snowden toward the new proposal on reparations, known as the Young Plan, which scaled down and fixed the total German payment but at the same time altered to Britain's disadvantage the percentages hitherto accepted. The sum in question was relatively small, but Snowden made it a matter of principle; he would accept a general cancellation of war debts and reparations, but, as long as the latter were paid, he insisted that Britain should receive its agreed proportion. His stand was widely applauded at home. The unpopular socialist propagandist suddenly found himself a national hero, but at The Hague everything was at a standstill. Henderson, however, thought that, as compared with evacuation and pacification, the question of percentages was of small importance, and exerted himself to obtain a compromise. He finally managed one, though Snowden got the bulk of his demands.

Once this question was out of the way and the Young Plan accepted, Henderson's political committee could act. It arranged for evacuation by zones; by Christmas the British and Belgians would be home, and by June 1930, five years before the time set in the Treaty of Versailles, the last French troops would be out of the Rhineland. Snowden returned home to receive cheers and the freedom of the City of London, while Henderson went on to continue his work at Geneva. Ominous, though, was the response of Germany, for in the election of September 1930, the Nazis scored heavy gains.[3]

Dr. Curtius, the German Foreign Minister, worsened matters, too, when on March 21, 1931, he announced the project of an Austro-German customs union. At once the French and their Little Entente allies, dreading it as a prelude to political union, took alarm. Henderson feared the effect upon his efforts to win the French to a conciliatory attitude. He urged the governments concerned to put the matter before the League Council to judge whether it was compatible with a protocol of 1922 which forbade Austria to violate its economic independence by granting any state exclusive advantages calculated to threaten its independence. The League Council in turn submitted it to the Permanent Court of International Justice, which in September—after the Labour government had fallen—decided that such a union would violate the protocol. Although in public Henderson appeared legalistic in this matter, he was actually concerned with keeping all governments involved from becoming so unfriendly that they would prevent cooperation in the prospective disarmament conference, which to him was of paramount importance.[4]

The restoration of good relations with the U.S.S.R. was another major Labour objective. Both *Labour and the Nation* and the election manifesto promised that a Labour government would at once take steps to restore diplomatic and commercial relations, to settle outstanding differences by treaty, and to revive trade. Admittedly, the Russians would be difficult. The steady outpouring of abuse and propaganda from Moscow could not be ignored; at home the Communists were denouncing Labour as the third capitalist party and the ministry as solidly capitalist. Yet Russia existed with its vast potential. As long as it remained outcast, it would inevitably be an unsettling factor; as such it would make impossible a peaceful atmosphere in Europe and also the effective measure of disarmament that was central in Henderson's policy. Henderson saw no value in using recognition and non-recognition as reward or penalty; on the contrary, the greater the strain between nations, the more the need for functioning diplomatic machinery. Always in the background was the fact that Britain without foreign trade was not viable, and any region subtracted from the area of trade was just so much of a handicap. In addition, there still lingered the optimism that something might be learned from a Russian experiment that should be allowed to proceed under favorable circumstances.

On July 5, 1929, the House of Commons was surprised to hear from the new Foreign Secretary that recognition of Russia had never been withdrawn; there had been only a suspension of diplomatic relations. All that was needed, accordingly, was to restore the machinery and to put it into operation.[5] Henderson then proposed to Russia that A. V. Dovgalevsky, the Soviet ambassador to France, be empowered to discuss the matter. Talks followed, but they did not go smoothly. The Russians wanted an unconditional exchange of ambassadors with solution of problems left to follow, but MacDonald had given a promise that no ambassador would be received without a ratification of the invitation by Parliament. Henderson knew that Parliament would not accept it without a prior understanding on propaganda.

Finally, on October 1, Henderson, then at the annual Labour party conference at Brighton, met Dovgalevsky at nearby Lewes, and there reached an agreement for resumption of diplomatic relations including the exchange of ambassadors. The protocol, signed on October 3, contained mutual guarantees to refrain from propaganda; on the Comintern, for which the Russians persistently disclaimed responsibility, the best Henderson could do was to insist unilaterally that Britain would hold the Soviet government accountable for Comintern propaganda. This basic problem remained unsolved, but the British government was left free to act should Moscow resort to this mouthpiece. The protocol also listed problems for negotiated settlement.

On November 5 the House of Commons formally ratified the invitation to exchange ambassadors by a vote of 326 to 201, with the Liberals and three Conservatives supporting the government. The Conservatives opposed, and in the House of Lords carried a contrary vote;

it was only a gesture, however, because the Attorney-General decided that the restoration was an executive act, which required approval of the Commons only. A few days later Sir Edmund Ovey, a career diplomat, was announced as British ambassador to Moscow, and when Gregory Sokolnikov arrived in London, Russia had a full ambassador there for the first time since 1917.[6]

The results of the resumption of relations were disappointing. There was an increase in trade, but it was too slight to do much to relieve British unemployment. The desired atmosphere of good will never really materialized; a few problems were dealt with, but there was no modification of the Russian attitude toward the West. Propaganda continued to provide material for Conservative criticism. The British Communist party under Pollitt and Dutt was more closely controlled than ever by the Comintern and Moscow. On January 1, 1930, it launched a new paper, the *Daily Worker,* the source of funds for which was not in doubt, and the very first number contained an inflammatory Comintern manifesto.

Henderson, nevertheless, sought to follow up resumption of relations and settle outstanding problems. Early in 1930 he initiated moves for a trade agreement. Negotiations were carried on against a background of controversy over reports of persecution of religious bodies in Russia, seized upon by Conservatives as a means of belaboring the government, and of pressure from the left, which always took the rosiest view of Russia as a market for all kinds of British goods, which in turn was looked upon almost as a specific cure for unemployment. On April 16 a commercial agreement was signed. Each country accorded most-favored-nation treatment to the other, and, because trade was a state monopoly, a limited number of the Russian trade delegates would have diplomatic immunity. While these negotiations were in progress, the Soviets also indicated a willingness to consider a long-standing dispute over fisheries in the waters off Murmansk. On March 22 an agreement was reached that permitted British trawlers to fish up to the three-mile limit; it placed in abeyance Soviet claims for a twelve-mile limit.[7]

A minor but annoying episode that illustrated the lack of Soviet response to Henderson's genuine efforts to create good will was the treatment of the Lena Goldfields Company. This British company held a concession granted in 1925 during the period of the New Economic Policy. Now by devious means the Soviets refused to accept arbitration and forced the company out.

In October 1930, Henderson took up the question of debt settlement. Optimistically, and unwisely, he insisted that all categories of claims, intergovernmental as well as private, be included; it made his case hopeless, because the Russians had long since indicated that they would meet any governmental claims with counterclaims for losses during the intervention. The Russians also insisted on linking a guaranteed loan with a debt settlement, but such a loan, so reminiscent of 1924, was something Labour was unwilling to consider. There the negotiations stalled and nothing was done. This effort by Henderson was the last serious attempt to settle the question of these debts. They had to be written off, in effect, as another war loss.[8]

With respect to the U.S.S.R., accordingly, Henderson achieved a return to normal diplomatic relations, a trade agreement that brought smaller returns than hoped, and a fisheries treaty. That his success was no greater was due to no lack of effort or good will on his part. The absence of good will on the other side was apparent in the steady stream of abuse and propaganda. It is noteworthy, though, that in the matter of diplomatic relations the succeeding government did not reverse Labour's policy.

From the meeting at The Hague Henderson went directly to Geneva, where he helped make memorable the tenth session of the League General Assembly. MacDonald made a speech that set the tone and won plaudits, but it was Henderson who stayed throughout most of the session, was on the best of terms with such prominent figures as Briand, Stresemann, Benes, and Politis, and made himself immensely respected because of his efforts and obvious sincerity. He was ably seconded by other members of his delegation, especially Under-Secretary Dalton, William Graham, Philip Noel-Baker, and Lord Robert Cecil. At this meeting British influence was high.

In 1929 the outlook at Geneva was hopeful. The clouds that darkened it in the 1930's were still low on the horizon. Henderson was optimistic on utilizing the League to create a system of alternatives to force, to minimize the danger of war, and to reduce armaments. Briand enthusiastically propounded his scheme for a European Federal Union. It stirred imaginations. Henderson feared, however, that it would be looked upon as a bloc by the Americans and peoples of other continents; it would cut across Britain's link with the Dominions; and, what was his chief objection, it might become a rival of the League, that cornerstone of his policy. The Assembly applauded Briand, but his grand proposal disappeared in a pigeonhole.

Henderson concentrated upon plans for arbitration which, if adopted, would clear the way for disarmament. Few countries had as yet signed the League's Optional Clause, whereby signatories bound themselves to accept the jurisdiction of the Permanent Court of International Justice in all disputes concerning the interpretation of a treaty, a question of international law, a breach of an international obligation, or the reparation due for such a breach. Britain's own difficulty had been the Dominions, who by this time were in full control of their own foreign policies and anxious to avoid involvement in Europe. Patient negotiations won their approval, though with reservations especially on intra-Imperial questions, so that MacDonald in his opening speech could announce Britain's intention to sign. That signature on September 19 was quickly followed by others, so that by May 1930 the Optional Clause was binding upon forty-two states.

An effort to close the "gap" in the Covenant that permitted war after a country had fulfilled all the requirements for delay was not successful, but Henderson fared better with the General Act for the Pacific Settlement of Disputes. It provided for arbitration of all justiciable disputes by the Permanent Court and of other disputes by special machinery. In September 1930 at the eleventh Assembly, Britain announced its intention to sign. The next Imperial Conference agreed, with the same reservation on intra-Imperial questions. In May 1931 Britain signed, and a number of countries followed.

At the tenth Assembly William Graham, with Henderson's support, made a strong appeal for a tariff truce, the lowering of trade barriers, and greater economic cooperation among the nations. He secured a conference at Geneva in 1930 with representatives present from thirty countries and an American "observer." The American Congress, however, was even then raising the barriers higher with the Smoot-Hawley tariff, an example followed by many other countries. This move for freer trade was, accordingly, frustrated; international trade worsened as the great depression spread.[9]

Henderson's League policy appeared successful. The Optional Clause and the General Act were available if the nations were willing to use them. The way seemed clear for the general disarmament conference upon which his heart was set. A date for it was agreed, and the League Council unanimously invited him to be its president. Willingness to disarm would be a test of the nations' confidence in their paper renunciation of war and in the new international judicial machinery.

The government meanwhile sought to reduce tension and to facilitate general disarmament by securing a measure of naval reduction. Thanks mainly to the efforts of MacDonald, it achieved some success. The initiative came from President Herbert Hoover, who instructed the new U.S. ambassador to Great Britain, General Charles Dawes, to broach the subject. In October 1929, MacDonald responded with a visit to the United States. In spite of fears in some quarters that it would rouse anti-British feeling, it was a triumph; he impressed with his dignity and idealism. He saw President Hoover at his fishing camp on the Rapidan, addressed both Houses of Congress, and contributed to the stock of good will. The old disagreement over cruiser strength remained unresolved, but President and Prime Minister issued a joint statement that all disputes should be solved by pacific means. The British government, meanwhile, indicated its serious intent by suspending work on two cruisers and by cancelling or slowing down work on other construction, including the great base at Singapore.

The negotiations prepared the way for a naval conference which met in London on January 21, 1930, with representatives from Great Britain, the United States, Japan, France, and Italy. Out of it came a three-power treaty signed on April 22 by Britain, the United States, and Japan. Britain yielded its demand for 70 cruisers and accepted the maximum of 50, much to the discontent of strategic-minded Conservatives such as Churchill, who thought in terms of the number necessary to defend the sea-lanes of British food supply. Tonnage of cruisers, destroyers, and submarines would be kept at a 5:5:3 ratio. Capital ships would be reduced to 15, 15, and 9, respectively—which involved the scrapping of four ships by Britain—and building would be suspended for five years. It proved impossible to bring France and Italy to agreement; with coasts on both the Atlantic and the Mediterranean and with an overseas empire, France refused to accept parity with Italy.

The agreement won wide approval. It afforded a contrast to the failure of 1927 under the previous government. The saving of £60 million annually was noted. The Prime Minister was given great credit; said the *Daily Express,* "To the principal actor of the piece— Mr. Ramsay MacDonald—there can be nothing but the laurels."[10] The Labour party conference expressed its pleasure. It again rejected an I.L.P. move for disarmament by example and turned to the concrete problem of providing for the thousands that would become unemployed. A board representing the T.U.C., the Labour party, and the parliamentary Labour party was set up to study the effect upon employment in shipbuilding, engineering, iron and steel, chemicals, and transport. Money compensation was suggested but rejected, because the increasingly serious unemployment problem would have to be considered as a whole. In days of depression alternative work was difficult; the committee could suggest only the expansion of trade with Russia and colonial development.[11]

The Labour party was thoroughly sympathetic with that development of the 1920's which, so far as the white Dominions were concerned, completed the evolution from Empire to Commonwealth. The pace at which the numerous mandates and dependencies should progress toward that status of equality under the crown was debated, but it was agreed that they were all on the march. The party program of 1929, however, contained only a declaration for increased cooperation with the Dominions and for the economic development of the Empire.

For the next Imperial Conference, scheduled for 1930, the government had no positive economic program, though that problem dominated the discussions. It was held during a strenuous agitation carried on by the "press lords," Beaverbrook and Rothermere, for "Empire free trade," which actually meant a close-knit association based on protection. MacDonald and Snowden, free traders, opposed protection. The *Daily Herald* voiced the view that tariffs were no panacea for the economic collapse; it pointed out that protectionist countries, such as the United States, Australia, and Germany, were suffering along with free-trade Britain.[12]

From the T.U.C. came another suggestion. Its economic committee prepared a report urging Britain to associate with some larger group of countries in which there would be a rough balance of raw materials and foodstuffs with manufactures; the whole would constitute a free-trade area. Externally there should be no system of protection, though, if circumstances made it necessary, the fiscal weapon might be used in defense. Because Europe was so divided by national rivalries and few Americans would be interested, ran the argument, the logical link was with the Commonwealth, already bound by ties of sentiment, language, and economics. To the 1930 T.U.C. Bevin put this case with his usual forcefulness; they should develop the resources of the Empire not only for their own benefit but for that of all its peoples and for all humanity.[13]

The Imperial Conference took no decisions on these economic matters, but in the political field it was more productive. It agreed that the Dominions' claim to equality should be recognized by positive legislation; it was accomplished by the Statute of Westminster, which was enacted in 1931, shortly after the fall of the Labour government. An imperial tribunal was set up to which disputes could be referred if the Dominions concerned so desired. It was also agreed that the appointment of the governors-general was a matter solely for the King and the Dominions concerned.[14]

The small but strategic islands of Malta confronted the Labour government with a problem that resulted in the unusual step of suspending a constitution. A dispute, somewhat trivial in origin, raised the issue of church and state, and it was carried on against a background of Fascist Italy's unconcealed territorial aspirations. It began with the proposed transfer by the Superior of a Franciscan community of a member of that order against his will. To the church the issue was its right to discipline; to Lord Strickland, the Catholic Prime Minister of Malta and half Maltese himself, the action also raised the question of the civil rights of a British subject. He protested and sought postponement of the action until he could communicate with the Vatican in the normal manner, through the British representative there.

The Vatican replied by sending a letter not through that representative but directly to the Maltese bishops, urging them to continue their opposition to the Maltese government. To British opinion this action appeared to overstep the bounds of diplomacy and aroused a suspicion of furthering Italian territorial ambition. The affair reached a climax in May 1930, when on the eve of a Maltese general election the bishops of Malta and Gozo issued a pastoral order forbidding their flocks to vote for Lord Strickland or his followers; in case of disobedience excommunication would be automatic. Lord Strickland postponed the election. The British government then suspended the constitution and ordered an investigation by a royal commission, but by the time the report was in, Labour was out of office. The constitution was then restored and an apology from Lord Strickland for his tactics smoothed over matters with the Vatican.[15]

In Iraq, which was a Class A mandate to be administered by Britain until ready for self-government, rising nationalism demanded early independence and admission to the League. In 1927 the Conservative government promised to support an application to the League, but made it conditional upon the ratification of a treaty that the Iraqis rejected. In 1929 the Labour government informed Iraq that it would support an application unconditionally, which allayed suspicions of a desire to prolong the mandate indefinitely. The improved relations then made possible a treaty whereby Iraq would safeguard oil interests and the air route to India. Iraq, assured of complete independence, entered into a defensive alliance with Britain. In 1932 it was admitted to the League of Nations.[16]

The Palestine mandate posed a far more difficult problem. The wartime Balfour Declaration confronted the mandatory power with the practically impossible task of creating a "national home" for the

Jews and simultaneously of providing for the development of the Arab population—all within the narrow confines of this land with religious associations sacred to both. Workable compromise was not in the thought of either side, and any proponent of it was subject to attack from both. In Britain Jewish voices were numerous and influential; Arabs there were negligible, but there were sympathetic Muslims, especially in Egypt and in India, with whom Britain had to deal.

Labour had a record of consistent support for Zionism. From the war-aims program of 1917 to the party conferences of 1930 and 1931, it affirmed that policy.[17] MacDonald, who had traveled in Palestine, together with Snowden and Wedgwood, was active in organizing a society to disseminate Zionist information in England. Wedgwood was among the advocates of Dominion status for a predominantly Jewish Palestine. In spite of generous sympathy for the Jews, however, there was reluctance to accede to extreme Zionist demands at Arab expense. When the disturbances of 1929 began, some questioned the wisdom of carrying on indefinitely the wartime pledge of Earl Balfour.[18]

In August 1929, the disorders that began at the Wailing Wall in Jerusalem claimed at least 133 Jewish and 116 Arab lives. The government sent troops to restore order and a commission under Sir Walter Shaw to investigate. While the commission's report placed immediate responsibility for the outbreak upon the Arabs, it found the causes ultimately in the political and economic animosities arising out of immigration at a higher rate than the country could absorb; it called for a definition of the government's policy on the second part of the Balfour Declaration, i.e., the safeguarding of the rights of the non-Jewish communities in Palestine. Despite lack of conciliatory feeling on either side, MacDonald stated the dual nature of the British obligation. On April 3 he said in the Commons: "A double undertaking is involved, to the Jewish people on the one hand, and to the non-Jewish population of Palestine on the other; and it is the firm resolve of His Majesty's Government to give effect, in equal measure, to both parts of the Declaration and to do equal justice to all sections of the population of Palestine."[19] A second commission under Sir John Simpson followed to investigate economic conditions in Palestine, while labor immigration was temporarily halted. The Simpson report dealt with the grievances of dispossessed Arabs and the prospect of better land utilization for the benefit of both sides.

On the basis of these reports, the government issued the so-called Passfield White Paper on October 20. It accepted the theory of equal obligation to Jew and Arab. It announced more vigorous measures to preserve order, the intention to establish a legislative council, an agricultural development for which a British loan of £2,500,000 would be available, an end to the eviction of Arabs, the restriction of Jewish agricultural settlement to lands already in Jewish hands, and the need for more stringently controlled immigration.

This effort to follow a middle way pleased neither side. To the Arabs it provided insufficient limitation on Zionist activity, and the proposed legislative council fell far short of the democratic government they demanded and, because of their numbers, would dominate. The Jews regarded it as hostile to their aspirations. In the West there were vigorous protests from Zionist sympathizers, and Dr. Chaim Weizmann resigned the presidency of the World Zionist organization. MacDonald and Lord Passfield (Sidney Webb) sought to quiet the storm by emphasizing that the White Paper did not prohibit all immigration and was not intended to frustrate the ideal of a national home, but they insisted that new entrants should not exceed the economic capacity of the country to absorb them. In a letter of February 13, 1931, MacDonald repeated the "absorptive capacity" idea and the fundamental principle that no solution could be satisfactory or permanent unless based upon justice both to the Jewish people and to the non-Jewish communities of Palestine.[20]

In this concept of dual obligation he maintained his consistency. Because of the reassurance of no ban on immigration, Dr. Weizmann and the Zionists were mollified; for the same reasons the Arabs called it a "black letter." The policy of holding the balance could not please either side. The final act of the Labour government was the appointment of a director and staff to survey the problem of resettlement of displaced Arabs.[21]

The Labour government's experience with the Palestine mandate was unhappy. Although predisposed to favor the Zionists, it honestly sought an equitable solution satisfactory to both parties. Arabs and Jews, however, had interests and aims that were irreconcilable. The former feared an immigration that would soon put them in a hopeless minority in a country that they regarded as their own. The latter, inspired by Zionist fervor, were bent upon converting the national home into a national state. Anyone who cited the two parts of the Balfour Declaration was regarded as an enemy by those who saw only one. The concept that one could be both pro-Arab and Pro-Jew was inconceivable to either claimant.

In Egypt Henderson sought to remove the sources of suspicion and replace friction with cooperation. His insistence upon abstention in Egyptian internal affairs brought him, as it had his predecessor Austen Chamberlain, into conflict with Lord Lloyd, the last imperial administrator in the "strong" tradition of Lord Cromer. The immediate causes of disagreement had to do with the proportion of British officials in Egyptian service, the Egyptian army, and the imposition of new taxes on British subjects, but the fundamental one was the obligation of a government's representatives abroad to carry out its policy regardless of personal views. Because Lord Lloyd resisted the government's insistence upon greater Egyptian autonomy, Henderson forced his resignation. Angered Conservatives, led by Churchill, accused Henderson of political motivation, but on July 26 in the Commons the Foreign Secretary presented his case so ably that he won a personal triumph and raised the government's prestige.

Henderson sought agreement with the Egyptians but with only partial success. In June 1929, Mahmoud Pasha came to England and a draft treaty was prepared, but it came to naught when Mahmoud lost the ensuing election to the intensely nationalist Wafd party. It was necessary to begin anew with Nahas Pasha, who arrived in England in 1930 to reopen negotiations. Agreement was reached on the maintenance of British troops in Egypt for the defense of the Suez Canal, utilization of Nile waters, and on the protection of resident foreigners as an Egyptian obligation. Left unsettled was the question of the Sudan, where Egyptian ambition demanded unrestricted Egyptian immigration, whereas the British policy was to maintain the condominium as it existed until the Sudanese could decide their own future. The temper of the negotiations was friendly, and Nahas left with expressions of good will. It required the threat in 1936 from Mussolini's Italy, however, to produce an Anglo-Egyptian treaty.[22]

The Labour government faced the great problem of India. The party had long accepted the goal of self-government, but though "India for the Indians" was a simple slogan, most members wanted a transfer of power under circumstances in which nationalism would become a cover neither for intolerance toward minorities nor for economic exploitation of the masses.[23] In office Labour had to deal with a worsening situation characterized by disorders, strikes, boycotts, caste and religious antagonism, Communist activity, civil disobedience, and bloody rioting. Deepest of all cleavages was the Hindu-Muslim rift; the former desired complete independence, the latter equality for India in the Commonwealth; the former wanted a unitary constitution that would place all under the Hindu majority, the latter a federal system that would preserve Muslim supremacy in several provinces.

Hopes for a solution centered upon a commission appointed in 1927 headed by Sir John Simon, a Liberal, but containing members of all parties. Clement Attlee and Vernon Hartshorn, a Miners' leader, were Labour members. Noncooperation by some Indian groups hampered the commission. The Indian radicals stepped up their campaign of boycott and civil disobedience which, as usual, quickly degenerated into violence, which the Indian government met with mass arrests. The resulting trade paralysis combined with the world depression, which now struck India, to produce great hardship; that, in turn, became a political weapon against the government. The report of the Simon Commission, published in June 1930, was, nevertheless, immediately recognized as a great state paper. The first volume contained a masterly survey of India and its problems; the second, in which were Attlee's main contributions, put forward constitutional recommendations, which included wider powers to the provincial governments and a central legislature on a federal basis.

To consider the report the Labour government prepared a round-table conference which, it hoped, would be representative of all British and Indian parties. In November 1930, it assembled in London. MacDonald presided and in such a position appeared at his very best, although Attlee complained that he gave not five minutes to ascertaining the views of his two Labour commissioners, an aloofness from colleagues only too characteristic of MacDonald.[24] Many Indian groups were represented, but not the great Congress party. Gandhi had demanded a pledge in advance that the British government would support Dominion status, but the government could neither anticipate the decision of the round table nor accept Gandhi's claim to speak for all India. The princes were represented, however, and agreed to enter a future federation. There was agreement for a federal central government and on an electorate in which the depressed classes would be treated as separate from the caste Hindus, but there was failure on the all-important question of the other communities. Further progress would have to await other conferences.

Early in 1931 the outlook appeared brighter. Indian moderates were alarmed at the seriousness of the Hindu-Muslim strife, and in March Gandhi ended civil disobedience. He agreed to attend a second round-table conference. Again MacDonald presided, but it was as head of a National government, because in the interval his Labour government had fallen. Labour's effort to further the political development of India, accordingly, was a failure, but it was due mainly to the inability of the Indians to agree among themselves.

Although this Labour government could look with some pride upon its conduct of external affairs, there was little reason to boast over its handling of domestic ones. It inherited an intractable problem of unemployment. It was overwhelmed by the great depression and became one of the first to be toppled by it.

Much was expected from this party of social reform, though dependence on the Liberals made it certain there would be little of socialism from it. The King's Speech outlining the government's program promised a vigorous attack on unemployment, improvements in transport, a reorganization in coal, slum clearance and better housing, an inquiry into the iron and steel and cotton industries in order to improve their position in the world markets, and an investigation of the social effects of the liquor traffic. Sensing the weakness of a minority position, MacDonald appealed to Parliament to deal with such matters in the spirit of a Council of State rather than in one of party warfare.[25] It suggested a timidity of approach when the situation called for bolder and positive planning, though whether such a program could have been carried through that Parliament was doubtful.

The curve of unemployment, which had remained steadily at a figure of over 1,100,000, in 1930 turned sharply upward and by the end of that year reached 2,500,000, or nearly 20 per cent of the insured population. This high figure was an index to the extent of the misery and suffering that intensified with the passing months. Especially hard hit were those mining and manufacturing areas mentioned in the opening paragraph of this book. They became lands of abandoned mines and idle mills, chronic and hopeless unemployment, and life on "the dole." The Labour government proved inadequate to solve the problems of the great depression. MacDonald began hopefully enough with the appointment of a special committee consisting of J. H. Thomas, the Lord Privy Seal, Sir Oswald Mosley, a recent aristocratic convert to Labour, and Lansbury, a veteran socialist. Thomas, who set to work with a good deal of initiative, sought to accomplish more than temporary relief; he wanted to increase productivity by "rationalizing" industry in order to strengthen Britain's position in the world market. As he wrote:

It is no use merely spending money on a job of work which when finished does not enable the country to provide more employment than it provided before . . . therefore, my object is to lay out money which will show a clear economic return to the country by increasing its productive efficiency. At the same time I am seeking, in connection with representatives of all our great industries, to stimulate a new interest in tightening up industrial organization and in strengthening the competitive power of the country in the export markets upon which we so vitally depend.[26]

In accordance with this policy unemployment benefits and pensions were liberalized for a limited period, but emphasis was placed upon road and railway improvement, public works, and the location of new industries in depressed areas. A Development Act authorized grants up to £25,000,000 plus an equal sum for public works, while a Colonial Development Act provided up to £1,000,000 a year for the colonies. Thomas made a trip to Canada and reported some success on a better market for British goods. Lansbury proposed schemes for land reclamation, colonization in Western Australia, and for a lowered retirement age, but they ran afoul of Snowden's financial orthodoxy. The former socialist agitator made a speech at Sheffield saying that government should encourage initiative but that private enterprise would have to be the primary factor in recovery.[27] The Thomas committee, accordingly, met the challenge with nothing bold or imaginative. It resorted to expedients, none of which touched the fundamental causes of the economic distress. It was quickly overtaken by events, and its slight successes quickly disappeared from view when Britain felt the full impact of the depression.

In January 1930 MacDonald appointed an Economic Advisory Council, intended to be an economic general staff, consisting of Cabinet members, economists, employers, and trade unionists. Among them were Colin Clark, Keynes, Cole, Tawney, Sir Josiah Stamp, Sir John Cadman, Bevin, and Citrine. They met regularly with the Prime Minister, but nothing tangible resulted. The industrialists, steeped in principles of thrift and balanced budgets, could never agree with those who proposed a program of spending to get out of a depression. Keynes, Tawney, Cole, and Bevin, on the contrary, urged the utilization of the resources of the State to further planned economic expansion; they would put increased purchasing power in the hands of the people so they might consume more. The two points of view were irreconcilable.[28] It was no wonder that Thomas's statements became increasingly gloomy as the unemployment figures mounted. It was clear that he had little hope, especially after his two colleagues showed open and fundamental disagreement with him.

Thomas's failure stirred the left to produce its own remedies. Maxton and the I.L.P., convinced that "rationalization" would only add to unemployment in the short run without ever providing a cure, demanded a socialist solution. They called for acceptance of the principle of work or maintenance, measures to increase purchasing power at home, the reduction of hours, a national housing program, credits to Russia, and, above all, the socialization of basic industries and services.

A different approach was that of Sir Oswald Mosley, Thomas's colleague on the commission. In February 1930, with the aid of Lansbury and Thomas Johnston, he prepared what came to be known as the Mosley Memorandum. When presented formally by Lansbury, it became a Cabinet document and therefore was secret, but its contents gradually became known. Its object was to expand purchasing power. It would control imports, either by tariffs or by direct limitation, make bulk purchase agreements, and develop agriculture in order to reduce dependence upon imports. It proposed a liberal credit policy, public control of banking, development of the social services, more generous pensions, benefits, and allowances, and a rationalization of industry under public control so as to secure expansion both for export and home markets.[29]

These schemes, involving measures of planning similar to those acceptable later to many parties and governments whether left or right, ran aground on the rock of Snowden's financial orthodoxy. The Chancellor of the Exchequer not only objected to their immediate cost but feared they would endanger the gold standard. Snowden carried the Cabinet against Mosley, whereupon the latter resigned. In the Commons, however, he made such an effective attack upon Thomas that MacDonald moved the latter to the Dominions Office and took charge of unemployment policy himself but failed to promote any bold and vigorous program such as the crisis demanded.

In October 1930, the left proposals were debated at the Labour party conference. Maxton presented the I.L.P. program, but was defeated by over five to one. Mosley, however, found so much support for his Memorandum that he lost by only 1,251,000 to 1,046,000, which was indicative of rank-and-file desire for a more positive policy. This desire was underscored when in the election of the party executive the veteran Thomas was unseated and Mosley chosen in his place.

At the moment Mosley's hope was to build up a following within the party. This threat to the leadership, together with manifestations of an arrogant and authoritarian temperament, led to his undoing. He issued manifestoes that in February 1931 culminated in *A National Policy,* which for the first time presented his complete program to the public. He had the support of 17 Labour M.P.'s, including John Strachey and Aneurin Bevan. When he discovered, however, that he could not win the Labour party, he broke away to found the New party. He was accompanied by only four of the Labour M.P.'s, including Strachey briefly, but not Bevan. The Labour party expelled him and those who left with him. When the New party failed, Mosley became an admirer and imitator of the dictators. As the founder of a fascist party, he was soon a prime object of Labour hostility.[30]

After assuming responsibility for unemployment, MacDonald's first step was to call a meeting of local authorities to discover why certain authorized public works were being held up by vested interests, as Mosley had revealed. It was followed by the quick passage of a bill to remove obstacles, and a royal commission was appointed to examine problems of unemployment insurance. MacDonald rejected a Lloyd George proposal for a Liberal-Labour coalition to deal with the emergency by means of vast development schemes; coalition was politically unacceptable to Labour, and Snowden would have nothing to do with the huge loan that would be necessary. The chancellor was likewise alarmed at Treasury warnings that the large loans to the insurance fund were drafts on the future to meet current needs; they could not be long continued, as he considered a balanced budget the primary objective.[31] In June 1931, the royal commission on unemployment insurance recommended increased contributions from employers and employees and reduced benefits. Such was the clamor from labor that it was not even considered, though a bill to eliminate abuses in the system was passed.

The Labour government ended with over 2,800,000 unemployed, an all-time high. Labour's misfortune was that its term of office coincided with a world economic crisis with which it, like other governments, was unprepared to deal. In spite of the fact that extreme suffering was eliminated or alleviated by benefits and pensions, the distress left a searing impression on working-class memories; for the next two decades nothing would draw such a hostile growl from a labor audience as a reference to unemployment.

The Labour government attempted legislation primarily in the interest of social welfare. It extended the Pensions Act to include widows between the ages of fifty-five and seventy. A Housing Act introduced by Greenwood, Minister of Health, provided subsidies for slum clearance and gave more power to local authorities to initiate long-term projects. Another act was designed to produce 40,000 cottages for rural housing. An act for Town and Country Planning enabled local authorities to further local and regional planning. A bill to establish a consumers' council with compulsory powers of investigation failed; the other parties objected to this attack on private enterprise.

Three efforts to aid education could not surmount the old obstacles of cost and the attitudes of religious bodies. A bill of 1929 to raise the school leaving age to fifteen was urged primarily on educational grounds but also because it would remove a few from the unemployment lists. It failed mainly because of a provision for maintenance allowances to parents who could not afford to keep children in school beyond the age of fourteen. A second bill in 1930 met Nonconformist opposition to subsidies to denominational schools, mainly Catholic and Anglican, to enable them to carry the additional pupils. A third bill, with financial aid omitted, went aground on the rocks of Catholic and Anglican opposition within the government's own ranks. It was mutilated in the Commons and lost in the Lords. Trevelyan, President of the Board of Education, thereupon resigned, though he made it clear that his action was based not on this failure alone, but on the fact that there was too little socialism in the government's policy.[32]

The government hoped to do something for the miners, who wanted to return from the 8-hour to the 7-hour shift without loss of pay, a concession the owners were unwilling to make. The Liberals were calling for "rationalization," which would involve the closing of the poorer mines and the expansion of the better; since that would have added to the number of the workless, however, it was a form of relief to keep all in operation. The Coal Mines Bill, accordingly, was full of compromises. It cut the shift to 7½ hours and proposed a National Wages Board. It set up production quotas for each district and mine, and proposed a levy to subsidize owners who exported, in order to enable them to compete abroad. It included compulsory amalgamation to please the Liberals whose votes would be needed. This bill had a long struggle in each House and emerged badly shorn. The Lords weakened the amalgamation proposals and destroyed the levy. The owners liked the power to regulate output and prices, but in practice refused to utilize the National Board and insisted upon district agreements, which frustrated the aim of a minimum wage. The miners were unhappy over the failure to return to the 7-hour shift. With its restrictionist schemes, quotas, and levies, this bill set a precedent followed in others in the thirties.[33]

An Agricultural Marketing Act likewise set precedents. This act established boards of producers of certain kinds of products, such as milk, cheese, cereals, hops, cattle, sheep, poultry, and fruit, to regulate their marketing. Once the majority of producers agreed to a board, the minority, too, were bound by it.

Some measures fared less well. A Land Utilization Bill to set up large-scale experimental farms and to place unemployed on small holdings met opposition in the Lords and finally passed with a life limited to eight years. The Trade Disputes Bill, intended to restore "contracting out" and to legalize the sympathetic strike, but not the general strike, was so nearly nullified by Liberal amendments that it was withdrawn. A measure for electoral reform, designed to abolish plural voting and separate university representation, provide the alternative vote, and set a lower limit on campaign expenses, was attacked in both Houses; it was still in dispute when the government fell.[34]

The problem of London transport came before the Labour government as a recognized case of inefficiency, duplication, and confusion. Therefore in March 1931 Morrison, the Minister of Transport, introduced a bill to buy the privately owned bus, train, and steam railway lines and set up a monopoly as a public corporation that would provide the entire metropolis with a complete and unified transport system. Instead of organizing it as a department of government under a minister, as the post and telegraph had been, there was substituted an independent corporation under a board, which would manage the industry but be responsible to a minister. There were precedents in the Conservative measures of 1926, the Central Electric Board and the B.B.C., both of which were generally accepted as having proved their efficiency. Morrison's bill went to a joint select committee, but its work was unfinished when the government fell. The succeeding National Government, after considering alternatives, implemented what was essentially Morrison's plan. The success of the London Passenger Transport Act of 1933 thereafter had great influence on Labour thinking.[35]

The budgets of Snowden were based on orthodox finance. For the first in April 1930, he fell heir to a deficit of over £40,000,000 and he had the cost of additional pensions and relief to meet. There was pressure for tariffs from the Beaverbrook and Rothermere papers and from the Federation of British Industries, but he was staunch for free trade and allowed some safeguarding duties to expire. He found the sums necessary to balance his budget by increasing the income tax from 4s. to 4s. 6d. in the pound, though alterations in exemptions put the increase mainly on the upper brackets. He increased the death duties and put an additional penny on a gallon of beer. This budget placed the burden on those most able to bear it. His second, a year later, was likewise balanced, with an increase in the petrol tax as the major change.[36]

In July 1931, two important committee reports were published. The government's Committee on Finance and Industry, appointed in 1929 and headed by Lord Macmillan, consisted mainly of economists and financiers with one trade unionist, Bevin. Its report, written largely by Keynes, dealt with British banking and investment. It emphasized that the return to the gold standard had overvalued sterling and thus handicapped British exports. The other was a report from a Committee on National Expenditure appointed by Snowden and headed by Sir George May. While this committee was working, the number of unemployed rose from 2,500,000 to over 2,750,000, and a financial crisis in Central Europe involved Britain. It began with the failure of a Viennese bank, the Credit Anstalt, and quickly spread to Germany, where there was a flight from the mark. Acceptance of President Hoover's proposal of June 20 for a moratorium on reparations and international war debts was delayed until July 6 by French insistence upon a favored position, a loss of time costly to all. During the last half of July the Bank of England lost gold at the rate of £2,500,000 a day. It was against this background that on July 31 the May Committee issued the report that precipitated the fall of the Labour government.

The report of the May Committee, with its estimate of a government deficit of £120,000,000, came as a shock to the Cabinet and the country. To meet this expected deficit the committee recommended new taxation to raise £24,000,000 and economies totaling £96,000,-000, though the two Labour members dissented from most of the latter. Two-thirds of the saving, or £66,500,000, would be at the expense of the unemployed, where the cut would be 20 per cent. The remainder would be found by reducing the pay of civil servants, teachers, and members of the armed forces, and by eliminating some public works designed to relieve unemployment.

The government set up an economy committee, consisting of MacDonald, Snowden, Thomas, Henderson, and Graham, to study the May Report. The situation was grave, but Parliament was adjourned on July 31, and most of the Cabinet went on vacation. The Bank of England secured loans of £25,000,000 each from the Bank of France and the Federal Reserve Bank in New York. The *Economist* stated that the report seriously overpainted the gloom.[37]

Very quickly, however, an atmosphere of panic developed, and after the first week in August bank withdrawals continued at a rate that within a month would exhaust the new funds. On August 11 MacDonald, called back from Lossiemouth, returned to London. What he and Snowden heard there from the officers of the Bank of England was that Britain was on the edge of a precipice and, unless the situation changed rapidly, would soon be over it; that the cause of the trouble was not financial but political and lay in the complete want of confidence in the government existing among foreigners; and that the remedy was in the hands of the government alone.[38] According to this view the cause of the crisis was not in the financial system and the cure not in such measures as control of exchanges or going off gold; instead, the cause was Labour's extravagant social policy, and the remedy would be to please the foreigners by balancing the budget, as suggested in the May Report. When the bankers asked to put "the facts" before the other parties, MacDonald assented.

The succeeding days, August 11–23, witnessed intense activity with much going to and fro, meetings, and conferences that involved the Cabinet, the Opposition leaders, the bankers, and the T.U.C. general council. There were differences on the causes and cure of the crisis, but the critical issue was that of the economies suggested in the May Report and, specifically, the cut in payments to the unemployed. It took place in an atmosphere of crisis and of newspaper build-up of a case against the government for extravagance. The general impression became that of a race against time.

The groups concerned behaved very much as might have been expected. The bankers of 1931 grew up on orthodox finance; their belief in the gold standard and a balanced budget was axiomatic. When invited to give advice, they rendered it in those terms. Snowden, although a socialist for ethical reasons, held the same view of finance as the bankers. He would consider neither the abandonment of the gold standard nor the restriction of imports. MacDonald trusted and relied upon Snowden; he would not listen to Keynes or others on the Economic Advisory Council who urged such alternatives. The Opposition leaders, Neville Chamberlain, Sir Samuel Hoare, Sir Herbert Samuel, and Sir Donald Maclean, thought likewise; they believed, too, in the necessity of drastic economies. They wanted the cuts, but were not anxious to upset the Cabinet; they thought it better, in fact, to have the economies implemented by a Labour government. Only in case the latter would not continue, would they consider an alternative.

Rejecting both the orthodox analysis and the proposed solution, the T.U.C. general council, led by Bevin and Citrine, maintained that the currency system based on the gold standard was breaking down, and that retention provided no remedy for the situation. It did not believe, as did MacDonald and Snowden, that if sterling went off gold, chaos and utter ruin would follow; nor did that happen when Snowden took it off just one month later. The general council's main objection to the proposals in the May Report was to the inequality of sacrifice involved; to make two-thirds of the economies at the expense of that section of the community least well off seemed the rankest injustice. When the Cabinet asked for the general council's views, it gave them. It suggested as alternatives: (1) a graduated levy on all incomes so that the whole community would share the burden; (2) new taxation upon fixed-income-bearing securities, the purchasing power of which had increased as prices fell; (3) a revenue tariff, although most members were free traders in principle; (4) the suspension of the £50,000,000 annual contribution to the sinking fund for the national debt. For giving advice when requested, the general council was accused of "dictation" by one side, as the bankers were of "a ramp" (plot) by the other.[39]

MacDonald and Snowden carried on the negotiations with the leaders of the Opposition and representatives of the Bank, which turned on the possibility of reaching a compromise on the economies in question. On this issue there was violent disagreement inside the Cabinet. Lansbury, Greenwood, and Johnston led the opposition to sacrifices at the expense of the unemployed, while Thomas, Webb, Sankey, and some others were willing to make concessions. The majority finally agreed upon economies totaling £56,250,000. MacDonald urged £78,500,000, a figure submitted for consideration by the Economy Council. The Conservative and Liberal leaders would accept nothing less. The gap between the two figures was never closed, although at one point the Cabinet suggested £68,500,000 as a basis for discussion, including a 10 per cent cut in unemployment allowances. Henderson, meanwhile, took the lead in opposing such cuts; there was a stiffening on principle, which was in danger of being compromised away. In the critical sessions of August 22–23 the Cabinet was almost evenly divided with ten ready to follow the Prime Minister and nine, or possibly ten, opposed. Among the minority, however, were definitely Henderson, Clynes, Graham, Alexander, Johnston, Addison, Adamson, and Lansbury, without whom no Labour government could be carried on.

During the meeting of August 23 a reply came from the Bank that in New York the prospects for a further loan were not good unless Parliament should have already enacted economy legislation. Mac-Donald appealed for his whole £78,500,000, but the minority would not yield. He thereupon asked the Cabinet to place their resignations in his hands and went to see the King. King George V urged reconsideration, and, as was constitutionally correct, he sought advice from Samuel and Baldwin. MacDonald, too, conferred with the Opposition leaders. On August 24 MacDonald again saw the King, and then returned to tell his colleagues—at the last meeting of the Labour cabinet—that there would be a National Government with himself at its head. According to a letter written by Sidney Webb to his wife immediately after this meeting, MacDonald made his announcement with great feeling and members uttered polite things, but accepted silently the accomplished fact. MacDonald then called together the junior ministers, told them he would be going into the political wilderness, and generously advised them for the sake of their future careers to dissociate themselves from the National Government. That afternoon he tendered the formal resignation, and the second Labour government came to its end.[40]

The course of the second Labour government strikingly paralleled that of the first. Again there were some successes in the field of foreign policy, where Henderson added to his reputation. At home the minority position and dependence upon the Liberals led to compromises, defeats, and frustration. Again there was no socialist advance. Unpreparedness in face of the unprecedented economic crisis brought another inglorious end. It completed the estrangement of MacDonald, so aloof but hitherto so indispensable, from the party to which he had contributed so much from the date of its founding. To those who had pioneered the labor and socialist movement the fruits of the MacDonald governments were a bitter disappointment. Something of the former high self-confidence disappeared in these experiences and the events of 1931 left scars that were long in evidence. Deprived of the best-known leaders, the shattered party appeared doomed to the role of a futile Opposition, while for nine critical years the country turned to Conservative leadership and policies.

10. Rout and Recovery

For the Labour party the aftermath of MacDonald's resignation was gloomy. An administration that opened in an atmosphere of good will and promise closed in one of disillusion and disaster. The best-known leaders were lost. In the election that followed, Labour suffered heavily in the country and was reduced to a fragment in the Commons. Internal strife brought further losses. The slow work of rebuilding began, however; the program was revised and confidence regained. The election of 1935 revealed a recovery of the 1929 strength in the country, and, although not proportionately reflected in the Commons, Labour was in a position to be a more effective Opposition.

On August 25, 1931, MacDonald announced his new Cabinet of ten members, the National Government of persons from all parties that would meet the emergency. Along with four Conservatives and two Liberals were three other Labour members, Snowden, Lord Sankey, and Thomas, who kept their old offices. Lord Amulree, Sir William Jowitt, and C. M. Aitchison remained in the ministry, and Malcolm MacDonald and G. M. Gillett stayed as junior ministers. MacDonald wanted to have Tom Shaw, Emanuel Shinwell, and Sir Stafford Cripps, but they would not serve. In fact, only seven other M.P.'s followed MacDonald, for a total of fifteen National Labour men. He did not resign from the Labour party, but waited in the hope that a greater response to him would develop within it. When it was not forthcoming, he was left with no solid basis of Labour support and a prisoner of his ex-enemies and new allies. On September 28 the Labour party executive formally expelled him and his following, and the long association came to an end. As distrusted and disliked in some quarters as he was admired in others, MacDonald had, nevertheless, seemed the indispensable leader. Henceforth there was a tendency to disparage his past services. His action in 1931 was interpreted as premeditated treachery and desertion; it was called "the greatest betrayal in British political history."[1]

Once again Henderson was the pivotal figure in the Labour party. He had been loath to part from MacDonald. When he concluded that it was no longer possible to follow him, however, he unhesitatingly went into Opposition, and by so doing saved the character and the identity of the party to which he had already contributed so much. At his suggestion there was a joint meeting of the parliamentary party and the T.U.C. general council at Transport House to preserve the unity of the movement. There, with only five I.L.P. members dissenting, Henderson was chosen party leader. Although it was a post he had never coveted, and in spite of the fact that he was now sixty-eight and already secretary and treasurer, he accepted the burden.[2]

Meanwhile, the National Government passed the budget, including cuts and economies amounting to £70,000,000, and then, to stop the run on sterling, went off gold. None of the freely predicted disasters resulted from the latter, though cuts in the seamen's pay ranging up to 25 per cent produced the first mutiny in the Royal Navy since the eighteenth century. Labour offered an ineffective opposition to the economies, and in the House many angry words passed between Labourites and their former leaders, especially Snowden, who was now on the Treasury Bench. The Conservatives began to press for a tariff and an election. Because the Liberals were divided on protection, with Sir Herbert Samuel's followers opposed and Sir John Simon's in favor, it was agreed that each constituent element of the Coalition would fight on its own program. Parliament was thereupon dissolved on October 7; for the election on October 27 MacDonald asked the country for a "doctor's mandate" to enable the National Government to deal with the crisis.

For this campaign, which had a resemblance to the one in 1918, Labour entered 489 candidates; there were 19 for the I.L.P., which fought its own battle. There were 517 Conservative, 121 Liberal, 39 Simon Liberal National, and 20 National Labour entries. There were also 26 Communists, who for the most part fought Labour men, and 24 for Mosley's New party. The Labour manifesto, drafted by H. J. Laski, had as its slogan "Plan or perish." Denouncing tariffs, it demanded a socialist solution with national planning of industry and trade, the national ownership and control of banking and credit, and the organization of power, transport, and iron and steel as public services, with such control of prices as was necessary to enable British industry to compete in the world market. It would reverse the harsh policy of the recent cuts made in the name of economy.[3] In this campaign radio broadcasting had an important place. There were eleven party broadcasts altogether, and, as all sections of Liberals had to be accommodated, Labour had but three of them; they were given by Clynes, Graham, and Henderson. On the platform there was intemperate language on both sides. The "plot theory," which held that the coalition was something long contemplated and well prepared by MacDonald, had an airing. There was a special effort to unseat him at Seaham. Sections of Liberals, headed by Lloyd George and Samuel, opposed the suggested tariff, and Lloyd George denounced the election as a mere Tory "ramp" to exploit the national emergency for partisan ends.

In the exchange of invective Snowden turned on his former colleagues. In a broadcast of October 17, generally stated to have been one of those that changed votes, he attacked the Labour program as "fantastic and impracticable," and one that "would destroy every vestige of confidence and plunge the country into irretrievable ruin." "It is Bolshevism run mad," he said.[4] At Seaham MacDonald waved German paper marks of the inflation period before his audiences. A misleading statement by Walter Runciman, the President of the Board of Trade, roused fears for the safety of postal savings.

The returns showed a landslide. Of the 615 seats the National Government won 556 and the Opposition a mere 56. The former were unequally divided with 471 Conservatives, 35 Simon Liberal Nationals, 33 Samuel Liberals, 13 National Labourites, 2 Nationals, and 2 Independents. The Opposition consisted of 46 Labour, 6 Independent Labour, and 4 Independent Liberal (Lloyd George's family group) members. One Independent was in neither group. The popular vote was less one-sided, but still decisive. For the government there were 14,539,403 votes, of which 11,926,537 were for Conservative candidates and 343,353 for National Labour. For the Opposition there were 6,754,129 votes, of which Labour received 6,362,561 and Independent Labour 285,462. The Communists received 74,824 votes and the New party candidates 36,377, but none approached success. To the Liberals coalition brought immediate gain, because with about three-eighths of the Labour vote the three sections captured a larger number of seats than the latter, but in the long run it cost them dearly through absorption by the dominant Conservatives. National Labour showed a loss of two.

For Labour it was the first serious setback in its march toward a popular majority. Its vote was down by approximately 1,700,000 from the 1929 figure, but it was up by nearly a million over 1924, so it was evident that the new recruits had not all deserted. It was a two-to-one defeat, nevertheless, and the system of territorial constituencies exaggerated it into something worse than nine to one. For the leadership it was even more serious. The only Cabinet member to survive the debacle was Lansbury; two minor ministers, Attlee and Cripps, did likewise. Among the defeated ministers and members were Henderson, Clynes, Greenwood, Morrison, Shinwell, Alexander, Shaw, Dalton, Margaret Bondfield, Tillett, Wedgwood Benn, Graham, Adamson, Addison, Johnston, and Jowett. It left an Opposition feeble in numbers and weak in debating strength. Of the 46 returned, 23 were Miners.

Geographically, Labour representation all but disappeared from certain areas. In Scotland it was down from 37 to 7 (including 4 Independent Labour men), in the Midlands from 47 to 3, in the London area from 54 to 7, in Yorkshire 47 to 7, in the Northeast 22 to 2; outside of Greater London it held not a single seat in the South, and there was only one success in the West country. Only from mining Wales and Monmouth were numbers returned.[5] By contrast MacDonald and Thomas won handily, whereas Labour organs had confidently predicted the defeat of the former.[6] Snowden went to the House of Lords.

The explanation of the measure of defeat lay in the depression, which presented problems too big for the Labour government to solve. Lack of confidence in it was intensified by fear that its policies would make matters worse. The spectacle of its wide-open split appeared to contrast with that of others abandoning partisanship to rally around the standard of national unity. The very name of "National Government" appealed to idealism and suggested sectionalism on the part of Labour. In such an atmosphere defeat for Labour was certain; the electoral arrangements that turned most constituencies into straight fights converted it into a rout. In other countries the collapse was viewed with amazement, but some of their governments soon suffered the fate of British Labour.

For a time the shattering of the political party brought the T.U.C. general council in to restore the broken front. Although in the British labor movement the spheres of the political party and the trade

unions were roughly delimited, during crises they were apt to overlap. Before and after 1918, for example, political issues were freely
debated in the T.U.C. The aftermath of 1931 again called the T.U.C.
into action through its general council. The parliamentary party had
lost its leaders and survived as a pitiful remnant. Henderson was not
only unseated but also was absent at Geneva as president of the disarmament conference; in 1932 he resigned the party leadership in
order to devote his last days to that heartbreaking task. Lansbury,
his successor, was a respected Christian socialist and sentimental pacifist, but was seventy-two and not an able parliamentarian.

In the T.U.C., however, was vigor and initiative; in Bevin and
Citrine it possessed men of outstanding ability. They now moved in
to fill the gap. They effected a reconstitution of the National Joint
Council, later known as the National Council of Labour, under
which the chairman and two members from the Labour party executive and the same from the parliamentary Labour party would meet
monthly with the chairman and six members from the T.U.C. general council. The chairmen of the Labour executive and of the general council would preside alternately. This extra-parliamentary body
for a time exerted great influence upon party policy. It posed a problem of appearing like outside dictation and a conversion of Labour
into a trade-union party, but that could change only with the general situation and the return to political life of those eliminated in
the recent collapse.[7]

In 1932 the Labour party lost by secession a constituent element
that might have been expected to assume a leading role in its rebuilding. In the late 1920's the I.L.P., which had been so prominent in the
founding and early years of the Labour party, became at odds with
the party over its program of "socialism now." Under Maxton and
Fenner Brockway it asserted its independence, so that in 1931,
although still nominally a Labour affiliate, it fought its own campaign on its own program. The parliamentary Labour party had a
clause in its standing orders that permitted a member to abstain from
voting on a matter of conscience, but it recognized no right to vote
in opposition. In 1932 the I.L.P. in its reaction against "gradualism"
brought out a statement of revolutionary policy calling for a new
class militancy in support of immediate socialist objectives and emphasizing that parliamentary methods would have to be supplemented by industrial action. The Labour party could accept neither
the policy nor the tactics. When negotiations proved only the incompatibility of view, the I.L.P. seceded in July 1932. At once it suffered

losses. A minority resigned; within a year the number of branches declined from 653 to 452. The I.L.P. lost all its former prestige and importance as the spearhead of a great party.[8]

While the I.L.P. was going its own way, other societies were brought into being to take its place. Labour was still in office when two organizations were founded, due mainly to the initiative of G. D. H. Cole. The New Fabian Research Bureau, with Attlee as chairman and Cole as secretary, was intended to do research for the development of a constructive program. It had the support of the Webbs and Henderson, but at first had no connection with the now nearly moribund Fabian Society. It pursued its independent course until 1939, when it united with and revitalized the Fabian Society. The second organization was the Society for Socialist Inquiry and Propaganda (S.S.I.P.), with Bevin as chairman and Cole as vice-chairman. Its objective was the diffusion of the results of the New Fabian research by means of a network of small but active local branches.

Although both new organizations were designed as planning and propaganda bodies unaffiliated to a political party, in 1932 the S.S.I.P. united with an I.L.P. minority that wished to remain in the Labour party to form the Socialist League. In it Cripps, Trevelyan, Brailsford, Laski, and William Mellor were the leading figures. It affiliated with the Labour party, sought to fill the place of the I.L.P., and found itself in the same difficulties, especially in the later thirties, because of its relations with the Communist party.[9]

The Communist party, now completely submissive to Moscow, continued to harass Labour. While Labour was still in office, the Communist party congress denounced it: "The Labour Government is the Government of war, rationalization, and starvation! . . . of imperialist war preparation against the Soviet Union! . . . of colonial slavery! . . . Down with the capitalist Labour Government."[10] In the tactics of "class against class" Labour was reckoned among the enemy. The Communist party redoubled its activity through its ancillary organizations, whose Communist character was perfectly clear to all except those easily duped. Naturally, Labour launched a counteroffensive. Because the National Minority Movement posed the greatest threat the unions moved first, and some, including the Railwaymen, General Workers, and Shop Assistants, excluded its members from officeholding. Antagonism to it heightened when at the insistence of the Red International of Trade Unions it abandoned all pretence of being a mere "ginger group" in favor of open revolt against official leadership and in favor of its own program.

Under these circumstances the T.U.C. ordered an investigation and report upon the character, policies, and methods of Communist satellites. This report, accepted by the 1929 T.U.C., became the basis of action by both great organizations of labor. For the time being the T.U.C. left each union free to deal in its own way with disruptive elements; but in February 1930, the Labour party executive listed seven organizations as unacceptable for affiliation, declared their adherents ineligible as members, delegates, or candidates, and warned against lending them any measure of support. The proscribed societies were the League Against Imperialism, the Left Wing Movement, the National Minority Movement, the Workers' International Relief, the National Unemployed Workers' Committee Movement, the Friends of Soviet Russia, and the International Class War Prisoners' Aid. Over very slight opposition the party conference of the following October upheld the executive's action.[11]

For the time being this action settled policy toward the Communists, so that for two years the issue ceased to feature the agenda of Labour party conferences. Renewed satellite activity then induced further legislation; the European Workers' Anti-Fascist Congress, the British Anti-War Council, the National Charter Campaign Committee, and a local Independent Labour Association were added to the banned list of bodies, membership in which was incompatible with that in the Labour party. The executive and the T.U.C. general council promoted a joint campaign to educate their followers upon the issue and to ask them to support no special organization for political or industrial purposes that could be pursued through the party or the T.U.C. With near unanimity the party conference of 1933 again upheld the executive.[12]

In October 1934 the T.U.C. council followed with two circulars. The first threatened the withdrawal of recognition from any trades council admitting Communists, Fascists, or members of ancillary bodies; the second requested the unions to exclude members of these disruptive groups from any official position. As this action was more specific than the very general request of 1929, which left each union to deal with the problem in its own way, a strong minority opposed. Especially among the Miners, Engineers, and Transport Workers, these "Black Circulars" were fought vigorously as dictatorial interference with union autonomy and an attempt to push the logic of the anti-Communist position beyond necessity. The T.U.C. ratified the circulars by a small margin of only 1,869,000 to 1,427,000, although on the general anti-Communist position it supported the general council by a vote of nearly four to one.[13]

At the same time the Labour party executive added the Relief Committee for the Victims of German and Austrian Fascism to the list of proscribed organizations. Lord Marley and Laski, who had been active on it, protested that their interest was purely philanthropic, but resigned from it when the Southport conference, by 1,347,000 to 195,000, upheld the official view. The same conference voted 1,820,000 to 89,000 to give the executive full powers in dealing with party members who, without authorization, associated themselves with Communist subsidiaries.

The executive was now in a position not only to stop the infiltration of Communists into the Labour party but also to restrain its followers from consorting with them. Insulation from the Communists was now as complete as could be effected by legislation. For a party as broadly based as Labour such legislation was exceptional, but as Morrison said in summing up the debate for the executive: "When we are dealing with a situation in which a body, by carefully planned underground organization, is deliberately trying to make the maximum of trouble for the Labour party, . . . the Labour party is entitled to take exceptional measures to protect itself from their activity."[14]

These defensive measures helped to frustrate the Communist effort to build "bridges to the masses." The Communists were able to stage spectacular "hunger marches" in 1931–32, but their satellites dwindled or disappeared; they tended to become little more than duplications of the party membership. After the collapse of the Labour government the Communist party registered gains, but not enough to warrant optimism on its part.[15]

In January 1933 the Nazi triumph and Hitler's accession to power in Germany profoundly affected the Labour-Communist situation. To democratic socialism it raised the twin threats of war and fascism; even in Britain there soon appeared Mosley's British Union of Fascists with their black shirts, anti-Semitism, and provocative demonstrations. Among Communists it aroused such fears that it produced a shift in the foreign policy of the U.S.S.R. and in the party tactics everywhere. The Comintern, weakened by the destruction of the German party, became more than ever the tool of Soviet diplomacy. Accordingly, the party line was changed again, and the policy of independent action gave way to that of cooperation against nazism. Orders went out from Moscow to the obedient national sections to cease their attacks upon leaders and parties of the Second International and, instead, to form a united front against the new enemy.

Following the receipt of these instructions, the British party promptly reversed its line and abandoned the policy of independence. Abusive attacks against Labour disappeared in favor of the drive for unity to repel "the offensive of capitalist reaction."[16] On March 11 the party broached the united front to the Labour executive, the T.U.C., the Cooperative party, and the I.L.P. Only the I.L.P. gave any encouragement. The National Council of Labour rejected the advances, and in *Democracy versus Dictatorship* (1933) proclaimed its aversion to dictatorships, whether of the right or left, and attributed a large measure of responsibility for the rapid advance of fascism to the Communists, because of the reaction against their continual advocacy of violence. The Labour party followed with a pamphlet, *The Communist Solar System* (1933), exposing the working of the Communist satellite bodies. By this time the labor movement had been so antagonized by Communist methods that the T.U.C. and the Labour party conference stood with the leadership almost without opposition.[17]

With the I.L.P. now separated from the Labour party, the Communists had a greater measure of success. Centering in East London was a self-appointed Revolutionary Policy Committee which, against the opposition of the I.L.P. branches in Wales and the North, entered into a united-front agreement which for about a year led to considerable activity. In February 1934 the two small parties approached the great labor organizations, only to be repulsed with the usual objections to the formation of any front behind which an intensified propaganda within the ranks could be conducted. It was then that the T.U.C. authorized the "Black Circulars" and the Labour party conference bestowed full disciplinary powers upon the executive. Even the I.L.P. leaders, Maxton and Brockway, who were generally regarded as on the far left of the British movement, noted the Soviet control of the Comintern and denounced its methods; in return they were labeled "Trotskyist." They then confined their cooperation with the Communist party to specific issues. The persistent Communists, however, continued faithfully on their new line and let it be known that, although uninvited, they would seek an electoral agreement with Labour for the next general election.[18]

Although firm in this stand against the Communists, Labour's mood after 1931 was, nevertheless, distinctly leftish. Its moves to redefine policy and methods took place against a background of theories of betrayal, of a bankers' "ramp," and of sinister Buckingham Palace influence as prime factors in the recent debacle. The ominous question was raised whether the holders of power would ever permit a Labour government, even backed by a Commons majority, to implement a socialist program. Marxist theories were voiced that all the weapons of counterrevolution, such as control of finance, the House of Lords, and the crown, would be utilized to prevent it. Such ideas appeared in the writings of Laski and Strachey.[19]

Catastrophic theories of social change were heard; Cripps reversed the dictum of Sidney Webb with the assertion that the one thing that was not inevitable was gradualness. Some of Attlee's utterances resembled those of Cripps. The two joined, in fact, in a memorandum questioning "whether it is possible to persuade Capitalism to hand over control to Socialism by gradual and restrained measures" and asserting: "So long as Capitalism holds the power and the control, so long will it use every weapon to retain it."[20] Cripps and the Socialist League were so firmly convinced of the inevitability of this adamantine resistance that they advocated the enactment of an emergency powers act by the next Labour government in order to overcome it. It was an atmosphere in which even the Fabian Webbs could look with such favor upon Soviet Russia and interpret it as a new civilization.[21] The *Left Review* became an outlet for young writers, and many young intellectuals turned to the Communist party instead of to Labour.

The Labour party executive, however, dominated by men of moderate views, set about preparing a positive program for the next Labour government. The generalizations of *Labour and the Nation* were insufficient; in order not to be caught unprepared, a program for action was needed. Accordingly, in December 1931, the executive appointed a policy committee under its chairman, George Lathan, to embark upon a series of studies of particular problems. Some hard work was done by a number of economists, politicians, and trade-union leaders, among whom were Tawney, Dalton, Greenwood, Pethick-Lawrence, Laski, Attlee, Morrison, and Citrine. They prepared a series of policy reports, the first four of which were on "Currency, Banking, and Finance," "The National Planning of Transport," "The Reorganization of the Electricity Supply Industry," and "The Land and the Planning of Agriculture." The series continued through the decade and laid the basis for the work of the 1945 Labour government.

The leftish temper was demonstrated at the annual Labour party conference of October 1932 at Leicester, where on several occasions the delegates differed from the moderate leadership. Trevelyan won a striking oratorical success in support of a resolution demanding that on assuming office, with or without power, the next Labour government must immediately promulgate definite socialist legislation and stand or fall on its principles. Attlee supported Trevelyan. Henderson opposed him on the ground that it was unwise to tie hands in advance, but the feeling against "MacDonaldism" ran so high that Henderson had a poor reception and the resolution was carried without the necessity of a formal vote.

The four policy reports were adopted, but the temper rose again over that on currency and banking, which touched emotions still vivid. The report demanded the nationalization of the Bank of England and the establishment of a national investment board, but made no mention of the joint-stock banks. Frank Wise, an ex-I.L.P. member, moved an amendment to include them on the ground that it was necessary to control short-term credit as well as long-term capital. Cripps supported him, saying that there should be no compromise with capitalists. Bevin and Pethick-Lawrence were opposed; they argued that, however good it might be in principle, it was unwise to commit a Labour government to so much during one term. Again the delegates opposed the leadership and carried the amendment by 1,141,000 to 984,000.[22]

A third point upon which leftist feeling was strong was that of workers' control, which in the 1930's took the form of advocacy of direct representation of labor upon the boards of nationalized industries. It led to a long contest between Bevin, who favored it, and Morrison, the chief exponent of the public corporation and of capacity as the sole qualification for members of the governing boards. Morrison won, and later the Attlee government adopted his view for the newly nationalized industries, while the trade unions shifted their preference to independence rather than responsibility. In the early 1930's, however, the advocates of direct representation showed great strength.

The public corporation, as championed by Morrison, would be run as a business and meet all ordinary obligations, including taxes and reserves for expansion. Maximum profit and dividends, however, were not objectives; once obligations were met, the ideal was public service. The governing board would be chosen solely on grounds of efficiency and would conduct day-to-day operations without interference from government. It would, nevertheless, be responsible to a minister, make annual reports, and be subject to parliamentary questions and criticisms on matters of policy. Morrison did not believe in workers' control; their place was in the workshop, not in top management or on governing boards. His own plan, he wrote, offered "a combination of public ownership, public accountability, and business management for public ends."[23] Acceptance of this concept of the public corporation quickly became so general that in 1935 Dalton could write that direct administration by a minister through a government department was now apt to be regarded as an old-fashioned form of socialization and unsuitable for new enterprises.[24]

When Morrison presented the report on the national planning of transport at the Leicester party conference, he was supported by the three railway unions but opposed by Bevin's Transport and General Workers. Morrison put the case for efficiency and pointed to the dangers of a statutory representation of trade unions on the board: such a provision would undermine the case for a board of capacity and ability; it would open the way to other demands and end in a board of interests with the general good forgotten by sectional minds. He feared the appointment of old and third-rate men, not from the trade unions, he was careful to say, though surely he had in mind the ex-officials rewarded for long and faithful service with a safe seat in the House of Commons. Morrison wanted a board of capacity and not of pressure groups.

The Transport Workers' case was put by H. E. Clay, prominent member of that union and of the Socialist League, who defined Morrison's plan as an efficient bureaucracy, but one that stratified society with the workers left powerless under perpetual dictatorship, whereas what they needed was an end to inferiority and a new social status. Democracy without democracy in industry was incomplete. Bevin agreed with Clay. A socialist member complained that, even should they get a few friends on the proposed boards, it would be no step toward socialism. As the manifest feeling of the conference was such that the acceptance of Morrison's plan was highly doubtful, the matter was not brought to a vote but postponed.[25]

Following the Leicester conference the Labour executive and the T.U.C. council arrived at a compromise statement that recognized the principle of workers' representation on the boards. It was submitted to the 1933 party conference at Hastings, but by a small majority the conference demanded something more definite; an amendment was carried to include trade-union representation on the boards as a statutory right.[26]

Morrison had to wait for his victory, but even after he won it in the measures of the Attlee government, there remained in many quarters a feeling that the place of the workers in socialized industry was still an unsolved problem.

At the Hastings conference Cripps and the Socialist League raised the question of how socialist legislation could be enacted. In order to overcome the mobilization of all the forces of resistance controlled by the possessing classes, which he regarded as inevitable, Cripps proposed that the next Labour government should immediately (1) abolish the House of Lords, (2) pass an emergency powers act to give the government authority over the financial system and to put into effect any measures necessary for the socialization of industry or to safeguard the supply of food and other necessaries, and (3) reform parliamentary procedure to facilitate a rapid constitutional change to socialism. Cripps had support from Attlee and Ponsonby, but Bevin opposed the plan as savoring too much of the methods of Mussolini and Hitler. It was referred back to the party executive for further study and report.[27]

The executive's recommendations, which were embodied in its report to the 1934 Southport conference, *For Socialism and Peace,* specifically affirmed the party's faith in parliamentary democracy and in change by consent, but it did propose to abolish the House of Lords; it would not resort to emergency powers so long as no emergency arose for which the normal powers of government were not adequate.[28] The difference between the Socialist League and the Labour majority on this point was that the League was so convinced of the necessity that it would act first, whereas the party majority and the trade-union leaders were equally convinced that constitutionalism was now so ingrained in Great Britain that the need would not arise. The conference upheld the leadership against the League by a ten-to-one majority.[29]

For Socialism and Peace summed up the work of the subcommittees whose many policy reports had been debated at the three preceding conferences. It was designed to supplement the general principles of *Labour and the Nation* with a statement of objectives, both in foreign and domestic affairs, to guide the next Labour government. It demanded a foreign policy based on the League of Nations, tax reform, equality of opportunity for both men and women, and improved social services—education, health, housing, pensions, and unemployment benefits.

What the nation required now, however, was stated as not mere social reform but socialism. Industry would have to be converted from a haphazard struggle for private gain to a planned economy carried on for the service of the community. It specified banking, coal, and iron and steel as now ready for socialization. It listed transport, electricity, gas, water, agriculture, textiles, shipping, ship-building, and engineering as ready for drastic reorganization, "and for the most part nothing short of public ownership and control" would be effective. Fair compensation would be paid to former owners. This document did not go far enough to satisfy the Socialist League, which offered 75 amendments, but the League was defeated by wide margins of usually ten or twelve to one. *For Socialism and Peace* was accepted by the party as a statement of objectives that would take more than one span of office to complete.

Labour's foreign policy in the early thirties was unhappily notable for its crosscurrents and confusion, although in these respects the party was not alone. In its analysis of the causes of war in 1914 first place went to capitalism, with its rivalries reflected in armament races and aggressive imperialism and buttressed by a perverted nationalism. How to prevent a repetition of the horror that had taken its toll from nearly every town and village in the land was a matter of fundamental disagreement. One line of thought led to disarmament, pacifism, and war resistance, while another led to organization to enforce peace.

As has been noted, support of the League was now Labour's accepted policy; in the event of sanctions, the concept of a police action reconciled many to it. Doubts remained, however: the League was controlled by governments that Labourites distrusted, including their own, for they never forgot their suspicion of designs upon Russia and their resort to Councils of Action. Many felt they dared not trust a Tory government with the force a League policy demanded. It was an ever-present dilemma, both horns of which could appear in the conflicting pronouncements of the same party conference. The confusion, which persisted throughout the decade, was accentuated by the fact that the party was always in Opposition; absence of responsibility made it easy to criticize the government for inaction without being precise upon what action to take. It required a series of aggressive acts by the dictators to clarify thinking, to put an end to vacillation, and in 1939 to bring Labour into war a united party ready to accept responsibility for its successful prosecution.

The long series of crises began with the Japanese invasion of Manchuria on September 19, 1931, and the attack at Shanghai the following January. In the Labour party sympathy with China and condem-

nation of Japan were almost universal, although there was an occa-
tional reference to Japan's special position in Manchuria and its
need for continental markets. One chairman's address to an annual
conference termed the invasion "one of the blackest pages in the
history of international brigandage."[30]

The Labour and Trade Union Internationals at once uttered their
protests and called upon their national sections to put pressure upon
their governments to utilize the League to secure the evacuation of
Manchuria. On February 23, 1932, the National Joint Council in
Britain issued a pronouncement charging Japan with responsibility
for the war and failure to observe its obligations to the League. The
future of the League was now at stake, it stated, and if no action were
taken, the collective system would be destroyed; the nations would
be unable to appeal to it in one part of the world if they allowed it
to be defied in another; the result would be a growth of insecurity,
the shattering of hopes for arms reduction, and the certainty of
future wars. The Council recommended that all League members
and signatories of the Peace Pact withdraw their ministers from
Tokyo, and, if that emphatic gesture went unheeded, they should, in
association with the United States, invoke the economic and financial
sanctions of the Covenant.

The recommendations of these official bodies were not followed
with any vigor in Parliament. There the party duly registered its protests and criticisms, but many shared the fears of the pacifist leader,
Lansbury, that interference in the Far East would extend the conflict to become another world war with all the attendant horrors so
vividly remembered.[31]

Military sanctions were not even contemplated. There was talk
of an embargo upon the shipment of arms and ammunition, but
some, like Cripps, thought that the stoppage of credit would be more
effective. Military sanctions were even less in favor after 1933, when
Japan and Germany left the League; there was no longer a possibility
of all against one, but a grave danger of group against group. There
were long-term hopes from the growth of Chinese nationalism and
political stability; meanwhile, Manchukuo should not be recognized.[32] In the T.U.C. a proposal was advanced, manifestly of Communist origin, to halt the Japanese invasion with its resulting threat
to the U.S.S.R. by stopping the production and transportation of
munitions of war. It was opposed by Will Thorne, a veteran of the
Gasworkers Union and a former member of the S.D.F., because it
meant another general strike, by Citrine, and also by Bevin, who

objected to putting his transport workers and the other unions always in the front line; they should not be expected to accept responsibility for the apathy, inertia, and Toryism of the British public. The motion was not even brought to a vote.[33]

The National Government ignored Labour protests. Foreign Secretary Sir John Simon followed what he called a "mediatory and conciliatory" policy, which Labour denounced as out of accord with Britain's obligations under the Covenant. In retrospect, Labour viewed the Manchurian crisis as a turning point; the inertia of the League powers in face of Japan's action in the Far East permitted the bad example to be set, which the European dictators were not slow to follow. At the time, however, the party was really no more ready to risk a war over Manchuria than were its opponents. It was left to the march of the European dictators to bring it to that point.[34]

After Manchuria crises followed in rapid succession. On January 30, 1933, Adolf Hitler became Chancellor of Germany, an event which Labour at once recognized as a serious threat to peace. In February 1934 the labor and socialist organizations in Austria were destroyed, and in October 1935 the Italian invasion of Abyssinia led to the crisis over League sanctions.

To Labour fascism and nazism, in spite of the latter's anti-Semitism, seemed very much alike. They shared the same aggressive nationalism and militarism. Mussolini's warlike speeches were noted: he called for preparation for war not tomorrow but today; he related the rise and fall of nations to their success or failure in the use of force; he identified the citizen with the soldier. The spectacle of small children marching in the Balilla della Lupa appeared ominous. Hitler's blunt assertions in *Mein Kampf,* such as that German living space could be won only by the sword, did not escape comment.[35] There was a tendency to deflate and ridicule Mussolini and his posturings, but not Hitler. In the latter was seen resurgent German nationalism backed by revived German power and imbued with the myth of the necessity of a war of revenge and expansion.

Hitler's rise to power, which was accompanied by the destruction of the German trade-union movement and of the most powerful Social Democratic and Communist parties in Western Europe, jolted the labor world. It produced a shift in Communist tactics from independence and "class against class" to collaboration and the united front. The Labour and Socialist International (L.S.I.) likewise was moved to common action. On February 19, 1933, during the brief interval between Hitler's accession to the chancellorship and the election that confirmed his power, the Bureau of the L.S.I. called for united working-class action to avert the menace of fascism. That it was ready to ignore the Communist abuse and attack extending over many years indicated its sense of urgency. Provided that an open and frank understanding could be reached, which involved a definite promise that alliance would not be used as cover for attack, the L.S.I. was ready to consider an agreement. The Comintern would not give that promise; its answer on March 5—polling day in Germany—was to cast doubt upon the sincerity of the offer and to insist upon separate negotiations in each country. As the L.S.I., in view of its long experience with Moscow's tactics, would accept nothing less than a general binding agreement, there was a deadlock, and this attempt at an international working-class front came to naught.[36]

As has been shown, the Labour party would have nothing to do with united-front tactics. Instead, it accepted a pronouncement on *Democracy versus Dictatorship* drawn up in March 1933 by the National Joint Council. It treated all dictatorships, right or left, as very much alike, and took its stand squarely upon the principles of democracy. It had no positive program to offer other than to call on the workers to strengthen their trade unions, their cooperative societies, and their own Labour party for the battle against fascism. It was not a very aggressive attitude to assume; however, no one in the Labour party was tempted to look upon Hitler with a kindly eye in the hope that he would be a bulwark against Bolshevism, as did many Conservatives.[37]

The trade unionists, likewise, were quick to respond to the Nazi danger. Their leaders, among whom were Citrine and Bevin, well understood the implications of dictatorship. At the request of the general council Citrine, who on repeated visits to Berlin on International Federation of Trade Union affairs had watched the Nazis' rise, prepared an analysis that revealed his grasp of the situation. His report on *Dictatorships and the Trade Union Movement* (1933) dealt with the suppression of the German Social Democratic party and trade unions, the confiscation of their property, the arrest of their leaders, and the abolition of collective bargaining and right to strike. He, too, regarded all dictatorships, right or left, as the same in principle; both kinds involved the ruthless suppression of opposition and of freedom of expression. Accordingly, the trade-union movement should oppose all dictatorships. Its members should prize democracy, which safeguarded the civil liberties and the freedoms so necessary for the workers in their struggle for justice; without them "the freedom and independence of the unions would not be worth a day's purchase."

When Citrine presented this report to the 1933 T.U.C. conference it was attacked by some, including Aneurin Bevan, who objected to bracketing Soviet Russia with the fascist dictatorships on the ground that they were not operating in the same interests, but Citrine was supported by an overwhelming majority. The presidential address and other frank condemnations of the Nazis abroad and of Mosley's Fascists at home indicated that British trade unionists were well aware of the implications of the Nazi revolution.[38]

The Cooperative Congress, the third great organization of the labor movement, joined the party and the T.U.C. in sounding the alarm. Wherever dictators secured control, the cooperative movement suffered. Even neutrality in politics was no defense; in fascist countries voluntary cooperatives were suppressed or compulsorily merged with fascist institutions and their democratic character abolished. The Cooperative Congress called for united action with the trade-union and political movements in order to bring pressure on governments.[39]

The Labour party followed up its denunciation with a campaign of protest against the Nazi policies, atrocities, and anti-Semitism. On April 12, 1933, it held a mass meeting in the Albert Hall, and the following May Day was devoted to demonstrations throughout the country. The National Joint Council instituted a boycott of German goods, which over a period of years appreciably affected their sale in Britain. Funds were raised to assist victims and refugees. Reports were issued to expose political and economic conditions in fascist countries and to counter the claims of extraordinary progress with accounts of increase in bankruptcies and decline in living standards; Labour hated fascism even if it were true that Mussolini "made the trains run on time." Hitler's slaughter of his own lieutenants in the purge of June 30, 1934, started another wave of emotion throughout the British movement; a few months later a similar one followed the summary executions in Russia after the assassination of Sergei Kirov, a prominent Stalinite and party leader in Leningrad. Brutality by Mosley's Blackshirts at the notorious Olympia meeting in June 1934 pointed to fascist danger closer to home.[40]

When dictatorship threatened to engulf the socialist and labor organizations in Austria, the Second and the Trade-Union Internationals sought to bring diplomatic pressure to bear on that government, but without success, and they met the fate of the German ones. When the Austrian workers took up arms in defense of the Karl Marx Hof and went down after four days of hard fighting, the British party could only watch the unequal struggle, voice sympathy, and raise funds for relief and legal defense. There was pride in the resistance of the Austrian workers, but there remained only a secret and illegal vestige of the movement that had made Vienna the great socialist citadel of Central Europe. In the gloom of 1934 it seemed that the only rays of hope came from Spain, where a republic had recently been established, and from Russia, which through fear of Hitler now joined the League of Nations.[41]

The conduct of the Nazis converted the British Labourites, and Liberals, too, from the chief advocates of reconciliation with Germany to its firmest opponents. It was not a matter of nationalism, but of horror and shock at Nazi methods and at the prospect of danger ahead. Nazi success was a blow to the easy assumption that socialism was inevitably the heir to capitalism. Some Labour leaders perceived that it might become necessary to take a stronger line against the dictators than a forceful expression of moral indignation.

To secure a frank and explicit statement of adherence to that firmer line, which involved the possibility of an ultimate resort to force, proved an arduous task for the leadership. The party contained no martial enthusiasts. There was one extreme of Christian pacifists and a handful of conscientious objectors to military service under any circumstances, but most Labourites were people who on rational and humanitarian grounds were primarily concerned with finding an alternative to war. Even when it became clearer that they were living in a world shaped not by men of good will but by men of violence and passion, they clung to the hope of discovering some means to avoid another life-and-death struggle, which at best could end only in a Pyrrhic victory. Accordingly, throughout this whole period of stiffening against the dictators, there was a yearning toward Geneva and a lingering hope that Henderson might accomplish the impossible and achieve peace through disarmament. The Labourites finally pinned their faith on collective security including sanctions, knowing well that sanctions might mean war, but only when it appeared certain that peace and security could not be had in the same world with Hitler and Mussolini.

In the conferences of 1933 the pacifist wing was active and antiwar feeling strong. In the T.U.C. there was a resolution from the floor for an organized refusal to assist in any way the prosecution of a war. As pacifists were weaker in the trade unions than in the party, that move was shelved in favor of one by the council for propaganda against war but with the general strike limited to the specific moment when an aggressor had been identified, when it should be called by the working class of that country. It would be the function of the world democratic movement to aid the section called upon for this definite action.[42]

At the Labour party conference at Hastings Sir Charles Trevelyan of the Socialist League moved a resolution committing the Labour party to war resistance and a general strike in the event of war. He argued that the gesture of the individual conscientious objector would be ineffective as a means to halt a war. The League of Nations would also be ineffective so long as it had to be worked by governments either skeptical of it or openly contemptuous; successful resistance could be interposed only by the whole labor movement. The debate that followed was on war in the abstract, and there was no mention of Hitler until Dalton concluded for the party executive. Under conference rules the executive could not amend a resolution, but had to either accept, reject, or withdraw it; such was the temper of the conference that Dalton, for the executive, accepted it, knowing that Henderson would follow with an exposition of the official view on foreign affairs. Henderson then made his statement emphasizing that a Labour government would base its foreign policy on the League and make use of all economic, financial, and other powers necessary to fulfill national obligations under the collective system. The conference accepted this statement and also a disarmament resolution of Clynes to abolish all weapons of the kinds forbidden to Germany by the Treaty of Versailles and the creation of an international police force.[43]

This Hastings conference confusedly looked in different directions for a road to peace. After the first expression of antiwar feeling in the war-resistance resolution it accepted a League policy with sanctions including "other powers," which were left undefined but were clear to all aware of Henderson's views. The explanation of the reception given Trevelyan lay in current Anglo-Russian relations, for Britain was embroiled with Russia over the trial of British engineers accused of espionage and sabotage. The sharp words of some statesmen and the angry tone of the press were sufficient to arouse the old suspicion of a Tory threat to Russia and the mood of the Councils of Action. Nevertheless, the acceptance of war resistance was the feature of the Hastings conference long remembered as the high tide of pacifist influence.

The leadership was careful not to be taken unprepared at the next conferences. When the executives of the party, the T.U.C., and the parliamentary party met, they decided to resist strenuously any attempt to involve Britain in aggressive war, but "in view of the recent events on the Continent, it was felt that there might be occasions when the Movement would assist defensive action taken to preserve the nation and its democratic institutions."[44] The outcome was a statement on *War and Peace* to be submitted in September to the T.U.C. and in October to the Labour party.

War and Peace opened with the comment that the war-resistance resolution of the previous year was not enough, because it failed to include Labour's policy of preventing war by organizing peace. It went on to restate the party's faith in the League and the collective system, with the Cooperative World Commonwealth as the ultimate goal. On the use of military force it drew a distinction between a war of aggression and one in defense of the collective peace system. It gave explicit support to the latter:

Labour is emphatically opposed to any form of aggressive War, but we recognize that there might be circumstances under which the government of Great Britain might have to use its military and naval forces in support of the League in restraining an aggressor nation which declined to submit to the authority of the League and which flagrantly used military measures in defiance of its pledged word.[45]

Ultimately, it was hoped, the League would develop into a world community, one to which the world citizen would owe certain loyalties. His duties would be limited, however, to three things:

(a) Arbitration-Insistence—the duty to insist that our government settle all its disputes by peaceful means and eschew force.
(b) Sanctions-Assistance—the duty unflinchingly to support our government in all the risks and consequences of fulfilling its duty to take part in collective action against a peace-breaker.
(c) War-Resistance—the refusal to accept our government's unsupported claim to be using force in self-defense; insistence on submitting this claim to the test of international judgment, or of willingness to arbitrate; refusal to serve or support our government if it were ever condemned as an aggressor by the League or designated itself as an aggressor by becoming involved in war after refusing arbitration.[46]

The tactic of the general strike was ruled out because it put the responsibility upon one section of the community and because no corresponding action was possible under the dictatorships where independent labor movements no longer existed.

War and Peace, with its clear statement of possible resort to military sanctions, was accepted by the Cooperators and by the T.U.C. after speeches from Bevin and Citrine, the latter reminding the delegates that their own previous votes for an international police force had meant not policemen but economic, military, naval, and air action.[47] In the Labour party conference at Southport Henderson initiated the debate with what proved to be his last speech before that body; he gave an exposition of the League policy for which he had stood so long and emphasized the necessity of honoring all the obligations of the Covenant. The opposition was voiced mainly by members of the Socialist League. William Mellor, one of its leaders, said it was illusory to rely upon a League of capitalist-controlled countries, and Ponsonby urged disarmament by example. Philip Noel-Baker and Bevin argued for a League backed by power. Attlee, who had once supported unilateral disarmament, now upheld sanctions. By a vote of 1,519,000 to 673,000, the conference accepted the commitments of *War and Peace.*[48] As mentioned above, this same conference also accepted the more general statement of policy, *For Socialism and Peace,* the international section of which also took a strong League of Nations line.

Faith in pooled security was manifest in other acts of the party. It was the theme of Labour's campaign in a famous and much misunderstood by-election in 1933 at East Fulham, where John Wilmot, a Fabian and champion of the League, reduced the Conservative vote by 9,000 and raised Labour's by 10,000 to win the seat. It was no "squalid election" lost in a "flood of pacifism," but one in which an able candidate who was no pacifist proved the popularity of collective security.[49] It was in behalf of a strengthened League that on May 14, 1934, the National Council of Labour, as the National Joint Council was now known, sent a deputation to the Prime Minister and the Foreign Secretary to express fears of a drift toward war, but received general statements in reply.[50] A Labour objection to the Anglo-German naval agreement of 1935 was that it undermined the League and divided Britain and France, two of its major powers. When the parliamentary party moved amendments to the arms estimates, it was to reaffirm adherence to collective security under the League. Labour did not, as Churchill charged, wish to disarm friends, have no allies, and neglect defenses.[51] Pooled security, it maintained, could provide allies and overwhelming force and do it without an arms race ruinous to all concerned.

In the early months of 1935 the National Council of Labour co-operated with the League of Nations Union in a peace ballot, the greatest private poll ever undertaken in Great Britain. More than 11,500,000 persons, about half the electorate, voted in this unprecedented effort to influence official policy. The wording of some questions was open to criticism and the sampling was not scientific, but the answers, because of their very number, had significance as a test of public opinion. There was practical unanimity on membership in the League, reduction of armaments by agreement, abolition of national military and naval aircraft, and prohibition of private traffic in armaments.

Three questions were very pertinent. On membership in the League the vote was 11,157,040 to 357,460 with 113,265 noncommittal; on recourse to economic and nonmilitary measures to repel aggression 10,088,312 favored, 638,211 opposed, and 901,242 were noncommittal; on the use of military measures, if necessary, 6,827,-699 approved, 2,364,279 opposed, and 2,435,789 abstained or were doubtful.[52] These figures afforded some measure of opinion. They indicated that a policy based on the League had great popular support, that given a lead the people would accept a policy of sanctions, and that a majority on this ballot approved military sanctions against an aggressor, if under League auspices. Certainly the verdict of the poll appeared to confirm an opinion that the foreign policy of the Labour party was that now preferred by a majority of the electorate.

This coincidence did not escape notice by the government. Whereas late in 1934 at Glasgow Baldwin disparaged a collective peace system as impractical and hardly worth consideration, on September 11, 1935, at Geneva, Foreign Secretary Sir Samuel Hoare assured the League Assembly that Britain stood for the collective maintenance of the Covenant in its entirety and for collective resistance to all acts of unprovoked aggression, although, as the event proved, he intended less than he implied.

Long before Hoare's speech it was clear that Italian ambition in Abyssinia would provide the League with a test of the efficacy of its sanctions. The crisis was long in the making, and Mussolini's intentions were obvious. Less certain were those of the governments that had to work the League machinery. The labor movement, however, had no doubt about its policy, and through its Internationals and the national sections strove to buttress the League. On July 24, 1935, the National Council of Labour called on the British government to utilize the League machinery. By the time the T.U.C. met on September 2 at Margate, the attack was felt to be imminent and the tension was high. On the initiative of the parliamentary party, the three national committees met on the eve of the conference and agreed upon a draft resolution to be presented by the general secretary, Walter Citrine, now Sir Walter.

The presidential address of W. Kean set the tone; the issue had to be faced squarely or the foundation of the League system would be destroyed. Citrine introduced the resolution approving sanctions, knowing full well that it might involve resort to force: "It may mean war, but that is the thing we have to face," he said. He said that there was no alternative, and that the future of the League and of peace was involved, because a successful flouting by Mussolini would be followed by Hitler, who had ambitions in eastern Europe. Bevin was as convinced of the need of sanctions as Citrine, but devoted his speech to a section of the resolution that discussed the need to deal with some fundamental causes of war by means of a world organization to provide access to necessary raw materials for all industrial countries.

There was a long debate in which ex-pacifists declared themselves now ready to accept the risks of sanctions. After an effective summing up by Citrine, the vote, 2,962,000 to 177,000, indicated the unanimity of the T.U.C. in support of full League sanctions against Italy. On the same day, September 5, at Geneva, the joint committee of the Second and Trade Union Internationals assured the officials of the League that the international labor movement would support the application of whatever sanctions were necessary to halt the aggressor.[53]

The debate on sanctions at the Dome in Brighton on October 1–2 was the longest in the history of Labour party conferences. The moment was critical, because the build-up of Italian forces on the Abyssinian frontier was obvious, and, in fact, on the very next day they crossed it. Chairman W. A. Robinson, general secretary of the National Union of Distributive and Allied Workers, expressed the prevailing opinion when he said that the existence of the League was at stake; should it fail in this test, it could hardly hope to survive. "Labour cannot now flinch," he said; "It must not shrink from the logic of its considered policy."[54]

Dalton introduced the resolution that had been prepared by the three executives and accepted by the T.U.C. at Margate. It was a call for full support of the League. It stated in part:

United and determined in its opposition to the policy of imperialist aggression, this Conference calls upon the British government, in cooperation with the other nations represented at the Council and Assembly of the League, to use all the necessary measures provided by the Covenant to prevent Italy's unjust and rapacious attack upon the territory of a fellow member of the League. The Conference pledges its firm support of any action consistent with the principles and statutes of the League to restrain the Italian government and to uphold the authority of the League in enforcing Peace.[55]

Dalton then spoke for Labour's policy of a League with power. He asked, "Do we stand firm in this crisis for the policy to which we have so often pledged ourselves, or shall we turn tail and run away?" He was convinced that Italy's economic weakness and the length of its line of communications, so vulnerable at Suez, would make Mussolini hesitate, but should he resort to force, "then so be it."

Dalton was supported by the trade-union chiefs, who made strong speeches and had the card votes of their big battalions to back them up; among them were Will Lawther (Mineworkers), Charles Dukes (General and Municipal Workers), George Hicks (Building Trades), and John Marchbank (Railwaymen). "Intellectuals" such as Attlee and Noel-Baker did likewise. A number of former pacifists, after a good deal of wrestling with their consciences, now came to the conclusion that "in a world of political gangsters" League sanctions were necessary. Trevelyan, who two years earlier at Hastings had stood for war resistance and a general strike in the event of war, now saw the League as the only hope. The weight of the speeches was all in favor of the resolution.

The opposition came from the Socialist League and the absolute pacifists. Cripps, who had recently resigned from the National Council of Labour, followed Dalton with a statement of the Socialist League's position. It mattered less what should be done, said Cripps, than who controlled the doing; unfortunately, it was not Labour in control but capitalist governments that could not be trusted. They had produced the last war, and "The capitalist leopard cannot change his spots." For this reason he had changed his views on the League; only a Labour government could be entrusted with sanctions. The situation was worsened for him by the absence of several major states from the League, which left it the tool of the sated imperialist powers. He concluded, rather inconsistently, that if they felt such a desperate urge to do something at all costs, they should use working-class sanctions, which could be kept under working-class control. William Mellor, also of the Socialist League, supported Cripps.

The pacifist position was stated by several speakers including Ponsonby, who had resigned the party leadership in the House of Lords on the issue; he also argued the practical danger of two armed camps and a world war, because of so many powers now outside the League. Dr. Alfred Salter, a well-known social worker and Christian pacifist from Bermondsey, put his faith in the ideals of the Sermon on the Mount and his conviction that ultimately that higher ideal would prevail. Miss Lucy Cox, general secretary of the "No More War" movement, stated the humanitarian pacifist position against bombing, killing, and starving.

The climax, though not the conclusion, came at the end of the first day's session. When Lansbury went to the microphone, he was greeted with prolonged applause and "For he's a jolly good fellow," a testimony of high personal regard and a tribute to service to the labor movement throughout most of his seventy-six years. Everyone knew his Christian pacifist faith; only recently, on August 19, he had published a letter in *The Times* with an appeal to all churches—Protestant, Catholic, Jewish—to unite in a conference at Jerusalem to declare a Truce of God and proclaim Christ's teaching to bring about a revolution in man's thought and action. He now presented his view that there was no difference between mass murder organized by the League and that conducted by the nations. He detailed his mental struggles as a leader no longer in agreement with his party on a fundamental issue. In this personal appeal, so emotionally presented that it moved women delegates to tears, he hinted at the possibility of severing old ties and resigning his post.

Among the trade-union leaders who had not joined in the sympathy and applause for Lansbury was Bevin. After listening with mounting anger to this emotional appeal, Bevin slowly lumbered to the platform and opened his attack. He objected to the diversion of the issue into a personal one, especially since the party had developed its policy over a long period and Lansbury had had a hand in the making of it. Bevin said that decisions democratically reached should be accepted, and he felt that Lansbury had betrayed them; he objected to his "hawking his conscience round from body to body" asking to be told what he ought to do with it. Although this last thrust brought cries of protest from the delegates, Bevin hammered away, recounted the development of the policy and Lansbury's share in it—essentially true, but with some inaccuracies—and finally had the delegates with him in the view that Lansbury should not accept responsibilities incompatible with his conscience. Bevin won the conference so completely that no one rose to defend Lansbury, and when he attempted a reply the delegates would not listen and the microphone was turned off.

In the same speech Bevin turned on Cripps whose slender ascetic figure was in such contrast to his own burly one. Cripps had attended the opening session of the three executives that prepared the resolution but had failed to appear for its vote, and on the eve of the party conference had resigned from the National Council of Labour. Bevin called it a cowardly stab in the back for him to participate in the making and not go through with the policy. Cripps's suggestion of working-class sanctions was another irritant to Bevin, who objected to the tendency to impose the burden of action upon the trade unionists and throw his transport workers into the front line. Throughout Bevin's speech flared his passionate hatred of the dictatorships, his resentment at the fate of his trade-union brothers in fascist lands, his bitterness toward those he considered unfaithful to agreements, and his contempt for those who could never resolve their own moral dilemmas. He set out to destroy the Lansbury leadership and did it brutally but effectively; the conference was shocked by his manner but convinced by his ruthless logic.

After Morrison summed up for the executive the next day, the conference accepted the resolution and all that it implied in the way of sanctions by a vote of 2,168,000 to 102,000. Seldom has a Labour party conference been so nearly unanimous.[56] To Lansbury this vote was final. A few days later he resigned the leadership. The parliamentary party chose Attlee to serve for the remainder of the session, while Lord Snell replaced Ponsonby in the House of Lords.

On October 23 Baldwin, who had been Prime Minister since MacDonald's retirement in June, had Parliament dissolved, with November 14 set as polling day. It was shrewd timing. It was the year of the King's Jubilee, and the international situation shifted attention from domestic problems, where the National Government's record was poor, to foreign affairs, where it could pose as champion of the League, a policy stolen from Labour. In spite of Labour's present high degree of solidarity, the spectacle of the three dissident leaders tended to conceal it from the public.

Nevertheless, Labour had grounds for optimism. It had an agreed program and knew that approval for its foreign policy extended far beyond its own ranks. Electoral support seemed to be returning; it had won ten by-elections, and the amazing upset at East Fulham in October 1933 was followed by the capture of the London County

Council in March 1934, thanks largely to Morrison's ability as an organizer, and by victories in many county, district, and borough councils. It was prepared with a general statement, *For Socialism and Peace,* and for the campaign brought out a brief *Programme of Peace and Social Reconstruction,* which put foreign affairs in first place and charged the government with undermining collective security in the Manchurian and Abyssinian crises. One former asset would be missing because of Henderson's death on the eve of the campaign.

Throughout the campaign Labour stressed the League issue, contrasting its own firm support with the government's belated conversion, which Attlee termed a "death-bed repentance."[57] There was great doubt about the sincerity of this conversion, suspicion of a post-election "deal" with Mussolini, and rumors of secret bargaining already in process.[58] On armaments Labour would maintain such defense forces as were necessary and consistent with membership in the League; it saw in Conservative rearmament the beginning of an arms race. Toward the end of the campaign attention was paid to domestic issues, with charges of failure to deal with the depression, unemployment, and the distressed areas, but with interest centered on foreign affairs, and in face of some economic recovery it made little impression.

The National Government denied that it would waver in support of the League; its manifesto affirmed that it would remain the keystone of British policy. It played down rearmament. Although Neville Chamberlain wanted to make it the issue, Baldwin gave assurance that he would never stand for a policy of great armaments.

In Opposition, too, were the independent Liberals under Sir Herbert Samuel and also Lloyd George, who made his last bid for a return with a "New Deal" of public works and economic planning. The I.L.P., with 17 candidates, fought separately. It hoped to profit from Labour's difficulties and predicted it would spearhead the rise of a new revolutionary socialism.[59] Because it shared Cripps's view that capitalist governments could never be trusted, it was antisanctions. The Communist party entered candidates in only two constituencies and elsewhere made itself into an unwanted ally of Labour.

The election was a disappointment to Labour. National Government parties won 431 seats: 387 Conservatives, 33 Liberal Nationals, 8 National Labour, and 3 other Nationalists. It was a majority of 247 over the combined Opposition. Labour secured 154 seats, a great improvement over the 46 (or 52, including the I.L.P.) of 1931 but far short of the 289 of 1929. The Samuel Liberals, the real losers, were down from 26 to 17, and the Lloyd George family party still numbered only four. The I.L.P. elected four and the Communists one in West Fife, where William Gallacher unseated William Adamson.

The popular vote was much closer. Government parties received approximately 11,500,000 votes and opponents just under 10,000,000, of which 8,325,260 went to Labour candidates, only slightly less than the 1929 total. The system of territorial constituencies exaggerated the victory; whereas each government seat represented 27,102 votes, a Labour seat represented 54,060. With about 53 per cent of the vote the National Government won 431 seats, while Labour with about 38 per cent had only 154. In 27 English counties Labour had no member despite a poll of over half that of the government coalition. Labour made its greatest gains in Greater London, Yorkshire, the Midlands, Lancashire and Cheshire, the Northeast, and Scotland.[60]

Of the successful Labourites 79 were trade unionists, including 34 miners. Of the others 12 were businessmen, 9 cooperators, 10 lawyers, 8 educators, and 5 journalists; clergymen, engineers, and other professions were represented, too. The trade-union group would be less dominant in the next parliamentary party.[61]

Most encouraging was the presence of debating strength. Attlee, Greenwood, and Bevan held their seats, and, to his satisfaction and pride, so did Lansbury. Back again were Dalton, Morrison, Clynes, Johnston, Shinwell, Alexander, and Pethick-Lawrence. National Labour, on the contrary, was reduced to eight. MacDonald lost to Shinwell. He was returned later by way of a safe seat, but in 1937 died while on a sea voyage. National Labour soon disappeared from the political scene.

Although doomed to more years of Opposition, Labour now appeared very different from what it did in the year of its great rout. It had kept the split to minimum proportions, and it was the seceders who had lost. In place of violent dissension there was an agreed program in both domestic and foreign affairs. A new generation of leaders was ready to replace the veterans who had passed away. There were promising young men available who had not been able to get into Parliament at this election; it was unfortunate that they would have to wait ten years for another opportunity in a general election.

11. Labour and the Dictators

For four years after the election of 1935 British Labour watched with deepening anxiety as the dictators made the moves that led to war. After Abyssinia came the successive crises over the Rhineland, Spain, Austria, Czechoslovakia, Albania, and Poland. As the prospect of peace diminished, Labour's hesitation and search for alternatives to force disappeared, so that in September 1939 it was a united party that accepted war in the conviction that the only way out was through.

In the new parliamentary party the first problem was that of the leadership. Clynes, who had once served but was now sixty-six, unselfishly eliminated himself. Three candidates remained: Attlee, who had been acting as "stop-gap" leader, Greenwood, an economist and a former Minister of Health, and Morrison, a former Minister of Transport. The first ballot gave Attlee 58 votes, Morrison 44, and Greenwood 33, but on the second most of Greenwood's supporters switched to Attlee.[1] This outcome was due in part to the rivalry between Bevin, who had backed Greenwood, and Morrison, and some did not expect the choice to be permanent. It was significant, however, that the reserved and unassuming Attlee had the support of most of the old parliamentary party with whom he had been working. He was appreciated as he grew in stature. Although he lacked great oratorical power and the expansiveness often associated with politicians, he impressed all with his ability to get powerful opposites like Morrison and Bevin to function as a team. At about the same time, J. S. Middleton succeeded Henderson as party secretary.

In 1937 some changes in party practice were effected. One change concerned the executive committee, an important body that met monthly, interpreted the constitution, conferred with the parliamentary party on political work and program, supervised the party machinery, and prepared a report for the consideration of the annual conference. It consisted of 23 members; 12 were nominated by the trade unions, one by the affiliated socialist, cooperative, and professional societies, and 5 by local Labour parties; there were also 5 women members, while the treasurer and the leader of the parliamentary party were ex officio members.

Although nominations for the first three classes were by their respective groups, the election, like that of the women members, was by the whole conference. The local Labour parties objected that they were swamped by the massive trade-union vote; the trade unionists retorted that they contributed the bulk of the membership and of the party funds. It was true that in 1937 the affiliated trade unionists numbered 2,037,071, as compared with 447,150 in the local parties and 43,451 in the cooperator-socialist-professional group; in fees to the central Labour organization the union contribution was four times that of the local parties. The local parties countered with the claim to activity far out of proportation to their numbers. Due to Dalton, who was party chairman in 1937, the number of local party representatives was increased from 5 to 7, and the first three classes listed above were allowed to elect, as well as nominate, their own representatives. As a result, the local parties returned a few more leftish intellectuals, but the moderates continued to dominate. In addition, the date of the annual party conference was moved forward to Whitsuntide in order to avoid following so closely upon the September conference of the T.U.C., whose pattern Labour sometimes gave a false impression of following. In order to avoid having two party conferences in quick succession the next one was scheduled for the spring of 1939, which, it was believed, would be a strategic moment to prepare for the next general election.

The party's League of Youth, an organization designed to recruit and train young people for the party, provided some headaches for the elders. It had made substantial progress, but the young enthusiasts wanted not only to discuss policy but to adopt resolutions and make decisions. But according to the constitution, control of policy lay with the party conference, so in 1936 some restrictions were placed upon the League of Youth. Membership was limited to those between the ages of sixteen and twenty-one, and the organization was encouraged to make a greater place for social and recreational activity. This did not end the matter. There were similar flare-ups in 1939 and in the 1950's; the seniors always feared that a party within a party would develop a program of its own.[2]

The series of policy studies continued with reports on such topics as broadcasting, the cotton industry, the socialization of coal, the depressed areas, and the gradual extinction of tithes. In 1937, looking forward to the next election, *Labour's Immediate Programme* outlined what a Labour government backed by a Commons' majority might accomplish in a single term of office. Unlike previous statements, it was brief and practical. There was a program of nationalization. The Bank of England received first mention, but the joint-stock banks, which had been included in 1934, were now omitted. A National Investment Board would be set up to mobilize financial resources and carry out large public enterprises. Transport, coal, gas, and electricity would come under public corporations. A Labour government would cooperate with the trade unions and with the International Labour Organization to raise standards at home and improve world conditions. It would deal with unemployment, locate industries in distressed areas, provide adequate pensions, shorten the working week with forty hours as the standard, extend health services, and raise the school leaving age to fifteen at once and to sixteen as soon as possible. It would reinvigorate the League and halt the arms race, but maintain such armed forces as were necessary for the fulfillment of League of Nations obligations, and provide a Defence Ministry to coordinate defense services. The manufacture of armaments would be monopolized by the state in order to take the profit out of war and end the alleged scandal of deliberately created war scares.

The Communists continued to present their perennial issue to the Labour party with pressures that were new but with problems that were constant. In the hope that loss of the election might dispose the Labour executive to a reconsideration of policy, the Communists immediately resubmitted their request for affiliation. Harry Pollitt's application of November 25, 1935, cited the ominous political situation abroad with the steady march of fascism. The failure in the general election, he argued, proved the futility of hope from a divided labor movement. While he admitted that his party would hold steadfastly to its ultimate revolutionary objectives, he insisted that its determination to fight the National Government, fascism, and war inspired it to work honestly for a working-class majority in the Commons. On January 27, 1936, the Labour executive replied that the fundamental differences so often emphasized still existed, and it refused to countenance any step that might be misinterpreted as a weakening of its stand on political democracy. A Communist effort to prolong the negotiations met with a pointed refusal.[3]

Meanwhile, on the Continent, the concept of the united front was broadened to include groups to the right of the socialists. In July 1935 the French People's Front, including the Radical Socialist, Socialist, and Communist parties, was completed on the premise that with the fascist danger so immediate and serious, it was a case of unite or perish. The Franco-Soviet alliance strengthened the bond. In February 1936 the Spanish People's Front of Republican, Socialist, Communist, and Syndicalist parties won an election. In May there was a similar victory in France. These successes were in striking contrast to the recent disasters in Germany and Austria.

These events abroad appeared to some Labourites to provide a lesson applicable at home. Among the middle-class intellectuals of the party, who were aware of movements abroad and were often less sensitive to fear of "Communist maneuvers" than the trade-union leaders so directly experienced with them, there was an active campaign for a popular front. The Fabian Society now reversed its position to favor Communist affiliation and the popular front. The Socialist League and the University Labour Federation approved a unity campaign.[4] In some of the largest unions, such as the Engineers and Miners, the movement found considerable support. In defense of a change of opinion a member of the Amalgamated Society of Engineers urged:

It is not so much what Radek or Bukharin or other people said in 1921, 1922, 1923, or 1924; what we have to appreciate today is what Hitler, Mussolini and Franco are doing against democracy in Europe, and because of this situation we are prepared to make any concession to bring about the unity of the working-class forces in Europe to fight against Fascism.[5]

The Labour leadership, however, refused to turn either left or right. It was convinced that cooperation with Communists would repel more votes than it would attract, while the experience of two Labour governments warned against reliance upon the Liberals. It sought the independent majority in the Commons that a turnover of 15 per cent in the popular vote would give, although the state of opinion hardly warranted that degree of optimism.[6]

Accordingly, the National Council met the clamor with a restatement of its position in a report, *British Labour and Communism* (1936). This document reviewed the historic principles of the party and its prolonged fight against penetration by a Communist party sponsored and financed by Moscow. It concluded that, however suitable the People's Front might be for countries like France, it was inapplicable to the very different political conditions and traditions of Great Britain. It rejected a fictitious unity in favor of its own principles and program:

The issue is plain. The Labour movement will remain firm to its principles. It will not attempt to achieve a spurious unity with those who hold principles so completely irreconcilable with Labour and who have no faith in democracy. The clear-cut refusal of the Executive Committee of the Labour Party to accept the Communist affiliation is a guarantee for the future development and progress of British Socialism.[7]

At Edinburgh in October the annual conference supported the executive. Communist affiliation was defeated by 1,728,000 votes to 592,000 and the popular front by 1,805,000 to 435,000, but the character and size of the minority gave the party cause for reflection.[8]

So long as the international situation moved from crisis to crisis, conference votes could not end this agitation. Intense feeling over the Spanish civil war influenced many. Laski, for example, who a few years earlier had condemned the united front as a "Machiavellian maneuver dictated by the necessities of the international situation," now came to its defense.[9] The drive for unity centered in the three small bodies on the extreme left of the labor movement. On January 18, 1937, the Communist party, the I.L.P., and—in spite of a warning from the Labour executive—the Socialist League agreed to join their forces in resistance to fascism and war, to work for the replacement of the National Government, and to further a program of immediate reforms.

This alliance proceeded uneasily, however, because of disagreement over the nature and extent of the front. The Communists were now the most ardent cooperators of all. In a new enthusiasm for democracy—the misfortunes of their party in some countries evidently brought conviction that democracy and civil liberties offered advantages—they were eager to include middle-class elements in the proposed coalition; the line now was that the class struggle could best be waged by the working class's combining with sections of the petty bourgeoisie to isolate the capitalist class.[10]

The I.L.P., which favored a purely working-class movement, opposed this rightward extension of the popular front; because the latter savored of class cooperation, it was denounced as a retreat from the class struggle. Indeed, as the Communist party developed moderate tactics, it yielded its post on the extreme left of the labor movement to the more uncompromising I.L.P., which now charged it with loss of revolutionary faith.[11] Within the Socialist League there was more diversity. Some members were ready to associate with anyone, including dissident Conservatives, in the pursuit of immediate objectives, but Cripps, an outstanding figure in the League, at this time (1937) opposed a widely extended front and favored a closer-knit one dominated by a class-conscious workers' party.

Since the Socialist League was affiliated with the Labour party, these maneuvers brought a quick response from the latter. Because the League had embarked upon its course in defiance of an executive statement, it was promptly disaffiliated. It protested, but continued its unity demonstrations regardless of the views of the local Labour parties in whose areas the meetings were held. The executive thereupon ruled adherence to it incompatible with membership in the Labour party, which virtually classed it with the proscribed Communist auxiliaries. Since the members of the League did not relish this position, they agreed to disband. Cripps, however, formed a unity committee composed entirely of Labour party men. The executive warned that, although it was free to advocate any policy within the party, neither a public campaign nor joint activity with the Communists would be tolerated. Again the issue was placed before the 1937 conference, and in spite of pleas from Cripps and Laski the delegates voted 1,730,000 to 373,000 to uphold the executive.[12]

During the spring of 1938 the rapid march of the totalitarian powers and the Prime Minister's policy of conciliating the dictators brought a revival of the popular-front agitation. On March 19, immediately after the German absorption of Austria, the Communist party called for a People's Government headed by Labour. A day later, Sydney Elliott, editor of the Cooperators' *Reynolds' News*, asked Labour to head a national peace alliance to defeat Chamberlain. Some Liberal papers supported the move. When in April General Franco's successful Ebro offensive divided Valencia from Barcelona, a conference in behalf of Loyalist Spain was organized by groups ranging from pro-League Conservatives to the extreme parties of the left. Many hoped, as did the Liberal *Manchester Guardian*, that although this conference was on a specific issue, it might lead to united action on the part of progressives irrespective of party affiliations.[13]

From several quarters the response was favorable. The annual conference of the Cooperative party, a close ally of Labour, overrode the opposition of its parliamentary representatives and accepted Elliott's resolution for a united peace alliance. The Liberal party, a poor third in the country and a handful in the Commons, had long urged an electoral agreement upon Labour. In May 1938 at Bath, the Liberal party's annual conference declared for cooperation upon the basis of a common foreign policy and of domestic measures upon which the Liberals and Labour could agree. Sir Richard Acland, mover of the resolution, would unite all those who believed in collective security from the radicals of the extreme left to the pro-League Conservatives and realists like Winston Churchill.[14] Every by-election afforded the Liberal press the opportunity to stress the impotence of a divided Opposition and the possibilities of success in the event of union for common objectives.

On these issues the Communists were now speaking the same language as the Liberals. They denounced Labour's independence as a boon to Chamberlain. Where a Liberal's chance of success in a by-election appeared the brighter, they urged Labour to withdraw. The "barrenness" of the two Labour governments was now attributed, in part, to the party's refusal to share a common program with the Liberals. Whereas the MacDonald governments had expected Liberals to be patient oxen, the proposed people's front would further their interests as well. Labour's policy of putting socialism in the forefront was ridiculed on the ground that the one overriding issue was the salvation of democracy. Dutt, the revolutionary known as "the Communist pope," now spoke like a Fabian gradualist: "Socialism is not the first stage, but the *crowning achievement* of a long process of social struggle."[15]

The Labour executive was unmoved. On April 22, 1938, on the eve of the conference in behalf of Loyalist Spain, it stated its case. It reiterated its conviction that early electoral success was possible, and that the party could risk neither the dilution of its program nor the practical disorganization that would inevitably result from coalition. It refused to commit Labour to an alliance with parties that did not share its socialist objective. Underlying this old policy of rejecting coalition with Liberals was, of course, the disinclination to preserve a party from whose disappearance it hoped to profit. Another statement, *The Labour Party and the Popular Front* (1938), developed these views further. The executive made clear its determination not to permit hope of temporary benefits to obscure its permanent objectives.

In January 1939 Cripps made a final effort to revive the project of a broadly based coalition. His memorandum to the executive proposed such an alliance to further a program of immediate social reforms and a foreign policy of rallying Russia and the western democracies in support of peace by collective action. By this time, however, the conduct of the Spanish Communists in attacking other elements in the republican coalition in Spain, together with a greater knowledge of Stalin's bloody purges in Russia, made coalition with Communists seem even less attractive. When on January 13 Cripps submitted his program to the Labour executive, it lost by 17 to 3; he was supported only by Ellen Wilkinson, an ex-Communist, and by D. N. Pritt, who often made common cause with Communists. On that same date, nevertheless, Cripps circulated his memorandum to all local Labour parties and to the trade unions.

Cripps's action was most embarrassing to the Labour executive. It coincided with the adoption of a joint program with the Cooperative party, which had reversed its decision of the previous year and opposed the popular front, and the initiation of a campaign in preparation for the next general election, which was expected in eighteen months or less. Athwart the executive's bid for an unhampered majority was now dragged the often rejected proposal, and the circularization of the memorandum on the very day of its repudiation appeared a particularly flagrant breach of party discipline. Cripps was promptly expelled, as were Trevelyan, Bevan, and G. R. Strauss, when they persisted in their campaign.

At the end of May the party conference allowed Cripps to present his case, but instead of dwelling upon the ideas of the popular front he argued the theoretical question of the rights of individuals and minorities in the party. The conference endorsed the executive by a vote of 2,100,000 to 402,000. In the majority were not only the trade unions but also the constituency parties, where Cripps assumed his greatest strength to be.

Later an ex-Communist, J. T. Murphy, brought a direct vote on the popular front but lost even more decisively by 2,360,000 to 248,-000. This issue was closed. The rank and file of Labour stood with the executive, which in these last stages of the contest had issued a manifesto repeating its unalterable opposition to the dilution of the Labour program that would inevitably result from such alliances. Confident of electoral success, it preferred to bid for power; and, if placed in office, it promised a bold application of socialist principles.[16]

In the early years of the Labour party, characterized by loose organization and vague objectives, the socialist and trade-unionist components had little in common, and sometimes members of the parliamentary party found themselves in opposite lobbies. By 1939 the organization had been tightened, objectives clarified, and a program developed. There were limits to differences that could be tolerated. The exclusion of Communists and the rejection of association with them was one aspect of this consolidation of an amorphous labor movement into a united Labour party.

The popular-front agitation and the Communist problem, however, were only reflections of the international situation, upon which attention was centered. The Italian invasion put in question the fate not only of Abyssinia but also of the League and collective security, now central in Labour's policy. The Baldwin government utilized the popular enthusiasm for pooled security to win the election, only to desert that policy.

Sir Samuel Hoare's famous speech in the League Assembly at Geneva on September 11, 1935, asserted his government's determination to fulfill its obligations to the League and the collective system. Actually, it was made the very day after he and Pierre Laval, the French Foreign Minister, had virtually abandoned effective sanctions; they had ruled out naval blockade, closure of the Suez Canal, military sanctions—everything that might lead to war—so the speech was a bluff.

Neither Hoare nor Laval thought Abyssinia worth a war, so when, on October 3, Italian forces crossed the Abyssinian frontier, there was no sign of military sanctions. Hoare, a realist, was convinced that no power would line up effectively beside Britain in case of a war on this issue. Accordingly, he and Laval entered upon a secret agreement on December 8. It allotted almost half of Abyssinia to Italy, together with special rights in the remainder. To the discomfiture of the British, Laval promptly leaked the agreement to the press. Such was the outburst of indignation at this policy of retreat that Baldwin sacrificed Hoare, who was succeeded by Anthony Eden.

Labour was unanimous in condemning the desertion of Abyssinia and the flouting of the League. In its desire to vindicate the League it ignored or minimized arguments that Abyssinia was not worth the risk of a major war, that other powers had shown no readiness to follow Britain in making naval dispositions, and that the British Navy could not escape losses that might handicap it in case of a more serious challenge. On December 12 the National Council of Labour denounced the agreement as a betrayal of the Abyssinian people, an encouragement to aggression, and the destruction of the collective system. It called upon the League to apply effective sanctions and to refuse a settlement based on conquest.

On December 19 the parliamentary party brought in a motion of censure and gave the government a very bad day. Baldwin, who had just sacked Hoare, was penitent, but some Conservatives were ready to express disapproval of his policy by abstaining from the vote. Attlee, making his first speech as party leader, was effective, but he pressed his attack a little too far when he asserted that the honor of the Prime Minister was at issue as well as the honor of the country. This personal charge brought Austen Chamberlain, who had been prepared to abstain, to the support of Baldwin, who thereby escaped censure, though the blot remained upon his reputation for honesty and sincerity.

In the following weeks the Labour party through all its national and international organizations urged the application of sanctions, with specific mention of oil, coal, iron, and steel, without which—especially oil—Italy could not have carried on the war. The Italians' bombing of civilians and use of poison gas was strongly condemned; at the same time they were noted as examples of the perils of any future war.[17]

The Abyssinian resistance soon collapsed; on May 2 the Italians were at Addis Ababa, and the country was annexed by Italy. On May 5 the National Council of Labour met to object to Italy's being allowed to gather the fruits of aggression; sanctions should be intensified, it urged, and the League vindicated. When on June 18 the government announced that it would abandon sanctions, the National Council, in conjunction with the London Trades Council, the London Labour party, and the Cooperative party, devoted Sunday, June 23, to a great protest meeting in Hyde Park. The parliamentary party tabled a vote of censure, and the Commons heard Greenwood's strictures against the government as trembling, vacillating, and cowardly. In October the annual conference condemned the government for its failure to support and strengthen the League, although by that date this issue was hardly a live one; the government had made it all too clear, even while there was yet time, that it would not give the lead necessary to implement collective security, and no amount of Labour pressure could induce it to follow the policy upon which it had won the election.[18]

The failure to stop the Italian conquest of another League member was a blow to the League and to Labour's foreign policy, which was based upon it. Some said pessimistically that the League had been tried and found wanting; they concluded that nations would not back military sanctions unless their own vital interests were at stake. The small nations began to contract out of sanctions; in September 1938 the Scandinavian countries indicated that they considered those clauses no longer binding. Labour voices that had never relished a

League backed by force and had opposed the Geneva Protocol were raised again to warn of the danger that sanctions might lead to a first-class war.[19] The Labour majority, however, persistently clung to its ideal and spoke of confronting an aggressor with overwhelming force, though hardly with its former confidence.

On March 7, 1936, while Britain and France were fully occupied with the Abyssinian question, Hitler suddenly denounced the treaty of Locarno and sent his troops into the demilitarized Rhineland. At the same time he sought to soothe and distract those powers by offers of a nonaggression agreement, an air pact, and the return of Germany to the League. Much later it became known that a show of resistance would have led to immediate withdrawal, but such were the doubts and hesitations in London and Paris that the bluff succeeded. Although Hitler's resort to force was widely condemned in Britain, excuses for inaction were easily found; after all, it was said, the Germans were going only into their own back garden; unlike the Italian action, it was no invasion of foreign soil.

The Labour leadership denounced Hitler's move and understood its significance. The National Council called a special meeting of trade-union and socialist leaders; on March 19–20 representatives from Britain, France, Belgium, Italy (exiles), Norway, Sweden, Holland, Switzerland, and Luxembourg met at Transport House. The statement of this conference, drafted mainly by Citrine and Dalton, condemned the breach of the treaty and the threat to collective security. Hitler's purpose was clear: fortification of the Rhineland and the establishment of air bases there were preparatory to attack on peaceful states both to the east and to the west; the professions of good will were camouflage. Members of the conference, however, as anxious as the government to avoid war, did not demand the use of force to oust Hitler from the Rhineland; their positive proposal again was to strengthen the League. Hitler could prove his sincerity by joining in arms limitation with international inspection and supervision; if he refused, the other powers should organize peace without Germany.[20]

Although not deceived by some fair words from Hitler about a possible non-aggression pact and German re-entry into the League, the Labour party, like most Britons, unwillingly accepted the accomplished fact with relief at a narrow escape from war. All the party could suggest was preparation to meet future aggression. The National Council of Labour issued a manifesto, *Labour and the Defence of Peace* (1936), which was a plea for a firm system of collective security in which Germany would be invited to participate as an equal.

The Spanish Civil War stirred British emotion even more than did Abyssinia or the Rhineland. In July 1936 there began a rebellion of army leaders and political rightists against a government composed of liberal republicans supported by a left coalition including socialists, communists, and anarchists, although none of these radical groups were represented in the ministry. Aided by supplies from Hitler and Mussolini, the rebel "Nationalists" quickly won most of the west and north of Spain, while the republican "Loyalists" held Madrid, Valencia, Barcelona, and a Basque-Asturias strip along the northern coast. Soon Italy and Germany were sending in troops, including two divisions of the Italian army, as well as supplies; the presence of troops, which the "Nationalists" denied at first, was finally admitted openly and even boastfully. To help the Loyalists individual volunteers went to form the International Brigades, while Russia furnished munitions. Madrid was saved, and for a time the battle line stabilized.

British sympathies were divided. Most Conservatives and Catholics disliked the republic. They regarded it as Bolshevist and guilty of condoning flagrant crimes against persons and property; they hoped Franco would win. Labourites, most Liberals, and some Conservatives supported the republicans. Labourites were deeply, even passionately, devoted to that cause. Although the Spanish brand of democracy was not theirs, they believed the future of democracy was at stake. Should Spain go the way of Italy and Germany, what would happen to France and the rest of Europe? If the countries toppled one after another like a row of dominoes, what would be the position of Britain? Spain appeared crucial. Life-long pacifists, as they watched the process, felt their confidence in moral suasion yield to a conviction that democracy and freedom might have to be defended by arms. So far as leftist excesses were concerned, they were regretted but excused as the response to long oppression and as exceeded by those of the "Nationalists." Accordingly, the Labourites, with Catholic exceptions, gave strong moral support to the republican cause; though few were prepared to risk a war over Spain, individual enthusiasts were willing to go there to fight and die for it.

Labour's first policy, naturally, was to preserve neutrality and to prevent the war from spreading. The party fully expected that the legal government with the right under international law and with the means to purchase arms abroad would be able to suppress the revolt. Soon, however, came disturbing reports that the Spaniards would not be left to settle their own affairs because the rebels had received aid from Portugal and the fascist powers. The socialist and trade-union Internationals met on July 28, 1936, and sent two observers to Spain to investigate. But on August 2 Leon Blum, the socialist head of the Popular Front government in France, fearful because of dissension in his own country and of the danger that another world war might grow out of the Spanish one, proposed a policy of nonintervention; Spain would be insulated and the rivals left to fight it out without involving other countries. Great Britain, Germany, Italy, Russia, and others agreed, so a committee was set up to enforce nonintervention.

Doubtful of this proposal, Citrine, Greenwood, and Middleton, for the National Council of Labour, saw Eden, the Foreign Secretary, and argued the right of the Spanish government under international law to buy arms. The official position, however, was that it was necessary to treat both sides alike in order to prevent the division of Europe into rival blocs and the spread of the war. On August 28 Citrine reported back to the National Council, which with a good deal of regret accepted the argument of expediency but was very dubious of the good faith of the fascist powers. In September Citrine presented this policy, admittedly distasteful, to the T.U.C. and, as at that time the extent of aid to the rebels was not known, nonintervention was accepted almost unanimously by a vote of 3,029,000 to 51,000.[21]

By the time the Labour party conference met at Edinburgh, October 5–9, reports were coming in of the one-sided operation of nonintervention. A minority of the National Council, including Morrison, opposed it, but the majority still accepted the unpalatable argument of expediency. Accordingly, Greenwood presented the resolution to that effect; although it was against all their sympathies and interests, it appeared the only way out of a bad situation and Blum wanted it. The alternative carried the threat of war: "Is this conference prepared to have the battle between dictatorship and democracy fought over the bleeding body of Spain? That is the question you have to answer," said Greenwood.[22]

Bevin and George Hicks of the Building Trade Workers took the same view. From the floor, however, came much opposition. Trevelyan chided the National Council for its timidity; the alternative was not intervention, but the upholding of the legal right of arms purchase; "sympathy accompanied by bandages and cigarettes" was not enough. Dr. Christopher Addison, Minister of Agriculture in the second Labour government, ridiculed a policy that depended for its enforcement upon the governments most interested in its violation and upon men who on Abyssinia were guilty of brazen duplicity. William Dobbie of the National Union of Railwaymen, who had just returned from an extensive trip through Spain, spoke of the desperate need for arms. Aneurin Bevan pointed to fascism's triumphant progress from country to country. Noel-Baker noted the new technique of aggression which, if allowed to succeed in Spain, would be repeated in Rumania and Czechoslovakia.

The debate was heated but Attlee, summing up, spoke coolly. He recommended acquiescence with nonintervention, however unwillingly, but said Britain should insist that it be honestly observed. This view was accepted by 1,836,000 to 519,000, but the size and composition of the minority indicated the displeasure with a course that followed too closely that of Chamberlain.

The conference was not finished with Spain, however, because next day two Spanish fraternal delegates were to speak, Señor de Asua and Isabel de Palencia, who was known as La Pasionaria and was a Communist member of the Cortes. De Asua's speech, in French, translated by Noel-Baker, detailed fascist breaches of nonintervention. Isabel de Palencia, in fluent English, electrified the delegates with a passionate speech that brought them to their feet in an ovation and the spontaneous singing of "The Red Flag," a song that at the moment expressed the emotion for Spain. With excitement high, delegates cried, "What about nonintervention now?"

Accordingly, the executive sent Attlee and Greenwood on a quick trip to London to consult with Chamberlain, who was acting Prime Minister in Baldwin's absence. After receiving Chamberlain's assurances that the British representatives on the nonintervention committee were fully conscious of the need to clear up the situation, they returned on the last day of the conference to report. The executive then proposed a resolution stating that if investigation proved deliberate violations of the agreement, the British and French governments should at once restore to the Spanish government the right to purchase arms. Attlee cautioned that abandonment of nonintervention involved the risk of war. Noel-Baker and Ernest Bevin repeated that they must be ready to face the consequences of their vote. Nevertheless, the conference unanimously accepted the resolution.[23]

Any shred of confidence in nonintervention disappeared within a month after the Edinburgh conference. Mussolini and Hitler made a farce of it with a steady flow of aid to Franco that sooner or later was certain to strangle the republic. The parliamentary party protested in scores of questions and with motions of censure that were easily voted down by the heavy Conservative majority. It repeatedly pointed to the evidence that not only arms but men by the tens of thousands were being supplied to Franco. Investigations were promised, but they were merely investigations of the obvious.

The Internationals were also active. On March 11, 1937, some 200 delegates from 19 countries met at Geneva to hear the Spanish republicans plead for the right to purchase arms and for the removal of foreign armies from Spain; they would include their own genuine volunteers if the expeditionary forces and the Moorish mercenaries with Franco were taken out. By summer the National Council was condemning nonintervention as a hopeless failure, and in October the party conference unanimously repudiated it.

The alternative of intervention was never a part of the Labour policy; what was desired was the restoration to Madrid of a government's normal rights. There were proposals, especially from Citrine, to get the League to act, but that organization was so incomplete and had so many members ready to contract out of collective action that the response at best could have been but partial. Labour therefore had to fall back on popular agitation. Its "Spain Campaign Committee" undertook to mobilize public opinion in order to pressure the government into abandoning nonintervention. Scores of demonstrations and meetings followed, but the government, secure in its majority, was unmoved. Chamberlain, who had been Prime Minister since May 1937, was more interested in coming to an understanding with Italy than with the rights and wrongs of the Spanish situation.[24]

Political frustration found vent in humanitarian aid to Spain. Food, clothing, and medical supplies were sent in great quantities. The National Council established and maintained a base hospital, while the Socialist Medical Association and a number of trade unions financed ambulances. Women knitted thousands of garments. A milk fund reaches £31,000; £120,000 was raised to aid refugees; the Mineworkers contributed £55,000 to be used especially for orphaned children of Asturias miners. People "adopted" Basque children, and by 1937 some 4,000 were in England for safety. As Jennie Lee later said, however, "Even the very best type of British bandage is not very much use against a German gun. The fascists won the war."[25]

There were some, especially in the League of Youth, who said that the cause of the Spanish workers called for action, and went to join the International Brigades. One battalion of that force was named for Major Attlee, and the Labour leader made the gesture of a visit to it. There was an I.L.P. contingent in Spain, too, but it was the

Communists who volunteered in the greatest numbers. Sixty per cent of the Britons in the Brigades became casualties, one-third of them dead. The efforts of the Communists to exploit the Spanish war for their own ends, however, did great harm to the cause and confirmed the Labour leadership in its resistance to all forms of united-front activity at home.[26]

The war dragged on for nearly three years. While Labour diligently sought by propaganda in the country and by speeches in Parliament to compel the government to change its policy, Franco built up his strength to launch his offensives down the Ebro and against the Basques. When in January 1939 Barcelona was threatened, Labour made an eleventh-hour plea for "Arms for Spain," but Chamberlain remained unmoved. After Barcelona was captured, he announced his government's formal recognition of the Franco regime amid Opposition cries of "Shame!" and "Betrayal!" After the fall of Madrid on April 20, all Labour could do was raise funds for refugees, commemorate the heroism of the Spanish republicans, and cherish a deep distrust of Neville Chamberlain.

While Labour's attention was centered on Spain, there was a distraction in the Far East when Japan stepped up its undeclared war on China. Soon after the incident at the Marco Polo Bridge on July 7, 1937, the Japanese armies were in Peking, Canton, and Nanking, with the Nationalists in retreat to Chungking. Labour and British opinion generally supported China. On August 24 the National Council denounced the Japanese for lawless and flagrant aggression. The T.U.C. and party conferences expressed the same view. At the Labour conference a resolution proposed by Attlee and seconded by Morrison called for economic and financial pressure on Japan accompanied by a boycott of Japanese goods. The Cooperators joined in the boycott. Many Labourites hoped that the United States and the League would join to impose economic sanctions on Japan. It was pointed out that the pacific powers were still the more numerous and possessed of superior resources; as Douglas Jay, economist and City Editor of the *Daily Herald*, noted, Japan was dependent upon the United States and Britain for the bulk of its oil, tin, and nickel. Others considered the League, since Abyssinia, moribund; when in September 1938 it did make proposals, the powers did not carry them out, because they would not risk war. Not much could be done in Britain then except to hold protest meetings and refrain from buying Japanese goods. Soon people were preoccupied with greater threats nearer home.

In contrast with the long drawn-out struggle over Spain, Hitler's absorption of Austria was done quickly. On February 12, 1938, he summoned Chancellor Schuschnigg to Berchtesgaden, and exactly one month later the annexation was completed. Under other circumstances, Labour would have welcomed this *Anschluss*, because it regarded the truncated Austria left in 1919 as not viable and the treaty provisions against union as a violation of the principle of nationality. Now it disapproved the manner of its accomplishment and expressed alarm at another example of the steady march of the dictators, which was heightened by the spectacle of brutalities against Social Democrats and Jews. The socialist and trade-union Internationals, meeting at Paris March 15–17, stressed the increased danger of general war and the menace to Czechoslovakia, now threatened from three sides by the Nazis.

On February 20, in the midst of this crisis, Eden and Lord Cranborne resigned from the Cabinet because of differences with Chamberlain, particularly over his conciliation of Italy. The parliamentary Labour party brought in a motion of censure contrasting the government's fair promises on the League with its subsequent desertion of it. It was defeated, but Conservative abstentions were significant. On February 22 the National Council of Labour denounced the policy that caused the resignations as "a crowning act of humiliation." It asked for a clear declaration that Britain stood for the enforcement of treaties against aggression, and that now Czechoslovakia, in particular, should be assured that Great Britain and the League powers would fulfill their obligations to maintain its integrity and independence.[27]

By this time it was clear that Czechoslovakia was next on Hitler's list, and that he would not rest until he had incorporated the German-speaking borderlands into the German Reich. The alleged grievances of the three million Sudeten Germans afforded him a convenient pretext to destroy the strongest bastion of democracy in Central Europe. In Konrad Henlein, head of the Sudeten German party, he found an ideal leader for a fifth column inside it. Prime Minister Chamberlain's assertions that British interests were not affected and his refusal to pledge support to the threatened country brought an immediate reply from Labour. On March 25 the National Council criticized his lack of a constructive policy and proposed that the peace-loving countries should unite to withstand the aggressor but simultaneously to promote negotiations toward a settlement of Europe's political and economic problems.

When on April 24 at Carlsbad Henlein demanded not merely local autonomy but a reorganization of the Czech state into a system of five or six national groupings, one of which would be, in effect, at Hitler's orders, Labour objected that it would put key positions in Nazi hands, destroy Czech power, and deliver the Sudeten Social Democrats to the Nazis. Its view was that not only Czech independence but Britain's vital interests were concerned. A statement issued by the Labour party shortly afterward emphasized that, should there be war, it was essential that Germany be compelled to fight on two fronts, and Czechoslovakia with its fortified mountain barrier was of immense strategic importance for an eastern front.[28]

When Henlein visited England, he was warned that violation of Czech independence meant war, but he was more impressed by the appeasement policy of *The Times* and the men about Chamberlain. On May 19 a border incident brought a war threat, but firmness on the part of France and Britain—the last prewar example—caused Hitler to back down. At the instance of the British representatives, the Labour and Socialist International then issued a statement that this success proved the need of a supreme effort to revitalize the League and collective security.[29]

The summer months saw German pressure on Czechoslovakia again stepped up, with corresponding danger of a general European war. Labour, convinced that Hitler was using the Sudetens to get control of the entire country, gave steady support to the threatened people. It was not more Czech than the Czechs, however, so from time to time it changed its position as the Czechs made concessions in the hope of conciliating Hitler. In July it sent Lord Snell, a Labour M.P., George Dallas, chairman of the party, and James Walker, M.P., as fraternal delegates to the Czech Socialist conference to demonstrate its sympathy. It opposed Chamberlain's policy as endangering the country's independence; it feared that Lord Runciman, who had been sent to Prague in August to mediate between Czechs and Sudetens, would sacrifice the future for the sake of temporary relief. There were protests that Runciman should have been sent to Berlin, where the real threat to peace lay, especially since Hitler's bellicose words were accompanied by military maneuvers on a gigantic scale. As the Czechs continued to make concessions to appease Hitler, the party could only assent. It would accept even the "Fourth Plan" dividing the country into linguistic areas, hitherto opposed as facilitating the creation of a Nazi dictatorship in the Sudetenland, if at the same time Britain and France would definitely guarantee the Czech frontiers.[30]

By September hope of satisfactory settlement was dwindling and the situation increasingly critical. Even the "Fourth Plan" did not satisfy Henlein, which really meant Hitler. "Incidents" occurred and tension mounted. France called up reservists. In Britain gas masks were distributed and bomb shelters dug in the parks. On September 12 Hitler spoke his demand for full self-determination for the Sudetens. The imminent prospect of war brought home even to those hitherto indifferent the relation between international affairs and their own lives.[31]

During the period of tension the National Council met almost daily. The next opportunity to consult a representative body of labor opinion would be at the September T.U.C. conference at Blackpool, because in anticipation of a general election the annual conference of the Labour party had been postponed until the spring of 1939. The three executives met and put their views before the T.U.C. in a manifesto of September 8, *Labour and the International Situation: On the Brink of War,* a forthright statement of policy in what was felt literally to be a "brink of war" situation. It pronounced the Nazi demands on Czechoslovakia incompatible with the latter's independence and denied the right of any government to pressure it into acceptance. "Britain Should Lead Against Aggression," said the document in capitals. It continued:

The time has come for a positive and unmistakable lead for collective defense against aggression. . . . The British government must leave no doubt in the mind of the German government that they will unite with the French and Soviet governments to resist any attack upon Czechoslovakia. The Labour Movement urges the British government to give this lead, confident that such a policy would have the solid support of the British people. . . . Labour cannot acquiesce in the destruction of the rule of law by savage aggression. . . . Whatever the risks involved, Great Britain must take its stand against aggression. There is now no room for doubt or hesitation.[32]

The next day, George Hicks presented this emergency statement to the T.U.C., saying that it was apparently a crisis exceeding that of 1914, and that Britain should join with France and Russia to defend Czechoslovakia if invaded; his belief was that the dictators would yield, but in any event no more democratic countries should be sacrificed. Other speeches were in the same vein; a collective stand must be made now or successively other Continental countries would succumb, leaving Britain to stand alone; the government must give a lead. The conference accepted the statement by an overwhelming majority.[33]

These words were in strong contrast to those of the Rothermere press and other apostles of appeasement. "Stand by the Czechs" was the burden of Labour speeches. Had the government given a strong lead, Labour would have accepted the risks. But the government did not; instead, it chose the course that gave the word "appeasement" an evil connotation.

When after Hitler's threatening speech of September 12 and an abortive revolt in the Sudetenland German intervention appeared imminent, Chamberlain decided upon the unusual step of a personal appeal. Labour, willing to try any honorable means of avoiding war, welcomed this dramatic move. Attlee and Greenwood, notified in advance, warmly approved, but warned the Prime Minister against any sacrifice of Czechoslovakia's integrity. Since the Czechs had just successfully ended the rebellion, it was fully expected that Chamberlain would stand fast. The National Council called for firmness and a strengthened collective system. What they soon heard, however, was an "Anglo-French plan" for the outright cession of certain Sudeten areas and plebiscites to determine preference in others with an Anglo-French guarantee of the new frontier.

The country was now stirred. On September 19 Labour held a protest meeting in Trafalgar Square. The National Council issued another manifesto on this "shameful betrayal" made under the brutal threat of armed force, which set "a dangerous precedent for the future," and hastened to consult the Internationals and to stiffen the divided French left.[34] Attlee and Greenwood told Chamberlain it was "an absolute surrender" and "one of the biggest disasters in British history"; another deputation spoke in similar terms to Halifax, now the Foreign Secretary.[35] Morrison proposed a voluntary exchange of populations as a solution. The National Council sponsored a series of demonstrations; it again asked that Parliament be summoned. By this time there was no doubt that public opinion was greatly aroused over the issue.[36]

On September 22 Chamberlain flew to Godesberg to implement the Anglo-French plan, but Labour protests continued. On the eve of the flight the three executives registered their "profound humiliation" at this pressuring of the Czechs into surrender. "This dishonour will not bring us peace," they stated. "Hitler's ambitions do not stop short at Czechoslovakia." They predicted, "Hitler's present triumph will be a new starting-point for further warlike adventures, which in the end must lead to a general conflict."[37] A national protest campaign of some 2,500 meetings followed. In the *Daily Herald* Attlee reiterated that Labour had approved Chamberlain's action only on condition of Britain's standing firm against aggression.[38] Accordingly, Labour was willing to risk war in defense of Czechoslovakian integrity right down to the time of Godesberg. But because on September 19 the Czechs had yielded, it was bootless to maintain the original position. Labour now had to strive for guarantees for the Czech minority in ceded areas and to save what was left of the country.

As Labour had warned, Hitler, never satisfied, made new demands; the surrender of the German areas must be immediate and without damage to military installations. The Czechs refused, and, at last, Britain and France conferred with Russia, which pleased Labour as a return to something like collective action. Attlee promised full support from his party and urged the goverment to give a strong lead.[39] A climax appeared in sight. The fleet was mobilized; trenches were dug in Hyde Park, and gas masks made available, while Hitler threatened force unless the Sudetenland transfer was completed by October 1. On September 28 the National Council telegraphed and printed for distribution in Germany an *Appeal to the German People*; Britain had no quarrel with them, it stated, but since the Nazi government showed no desire for a peaceful settlement, British Labour would have to support a united stand against aggression; the German people should revolt against their Nazi tyrants and cooperate in building a peaceful and prosperous world.[40]

Again it was a verge-of-war situation when on September 29 Parliament finally met, and during its session Chamberlain received and read Hitler's invitation to meet him the next day in Munich. There might be a way out, after all. Relief from tension was such that the Commons gave the Prime Minister a highly emotional ovation. Just how fully Labour members joined in it is disputed; some, at least, sat silent. Attlee, nevertheless, welcomed the opportunity even at that late hour for further discussions to preserve peace "without sacrificing principles."[41] After the debate he and Greenwood interviewed Halifax in order to press their view that no more sacrifices should be imposed upon the Czechs than those already accepted in the Anglo-French plan; they also expressed dissatisfaction at the absence of Czech representatives from the conference and the lack of any reference to Russia.[42]

Confronted with an accomplished fact and with the evacuation of the Sudetenland already in progress, Labour viewed the Munich settlement with mingled feelings of relief at the narrow escape from immediate war and disgust at the means by which it had been achieved. The harsh terms of Godesberg appeared but little softened in the manner of their execution. In the debate that began on October 3, Attlee called Munich "one of the greatest diplomatic defeats this country and France have ever sustained . . . . Without firing a shot, by the mere display of military force, he [Hitler] has achieved a dominating position in Europe."[43]

Morrison denied that Chamberlain had laid a basis for peace. Others denounced the "appeasement" policy as having so enhanced Hitler's strength that it might be impossible to stop further aggression. They condemned the government's failure to support the Czechs or to consult the Russians, and harked back to the failure to stand by and strengthen collective security. The National Council issued a manifesto expressing sympathy for the Czechs and promised efforts to preserve what was left of their country.[44] Lansbury and the handful of pacifists praised the agreement, but solely on the ground that any settlement was better than a war. With Czechoslovakia all but lost, attention shifted again to Spain, where the republic was making its last desperate stand.

The successive challenges from the dictators belatedly but finally ended Labour's confusion on rearmament. Absolute pacifism, exemplified by Lansbury, was now negligible, and few expected any tangible good from his personal appeals to Hitler and Mussolini. The position was that a Labour government would maintain such defense forces as were necessary and consistent with membership in the League. Yet Labour was not in office but in Opposition, and such was its distrust of the National Government, rooted in an exaggerated suspicion that the government would rather enter into an imperialist deal with the Fascists than resist them, that it was loath to entrust it with arms.

On this ground the parliamentary party regularly voted against the estimates for the armed services, not as a sign of opposition to all armaments but as evidence of disapproval of policy. Its votes and amendments, which were easily overwhelmed by the government's majority, were in line with recognized parliamentary procedure as a method of registering such disapproval, but they were badly misunderstood and open to misrepresentation as simply opposition to arms for Britain. Some of the leaders, especially Dalton, Citrine, and Bevin, had quickly become conscious of the futility and danger of this position. They urged and supported rearmament regardless of the party in power, but it required the pressure of events to convert the party to their position.

Hitler's unilateral denunciation of Locarno and occupation of the

Rhineland led the National Council to produce *Labour and the Defence of Peace* (May 1936), which contained a strong expression of the case for providing the necessary force to make collective security "an effective deterrent." The concession of force, however, was still coupled with hope of disarmament. Hopes died hard in spite of the revelation of League weakness over Abyssinia and the long drawn-out disarmament failure at Geneva.

The National Council attempted to answer the question of what to do next by a resolution presented to the party's October conference at Edinburgh. It was still a compromise. It took a firm stand for collective action with automatic sanctions; it proposed that the armed strength of those countries loyal to the League be conditioned by those of the potential aggressors; it reaffirmed the policy of Britain's maintaining such defenses as its League responsibilities demanded. Dalton, who moved the resolution, voiced his alarm at the speed and extent of German rearmament, Hitler's theory of striking like lightning in the night, the new Rome-Berlin "axis," and Britain's vulnerability. The time had come, he reiterated, to take a bold stand against the fascist states. A Labour government with power would have to rearm.

The debate, which lasted an entire day, revealed a wide range of views. Lansbury and Lord Arnold put the pacifist position. Some speakers had no confidence in a capitalist-controlled League; others demanded properly equipped armed forces. Morrison said he supported the resolution, and approved arms for collective security, but declined to be a party to the government's rearmament program on the ground that to do so would implicate Labour in its foreign policy. Cripps opposed the resolution; he could not put arms into the hands of people responsible for present world conditions. He also pertinently noted one omission; the resolution failed to state specifically a position on rearmament under the National Government.

Bevin, who agreed with Cripps on nothing else, also fastened upon this crucial point and demanded a definite lead on what must be done now. He rudely characterized Morrison's position as "tightrope walking." Pointing to the fate of his brother trade unionists in some countries abroad, he stressed the dangers of confusion and delay at home. He was prepared to face the question of arms and say to Hitler, "If you are going to rely on force . . . we will stand four-square to it"; he hoped for peace, but said, "I am afraid, however, that we may have to go through force to liberty."[45]

The conference accepted the resolution, 1,738,000 to 657,000, but the ambiguities remained. When Dalton could imply one thing and Morrison another, it was no guide for the parliamentary party; as Bevin said, it "passed the buck" to the latter. The parliamentary party continued to vote against the estimates to demonstrate disapproval of the government's foreign policy.[46]

In the course of the next twelve months the ambiguities disappeared. The Spanish war converted many utopians into realists, and two outstanding advocates of rearmament were in a position to influence policy, Dalton as chairman of the Labour party executive and Bevin as chairman of the T.U.C. general council. Both were purposeful on defense. Dalton, who was backed by most of the trade-union M.P.'s, though opposed by Attlee, Morrison, and other front benchers, ended the parliamentary party's practice of demonstrating disagreement with policy by opposing the estimates for the fighting services. Accordingly, this majority decision was loyally accepted in July 1937. Only six leftists followed the traditional practice which in retrospect appeared so unwise.[47]

Party pronouncements were firm. *Labour's Immediate Programme,* published in March 1937, restated that a Labour government would maintain the armed forces necessary for home defense and their League and Commonwealth obligations. It urged the establishment of a ministry of defence to coordinate the armed services, the democratization of the army by promotion on merit alone, and the improvement of conditions in the services—ideas that came from the party's committee on defense, for which Attlee was mainly responsible.[48]

The National Council's *International Policy and Defence,* issued in July, described the situation as highly dangerous to a Britain terribly vulnerable to attack by air or sea. It recognized the present weakness of the League, but urged its reinvigoration, so that aggressors could be confronted by an emphatic superiority of force. It called for a Labour government, which must be strongly equipped for defense; such a government "would be unable to reverse the present program of rearmament." It was a statement that revealed a thorough understanding of the situation, though it fell short of stating the need for arms in the positive terms in which leaders were thinking.

This statement was presented in September to the T.U.C. at Norwich, and a month later to the Labour party conference at Bournemouth. With Bevin in the chair at the T.U.C. meeting Citrine, with his usual clarity and incisiveness, analyzed the international situation and the necessity of rearmament; it was absurd to wait two or three years for an electoral victory and a similar period thereafter before an arms program could bring results. The dictators might not conveniently wait. The congress passed the resolution by 3,554,-000 to 224,000.[49]

At Bournemouth Dalton's address keynoted that in this grim situation "our country must be powerfully armed," and it needed a foreign policy that would "breathe new life into the League of Nations," though it was always ready for peaceful solutions. The few pacifists spoke out of proportion to their numbers, and Bevan feared that collaboration endangered party independence, but Clynes, Noel-Baker, R. H. S. Crossman, and Bevin effectively supported Dalton. The resolution passed easily by 2,167,000 votes to 228,000. There was now no doubt where the party stood; the speeches were an even clearer indication of Labour's mood and intention than the document's wording. Dalton rejoiced that he had won his long battle for immediate rearmament.[50]

The parliamentary party showed great activity in criticizing alleged governmental shortcomings. The estimates were made the occasion to condemn the government for failure to organize a Ministry of Supply, for permitting profiteering, for undemocratic officer selection, and for delays and deficiencies in aircraft production and in antiaircraft defense. Dalton's speech of May 25, 1938, on these matters of air power presented what Churchill, who followed, called "a formidable case" that should be read by all who were awake to the impending dangers.[51] Shortly after Munich a party statement, *Labour's Claim to Government* (1938) likewise demanded better defenses against air attack and a rapid increase in air power, while *A.R.P., Labour's Plan* urged a speed-up of evacuation schemes in the event of air raids.

The trade unions showed concern for the establishment of machinery for consultation and for better cooperation in defense production between government, employers, and labor. A government White Paper of 1936 mentioned the necessity, but not until March 1938, after the Austrian crisis, did the Prime Minister make a move. He then invited the T.U.C. general council to a conference, but still had no specific proposals. The council, conscious of the need for adequate defense equipment, wanted joint consultations with the government and employers. Matters were left to individual industries, where some employers could suggest only dilution, which revived memories of 1914 and the sacrifice of trade-union conditions.

The much desired Ministry of Supply was not set up until July 1939, and, when Sir Thomas Inskip, the minister, announced an advisory panel, to the indignation of the unions, it consisted exclusively of businessmen. Not until after hostilities began were labor representatives added.[52]

On manpower Labour gave full support to the National Voluntary Service Scheme to secure recruits for essential services and a register of essential occupations, but opposed the conscription bill introduced April 26, 1939, after the German occupation of Prague. Labour's attitude on conscription had no relation to pacifism. It held to the traditional faith in the voluntary system and urged every effort to ensure its success. Conscription was thought unnecessary; one theory held that modern armies needed smaller forces of highly skilled men, not huge masses. Also, like others, Labour did not foresee a struggle with one whole front soon to collapse before the mighty German military machine. It regarded conscription as a breach of the repeated promises that there would be no resort to it in peacetime. Labour feared it as an entering wedge for industrial conscription and resented the lack of any corresponding proposal for the conscription of wealth. So, except for Dalton and a few others, the parliamentary party, a special conference of trade-union executives, and the annual party conference all registered disapproval.[53]

This party conference—the same one that finally expelled Cripps on the popular-front issue—met May 29–June 2 at Southport. Dalton submitted a report on *Labour and Defence,* which was devoted to efficiency in defense. Again Labour asked for improved conditions for service men, promotion by merit, a Ministry of Supply, and a Ministry of Defence. When this report was accepted with practical unanimity, Morrison, a former conscientious objector, congratulated Dalton, who had seen active service in the war, saying that five years earlier such approval would have been wanting. This was true, but now, as Churchill noted, when it finally came to standing up to the Nazis and the Fascists, there were fewer doubts and divisions in the ranks of labor than in those of the other social classes.[54]

The respite purchased at Munich was brief. When on March 15, 1939, the Germans marched into Prague, the parliamentary party immediately called for a debate and showed a better comprehension of what had taken place than did Chamberlain. Although the Prime Minister manifested bitterness at German methods, he maintained that his course had been right, and would not be deflected from it. But Labour speakers condemned appeasement as a failure. Dalton, to cries of "Oh!" from unconverted Tories, said that the Prime Minister had been "outmaneuvered, hustled, and humbugged by Herr Hitler," while not until two days later did Chamberlain admit violation of the agreement.[55]

On March 21, the day Memel was occupied, the National Council denounced appeasement as a disastrous delusion and called for immediate British initiative in organizing a peace bloc to resist aggression. It convened a meeting of the three executives, which in turn sent a deputation to the Prime Minister to hasten such an alliance. It heard a statement of hopes for joint action with France, Russia, Poland, and Rumania, but also the objections of Poland and Rumania to the presence on their soil of Russian forces that might never depart.[56]

The government's bold guarantee to Poland on March 31, promising full support in the event that its independence was threatened, found the parliamentary party divided. There was general approval of the guarantee as a step toward a kind of collective action, but some members opposed unless Russia participated. Dalton convinced his colleagues of its necessity, so in a full-dress debate on April 3 the party supported it. In the absence of Attlee, who had been out for some months because of illness, Greenwood, the deputy leader, welcomed the move but warned that it would not be enough until other states, especially Russia, were included.[57] Twenty years earlier the Polish "corridor," which separated East Prussia from the rest of Germany, had been a much criticized provision of the Treaty of Versailles, but now Labour emphasized more Poland's ethnic and historic claim to Pomorze, the "corridor," and the economic importance of Danzig to Poland.[58]

Following Italy's occupation of Albania on April 7, Good Friday, Labour approved the guarantees extended to Greece and Rumania. While the Cabinet was still undecided on the guarantee to Rumania, Attlee and Dalton visited Chamberlain to urge it in order to forestall German occupation.

Labour viewed the government's course as a belated acceptance of its own policy of collective action, although attempting to implement it with weaker states, including some whose geographic location was a handicap. To yield to Polish fears and objections against Russia was, in effect, unrealistically to put the latter in second place. What Labour wanted was a strong system of mutual aid with specific military undertakings. Chairman George Dallas keynoted the party conference May 29 at Southport with insistence upon a firm peace pact resting upon a triple alliance of Great Britain, France, and Russia. Introducing the resolution, Noel-Baker, a prominent supporter of the League, said that with that organization in ruins the best alternative was to construct an alliance of greater power than the axis could command. "We have reached a moment where at every cost brutal aggressive armed force has to be restrained," he said.[59] Whatever the occasion of conflict—it might be Danzig or a single country—the real factor was the need of making a stand now; the League could be reconstituted later. The conference showed its unity, 2,363,000 to 55,000, in accepting the policy with all its implications.

To implement the policy, however, Russia was needed, for only Russia could make a strong eastern front. Here it was felt that the government was laggard; in spite of its allusions to "contacts," "consultations," and "close touch," the conviction grew that the Russian alliance was not being pursued with vigor. What Labour wanted was a principal member of the government in Moscow to emphasize the importance of the negotiations. It wanted Halifax there in person, as Ribbentrop was later, but the government sent William Strang, an able man, but only as adviser to the ambassador.[60]

At the same time that Labour advocated stern measures to check Hitler, it extended the olive branch to the German people. A declaration of June 30, *Why Kill Each Other?*, was an effort to destroy the myth of encirclement. It asserted that the policy was directed solely against the aggressive dictators whose appetites only grew with the feeding; it invited the Germans to come into the circle themselves to join in making a friendly world because "For All of Us Butter Is Better Than Guns."[61]

The signing of the German-Soviet pact on August 23 came as a surprise and a shock to Labour. It produced not only resentment as a double-cross and betrayal but also dismay, because it upset the calculations upon which collective security was based. However, it did not affect Labour's determination. On that same day the National Council decided upon a meeting of the three executives, which two days later broadcast another *Message to the German People;* again the Council drew a distinction between the people and their rulers, but stated emphatically that Britain and France would honor their pledges to Poland. At Paris Citrine presided over a meeting of the International Federation of Trade Unions, which said that the workers would defend their liberties.

When Parliament reassembled on August 24, an Emergency Powers

(Defence) Act was rushed through, with only Lansbury and one other Labour member in the minority of four. At this time Greenwood, still acting as deputy for Attlee, made the first of a series of impressive speeches in support of decisive action, saying that in spite of past disagreements Labour would give unreserved support to the government if it implemented its present policy. That aggression would have to be brought to an end now, was the theme of Labour speakers and leader writers.[62]

When on September 1 Hitler sent his troops into Poland and Danzig, Labour had no doubt about its policy. Meetings of the party executive and parliamentary party were held to consider it, but by this time opposition was confined to a negligible few peace-by-negotiations people and the tiny I.L.P., which was no longer an affiliate. The party executive issued a manifesto pledging support, and the next day the parliamentary party accepted a bill extending the age of conscription to forty-one, although it would have preferred to raise the starting age from eighteen to twenty. At the same time, it unanimously rejected an invitation to join the Chamberlain government.[63]

Late in the session of September 2, in a singularly detached manner, Chamberlain related the recent events, and said that he had as yet received no reply to his warning and nothing on a German withdrawal. Mutterings in all parts of the House indicated dissatisfaction with the speech. As Greenwood stood to reply, Amery cried "Speak for England!" from the Conservative benches. Greenwood rose to the occasion with the noblest speech of his career. He spoke the words that men of all parties wanted to hear. He confessed himself gravely disturbed that, thirty-eight hours after the act of aggression had occurred that automatically should have brought into operation Britain's pledge, the government had done nothing. How much longer would there be vacillation when Britain and all civilization were in peril? He demanded an end to wavering: "I believe that the die is cast and we want to know in time," he said. This speech brought the promise of a reply the next day.[64]

On September 3 the Prime Minister announced that as of 11:00 A.M. Britain was at war. Greenwood followed with the promise of Labour's support in keeping the pledge to Poland and in defending the liberties of Europe. The T.U.C., in session at Bridlington, with but two dissentients gave the same promise.[65] As Greenwood said, Britain entered this war in an atmosphere of relief, composure, and resolution. All Labour doubts about armaments, alliances, and war had been resolved by the acts of the dictators.

12. Labour in the Second World War

The history of the Labour party from 1939 to 1945 is found mainly in the history of the nation. Even before it joined the Coalition party strife had been largely eliminated, and, as an Opposition, it was loyal. Not until the defeat of Germany was politics resumed. Meanwhile, Labour's contribution to the war effort and its participation in the Churchill government not only provided its leaders with valuable experience, but so impressed the country that after victory in Europe the electorate gave Labour a surprisingly strong mandate to guide Britain in the postwar reconstruction.

In 1939, as in 1914, Labour immediately entered an electoral truce whereby the party holding a parliamentary seat would retain it if it fell vacant. The parties agreed that the truce could be terminated at will, and that it did not affect the right to carry on propaganda. So far as the main parties were concerned the agreement was observed, though some small minorities did not feel bound. Of the twenty-four by-elections held before May 1940, eleven were contested by I.L.P., Communist, "Stop-the-War," Pacifist, Fascist, Scottish Nationalist, or Progressive candidates, but their polls were usually negligible.[1]

The Labour leaders did not become deeply involved in the strategy and direction of the military effort. Until the Norwegian fiasco no serious opposition developed on this score. There was some hopeful thinking that the blockade designed by the Ministry of Economic Warfare might lead to a German economic collapse and that an internal revolt would displace Hitler. Much attention, however, was devoted to the home front, especially in the direction of greater production, economic controls, social welfare, and equality of sacrifice.[2] Labour wanted to speed up production for defense. It noted the waste of manpower due to unemployment, which mounted higher in October than it had been in June and until April 1940 remained well above the million mark.

The parliamentary party repeatedly stressed the need for an economic general staff or a minister to direct the economic aspects of the war, but its proposals were rejected. The party wanted effective price controls and rationing, for by December prices were at their highest in thirteen years. Although gasoline and fuel were rationed from the beginning, such control was only slowly applied to food; it was January 1940 before plans for bacon, butter, and sugar were implemented. On grounds both of war necessity and equality of sacrifice the parliamentary party proposed comprehensive rationing, but was defeated. It also, with more success, criticized inequalities and inadequacies in pensions and allowances.[3]

In order to define its position, the party early announced its war aims or peace program. On October 12, 1939, Attlee, who had returned to active leadership, outlined the broad principles of the program in the House of Commons. After discussing it with the Labour executive, he developed the program in a speech of November 8 before party M.P.'s and potential Labour candidates; it was printed as a pamphlet (*Labour's Peace Aims*) and widely circulated.[4] *Labour's Peace Aims* was an effort to avoid the mistakes commonly attributed to the Treaty of Versailles and to prepare for a more cooperative postwar world. It insisted upon replacing the Nazi regime with a government that could be trusted; there would be no dictated peace but one of reconciliation. Laid down as basic principles were the right of every nation to develop its own civilization, the rights of minorities, the renunciation of war as an instrument of policy, the federation of Europe, a strengthened international authority, world economic planning, and the abandonment of imperialism.

In February 1940 the Labour executive restated this program as *Labour, the War, and the Peace* for presentation in the following month to the annual conference at Bournemouth. It emphasized the call to the German people to overthrow Hitler: "Until this accursed Nazi regime is overthrown, there is no hope of Peace between us." Yet it denied any desire to humiliate Germany. It also stigmatized Russia because of the pact with Germany and the recent assault on Finland. Although a few voices were raised against the criticism of Russia and the "fight to a finish tone," the conference approved the statement.[5]

Labour condemned the Russian invasion of Finland of November

30, 1939, as wanton aggression by a great power against a small one. The National Council expressed its horror and indignation that the Soviet government should adopt Nazi methods, and called upon the free governments to give all practicable aid to the Finns. At the invitation of the Finnish trade unions and Social Democrats, it sent to Finland a delegation consisting of Noel-Baker for the Labour party, Citrine for the T.U.C., and John Downie for the Cooperative Union. The delegation brought back a report that, contrary to Communist claims, Finland was a democratic state with a program of social and economic reform. Accordingly, Labour set up a Finland Fund and supported the government's move to send material aid and an expeditionary force. Just how it would have been possible to help Finland without fighting Russia as well as Germany was not made clear. Labour was consistent in opposing aggression, though some, like Dalton, thought that under the circumstances active intervention was quixotic, even "political lunacy" that might lose the war. Fortunately, the insistence of Norway and Sweden upon firm neutrality prevented intervention and an Anglo-Russian conflict.[6]

From the outset of the war the I.L.P. and the Communist party were sources of irritation to Labour. The I.L.P., which interpreted the conflict as a struggle between rival imperialisms, immediately issued an antiwar manifesto calling on the workers to refuse support to any war not waged by a workers' government. It opposed conscription, condemned coalition as "class collaboration," and demanded a negotiated peace, a policy that to Labour seemed unrealistic.[7]

While the I.L.P. adhered consistently to its views, the Communist party twisted and turned as it sought to follow Moscow's changes of direction, on which it was not informed in advance. Its first manifesto on September 2, 1939, heartily approved the war as one for democracy against fascism. In the Commons William Gallacher promised every sacrifice to ensure the defeat of Nazi aggression; the *Daily Worker* would support all measures necessary for the victory of democracy; Pollitt, the party secretary, wrote a pamphlet on *How to Win the War* (1939).

When it appeared, however, that the soviet Union, instead of opposing Hitler, was actually cooperating in the partition of Poland, there was a long debate in the party's central committee. Pollitt and J. R. Campbell upheld the original interpretation, and Palme Dutt and William Rust maintained that the western Allies were fighting an imperialist war. As the latter view prevailed, the first was now "incorrect." Pollitt and Campbell "confessed error," and Pollitt was removed from his office.

On October 7 the party issued a second manifesto that flatly contradicted the first. Many members, unable to stomach this reversal, left the party, and some of them, veterans of the International Brigades in Spain, assisted in training the home guard to resist threatened invasion. For the next twenty-one months, however, the Communist party opposed the war and attempted to sabotage the national effort by exploiting every political, economic, and industrial grievance. It ran some "Stop-the-War" candidates in by-elections. The Labour party retaliated by adding the Russia Today Society, Ltd., the Anti-Fascist Relief Committee, and other satellites to the list of societies whose members were ineligible for membership in the Labour party.[8]

Hitler's sudden invasion of Denmark and Norway on April 9, 1940, put an end to the uneasy quiet of the "Phony War." The disasters on land and sea that followed the Allied attempt to recover Norway left Prime Minister Chamberlain still unruffled and confident, but created a tide of resentment in the country and a division in the Conservative ranks. In confidential meetings with the Tory rebels, who included Amery, Duff Cooper, Harold Macmillan, Lord Cranborne (later Lord Salisbury), and the Liberal Clement Davies, Attlee discovered the depth and extent of the discontent. It was fully revealed on May 7–8, when a tense and angry House of Commons debated the Norwegian fiasco. M.P.'s who were in the armed services came in uniform to put the views of those who had suffered directly from the bungling. When Chamberlain opened with a recital of events and his explanations, the interruptions from both sides indicated the general temper. Attlee followed critically, and concluded by demanding the replacement of the present government with one that could win the war. Conservatives joined in the attack. Amery was particularly devastating in a speech that ended with a famous quotation from Cromwell, now directed to the Prime Minister: "In the name of God, go!"[9]

Although Labour with its quarter of the seats in the House could not alone unseat Chamberlain and form an alternative government, it was now clear that in combination with the dissident Tories and Liberals it might do so. At this point Attlee expected, and Dalton favored, Halifax for the succession, for many Labourites were still suspicious of Churchill, their old antagonist in the days of the General Strike and Trade Disputes Act. But a visit from Brendan Bracken, a rebel Tory, persuaded Attlee not to refuse to serve under Churchill.

Early on May 8 Attlee met with the parliamentary party executive. They determined to press the debate to a division, an important decision, because Chamberlain still had no intention to resign. Therefore, when the debate was resumed, Morrison announced that the vote on the adjournment would be one of censure. Chamberlain accepted it as such. The Conservative majority, some reluctantly, still stood by him, but his normally huge one shrank to 81. Among the 200 who voted against him were 37 National Government supporters, and significantly, some 65 Conservatives either absented themselves or abstained. The result was greeted with cries of "Resign!"

Still hopeful of escaping his difficulties by bringing Labour into a coalition under himself, Chamberlain invited Attlee and Greenwood, along with Churchill and Halifax, to confer with him. Both Attlee and Greenwood refused his offer, but they did agree to go before the Labour party conference, scheduled for Bournemouth on May 13, to submit the question of entering a coalition either under Chamberlain or under someone else. It was a grim moment, because on the next day the German armies moved into the Low Countries. In view of this new crisis Sir Archibald Sinclair, the Liberal leader, tried to convince Attlee that Chamberlain should continue. But Attlee joined Greenwood in a manifesto calling for drastic reconstruction of the government. They went on to Bournemouth, consulted the party, and agreed to enter a coalition, provided that it was not under Chamberlain. This decision, telephoned to London, settled the Prime Minister's fate. He immediately resigned, and Churchill was asked to form a new government.

In Churchill's War Cabinet of five, Labour held two places, Attlee as Lord Privy Seal and Greenwood as minister without portfolio. Chamberlain remained as Lord President of the Council and Lord Halifax as Foreign Secretary. Other Labour men in important ministries were Bevin as Minister of Labour and National Service; Morrison, Minister of Supply, though in October shifted to Home Secretary; A. V. Alexander, First Lord of the Admiralty; Dalton, Minister of Economic Warfare; and Sir William Jowitt, Solicitor-General.

In September 1940 the War Cabinet was enlarged to seven, and Bevin was brought in to raise Labour's number to three. In February 1941 Thomas Johnston became Secretary of State for Scotland. In February 1942 Attlee, now Deputy Prime Minister, took the Dominions Office, and Dalton went to the Board of Trade. Greenwood, who was not a success as a minister, was replaced by Cripps, who was still under expulsion but regarded as Labour. Cripps was also to lead the House of Commons. In November he became Minister of Aircraft Production. Morrison took his place in the War Cabinet, so Labour continued to have three members.

On the whole, this Coalition functioned smoothly, effectively, and without division along partisan lines, even with Chamberlain, who, however, retired on September 30, 1940, and died six weeks later. Attlee and Churchill cooperated fully, and during the Prime Minister's frequent and prolonged absences Attlee presided over the government with an efficiency that won the confidence of his colleagues and raised his prestige in the country.

Other Labour ministers made impressive records. Morrison was an effective chairman of the Cabinet civil-defense committee. Johnston put through a hydroelectric project for the Scottish Highlands. Bevin, whose tremendous energy and ability had hitherto been devoted to the trade unions, now made a great contribution in mobilizing the nation's manpower both for war service and for industry. Dalton was a vigorous head at the Ministry of Economic Warfare, designed to strangle the German war effort; it had its own intelligence service and foreign-relations divisions, and thus could operate independently. In addition, he was the first head of the Special Operations Executive, which was designed to carry on sabotage and subversion in enemy-occupied countries. Two young economists, Hugh Gaitskell and Harold Wilson, made their mark while serving with Dalton. In all this activity a new generation of Labour men received valuable experience in office.

Attlee's acceptance of office was ratified by the party executive and the T.U.C. general council. On May 13 the party conference approved by 2,143,000 to 170,000, and later the same day the parliamentary party did so unanimously. In the Commons the only opposition to the new government came from two I.L.P. members.[10]

Since the duties of a responsible Opposition could not be left to the only M.P.'s outside the Coalition, the four I.L.P.'ers and the one Communist, a new one had to be invented. Attlee therefore omitted some of the older Labour leaders from the ministry so they could fulfill the function of constructive criticism. H. B. Lees-Smith undertook the task of leading the Opposition until his death in 1941, whereupon F. W. Pethick-Lawrence succeeded him.[11]

In 1941 the party conference reaffirmed the coalition decision by

2,430,000 to 19,000. In 1942, the proponents of independence showed slightly greater strength, but were easily voted down by 2,319,000 to 164,000. Not until victory was in sight did the leadership give attention to a method of ending the Coalition.[12]

Due to the far greater national unity about the causes and object of this war than had been the case in the previous one, there was less friction on the home front and a willingness to accept sacrifices. Hence Attlee was able to pilot through the Commons in one day a new Emergency Powers Bill that gave the government unprecedented control over persons and property, while Bevin presided over a redistribution of manpower in spite of all that it meant in the way of state direction and the suspension, where necessary, of trade-union conditions. There was a conviction, however, that out of this war would come great changes; it would destroy old ideas as well as old buildings, and out of all the evil would come something good in the opportunity to build anew and better. Much would be learned from the enforced collective action of the war that socialists could utilize in the peace. Even for the war effort, however, the home front was important, and the civil liberties and social justice were matters of concern.[13]

In the matter of civil liberties Labour found little cause for complaint. It had occasion to protect some anti-Nazi Germans and anti-Fascist Italians, but when Morrison went to the Home Office there was general approval of his handling of problems. The greatest criticism arose over his leniency to the British Fascist leader, Mosley, whom he released from prison on grounds of ill health but left under house arrest. In this instance a large minority of the party wanted to censure Morrison.[14]

When the increased cost of living threatened the standards particularly of those who lived on small fixed incomes, the parliamentary party sought remedial action. It secured rises in the level of pensions. An act of 1941 ended the hated family-means test, under which the resources of an entire family were counted in assessing individual needs, and a personal test substituted. It sought better pay for servicemen and better allowances for their dependents, for a private's pay was only 14 shillings a week and the allowance of a wife and two children, even including the compulsory deduction from the soldier's pay, was only 38 shillings. The party was successful on both scores, so that by 1944 there was no longer a marked disparity between servicemen and civilians. In 1945 it secured the passage of a family-allowance act, which, incidentally, ended a long argument within labor ranks, because some trade unions had long opposed it for fear employers would use it as an argument against wage increases.[15]

Because wartime need showed how costly illness was to the national effort, there was a greatly increased interest in the problem of national health. Labour sought to take advantage of this interest to liberalize and improve the system of national health insurance. The small concessions it won were not enough; Labour wanted a comprehensive medical scheme. At the 1943 conference the party executive proposed a plan to provide medical service for the entire nation. This service would be directed by a minister of health and financed through taxes and rates; doctors for the service would become full-time government servants paid out of public funds. Medical attention would depend upon need, not upon ability to pay.

The government scheme, embodied in a White Paper published in 1944, did not quite meet Labour's wishes, but it was welcomed by the parliamentary party, by the 1944 general conference, and by the doctors of the Socialist Medical Association. Nothing was done before the end of the war, however, and there were indications that the Conservatives and the British Medical Association were not as enthusiastic about a complete health service as Labour wished.[16]

Since the government's piecemeal approach to social security was unsatisfactory to Labour, the party and the T.U.C. pressed for something comprehensive. In June 1941 Greenwood appointed as chairman of an interdepartmental committee to survey the general problem Sir William Beveridge, a Liberal who had contributed much to the social legislation of the Asquith government. His famous report outlining a scheme of social security "from the cradle to the grave" would insure against interruption of earning power and for special expenditures arising at birth, marriage, and death. For this complete coverage of risks, with benefits for unemployment, disability, retirement, medical care, and funeral expenses, the insured would make a weekly contribution to the government.

Labour had nothing but praise for the plan. The government accepted the principles, but postponed implementation until after the war. This decision caused much dissatisfaction; in spite of a conciliatory speech by Morrison, all but two of the nonministerial members of the parliamentary party registered disapproval by voting against the government on an amendment. It was the parliamentary party's one revolt during the Coalition.[17]

Britain's problem of slum clearance and housing, which had been only partly solved before the war, was intensified by wartime destruction and by the virtual cessation of building. In 1943 the Labour executive outlined a program for the future that would be national in scope, provide for planning and controls, and involve public ownership of land. In 1944 it proposed a minister of Cabinet rank to supervise its execution. It was clear that after the peace housing would have high priority on a Labour program. Meanwhile, the party would be watchful that landlords did not take advantage of wartime shortages in order to exploit tenants.[18]

Education suffered from the destruction of school buildings, the enrollment of thousands of teachers in the armed services and war work, and the inadequate equipment of evacuation areas. Although not much could be done in wartime, Labour pressed for a comprehensive postwar scheme. One such scheme was proposed at the 1942 conference, and early in the next year the minimum demands were presented to R. A. Butler, President of the Board of Education. Labour would raise the school leaving age from fourteen to fifteen and ultimately to sixteen, provide nursery schools, limit the size of classes, make medical inspection of pupils mandatory, and set up a unified education authority. The aim was a system that with the aid of financial grants, would enable every child to receive an education determined by his ability rather than by the means of his parents.

The outcome of such pressure was the Education Bill of 1944, which incorporated the above minimum and laid the basis for the present system. The measure was debated and carried even while the war was yet in a critical stage. A compromise on the religious issue, which involved government aid where sectarian religion was taught, violated some principles of Labour's old Nonconformist inheritance, but the party supported the measure as the best compromise obtainable.[19]

Labour's refusal to utilize the emergency to force a program of socialization saw a practical example in 1942 when the parliamentary party, except for four members, joined with the Conservatives to vote down, 329 to 8, an I.L.P. proposal to nationalize the coal mines, a proposition to which, in principle, it was committed.[20] It did, however, note the usefulness of planning and controls that made for increased production, as in agriculture, or for better distribution, so that even in wartime the poorest suffered less from want than they had in peace.

In 1942 the party produced a new policy statement, *The Old World and the New Society,* which was more of a political pamphlet than the *Immediate Programme* had been. It advocated the retention of all useful controls, planned production for community consumption, and public ownership and operation of the essential instruments of production. On the matter of operation the T.U.C. changed its opinion during the war. In 1942 it favored a share in management for workers, but in 1944 it reversed its position. It now took a stand against direct trade-union representation on the boards of nationalized industries; trade-union officials appointed to them should resign their posts in order to avoid an irreconcilable clash of loyalties. The unions preferred their independence and the position of outside pressure groups.[21]

The tiny minority groups continued to be irritants. The I.L.P. did not oppose Labour candidates in by-elections, but called for a peace-by-negotiations, which seemed to Labour utterly unrealistic. In 1945 it bid for reaffiliation but was rejected. A new movement was that of the Common Wealth, founded by Sir Richard Acland, an ex-Liberal, who now believed socialism to be the embodiment of Christian principles. The Common Wealth program resembled Labour's in its support for public ownership of productive resources and the Beveridge social-security plan, but it criticized the Labour leadership and denounced the electoral truce. It appealed to those leftists who under the terms of the truce were prevented from voting for Labour candidates in Conservative seats. In 1943-45 it captured two seats, and in a third by-election aided the success of a "Progressive." The Labour executive banned association with the Common Wealth party, and the 1943 party conference upheld its action.[22]

The Communist party continued to denounce the "imperialist" war. It was instrumental in organizing a so-called People's Convention, which met January 12, 1941, in London. It won the support of such leftists as Dr. Hewlett Johnson, Dean of Canterbury, J. B. S. Haldane, biologist, D. N. Pritt, expelled from Labour for popular-front activity, and V. K. Krishna Menon, then a Labour candidate for Dundee. Actually, it was a Communist satellite. Its demands included higher wages, improved social services, the use of emergency powers to take over large industries, independence for India, friendship for the Soviet Union—which was still in the pact with Germany—a people's peace, and a people's government. A National Council of Labour circular immediately denounced it as another "Innocents' Club" and Communist maneuver. Most Labour members involved quickly dissociated themselves from this move, but a few recalcitrants were expelled and two local parties disaffiliated.[23]

Opposition to the Coalition led Communists to challenge Labour in by-elections, but without success. Upon Lansbury's death, for example, they attempted to capture Bow and Bromley, only to suffer overwhelming defeat by 11,594 votes to 506. The *Daily Worker* carried on a steady campaign against the Labour leaders with charges of chauvinism and deceiving the workers. It exaggerated Britain's failures and misfortunes, magnified losses, and fomented unofficial strikes. It was considered so generally untruthful that on January 22, 1941, Morrison, the Home Secretary, banned further publication on grounds of direct damage to the war effort. The Commons upheld him, 297–11, with only 6 Labourites in the minority. Although the party conference uniformly supported the executive on the Communist issue, on this one it disagreed with its recommendation. Suppression of a newspaper raised the question of freedom of the press, so in an extremely close vote—the margin was only 13,000 in a total vote of 2,475,000—a protest against the ban was carried. In September the *Daily Worker* resumed publication.[24]

When on June 22, 1941, Hitler launched his attack on Russia, the Communist line was again abruptly switched. No longer was the war denounced as "imperialist"; it was now a crusade for freedom and the workers. Thenceforth none surpassed the Communists in their militant support. The *Daily Worker* was as enthusiastic as it had been critical; it campaigned vigorously for the opening of a second front to relieve the pressure on Russia.

Though happy to be relieved of one source of annoyance, Labour again found this unsought ally an embarrassment. The National Council joined the party and T.U.C. executives in a statement welcoming the cooperation of Britain and Russia, but branding the Communist party as so unstable and irresponsible that association with it was impossible. The 1942 party conference sustained this view, and by 1,899,000 votes to 132,000 turned down a plea for working-class unity. A year later the atmosphere was slightly different. The impressive deeds of the Red Army, the dissolution of the Comintern, and the optimism about postwar coexistence modified somewhat the distrust of Communists. Once more that party sought affiliation with Labour, and Pollitt was profuse in promises to loyally accept all the conditions and obligations of membership. Some Labourites, including the Mineworkers, were ready to take these words at face value, but after Morrison's full and effective refutation of the Communist argument the conference rejected the request by 1,951,000 to 712,000. Too often the British party had revealed its subservience to Moscow.[25]

Labour had little to do with the shaping of Britain's foreign policy during the war. That matter was left to Churchill and Halifax, the Foreign Secretary, both Conservatives. Such was the urgency of the situation, however, that there was far more agreement than disagreement in this sphere.

Labour recognized Britain's need for allies. Before the war it pressed for alliance with Russia, partly because the isolationism of the United States appeared unshakable. Events soon altered the possibilities, because the Russo-German treaty put alliance with Russia out of the question, while ties with the United States grew stronger. Long before the United States entered the war, the destroyer-bases deal, the lend-lease legislation, and the military staff talks rejoiced all Britons. Chairman James Walker told the Labour conference of June 1941 that for all practical purposes America was in the war. The Roosevelt-Churchill Atlantic Charter (August 1941) united the countries ideologically in terms Labour approved. After Pearl Harbor the party denounced the Japanese action and declared its pride that the United States and Great Britain should be standing together in the momentous struggle for freedom.[26]

With the German invasion of Russia, anti-Soviet feeling in Britain yielded to the need and desire for cooperation. The National Council of Labour condemned the German aggression, sent warm greetings to the Soviet people, and promised support against the common enemy. Party sentiment now considered the future of Europe and of civilization dependent upon the continuation of good relations with the Soviet Union. Labour welcomed the Anglo-Soviet treaty of May 26, 1942, with its promises of collaboration in war and peace. The executive planned a mission to Russia, but it had to be postponed until after the war.

Now that the three great powers were joined in a common cause, the chances of future cooperation appeared bright. Much was hoped from the "summit" conferences of the leaders. The Tehran meeting of November 1943, at which the heads of Britain, the United States, and Russia met for the first time, was viewed hopefully as providing the necessary personal understanding. Labour was pleased, too, when Roosevelt and Churchill met Chiang Kai-shek at Cairo, because like most Westerners it overrated Chiang's strength. The Yalta conference, though later a subject of violent controversy, was at the time welcomed as further proof of the desire for complete and wholehearted cooperation.[27]

On intervention in the affairs of Greece and Italy differences rent the Labour party. On Greece the Labour members of the War Cabinet and most of the parliamentary party accepted the official policy of restoring the King to the throne and even the use of British troops in Athens to suppress E.L.A.S. (National Popular Liberation Army), the military arm of E.A.M. (National Liberation Front), a resistance group dominated by a communist minority manifestly intent upon a seizure of power. E.L.A.S. often attacked and even destroyed other resistance forces and terrorized the populations in areas under its control.

Since the press tended to give an idealized buildup to all forces of the resistance, there was little understanding in Britain of the real nature of E.A.M.–E.L.A.S. In the belief that E.A.M.–E.L.A.S. faithfully represented democratic Greece, many Labourites gave it their sympathy and accused Churchill of using British troops to impose an unpopular monarch upon an unwilling people. The Labourites in the War Cabinet, however, shared responsibility for the official policy. Churchill's visit to Athens, the installation of Archbishop Damaskinos as regent, and British advice to the King not to return until authorized by a plebiscite reconciled most of the parliamentary party.

In the case of Italy there was discontent when it was reported that the British government opposed the inclusion of Count Sforza as Foreign Minister in the new Italian cabinet. Count Sforza was popularly admired for his long and courageous stand as an anti-fascist, but British official circles disapproved of his demand for the immediate abdication of the King as his price for entry into an Italian government. The Churchill government held that since the existing combination of the King and Marshal Badoglio was proving useful, it should continue until the liberation of Rome, which would enable a large segment of the Italian people to decide for themselves the question of the monarchy. Although the leaders of the anti-fascist parties in Rome sent the British government a message of agreement with this policy, there was in Britain a suspicion that Churchill was motivated by sympathy for the King.

At the Labour conference of 1944 there were rank-and-file objections to the government's policies on these two issues. They were linked in a resolution that the administration of liberated territories should be left to the democratic control of the inhabitants without interference from or direction by outside forces, either political or military. Even though Bevin gave a full explanation of the government's Mediterranean policy and of the Labour ministers' responsibility for it, this resolution was carried. It was in accord with Labour's ideal of self-determination, but it was based on lack of knowledge of

the true character of E.A.M.–E.L.A.S. and of what it might mean in
the way of future Communist control of Greece. The British government was partly to blame for failing to make known the totalitarian
aims and terroristic methods of the E.A.M.–E.L.A.S., and in the case
of Count Sforza that the motives for opposition to his maneuvers were
not imperialist.[28]

In 1944, when victory appeared probable, Labour issued a new
statement of peace aims, *The International Post-War Settlement,*
based upon a draft by Dalton. Labour had no interest in a vindictive
peace, the dismemberment of Germany, or its relegation to the status
of a minor agricultural country. It expected Germany to remain a
major industrial power. It hoped to avoid the features of the Treaty
of Versailles it had found objectionable, but it intended to make a
repetition of German aggression impossible. Accordingly, the document sought to strike at the roots of fascism and war, provide for collective defense against possible aggression, lay foundations for general
economic well-being, and promote democracy and freedom.

On the question of responsibility for the war, the early theory that
the German people were innocent victims of a few Nazis had yielded
to one that a large proportion of them shared the guilt. There were
good Germans, the document said, but "The trouble is, not that good
Germans don't exist, but that they are singularly ineffective in restraining the bad Germans." Although it would be difficult to determine how many were guilty, the war criminals should be tried and
punished. Repetition of the aggression should be made impossible by
disarming Germany and by a period of military, economic, and financial control, to be accompanied by an educational program to counter
the effects of Nazi teachings. Reparations should be exacted, but the
prolonged and futile aftermath of Versailles should be avoided by
limiting them to a brief period of five or six years during which Germany should return all identifiable loot, provide materials and labor
for the reconstruction of devastated areas, and pay the costs of armies
of occupation. It was considered premature to redraw boundaries in
Europe, but when done it would be advisable to repatriate German
minorities left outside Germany.

Dalton, who had long been interested in the Zionist cause, felt that
the unhappy situation of the surviving Continental Jews called for
an end to hesitation on the Palestine issue. He included a statement
in the document calling for unlimited Jewish immigration; as Jews
came in, the Arabs should be encouraged to move out. Since the Arabs
had such wide domains elsewhere, ran the statement, "they must not

claim to exclude the Jews from this small area of Palestine, less than the size of Wales"; indeed, by agreement with the neighboring Arab states, the existing Palestine should be expanded. It was a facile suggestion that overlooked the unwillingness of Muslim and Christian Palestinians to move out of Palestine as well as the bitter opposition of the neighboring states to expanding Palestine at their expense.

Instead of the straight anti-imperialism often voiced by Labour spokesmen in the past, this document stressed the constructive side of the Commonwealth and its possibilities for good in the postwar world, especially if enhanced by close cooperation and the strengthening of consultative machinery for external policy. It urged the planned exploitation of colonial resources with an increased development fund, but primarily for the benefit of the peoples of those areas. At the same time, these peoples should be guided toward self-government with the hope that they would remain within the Commonwealth as the former Dominions had done.

This policy included India. Earlier Labour had approved the Coalition's offer of August 1940 to grant India full Dominion status after the war, and was deeply disappointed at the failure of the Cripps mission to get the mutually hostile Indian groups to accept it. In *The Old World and the New Society* (1942), Labour showed a readiness to give the Indians full responsibility, both in the central government and in the provinces; independence, however, should await the outcome of the war and the agreement of rival parties, Hindu and Muslim. As the possibility of independence drew nearer, however, those communities revealed an increasing distaste for uniting in it.

The 1944 statement urged the projection of the Anglo-Soviet-American partnership into the postwar world, which would surely be troubled without it. The three big powers, however, should not dominate, but become the nucleus of a world organization, which should be provided with a sufficient and readily available armed force to deter aggression. But absence of war was not enough; the international organization should further world cooperation through a greatly strengthened I.L.O. and new agencies to facilitate production and exchange. In April 1945 Attlee, Ellen Wilkinson, and George Tomlinson were Labour members of the British delegation that helped to draw up the charter of the United Nations in San Francisco.[29]

Just as after the First World War, the socialists of western Europe looked to British Labour to take the lead in reconstructing the Labour and Socialist International. The first steps were taken in March 1945 at a conference in London under the chairmanship of Dalton. The conference also issued a declaration of policy which followed closely that of the recent Labour statement.[30]

When the Coalition was formed, its members assumed that with victory in the field it would be dissolved and normal constitutional procedure restored. Japan's entry into the war raised the question of whether victory applied to the European war alone or would await the outcome in the Pacific. When delegates concerned over the future of Labour's social program raised this issue at the 1943 party conference, Attlee pledged that the matter would be submitted to the conference at the end of the war with Germany. In 1944 the executive committee promised that there would be no repetition of the 1918 "coupon" election designed to prolong the Coalition into the peace. Labour, it was felt, could not continue indefinitely as a junior partner, dependent upon a Tory majority for the implementation of its social program.[31]

After the failure of the last German offensive in the winter of 1944–45, the outcome was so little in doubt that party differences reappeared. While Attlee asserted that only Labour could successfully meet the problems of reconstruction and that a planned economy was essential, the Conservatives demanded the speedy removal of wartime controls. Although the Conservatives had a program of social reform, they would wait to see what postwar conditions were before proceeding with it; the Labourites wanted to take first steps immediately.

Churchill wished to keep the Coalition and to postpone an election until the end of the war in the Pacific, but met disagreement both in his own party and from Labour, partly because of the belief that the Japanese defense would be stubborn and the conquest piecemeal. Conservatives like Beaverbrook wanted a June election in order to cash in on the victory in Europe and the immense prestige of their leader. Attlee showed an inclination to accept the Prime Minister's view, but Morrison, an astute politician, and nearly all the party executive wanted an October poll. An October election would give both parties time to make up a more complete voters' register and give servicemen a better opportunity to acquaint themselves with issues and candidates.

Attlee went to the Blackpool conference, which opened May 21, 1945, to sound party opinion. It was definitely against awaiting victory in the Pacific, for the present Parliament had already lasted nearly ten years, or double the legal term. This decision ended any prospect of postponement. The national executive rejected Churchill's suggestion of a referendum on the issue, which would have been a constitutional innovation, so on May 23 the Prime Minister resigned and the Coalition came to an end. He formed a "caretaker government," which was mainly Conservative with a few National Liberals and nonparty men, and set June 15 as the date for dissolving Parliament and July 5 as polling day. Labour went into Opposition.[32]

So ended the famous Coalition. The members parted on friendly terms. The Labourites acknowledged the dauntless courage and inspiring leadership of the great Prime Minister who was mainly responsible for the harmonious cooperation through the time of trial to final triumph. Churchill responded with a generous testimonial to the services of the Labour ministers. "No Prime Minister," he wrote, "could ever have wished for more loyal and steadfast colleagues than I had found with the Labour party."[33]

Let Us Face the Future, a Labour policy statement based on a draft by Morrison and adopted in May at the Blackpool conference, contained the program upon which the party fought the election. The statement was general on foreign policy, where it urged the continued cooperation of the three great powers within an international organization, but specific on domestic issues. It said that a Labour government would provide full employment and high production by maintaining purchasing power through good wages, social services, social insurance, and a system of taxation that would bear less heavily on the lower-income groups. It emphasized that the wartime experience should be used as a basis for developing a plan to promote British industry. New industries should be located to benefit depressed areas. The test of efficiency should be applied to individual industries; if they were not serving the nation well, the government should intervene. Most small businesses rendering good service could be left to continue their work, but some large basic ones were ripe for public ownership and management. Among the latter were fuel and power (coal, gas, and electricity), inland transport (rail, road, air, and canal transport), and iron and steel. All had been mentioned in the prewar nationalization program, though not clearly in the case of iron and steel.

Efficiency was the objective most emphasized; nationalization was stressed as a practical remedy rather than as a political end. In the case of the Bank of England, likewise marked for nationalization, the objective was effective control over capital investment and, incidentally, insurance against political obstruction. For other monopolies and cartels there would be firm controls. The statement warned further that these proposals for a single Labour government were only an installment; they placed no limit upon later socialization. No attempt was made to define that limit; for the moment Labour would keep to key industries.

Among the issues emphasized housing had a high priority; Labour would stress it until every family had a good standard of accommodation. Wartime controls of rents and prices would be kept. Agriculture would be planned to increase the supply of foodstuffs. The principle of land nationalization was affirmed, but the program was limited to acquiring land for public purposes where necessary. Labour promised the implementation of the Education Act of 1944, a national health service, and legislation on social insurance.

Labour entered the campaign a united party. Moves by Ellen Wilkinson and Laski, who wanted a more colorful leader, to replace Attlee with Morrison came to nothing. The success of the Common Wealth party in recent by-elections gave reason for optimism. Accordingly, Labour put up 604 candidates for the 640 seats in the new House of Commons. It was allotted 10 of the 24 political broadcasts, for which it arranged a coordinated presentation of its program by as many different speakers in a manner that bettered its chief competitor's performance.

Churchill opened the series on June 4 with a broadcast in which the atmosphere of good humor gave way to one of bitter invective. Instead of dealing with the Labour program, he launched a virulent attack on socialism, which he described as abhorrent to freedom and inseparably interwoven with totalitarianism; he charged that socialists found a free Parliament odious, would resort to a Gestapo, and would threaten the savings of the humblest. His diatribe might have carried an excited public meeting, but not people listening quietly in their own homes. Attlee's response next evening was in complete contrast. He easily disposed of the vague charges that few had taken seriously and gave a reasoned exposition of Labour's constructive proposals. The exchange was all to the advantage of Attlee, whose prestige was much enhanced by it.

A few days later attention centered on the "Laski affair." When Churchill let it be known that he would invite Attlee to accompany him to the forthcoming Potsdam conference, Laski, chairman of the Labour executive for the year, issued an indiscreet statement that, in order not to bind a future Labour government, Attlee should go solely as an observer. Although Attlee promptly gave the assurance that Churchill asked, namely, that he would be no mere observer, the Conservatives seized upon the matter, raised great clamor, and charged that the leader of the parliamentary party would be controlled by an outside socialist caucus headed by "Gauleiter Laski."

On June 30 Churchill featured the issue in the last of his four broadcasts, in which he portrayed a Labour Prime Minister as a tool of a non-parliamentary body, an outside committee (i.e., the Labour party executive committee, now 27 in number) to which State secrets might be communicated. Interchanges of letters followed, all published in the press, in which Churchill repeated his charges, while Attlee, saying that Churchill was exercising his imagination, tolerantly and patiently explained the Labour party constitution and flatly asserted that a Labour government would be under no extra-constitutional control. Again the advantage was with Attlee.[34]

Yet Churchill was not entirely without grounds for his doubts. Ordinarily, the parliamentary Labour party has been independent in its operation, and the subtleties of its relation to the party executive and party conference have not been widely understood. But it was true that in the post-1931 reaction against MacDonaldism the National Council on occasion asserted the right to control Lansbury's actions, and the dispute between Hugh Gaitskell and the annual conference over unilateral nuclear disarmament (1960–61) showed that internal conflict over the relation between the parliamentary party and the party conference could still arise.

The issue that most concerned the electorate was housing, which was mentioned in 97 per cent of the campaign speeches of Labour candidates and almost as frequently by their rivals. In a Gallup poll 41 per cent of the voters gave it first place, which put it far ahead of any other issue; it was of significance, too, that more of them thought Labour would handle this problem better than the Conservatives. Food rationing, full employment, social insurance, pensions, and agricultural production were all debated. The Conservatives played up their leader. On the basic issue of private enterprise versus nationalization, Conservatives had more to say about the latter's defects than Labour did about its merits. Labour devoted much attention to the social-reform proposals, and emphasized its doubts that the Conservatives could be trusted to implement such a program.

Rivaling Labour in insistence on a social program were the Liberals, who had the advantage of claiming Beveridge as a member. The Communists now spoke much of democracy and of what could be accomplished under it. The Common Wealth, farther left than Labour, stood for full socialism. The I.L.P., which was pacifist, termed the Pacific war "imperialist."

Polling day was followed by three weeks of suspense pending the arrival of the servicemen's ballots. Churchill and Attlee left to attend the opening sessions of the Potsdam conference, where both noted with some surprise how Attlee was cheered by the soldiers. Churchill fully expected to win, and most predictions were for a Conservative victory. Even the *Daily Herald* and the *New Leader* thought that Churchill's personal popularity would return him to office, though narrowly. Too few paid attention to a Gallup survey taken about ten days before the poll which revealed 47 per cent for Labour, 41 per cent for the Conservatives and allies, and 10 per cent for the Liberals, which came within about one per cent of accuracy.[35]

On July 26 Churchill and Attlee were back in London for the count. To the amazement of both, it became clear soon after the first return that the result was not only a Labour victory but a Labour landslide. The party captured 393 seats, a majority of 146 over all others. The Conservatives and their allies won 213, the Liberals 12, the Independents 14, the Irish Nationalists 2, the I.L.P. 3, the Communists 2, and the Common Wealth one. The Labour candidates polled 11,992,292 votes, the Conservatives and their allies 9,960,809, and the Liberals 2,239,668. The prosocialist total was about 12,008,-512 and the anti-socialist 11,942,632, so adherents of the socialist policy could claim a balance of about 65,880. Of the total poll Labour, with its 48 per cent, won nearly two-thirds of the seats; the Conservatives with two-fifths received fewer than one-third of them, and the Liberals with one-tenth secured less than one-fiftieth. Accordingly, Labour got the benefit of the British electoral system, which exaggerated the victory and enabled the winning party to govern.

Most of the large towns, including London, Manchester, Liverpool, Leeds, Bradford, Bristol, Cardiff, and Edinburgh, returned a majority of Labour men; some sent solid delegations. Most striking was the case of Birmingham, which, though solidly Conservative in 1935, now chose 10 Labourites and 3 Conservatives. As compared with 1929, Labour's previous high, its greatest gains were in the London area, the Eastern counties, Lancashire and Cheshire, and the Midlands. It held its own or slightly improved its position in Wales, Scotland, Yorkshire, and the Northeast. It made no great inroads in the wealthier areas—Bournemouth was still Conservative by over 20,000—but even in the Southwest it won 25 per cent of the vote. The servicemen voted Labour.

This great victory gave the younger Labourites their opportunity. The party was encouraged to see returned so many able men, still in their thirties or even in their twenties, who had been compelled to fight in constituencies hitherto hopeless. There were 121 trade-union-sponsored candidates elected, 23 Cooperative party, and 248 divisional Labour party. The number of this last group indicated the greater diversity of occupation; professional men were now represented in great numbers—28 journalists, 54 educators, 41 lawyers, 31 businessmen, 11 medical men, and 31 other professions.[36]

Labour had swept to victory like the Whigs in 1832 and the Liberals in 1906; everyone knew it was a revolution—British style. The Conservatives paid for their prewar diplomatic record, including Munich, and for their conduct of the election campaign. More important, looking ahead, the country felt that it could better trust Labour with the task of rebuilding and in sharing equitably the burden of doing it.

On the evening of the count, Churchill went to Buckingham Palace to tender his resignation. A few minutes later Attlee followed to receive his appointment as Prime Minister. The transfer of power had taken place.

13. Labour's Great Ministry

The third Labour government, the first to have majority backing in the Commons, implemented its short-term domestic measures outlined in *Labour's Immediate Programme* (1937). Its legislative record rivaled that of the first Gladstone and Campbell-Bannerman ministries. It had an important role in international affairs and took decisive steps toward transforming the Empire into the Commonwealth. Not all went well. Its years in office were associated with shortages and "austerity," but any government would have found problems baffling in the political and economic distortions of the postwar world, in which Britain was peculiarly vulnerable. Insofar as by-elections were a test of popular approval, it is notable that this government in its four and one-half years did not lose a single parliamentary seat.

Attlee, the new Prime Minister, was now experienced in governmental affairs. As party leader for ten years and as wartime Deputy Prime Minister, he had gained stature, prestige, and acquaintance with both politicians and civil servants. After the election Morrison tried to postpone his forming a government until the parliamentary party could debate the leadership and select colleagues to help him form it. But when Attlee refused to comply, this procedure, laid down after 1931 to check another arbitrary MacDonald, was tacitly dropped.

Attlee decided to abandon the small War Cabinet, and return to the larger one, twenty in this case, though Bevin, Foreign Secretary, Morrison, Lord President and Leader of the House of Commons, Greenwood, Lord Privy Seal, and Dalton, Chancellor of the Exchequer, would have duties broader than any department and constitute an unofficial inner Cabinet. Attlee hesitated briefly over the assignments of Bevin and Dalton. At first he intended to give Bevin the Exchequer and Dalton the Foreign Office, which was in accordance with the expressed desires of each. In a matter of hours he reversed the assignments. It is true that King George VI, when consulted, exercised his right to make suggestions; since foreign affairs were so important, his hope was that Bevin would take that office.[1] The major reason for the shift, however, was not royal intervention, but something more personal. Morrison, who would become a coordinator of home affairs, never got along well with Bevin, and if Bevin went to the Foreign Office, the two would not clash. So Attlee made the change, and Dalton, an authority on public finance, went to the Exchequer. For a time, Attlee doubled as Minister of Defence.[2]

Other Cabinet members were Sir Stafford Cripps, recently readmitted to the party, President of the Board of Trade; Lord Jowitt, Lord Chancellor; A. V. Alexander, First Lord of the Admiralty; J. Chuter Ede, Home Secretary; Viscount Addison, Dominions Secretary and Leader of the House of Lords; Lord Pethick-Lawrence, Secretary of State for India and Burma; G. H. Hall, Colonies; J. J. Lawson, War; Viscount Stansgate, Air; J. Westwood, Secretary for Scotland; G. A. Isaacs, Minister of Labour; Emanuel Shinwell, Fuel and Power; Ellen Wilkinson, Education; Aneurin Bevan, Health; and T. Williams, Agriculture and Fisheries.

Changes later reduced the size of the Cabinet to seventeen. In October 1946 the three service ministries were united under one Cabinet Minister for Defence, A. V. Alexander. In 1947 Greenwood was dismissed and replaced by Addison, whose office was filled by Noel-Baker as Secretary of State for Commonwealth Relations. Shinwell was dropped from the Cabinet but remained in the ministry. Ellen Wilkinson, who died in 1947, was succeeded by G. Tomlinson. Pethick-Lawrence was replaced by Lord Listowel (for Burma only), and G. H. Hall by A. Creech Jones. Because of a budget indiscretion Dalton yielded to Cripps in November 1947, and Harold Wilson, aged thirty-one, went to the Board of Trade. A year later Dalton rejoined the Cabinet as Chancellor for the Duchy of Lancaster. It was a Cabinet to which all sections of the movement contributed—veterans and new men, trade unions, cooperators, and left wing. In spite of this diversity, the Cabinet members functioned as a team.

At times some of the team wished for greater drive at the center, and in 1947 Cripps maneuvered to replace Attlee with Bevin. Although the move gained the support of a group of M.P.'s, Bevin rejected the suggestion with some indignation, so nothing came of it. Attlee was unperturbed. No one else enjoyed as much confidence and support in all sections of the party.[3]

Labour now had office with power, but it was apparent that economic and social change would have to be effected under most unfavorable conditions. Peace was accompanied not by plenty but by shortages and controls, restrictions and "austerity," for Britain had knowingly thrown all its resources into the war effort.

The basic reason behind this situation was the unbalanced nature of the British economy. For over a century Britain had lived by exchanging goods and services for the food and raw materials it could not produce. About two-thirds of the food and most of the raw materials had to be imported. The exceptions were coal, a third of the iron ore, and a sixth of the wool. The imports were paid for by the export of manufactures, the income from investments abroad, and by services such as shipping, banking, and insurance. The war sadly diminished all these sources of income. With world trade disorganized, many former markets were gone and services idle. More than one-fourth of all foreign investments had been relinquished and sold for munitions. Factories, docks, and shipping facilities had been largely destroyed. Britain owed nearly three billion pounds, mainly to the United States but also to India and Egypt. Over four million houses, one-third of all in Britain, had been destroyed or damaged. Victory in the field could not conceal the fact that Britain had suffered great losses at home.

Given time and transitional aid, the government might hope to guide the restoration of the shattered economy. But it had hardly taken office when on September 2, 1945, the American lend-lease program was abruptly ended. The decision to halt the program was taken in Washington in accordance with the terms of the wartime measure, but—as it transpired later—without perceiving the consequences in Britain or giving the British government an opportunity to suggest alternatives. The decision was a shock and a body blow to the government.[4] It had to seek loans to tide the country over until industry could be rebuilt and exports revived and expanded, which appeared the only way of quickly effecting a balance of payments. Lord Keynes was sent to Washington as principal negotiator, but met some hard bargaining. A loan of $3,750,000,000 at two per cent was finally granted in July 1946, but on condition that within a year sterling would be made convertible and trade discrimination ended. The stipulation on trade discrimination referred to imperial preference and to the reciprocal-trade agreements to which Britain had resorted when confronted by a world of protective tariffs.

This loan, together with a loan of $1,250,000,000 from Canada, relieved immediate anxieties and provided some time for planned recovery. But the dollars ran out faster than anticipated, partly because of depreciation, which sent dollar prices up by over a third, and partly because a portion of Britain's share of food for occupied Germany had to be paid in dollars. Instead of lasting five years, the loans would be gone in half that time.[5]

It was against this background of urgent need to expand exports and cut imports that the Labour government decided to retain war-time controls over industry and the rationing of most consumer goods. Licenses were required for exports and imports. The government controlled the importation and distribution of raw cotton. It allocated supplies of coal, steel, machine tools, and other essentials for industry, giving preference to firms manufacturing for export. Many famous lines were now earmarked "for export only."

In order to decrease food imports, wartime controls on agriculture were maintained. The farmer received an assured market and guaranteed prices, but in return had to accept crop control and inspection for maintenance of standards. Consumer goods were rationed, both to decrease imports and to ensure "fair shares." Even bread, unrationed during the war, was on the list. Few labor controls were kept, but on the whole labor responded to persuasion and to the slogans of "Export or Die" and "Work or Want." The trade-union leaders were generally in line with a policy of wage restraint and increased productivity. Days lost in strikes amounted to about one-sixteenth of those of the post-1918 years.

The budgets of Dalton, Chancellor of the Exchequer, had social and equalitarian objectives. He raised income-tax allowances to a point where some two million persons were wholly relieved and decreased the standard rate from ten shillings in the pound to nine, but raised the surtax. He remitted the purchase tax on some essentials. He lowered the death duty on smaller estates and raised the exemption limit to the point where only about 50,000 of 600,000 estates left each year would pay the duty. He provided for the government's acceptance of land in payment for taxes, so that it could be used for national parks and the purposes of the National Trust and the Youth Hostels Association. His cheap-money policy encouraged local authorities to proceed with rehousing. More was provided for education, the social services, and food subsidies. Such budgeting, followed also by Cripps, Dalton's successor, tended to redistribute the national income.[6]

The year 1947 was a difficult one. It began with an exceptionally severe winter in which a considerable number of livestock perished. A heavy snowfall disrupted transport, accentuated a coal shortage, and caused loss of production. In the summer free convertibility between the pound and the dollar, of which Dalton was so fearful, resulted in such a rapid drain of gold and dollars that within six weeks of its introduction it had to be suspended. In order to cut imports and close the dollar gap Cripps, who became Chancellor of the Exchequer in November 1947, imposed a regime of austerity upon all classes. One could buy 14 pence worth of meat a week, 2 ounces of bacon, 3 or 4 of butter or margarine, and 8 of sugar. In 1950 the meat ration was even less, 8 pence worth. It was the same with clothing and fuel. There was some inevitable grumbling over the paper work, the ration cards, and the coupons, but observers generally commented approvingly upon the patience with which the system was accepted and the fairness with which it was administered; it was a spirit that inspired many Americans to send an "unsolicited gift" or a CARE package.

From 1948 to 1950 the situation was eased by Marshall Plan aid from the United States, which was, in effect, a resumption of lend-lease. The Marshall Plan took its name from a suggestion of General Marshall, but owed much to Bevin for seeing its possibilities and actually bringing it into existence. It enabled Britain to secure the necessities to get production going again. In 1949 devaluation of the pound from $4.03 to $2.80 gave a momentary advantage, too. By 1950 the export target of 175 per cent of prewar volume was achieved. It had to be done by completely reorienting exports. Whereas in the nineteenth century the staples were coal and textiles, those items were now surpassed by chemicals, motor cars, electrical and engineering equipment, iron and steel manufactures, and aircraft. The adaptability and enterprise of British industry was heartening, but much of the gain was cancelled by the inflated cost of imports and in 1951 and after by the demands of rearmament.[7]

Backed by a strong majority in the Commons, the Labour government proceeded to enact the program outlined in *Let Us Face the Future* (1945). Nationalization was something upon which the parties were in basic disagreement. To Labour it was desirable, not as an end in itself, but as a useful tool both for planning for high productivity and for a better distribution of wealth and greater social equality. The Conservatives and Liberals were opposed on principle, although they were willing to accept and use it when the occasion demanded. Indeed, it was a Conservative administration that in 1926, when it inaugurated the B.B.C. and the electric grid, set the pattern of nationalization with control by government boards, and a Conservative-dominated government that nationalized coal royalties in 1938 and the British Overseas Airways Corporation (B.O.A.C.) in 1939. Labour now nationalized the Bank of England, the coal-mining industry, civil aviation, telecommunications, electricity and gas supply, inland transport, and iron and steel.

This short list was selective; Labour had no plan to do everything at once, as in Russia. The industries concerned were basic to the economy or in the nature of public utilities. Except in the case of the Bank of England, the reasons emphasized were the old Fabian ones of economy and efficiency. Consumer interest was important; Guild Socialist ideas and thoughts of workers' control were absent. The program was Fabian in its insistence upon compensation and in its experimental character. The results would have a bearing upon future policy, but the program was not regarded as a step toward total nationalization.

The Bank of England, the only central bank in private hands, was first on the list. Dalton introduced his bill to nationalize the Bank in October 1945, and on March 1, 1946, it went into effect. The Bank was continued as a corporation under a board of directors consisting of a governor, a deputy governor, and sixteen directors appointed by the government. This board would supervise the daily operations, but, when necessitated by the public interest, the Chancellor of the Exchequer in consultation with the governor could decide policy. Likewise in the national interest it would be possible through the Bank for the board to control the joint-stock banks. The stockholders were compensated with government stock in an amount that at 3 per cent per annum would yield an income equal to the average received over the past twenty years. Since the dividend rate had been constant for a somewhat longer period, this settlement meant that the former holders had exactly what they had been accustomed to receive.

The measure met with little opposition. Churchill, now leader of the Opposition, said the bill raised no question of principle. He gave no call to oppose and did not vote against it, though some Conservatives condemned it as unnecessary and dangerous. The citadel of finance was socialized without difficulty, which falsified the predictions of some Marxists who held that in order to frustrate any such step in socialization, the forces of reaction would mobilize all resources from the House of Lords to physical force against it. Instead, Lord Catto, the governor of the bank, agreed over a cup of tea with Dalton to continue in that office under the new regime, in which he proved most loyal and cooperative.[8]

Coal was next on Labour's list. Here the government began its nationalization-of-industry program, not with an industry flourishing and profitable like chemicals, but with a most difficult and unpromising one. The problem was to rescue what had been neglected, modernize what had been chaotic and backward, and administer what was notorious for a long record of bad labor relations. Yet the need was not seriously questioned; coal was so vital to every industry and service that the British economy could not prosper unless the industry was doing well. Modernization and mechanization could come only with unification. Nationalization had been seriously proposed ever since the 1919 Sankey commission, and was now supported by the Liberals as well as by Labour.

The task of preparing a measure fell to Shinwell, Minister of Fuel and Power, who noted that in spite of many years of discussion, Labour had nothing tangible in the way of a plan. His Coal Industry Nationalization Act was passed in July 1946, and January 1, 1947, set as vesting day. The entire coal-mining industry passed into the ownership of a board of nine, consisting of a chairman, a deputy chairman, and seven directors, all full-time salaried officials chosen by the Minister. Operation rested with the board, but the Minister of Fuel and Power could give general directions on matters affecting the national interest, and the board had to reach agreement with him on all large-scale planning activities. Two consumers' councils, one for industrial and one for domestic users of coal, were to be set up under the Minister. Compensation to ex-owners was determined by a special arbitration tribunal, which fixed upon a global sum of £164,660,000, to be divided among the individual companies by special valuation boards.[9]

The railways, like coal, presented a task of rescue from distress, financial solvency where a subsidy had been necessary—they lost £60,000,000 during their last year under private ownership—and restoration after long neglect. There had been much sentiment for nationalization during the earlier war; it was strong after the second war when the prospect of vast expenditure for new equipment became apparent. Labour wanted a service that was not only nationalized but unified and coordinated to include all forms of inland transport—railways, canals, and long-distance road haulage. Because long-distance haulage was very profitable, the measure roused stiff Conservative and Liberal opposition.

The Transport Bill, introduced in December 1946, became law on August 6, 1947. It set up a Transport Commission to consist of between four and eight members appointed by the Minister of Transport and responsible to him. Five executives would manage the railways, docks and inland waterways, long-distance road transport, London transport, and the railway hotels and catering services. Consultative committees, central and regional, were authorized for the protection of the public interests. Compensation to former owners would be paid according to the average market value of their securities on certain specified dates; it proved to be a 3 per cent stock. Soon a new sign, "British Road Services," appeared on trucks on all public highways.[10]

The nationalization of civil aviation, telecommunications, electricity, and gas brought little opposition. The previously nationalized B.O.A.C. continued its service throughout the war, but the domestic airways were taken over by a government agency and most of them closed down. Labour's Civil Aviation Act, which went into effect on August 1, 1946, set up two new corporations, British European Airways and British South American Airways (the latter merged with B.O.A.C. in 1949), which with B.O.A.C. would be given a monopoly of scheduled air services. Telecommunications likewise raised few objections; they closely resembled the postal and telegraph services, long since nationalized. The Cable and Wireless Act, which went into effect on January 1, 1947, kept in being, as a government-owned company, the British company that had operated those services. However, control passed into the hands of a government board responsible to the Postmaster-General, while ex-owners received government stock in return.

The production of electricity had been in the hands of private companies and local authorities, who sold it to the Central Electricity Board, the government-owned body set up in 1926 to operate the national grid; this board, in turn, sold it to local authorities and companies for retail to consumers. The Electricity Act, which became law on August 13, 1947, brought all three stages of the industry under public ownership. A central authority was set up consisting of a chairman and 9 to 11 members under the Minister of Fuel and Power. It would have charge of generating and supplying electricity, conduct research and training, and supervise the fourteen area boards that were in charge of distribution.

The Gas Act, which went into effect on July 30, 1948, set up a similar but—because of the different nature of the service—less centralized system. It provided for a central council and twelve area boards, but the council would serve mainly as a common meeting ground for discussing policy with the Minister of Fuel and Power. Area consultative committees would be set up for both electricity and gas. In both instances compensation followed the example set in the case of transport; former owners were issued guaranteed 3 per cent stock on the basis of the average value of their holdings during a specified recent period.[11]

In the case of iron and steel the government had made no prewar commitment to deal with the entire industry. No need for rescue or rehabilitation could be urged; it was a major industry that had been meeting the demands made upon it. Through the Iron and Steel Board there was already supervision. The industry presented an unusual difficulty to nationalization in that, in addition to its sheer dimension, it lacked definite boundaries, because many firms not only supplied essential materials for a wide range of industries, but also manufactured finished products. The proponents of nationalization, however, held that a question of principle was involved: did, or did not, the Labour government intend to build a socialist economy? If it did, it could not stop with utilities, which were publicly owned even in capitalist countries.

There was an efficiency argument, too: steel, while doing well, was not doing well enough; the nation could no longer entrust it to those who set their sights on the low target of fifteen and one-half million tons per annum, as the steel owners did, when within five years the minimum need would be for twenty-six million. An industry so basic to the country's economy and security could not be left in private hands. Some regarded nationalization of iron and steel as a test of power; since steel was the very citadel of capitalism, there was a strong political reason for its capture.[12]

In the Cabinet Dalton, Bevin, Cripps, and Bevan took the lead for an early move on steel. A minority hesitated; either they wanted to give priority to the utilities, with which they felt already fully occupied, or, like Morrison and Attlee, they considered, and would have been content with, a half-way step of greater control coupled with the acquisition of firms performing unsatisfactorily. The advocates of implementing the election promise won. A bill introduced in 1948 proposed to take over ownership of all substantial firms, which were defined as those producing 50,000 tons or more of iron ore or 20,000 tons or more of iron or steel. Although they would be placed under a national Iron and Steel Corporation, the individual firms would be left intact, free to compete with one another, and, as far as possible, with the same directors in charge. Although free in their day-to-day management, they would conform to the general policies of the corporation, which would be subject to direction from the Minister of Supply. That minister would appoint the chairman and the four to ten other members. Former owners would be compensated on the same stock-exchange criterion as transport.

In order to facilitate passage of this bill, introduced late in the government's life, the Parliament Act of 1911 was amended in 1949 to shorten the suspensive veto of the Lords from three successive sessions to two and from a minimum of two years to one. It was not necessary to invoke the act, however, because the Lords amended but did not obstruct. One amendment, accepted by the government, insisted upon setting a vesting date that would be after the next general election. Consequently, it was February 1951 before nationalization of iron and steel was completed. Meanwhile the Conservatives threatened to denationalize the industry at the earliest opportunity.[13]

The post office did not serve as a model for the newly nationalized industries; none was run as a department of government. The organization provided was that of the public corporation, adapted to the individual case, so that there was no uniformity of structure. Professional managers were in control; there was no transfer of power to workers' representatives, though provision was made for joint consultation. The completion of the program left Britain with a mixed economy, of which a basic portion, estimated by Cripps at 20 per cent, was publicly owned. But the professional managers were concerned with efficiency rather than socialism, and the structure of British industry remained essentially capitalist.

Other aspects of the Labour program had a greater immediate effect upon the character of British society. The policy on education and the legislation on housing, planning, national insurance, and national health were notable. They had a long history of support from social reformers of all parties, though more immediately they stemmed from the Beveridge plan, accepted in principle by the Coalition.

A first care was to ensure that the Education Act of 1944 did not meet the fate of the Fisher Act of 1918, a victim of Tory economy. Ellen Wilkinson, Minister of Education, at once announced an intention to carry out the proposal to raise the school leaving age to fifteen, even though it would withhold about 160,000 young people from work at a time when all available manpower was needed. There was a shortage of teachers and classrooms. Nevertheless, she took the long view and won. All fees were abolished in primary and secondary schools under local authorities. School meals and school milk services were extended. At the same time, aid to the universities was increased fivefold. State scholarships were more than doubled in number and increased in size so that, together with grants from local authorities, many students received maintenance. It became possible for the poorest, if qualified, to receive a university degree; Oxford and Cambridge ceased to draw only from the wealthier classes.[14] But it was not long before aspects of the act drew criticism, especially the provision to channel children into three different types of schools on the basis of an examination given in their twelfth year—the "eleven-plus" examination.

Housing presented a problem as pressing as it was difficult. Building was at a standstill; deterioration and the blitz had taken their toll; brickyards had stood idle and British timber had been sacrificed to wartime necessity, so that all materials were in short supply. On new building there was a party difference. The Conservatives argued for the efficiency of the private builder and for the construction of houses for sale. Labour insisted on rehousing the greatest number in the shortest time with the greatest conservation of materials by building small houses for low rental—"houses before mansions." Accordingly, Bevan's Housing Acts of 1946 and 1949 provided government aid to local authorities so they could construct such houses. Private building was strictly limited and a ceiling placed on the cost of privately built houses. The 1949 act permitted local government authorities to meet the needs of all sections of the community, not just the working classes. It also offered landlords inducements to modernize large old town houses, relics of the bygone days of unlimited cheap domestic help, but in return for aid the rents would be controlled. The program fell short of its goal of 200,000 new houses annually, but by 1949 repair, temporary prefabricated dwellings, and new homes had produced a total of one million houses.

The Town and Country Planning Act of 1947 was intended to provide for planned development of urban areas and prevent the haphazard sprawling of dormitory suburbs and ugly "shoestring" building along highways. It required all county councils and larger towns to survey their areas from the point of view of population trends and to submit a development plan to the Minister of Town and Country Planning. If the plan were approved, the local government authority would be given all necessary powers to acquire the needed land. Industrial, residential, and recreational areas must fit into the plan.

The New Towns Act of 1946, designed to halt the growth of over-large metropolitan areas, contemplated whole new towns of about 50,000 inhabitants each at a distance of 30 or 40 miles from London or other metropolitan centers. Each town would be an entity with its industry, homes, business and community centers, and parks. The National Parks and Access to the Countryside Act of 1949 was an effort to make natural beauty spots available to the public of heavily urbanized Britain.[15]

A national insurance plan, based on the Beveridge recommendations, consolidated existing legislation and expanded it to cover the whole population. It consisted of a new workmen's compensation act, insurance against loss of income through accident or illness, and old-age pensions. The Industrial Injuries Act of 1946 substituted a national system for the liability of an individual employer. It was intended to be wholly self-supporting with weekly payments to a central fund from both employer and employee. Although the act placed part of the burden on the employee, it increased the compensation and relieved the accident victim of having to resort to legal proceedings to establish his claim. Compensation was set at 45 shillings a week, or, in case of permanent incapacity, at 65s. with 16s. for a wife and 7s. 6d. for the first child.

The National Insurance Scheme of 1948 covered all employed persons between the school leaving age and the pensionable age of sixty-five for men and sixty for women. All persons earning over £104 a year made contributions to a central fund at a rate intended to cover the cost of benefits and administration. In return, the individual would receive benefits in case of unemployment, illness, or accident, and a pension upon retirement. The unemployment benefit was 26s. weekly for a single person, 42s. for man and wife, and 7s. 6d. for one child. In addition, there were widows' benefits, maternity benefits, and a grant for funeral expenses. Old-age pensions were increased.

The National Health Service Bill of 1946, with Aneurin Bevan in charge of its passage, roused greater controversy than the other measures, especially because most doctors feared for their independence. But Labour was determined to end the maldistribution of medical service, which had tended to gravitate toward the centers of wealth; to end the discrepancy of treatment between that accorded the rich and the poor; and to relieve individual anxiety over costs that might be ruinous. The government endeavored to meet objections, however, by preserving the patient's freedom to choose his doctor, and by making a doctor's entry into the service optional; doctors could continue to practice independently. The greater part of the service was placed under regional boards, upon which both local authorities and doctors would be represented.

The act provided for a medical and dental service freely available to all; drugs, medicines, and artificial limbs would also be free. Public clinics where groups of doctors would be available for advice and treatment were to be set up. All hospitals, whether owned by local authorities or by voluntary organizations, were to be taken over by the government. Doctors were to be compensated with a basic salary of £300 plus a capitation fee for each person on their list. The dental association, however, insisted upon compensation on the basis of work done, which resulted in gross incomes so high that they had to be reduced.

Over 90 per cent of the population quickly enrolled for the service, as did a majority of the doctors, and the number tended to grow. There were problems. The demand was greater than doctors and hospitals could meet, which, a Labourite would contend, afforded an indication of need hitherto unknown or neglected. The cost surpassed all estimates. The demand for spectacles and dentures was unexpectedly high, which again was probably a measure of need; certainly in the past the obvious dental neglect had been remarked even by the friendliest of foreign visitors. The public appreciated the service, as evidenced by Gallup polls. The principle of equality on something as essential as medical care appealed to idealists; others pointed to the national gain from days saved for productive work. It was significant that in the next general election the Conservatives promised, if returned to power, to maintain the service; the major party difference today seems to be on which can run it better.[16]

The system of social security, Beveridge's "cradle-to-grave" plan, was rounded out by the family allowances scheme, enacted by the Coalition, whereby a mother received a payment of five shillings a week for each child under sixteen except the first. The Labour government added two more acts. A National Assistance Act (1947) met cases not otherwise covered and provided for weekly payments to supplement other sources where needed. It ended the old Poor Law system, which left the problem of indigence to local authorities. The Legal Aid and Advice Plan of 1949 enabled those below a certain income level to receive legal advice from centers under control of the Law Society.

One of the Labour government's first acts in 1946 was to repeal the

1927 Trade Union Act and to restore "contracting out." To both unions and party these changes brought deep satisfaction, because the Tory measure had been regarded as partisan and vindictive. To the unions it meant full recognition; to the Labour party it meant more adequate finance. The number of trade unionists paying the political levy almost doubled, while the trade-union contribution to the central Labour party funds increased from £50,663 in 1946 to £129,476 in 1948. By Conservative standards Labour was still poor, but it could now build up a war chest.[17]

The Labour government contributed much to the evolution of the Commonwealth. To emphasize equality of status among the members, the title of the Dominions Office was changed in 1947 to Commonwealth Relations Office. The Prime Ministers met frequently to discuss matters of trade, finance, and defense. The voluntary nature of the relationship was emphasized when in 1949 the Irish Free State seceded and, as Eire, became an independent republic. The effects of the change were minimized, however, by legislation providing that Eire would not be treated like a foreign country. The thousands of its citizens resident in Britain were not to be regarded as aliens, but were to receive such privileges as the right to vote in British elections. The republic gave reciprocal rights to British citizens. Other members of the Commonwealth accorded Eire the same treatment and received reciprocal rights. The secession did increase the disunity of Ireland by accentuating the difference between Eire and Ulster. In South Africa, too, the Nationalists' victory over Smuts in 1948 set that dominion on the road to secession and foreshadowed a conflict over racial policies, but it was not for the Labour government to question the decision of that electorate.

The character of the Commonwealth was changed when in southeast Asia the three new dominions of India, Pakistan, and Ceylon were added. Unlike the earlier ones, they were not settled largely by peoples of white British stock. National independence of the new dominions had been long in the making, but the successful completion of the process and the inclusion of India and Pakistan within the Commonwealth owed much to Prime Minister Attlee himself.

In keeping with the wartime promise of independence, a Cabinet mission of A. V. Alexander, Pethick-Lawrence, and Cripps went to India, but came up against the old obstacle of communal antagonism and distrust. As independence came closer, the feuds heightened. The Muslims, their ninety millions constituting the world's largest minority problem, positively refused to unite with the Hindus. They demanded Pakistan, which would be a separate state consisting of Bengal, where they had a narrow majority, and three provinces in the northwest, where they had large ones. Negotiations were fruitless. Attlee, who knew India at first-hand from his service on the Simon Commission, concluded that as long as Britain held power, the Indians would dispute among themselves and attribute failure of negotiations to Britain; his solution was to thrust responsibility on them. He announced that the British administration would depart in June 1948, and appointed Lord Mountbatten to be the last viceroy and to effect the transfer of power.

This decision compelled the Indian leaders to effect a settlement, but because they still could not agree upon a single government, a division of the peninsula into two countries took place. In July 1947, Parliament passed the Independence of India Bill, and on August 15 India and Pakistan became members of the Commonwealth. India, though a republic, accepted the Queen as Head of the Commonwealth, a formula devised by Attlee that made it possible for republics to stay within the Commonwealth.

It was a tribute to the smoothness with which Mountbatten effected the transfer that the Indians requested him to remain as the first governor-general. Other aspects of the transition were less pleasant. Although the states governed by native princes were to opt freely for India or Pakistan, there were instances in which India did not hesitate to exercise force. The old Hindu-Muslim feud flared with such ferocity that the number of dead and refugees in Bengal and the Punjab exceeded that of many major wars elsewhere.[18]

In neighboring countries there were corresponding changes. In 1946 self-government in Ceylon, suspended during the war, was restored. When independence followed in 1947, the country remained in the Commonwealth. Burma, however, chose to become completely independent. Malaya, whose tin and rubber were valuable dollar-earners in this day of shortages, advanced a step with the formation of a federation in 1948.

In many other colonies the government furthered constitutional advance toward self-government. In 1947 Malta received an elective legislature. Cyprus was offered a new constitution with an elective majority in the legislature, but it could not be implemented because of friction between the Greek majority and the Turkish minority. In 1951 British Guiana received internal self-government, but two years later disorders led to its suspension. Some West Indies islands and African territories received new constitutions, and a federation movement in the West Indies was encouraged. The pace of change was rapid. Demand from colonial peoples was matched by the Labour government's willingness to aid and guide them, preferably into a voluntary association of free nations but to independence if they insisted.

In the tropical African colonies constitutional development, hitherto slow because of the primitive state of so many of their peoples, now speeded up. Labour sympathized with African aspirations. The British humanitarianism that had produced the antislavery movement and missionary activity was strong in the party; it now focused on political and economic needs. In 1940 the Fabian Society had organized a Colonial Bureau for the study of colonial problems; the Bureau's journal, *Empire,* disseminated its ideas. In 1947 its secretary, A. Creech Jones, went to the Colonial Office. In a brief period, new constitutions with elective majorities were granted to the Gold Coast, Nigeria, Sierra Leone, Gambia, and Mauritius.[19]

The Gold Coast was the pacemaker among the African colonies. It was economically prosperous; it had an urban middle class in the coastal towns and, thanks partly to Achimota College, graduates capable of filling responsible posts. A new constitution of 1946 made it the first African dependency to achieve an African majority in its legislative council and gave a corresponding advance in municipal government. But unrest followed, originating largely in the inability of illiterate cocoa growers to understand why producing trees had to be destroyed to halt the "swollen shoot" virus that threatened this basic crop. The government appointed an all-African committee headed by an African judge, Henley Coussey, knighted for his services, to make suggestions, most of which were accepted in a constitution that set a new standard for colonial Africa. Except for three officers who controlled external affairs, finance, and justice, and for the emergency powers left by the committee with the governor, it provided for complete self-government. Still the extremists were unsatisfied, and Kwame Nkrumah, their leader, demanded complete and immediate self-government. Disorders led to his arrest, but when in February 1951 his Convention People's Party decisively won the election, he was released to become the first Prime Minister of the Gold Coast, later independent as Ghana.[20]

Elsewhere the rate of change was slower. Nigeria was larger, more diverse, and more backward than the Gold Coast, and therefore remained dependent longer. In East Africa the situation was complicated by the presence of minorities of whites, Arabs, and Indians.

The Rhodesias, too, presented the problem of races on different levels of civilization. The government favored a federation with Nyasaland, though African opinion did not. Along with constitutional advance everywhere went a policy of Africanization of the civil service.

There was general agreement on the main lines of political development but not on the rate of change. To doctrinaires in the party and to ambitious Africans, it seemed too slow. To white administrators confronted with masses still backward and uneducated, and aware of the survival of barbaric practices, the policy seemed to involve a high degree of risk. To those whites who now called Kenya or Rhodesia their home it appeared to contain a threat to personal safety and to the permanence of their civilization. These factors combined to make a smooth and even application of Labour's policy impossible.

Insofar as Britain's own difficulties permitted, the government facilitated economic development in the Commonwealth. Allotments were made under the Colonial Development and Welfare Acts, which provided better communications, industrial development and power, medical aid, education, and social welfare. Interest in the colonies, combined with postwar shortages and the need for nondollar necessities, led the government into some unwise and costly ventures. The British trade unions and the cooperators also sent missions to aid in extending their systems to the colonies. The hope was that the relation between Britain and the dependencies might be one of mutual advantage.

The Middle East, second in importance only to Europe in British foreign policy, made heavy demands on the attention of Prime Minister Attlee and Foreign Secretary Bevin. Defense of the Suez Canal was axiomatic in British strategy, and the whole area was of great concern in the developing "cold war" with Soviet Russia. The Labour government was anxious to come to terms with rising Arab nationalism and with the Arab League, formed in 1945 by Egypt, Saudi Arabia, Yemen, Syria, Lebanon, Transjordan, and Iraq. Britain might thereby hope to reduce its heavy commitments, but could consider no withdrawal until some regional organization was ready to assume the obligation of defense. When the Palestine problem violently erupted, it handicapped the solution of all these problems as well as relations with the ninety million Muslims of India.

Bevin was deeply interested in the welfare of the masses in the Arab lands. "Peasants, not pashas" was his slogan, and one of his first acts was to direct officials to view problems from that angle. At the end of 1945 he announced the establishment of a British Middle East Office to furnish the Arab states, upon request, with commercial and technical information, technicians, and experts. He would spread the benefits among all classes, not just the few at the top.

Egypt, most populous of the Arab states, was the primary object of Bevin's attention, but good relations suffered from conflicts arising out of the war, political instability, an irresponsible press, the Palestine war, and control of the Sudan, where a strong nationalist movement existed. The Egyptians demanded revision of the treaty of 1936 though it had another ten years to run, evacuation of British troops, and unity with the Sudan under the Egyptian crown.

In the negotiations that started in April 1946, Bevin was prepared to make any compromise that would provide security in the Middle East and the freedom of the Sudanese to decide their own future. He went so far as to offer withdrawal even from the Canal zone, subject to the right of re-entry in case of need. Actually, the troops were soon out of Cairo, and Alexandria ceased to be a British naval base. Bevin even cherished hopes that defense of the Canal might become a matter for the United Nations, for like many others in 1946 he expected much from that organization.[21]

In October the Egyptian Prime Minister, Ismael Sidky Pasha, came to London, where he and Bevin reached agreement on a treaty of mutual assistance and evacuation, together with an ambiguous and illusory agreement on the Sudan. Obscurity on the Sudan roused vehement Sudanese protest against any subordination to Egypt, an inference which Bevin promptly denied. In Egypt extreme nationalists forced rejection of the proposed treaty and the resignation of Sidky. Negotiations with his successor, Nokrashy Pasha, broke down over the Sudan issue.

The Palestine war monopolized attention for a time. The defeat of the Arab League by the Israelis revealed how slight a resistance it could interpose against any serious attack on the Middle East. Therefore, when Egypt unilaterally abrogated the treaty in 1950, Bevin denied its right to do so and reinforced the Canal garrison. When Morrison succeeded Bevin in 1951, he continued Bevin's policy. Egypt remained uncompromising. It rejected a scheme for a defense pact in which it would join as an equal partner with France, Turkey, the United Kingdom, and the United States. On October 15, 1951, in the last days of the Attlee government, it abrogated the 1936 treaty, which left the problem to the succeeding Conservative Cabinet. Egyptian intransigence had made impossible an agreed provision for Middle East defense and self-determination for the Sudan. Bevin's failure in Egypt had an adverse effect upon his relations with other Arab states.[22]

Bevin had some success with Transjordan, although nationalism produced strain. Keeping a wartime pledge, he raised the country from a mandate to an independent and equal partner in a treaty of mutual assistance. Because of the poverty of the country, Britain lent financial aid. It received the right to station armed forces there, but to meet Arab League objections this privilege was limited to two R.A.F. bases. It met Bevin's objective of keeping Transjordan solvent and friendly and of making a contribution to Middle East security.

In Iraq, however, a similar effort received a setback. In January 1948, Bevin negotiated a treaty for joint defense and a close military alliance, only to see it nullified as a result of a violent nationalist outburst, stemming partly from hostility to Britain's role in Palestine as too pro-Zionist and partly from Communist propaganda. As a result, a friendly Prime Minister was compelled to flee. Nevertheless, Bevin continued British aid for constructive projects and for education. In the French mandates of Syria and Lebanon, he demonstrated his sympathy for Arab independence and acted as mediator in persuading the French to withdraw.[23]

In Palestine the Labour party was deeply committed to the Zionist cause. In the party, as in the country, were many Jews, organized and in a position to influence opinion, whereas the Arab case was seldom stated and little known. The plight of the Jews who survived Nazi persecution and the death chambers excited compassion. The Labour party conference of 1944 had easily accepted the report on the *International Postwar Settlement,* which reflected Dalton's vision of a Jewish Palestine with expanded borders, where Jewish energy backed by British aid would develop industry and through irrigation projects work miracles in agriculture. A revitalized Palestine would not only provide greater happiness for a future Arab minority but set a standard for the entire Middle East. Such a Palestine, thought Dalton, would provide a friend, possibly an ally and a base, and, perhaps, a new member of the Commonwealth.[24]

Attlee and Bevin did not pursue this policy. Neither was anti-Semitic, but both regarded Jews as members of a great international religion, not as a race or nation. They disagreed with Dalton's assumption that Arabs should move out as Jews moved in. Like Mac-

Donald and Lord Passfield during the Second Labour government, they saw the problem as having two sides. Bevin, who prided himself upon his ability as a negotiator, approached the problem with confidence. In his long experience as a trade-union official, he had solved scores of disputes by patient negotiation, which often involved a compromise that gave neither party all it wanted yet left each with some feeling of satisfaction. If he could only get Jews and Arabs around a table together, he thought, he could persuade them to reach an agreement. But he forgot how uncompromising nationalism and religion could be, and in this case he was confronted by two peoples inspired by both.

The matter was complicated by the policy of President Truman. Truman was more in agreement with his party managers, who stressed the importance of Jewish campaign contributions, than with his own State Department, which in view of the strategic importance of the Middle East in the "cold war" and the increasing American need for oil saw the necessity of friendly states in the Arab world.

On August 31, 1945, Truman wrote Attlee requesting the lifting of restrictions upon Jewish immigration into the mandate and the immediate admission of 100,000 refugees. Attlee replied that his government had to consider the interests of both sides, and reminded Truman that both Roosevelt and Churchill had pledged that no final decision would be taken without consulting the Arabs. He also mentioned the repercussions that would follow throughout the Middle East and India if the pledges were repudiated. In conclusion, he suggested that a joint Anglo-American commission of inquiry be formed to review the questions. Meanwhile, an emergency quota of 1,500 immigrants monthly would be permitted, though even that low figure aroused strong Arab protests. The Arabs were naturally dismayed over the Zionist intention to swamp their majority with a flood of Jewish immigrants, and they resented the British failure to extend to Palestine the measures of self-government now so rapidly being shared by other parts of the Commonwealth.

In November the Anglo-American commission was set up. Its report in April 1946 expressly disapproved the idea that Palestine had in some way been ceded to the Jews. It made ten recommendations, one of which proposed the creation of a state in which no religious group would dominate, while another suggested the immediate admission of 100,000 Jewish immigrants. Truman singled out the last point for consideration, whereas the British would first settle the question of the status of Palestine. When Attlee raised the question of sharing the military and financial responsibility, the United States showed no willingness to accept obligations. In Palestine the Jewish extremists resorted to a campaign of terrorism and violence which culminated in the blowing up of the King David Hotel in Jerusalem with over one hundred casualties.

Bevin strove to bring the two parties together in round-table conferences, but the Jews refused to sit down with the Arabs unless the conference were committed in advance to a Jewish Palestine. Bevin was willing to put any Jewish plan on the table, but could make no advance commitment. He then found that he could only speak separately with the two parties, and so he failed to secure the agreed settlement upon which he had set his heart. He deplored the intransigence of both and the violence to which both resorted, but he would impose no solution that he felt would be unjust to one or the other. Unwilling to sacrifice more British lives and treasure on a mandate so costly and unrewarding, he referred the matter to the United Nations in April 1947 and in December announced that British troops would be withdrawn by August 1, 1948.

Meanwhile, in Palestine, the disorders worsened, and such incidents as the deliberate decoying and judicial murder of two young sergeants by Jewish terrorists and the conversion of their corpses into booby traps alienated opinion in Britain, including even Dalton. On May 15, 1948, after the failure of a United Nations proposal to settle the Palestine problem by partition, the Labour government brought the mandate to an end and British troops were withdrawn. Bevin's policy of mediation without force ended in failure, and the problem of Palestine was settled by war. But Britian felt relieved to be rid of an expensive, troublesome, and thankless mandate. On the day the mandate ended, the Jewish National Council and the General Zionist Council at Tel Aviv proclaimed the State of Israel, which the United States immediately recognized. In April 1950, after the Arab-Israeli war made the new state an accomplished fact, Britain gave it formal recognition.[25]

The Middle East was not the only difficult area of foreign policy for the Labour government. Hope had been high that the wartime alliance of the Big Three would continue constructively into the peace, and that the United Nations would become not only an international forum but a powerful and effective instrument for security and stability. Its existence would enable countries to substitute good will and cooperation for power politics as the basis of foreign policy. To a country that depended for its livelihood upon the ability of others to produce and exchange, such a world held bright promise. But the actuality was in grim contrast. Even before the end of Hitler there were symptoms of noncooperation by the U.S.S.R. After the war, these symptoms became increasingly pronounced. This situation was the primary factor in determining Labour's foreign policy. Britain still had to be prepared to protect itself from a possible one-power domination of the Continent and from threats to the sources of its food and raw materials and the sea lanes through which they were transported. This situation made for more continuity than change in foreign policy.

In spite of decades of conflict with Communists, one of Labour's slogans in the campaign of 1945 was that "left could speak best with left." Bevin found, however, that Stalin's words lessened no tension and that Molotov usually said "No." One of Bevin's first tasks was to resist a Russian effort to penetrate the Mediterranean by securing a trusteeship of Tripolitania, where Britain had given a promise of independence. He also supported Turkey's refusal to make concessions to Russia in the Straits and to let it establish bases in Anatolia, and Iran's effort to get the Russians out of Azerbaijan. As a result, Britain found itself not the partner but the chief target of the U.S.S.R. in the Near and Middle East.

It was apparent, too, that Russia had no intention of relinquishing its hold upon the border states or of facilitating agreement on a peace treaty with Germany. When Stalin made clear his disbelief in the possibility of the coexistence of capitalism and communism, and when Churchill answered in March 1946 with a call for the fraternal association of the United States and Britain, the disunity of the Big Three was admitted and the "cold war" was on. Bevin had no wish for it and personally offered to turn the wartime treaty into a fifty-year alliance, but Russian intransigence gave him no choice. The facts of the international situation, coupled with economic necessity, compelled Britain toward close association with the United States.[26]

Accordingly, the Labour government carried on what was virtually an unwritten Anglo-American alliance. The task was not always easy. British pride had to adjust to the role of junior partner, but the country's exhaustion by the war effort compelled it. Some leftists resented "the American yoke." On the American side were many who would have preferred to withdraw into isolation, and who regarded financial aid as a subsidy to Labour's economic program; they feared "creeping socialism." British "colonialism" was an obstacle to those who were unaware of the changes and development in the policy over the preceding hundred years, though Britain's granting independence to the Asiatic dominions in 1947 did much to lessen that feeling.

Nevertheless, the American loan did tide Britain over its worst period, and Marshall aid was an enormous help. Thanks to Bevin, Secretary of State Marshall's general suggestion of the United States' willingness to aid European recovery, made in a speech at Harvard University on June 5, 1947, was taken up and developed into a "Marshall Plan." Bevin, who at once sensed the possibilities, promptly called for a conference of European nations to consult upon it. The outcome was a plan for recovery that, although the Soviet bloc refused to participate, was of immense benefit to the rest of Europe.

The Labour government also sought to persuade the United States to shoulder economic and strategic burdens where an exhausted Britain could no longer support them. In 1947, when Dalton reported the sheer impossibility of further exchequer aid to Greece and Turkey, the United States, moved by fear of a communist penetration there, stepped in to assume a responsibility hitherto beyond consideration.[27]

Attlee met with a rebuff in his attempt to secure a continued joint effort in the development of atomic energy. Shortly before the war, Britain had begun atomic research and during the war planned a project in connection with Canada. In 1941 the project became a combined effort with the United States, in accordance with which accumulated information was passed on and British scientists sent to the United States. Attlee wished to possess atomic power for peaceful purposes, and ultimately to place it under United Nations' control. Meanwhile, he wanted to continue the exchange of information between the three countries. A visit to Truman and Canadian Prime Minister Mackenzie King in November 1945 resulted in an agreed memorandum for "full and effective cooperation in the field of atomic energy." But Congressional opinion was against it, and the McMahon Act of August 1946, which set up the Atomic Energy Commission, contained restrictions upon the dissemination of information that ended hope of continued cooperation. Consequently, Britain was denied reciprocity of information and had to duplicate costly experiments in the development of nuclear power.[28]

In Germany, Russia and the Western powers were in fundamental opposition. Bevin opposed the transfer of parts of East Germany to Poland, partly because it cut off the other zones from their normal food supply. The British zone, which included the Ruhr, was not only the most industrialized and densely populated, but also the most devastated. Occupation costs were high. Instead of getting the expected food from Germany to relieve serious shortages at home, the British had to find it elsewhere to keep Germans alive and pay for it with scarce dollars. Reparations in kind presented a dilemma. Some German plants and machinery went to make good losses in Britain and France. But the dismantling of factories and ports had to be stopped and coal production and manufactures for export revived, for unless Germany recovered, prosperity could not return to Europe. When in 1946 Bevin stated that obligations in Germany, largely to restore production, were costing the British taxpayer £80,000,000 a year, the question of who was paying reparations to whom was raised. Soviet demands had to be resisted, too, because Russia strove to exact reparations that would, in effect, have to be paid by the other occupying powers. In December 1946, Bevin and James Byrnes, American Secretary of State, agreed to the bizonal policy whereby the American and British zones were joined as a move toward a self-supporting Germany. The two countries disagreed on the mines question; the Labour government favored nationalization, but the Americans did not. As a result, that matter was left to the Germans.[29]

By 1947 the severity of the "cold war," together with stresses in the Middle East, necessitated new defensive measures. The war against the communist guerrillas in Malaya and the disorders in Palestine called for large forces. The Berlin blockade with its fantastic airlift intensified the danger in Europe. In February 1948 the communist take-over in Czechoslovakia, which had hitherto been regarded as democracy's showpiece and bastion in central Europe, appeared a disaster to the West. A special statement from the Labour executive called it a lesson and a warning.[30] It appeared that, should the Russian armies move, they might roll with little resistance to the Atlantic. The Labour government had to resort to conscription. In 1947 it proposed a term of service of eighteen months, but objection from its own backbenchers reduced it to twelve. A year later it was raised to eighteen, and in 1950, at the time of the Korean War, to two years.

In March 1948 Britain joined France, Belgium, Holland, and Luxembourg in the fifty-year defensive Treaty of Brussels. Just before it was signed, Bevin proposed to General Marshall that on this basis they build a broader structure to cover the whole Atlantic-Mediterranean area. This initiative, taken up and carried through by the United States, culminated on April 4, 1949, in the North Atlantic Treaty Organization (N.A.T.O.), which brought the United States, Canada, Italy, Norway, Denmark, Iceland, and the five Brussels powers into a security system. At first Bevin resisted proposals to rearm

West Germany to aid in this mutual defense, but finally, though with great misgivings, he and the Cabinet accepted the proposition in principle; they specifically rejected any attempt to proceed with it until assured of adequate safeguards against a possible resurgence of German militarism. Accordingly, it was another five years before West Germany became a member and contributed its own forces.[31]

External pressure was mainly responsible for moves toward a closer union of Western Europe. In the past Attlee and Churchill had both mentioned such a union; Attlee once said that Europe must federate or perish. In November 1948 Dalton headed a British delegation to a conference at Paris called by the Foreign Ministers of the five Brussels-treaty powers; the next year a Council of Europe was seated at Strasbourg. Opinion differed over the degree of unity desirable. Some, especially among the French and Italians, pressed for a federal union. The British would not merge their identity with Europe if it meant the sacrifice of Commonwealth ties; Bevin and Dalton were firm on that question. They and the party declared for a "functional" approach rather than a constitutional "federal" one.

The Brussels treaty provided for kinds of cooperation other than military; Labourites would extend the list as a means of binding Western Europe together. They feared a supra-national authority that might endanger the national controls to which they attributed the benefits of social security, fair shares, full employment, and price control. It appeared dangerous to tie too closely to countries in which unemployment was as high as 10 per cent while their own had been reduced to two. A decade later, when the Common Market had shown its immense potentiality, Labour and Britain faced these same issues.[32]

In the Far East the Labour government disagreed with the United States on the question of China. At the conference to form the United Nations in San Francisco, Attlee had thought it absurd to consider "Nationalist" China as a great power worthy of a seat on the Security Council. Now the difference was over the recognition of the new communist regime, which had overthrown Chiang. To the Labour Cabinet it was not a question of like or dislike of a particular government. Just as it recognized the Franco regime, though nearly every Labourite felt a particular aversion to it, so it would recognize China. It hoped that recognition would at least permit the discussion of practical problems, though ultimately it found the results disappointing. Moreover, it was convinced that Red China would not remain a tool of Soviet policy indefinitely. In Indonesia it exerted pressure on the

Dutch to relinquish their former possessions, and in November 1946 gave *de facto* recognition to that new republic. It also participated in the Colombo plan for the economic development of Southeast Asia.[33]

Labour's foreign policy suffered as much criticism from its own left wing as it did from the Opposition. Among the relatively few pacifists Emrys Hughes, editor of *Forward*, carried on the tradition of Lansbury. A few crypto-communists and fellow travelers invariably followed the Moscow line. More numerous were those who opposed aspects of Bevin's policy from conviction, sincerely held, but often accentuated by personal dislikes. Their opinions were voiced in the *New Statesman and Nation*, edited by Kingsley Martin, and the *Tribune*, whose policy was determined by Michael Foot, Ian Mikardo, Jon Kimche, Jennie Lee (Mrs. Aneurin Bevan), and Mrs. Patricia Strauss. G. D. H. Cole and Laski were among the widely read leftist writers. In 1946 a group of M.P.'s began to meet regularly; in May 1947, *Keep Left*, a pamphlet by R. H. S. Crossman, Foot, and Mikardo, provided a statement of their principles.

The left complained that Bevin pursued not a socialist foreign policy but one of continuity. Having assumed that the accession of Labour to power would facilitate the much desired exit of Franco, they were indignant at the continued recognition of the Spanish government. Greece was a particularly sore point; they would shift support from the royalist side even if it meant, in effect, risking the installation of a communist regime. They were highly suspicious of the American government, which they sometimes portrayed as sensitive to Wall Street and at the mercy of generals in the Pentagon, with Wall Street hoping for the failure of the British social revolution and the Pentagon under temptation to use the atom bomb. At first some sensed danger to Britain's independence in Marshall aid. Laski, for example, feared it would be incompatible with freedom and democracy in Britain, but by 1948 the plan was generally approved. Leftists were suspicious of American aid to Greece and Turkey as a cloak for economic imperialism with Middle East oil a special objective. Rather than depend on America, the leftists wanted to create a "third force" by cooperating with other socialist states in Western Europe. But after the elections of 1946, few such states survived.

Above all, the leftists wanted friendship and close relations with the U.S.S.R. They found it as easy to place favorable interpretations on Russian policy as to place the opposite on American. Soviet truculence or noncooperation was attributed to a justified fear of a hostile capitalist West. Like G. D. H. Cole, many accepted the Soviet system as a legitimate form of democracy, and rejected the view that it was autocracy in disguise. Like Laski, they would facilitate a trade agreement with Russia in order to obviate the need of dependence upon America. Except for the *Tribune* group, they opposed Western policy on the Berlin blockade. In contrast to the official indignation, again except for the *Tribune,* they were undisturbed by the communist coup in Czechoslovakia, which was interpreted as a voluntary acceptance of the communist way.

Conflict between left and leadership was continuous, because the latter, irritated and resentful at breaches of unity and party discipline, naturally fought back. Labour's accession to office coincided with Laski's year as party chairman. In this position his steady flow of speeches and interviews was embarrassing, because outside the party and abroad they were taken as expressions of official policy. Attlee, who could be very blunt, thereupon requested him to desist from "irresponsible utterances," saying that foreign affairs were in the capable hands of Bevin and "a period of silence on your part would be welcome."[34]

At the 1946 party conference the left assailed Bevin's policies, but overwhelming majorities supported him on all points. On November 13 in the Commons Richard Crossman led a similar attack, and amused Conservatives watched while back-bench rebels accused their own government of following policies that smacked too much of those enunciated by Churchill in March.

In 1947 the leftist M.P.'s had a hand in securing the reduction of the proposed term of military service from eighteen months to twelve, but the annual conference again stoutly approved Bevin. The "Keep Left" movement then declined. In 1948 the extreme procommunist J. F. Platts-Mills was expelled from the party; Leslie Solley and Konni Zilliacus followed him in 1949, and others disappeared in the next general election. In 1950 the Korean War brought a revival of leftist activity. But behind the manifesto *Keeping Left* was a new group that, while friendly to the Soviet Union, was more pacifist in character. It opposed British participation in N.A.T.O. and regarded rearmament as politically dangerous and economically ruinous.[35]

On February 23, 1950, as the constitutional maximum of five years drew to a close, the government took its case to the country in a general election. Labour contested all of the 625 seats except the speaker's, traditionally unopposed, and 5 of the 12 in the Unionist Ulster stronghold. All its candidates faced opposition, because not only did the Conservatives determine to unseat Labour but the Liberals made a supreme effort to stage a political comeback, while the Communists, largely for propaganda purposes, entered 100 candidates. In this election votes were more equal in weight than ever before, because Labour had abolished the university seats and the dual vote for business premises, which had given extra members to the Conservatives. In the interest of equalization it had redrawn boundary lines so that only 80 of the 625 constituencies remained unchanged. This latter bit of altruism cost Labour many safe borough seats, especially in London's East End, while it multiplied middle-class suburban seats where Conservatism was dominant.[36]

Labour's campaign manifesto, *Let Us Win Through Together,* written by Morrison, had a significant title; it was an appeal for middle-class support and a reminder that the party stood for cooperation and not for the class war. It emphasized the achievement of full employment and "fair shares," by which it meant the abolition of abject poverty, progress in education, the comprehensive system of social security, and the national health service. Looking ahead, it faced squarely the economic problem and the need for greater production and increased exports if Britain were to maintain a decent standard of living. It would maintain controls, rationing, and subsidies where necessary.

Nationalization was not emphasized, which was a victory of Morrison and the advocates of cautious, pragmatic advance over Bevan and the proponents of a more rapid pace, but there was a select list of candidates for nationalization in sugar, cement, cold storage, meat importing and wholesaling, and water supply. Industrial insurance would be "mutualized," a scheme whereby ownership would be transferred from shareholders to policy holders. There was an ambiguous statement that the chemical industry would be "carefully examined." At the same time, there was a promise to encourage private enterprise in the non-nationalized sector.

Commonwealth and foreign affairs received brief mention. Labour could reasonably claim credit for the three new Asiatic members. In foreign affairs it maintained its allegiance to the ideals of peace and collective security, but the results of the "cold war" were manifest in a promise that, although prepared for full cooperation with Russia, Labour would stand firm against intimidation.

The campaign was quiet and dominated by domestic issues. The Conservatives and Liberals would put a full stop to further nationalization, but would engage in no general denationalization. They would, however, refuse to implement the Iron and Steel Act and would restore the profitable road haulage to private ownership. Significantly, neither party would undo the measures of social security and social services; they promised, instead, to maintain and improve them.

An argument heard from every Labour platform was the existence of full employment, while any reference to the dark days of unemployment and "hunger marches" was very effective in South Wales, Lancashire, the West Riding, Tyneside, and Clydeside. Housing was also a frequent topic. Although here on the defensive, Labour could point to a record of accomplishment. In spite of shortages of both materials and labor, houses were being built at the rate of about 190,000 a year. Conservatives demanded the removal of restraints upon the private builder.

Foreign affairs had little part until February 14, when Churchill proposed a "summit conference." In the hope of lessening tension and ending the H-bomb menace, he suggested a return to the wartime practice of direct conversations among the heads of states. Conservatives and Liberals at once enthused over this initiative. Some Labourites dubbed it an election stunt. Attlee answered that he preferred to utilize the machinery of the United Nations.

In spite of the quiet campaign and unfavorable weather, a record 84 per cent of the electorate voted. Labour secured 13,295,736 votes and 315 seats; Conservatives and their associates 12,501,983 and 298; Liberals 2,621,489 and 9. The Communists polled only 91,815 votes, and both their M.P.'s lost their seats. Labour could boast the largest poll ever received by a British party. Nor had it lost a single election deposit, which indicated that its strength was now distributed somewhat more evenly throughout Great Britain than it had been in the past. Yet its percentage of the total poll was down by 2.5 per cent as compared with 1945, and with the narrow margin of 6 seats in the Commons it lacked a working majority.

In the country it had failed to dent the Conservative strongholds of rural Britain, the middle-class suburbs, the seaside resorts, and Ulster. It held its own in the mining and industrial regions and even improved its position in those parts of Wales and Scotland. It continued to hold most of the large towns except Liverpool. It sustained losses in the East and in the Northwest, but more in the London area. Seventeen seats there, most of them perfectly safe for Labour, disappeared in the redistribution, while the new "dormitory" constituencies that encircled London voted Conservative. In the five counties surrounding London, the representation changed from 53 Labour and 34 Conservative to 28 Labour and 68 Conservative. This result exemplified Labour's failure to hold the middle-class vote, a large proportion of which had supported it in 1945, but now, associating the party with controls and "austerity," deserted it.

The lack of a working majority virtually ended the effectiveness of the Labour government, so that henceforth it could only mark time. But it could look back with satisfaction on its fulfillment of the campaign promises of *Let Us Face the Future*. It had carried through a social revolution greater in scope and significance than many political revolutions, and had done so peacefully and constitutionally. As the instrument of change it had carried on its work with due regard to continuity and in a manner that reflected credit on government and Opposition alike. This achievement was all the more noteworthy because it was accomplished during the difficult and unfavorable aftermath of a destructive world war.

14. Defeats of Yesterday: Debate on Tomorrow

The 1950's were a time of trouble for Labour. The party set a new record, but it was the unpalatable one of three successive general-election defeats. Labour suffered much internal strife, and, to the delight of its opponents, the party's acrimonious debates over unilateral disarmament and the constitutional statement of socialist objectives took place in public. But thanks to the skill and determination of Hugh Gaitskell, unity was preserved, and upon his untimely death in January 1963 Harold Wilson succeeded to the leadership of a party apparently in the best position to strike for power that it had enjoyed since 1945.

The second Attlee government lasted for twenty months, but it was recognized as a stopgap until opinion could jell and another election give one party or the other a majority that could govern. Churchill and the Conservatives repeatedly tried to bring the government down, but its slender majority held. But the Cabinet survived unhappily, because it was beset by problems abroad and by the inflation and budgetary difficulties of the Korean War period at home. It early lost its ablest members, Ernest Bevin by death and Cripps through mortal illness. Aneurin Bevan and Harold Wilson resigned. Under these circumstances the government could add nothing to its laurels.

The record in domestic legislation was barren. The Iron and Steel Act was implemented in the face of Conservative threats to undo it at the first opportunity. The problem of rearmament, owing mainly to the Korean War, was so pressing that in 1951 the defense estimate was raised from £3,600,000,000 to £4,700,000,000. Since this suddenly increased expenditure coincided with the end of Marshall aid, it presented a serious problem to Gaitskell, who succeeded Cripps at the Exchequer in October 1950. When in April 1951 he proposed to check the rising cost of the national health service by putting a charge on dentures and spectacles, it brought a clash with Bevan and Cabinet resignations.

Bevan, Labour's stormy petrel, was also its most popular orator and a most formidable debater in the Commons. Although he sometimes appeared truculent and arrogant, he sincerely desired an absolutely free health service, which as the minister in charge he had helped to initiate. Perhaps he was also piqued at being passed over twice within five months when Gaitskell replaced Cripps at the Exchequer and Morrison followed Bevin at the Foreign Office. He was accompanied in his breakaway by Wilson, President of the Board of Trade, and by John Freeman, Parliamentary Secretary to the Ministry of Supply. Attlee, ill at the time, could not prevent the breach, which became so wide that the Bevanites carried on a duel with the leadership for about six years. They established a hold on the constituency parties, where the active socialists had great influence, but made slight impression on the trade unions.[1]

When the Korean War broke out in July 1950, British and Commonwealth forces were the first to join those of the United States. The government acted with some reluctance, however, fearing that the Soviet Union might seize the opportunity to make moves elsewhere, possibly in the Middle East. It feared, too, that this war could not be contained and might become general. The appearance of Chinese "volunteers" intensified the danger. Attlee went to Washington to put his views before President Truman.[2]

The party leftists took their own line on Far Eastern affairs. They attacked the United States for rearming Japan and for supporting Chiang Kai-shek. On Korea the *Tribune* group approved the United Nations' action, but others opposed and leftists generally distrusted American policy. They charged the United States with propping up reactionary landlordism in South Korea and endangering the social revolution of the Asian peoples. They regarded General Douglas MacArthur as so dangerously aggressive that Britain might be dragged into an unwanted war with China. A Peace with China group, which included Kingsley Martin, editor of the *New Statesman,* urged the return of Formosa to China and the admission of China to the United Nations. A Victory for Socialism group, in which Victor Gollancz, the publisher, and Fenner Brockway, a former chairman of the I.L.P., were members, held similar views. On all these aspects of foreign policy except the recognition of China, the government was more harassed by its leftists than by the Opposition.[3]

Morrison's brief tenure at the Foreign Office from March until October 1951, was rendered memorable but unhappy by events in the Middle East. Persian oil was one of those overseas investments that, unlike some in Tanganyika and elsewhere, brought a good return. A treaty providing that the profits be shared equally by the Anglo-Iranian Oil Company and the Iranian government was unfortunately nullified by the assassination of Iranian Prime Minister Ali Razmara. His successor, the fanatical Dr. Mossadegh, intent upon ejecting the company, ignored a clause in its concession stipulating that any dispute between the company and the government should be submitted to arbitration, and proceeded to nationalize the oil industry without negotiating the issue or discussing compensation with Britain. At stake were the oil necessary for British industry and the great refineries at Abadan, Britain's most valuable foreign investment.

Morrison, who like Bevin understood that the standard of living at home depended upon such investments abroad, advocated sharp and forceful action, claiming it was as important to have justice against small nations as against large ones. But Attlee disagreed with him on the ground that quick and decisive action on the requisite scale not only was impracticable but would alienate Asian and world opinion. The outcome was a great loss to Britain, and the incident was a blow to Morrison's prestige. It was followed by demands from Iraq, although here the oil settlement accepted was on the fifty-fifty basis. Ten days before the election of 1951, Egypt unilaterally annulled the treaty of 1936. In this instance, Attlee and Morrison agreed to resist expulsion from the Canal zone, but the succeeding government yielded the point.[4]

In preparation for the next general election Labour adopted a policy statement, *Labour and the New Society,* at the Margate conference in October 1950. The specific nationalization proposals of the previous campaign, which had not been vote-getters, here disappeared in favor of a more general approach. It was suggested that the suitability of industries for public ownership be determined according to whether they were basic, monopolies, or inefficient and "failing the nation." There was also a specific statement that private enterprise, properly controlled in the national interest, had a place in the British economy. The emphasis was upon efficiency and a period of consolidation.

A supplementary statement of August 1951, *Our First Duty—Peace,* developed the same views, but also reflected the crisis over Korea and rearmament. It staunchly upheld the government's policy of peace through strength and the commitment of £4,700,000,000 for rearmament as the minimum required to deter aggression. It expressed confidence that rising production would enable Britain to carry the burden. It expressed Labour's pride in its contribution to the welfare state.

Earlier, in July, the Bevanites stated their case in a *Tribune* pamphlet, *One Way Only*. They disclaimed any intention of party schism, a course they labeled "frivolous and barren." They stressed their belief that a measure of rearmament was necessary to prevent repetition of the aggression in Korea: "No one except a pacifist or partisan of the Kremlin would argue that military strength is not needed to deter the rulers of Soviet Russia from attempting similar adventures elsewhere." However, they did differ on the degree of rearmament, partly because they feared an arms race as a threat to peace and partly because they believed Russia's strength was overestimated. Primarily, however, they believed that commitments on the proposed scale would threaten the economies of all countries concerned, particularly that of Great Britain, where life depended upon exports that could not be maintained in the face of such heavy rearmament. They contended that in the struggle with communism force was not enough; equally important was the maintenance of a high standard of living at home and assistance to the world's backward and underprivileged peoples. Otherwise the way would be open to communism in a manner that no armies could prevent. They urged that the Anglo-American alliance, which they accepted despite some distrust of American policies and leadership, direct its energies to this end more effectively than in the Point Four and Colombo plans. At home, the Labour party should carry on the war against poverty and make more rapid progress toward a socialist Britain.

On the economics of rearmament the Bevanites were right, but at the moment Britain's remarkable achievement in production and apparent establishment of a trade balance made for high confidence that the country could have both "guns and butter." *One Way Only* was received very unfavorably, but in the weeks that followed the financial situation deteriorated so rapidly that a second Bevanite pamphlet, *Going Our Way?*, restated their argument. Moreover, it directly attacked certain prominent trade-union heads, mentioned by name, for allegedly directing the Labour party's policies along lines not supported by their own members. The publication of this document could not have been more ill-timed. Evidently the Bevanites were unaware of the coming election date when the pamphlet was authorized. Its appearance on September 21, only two days after Attlee announced October 25 as election day, made a tremendous sensation. The trade-union leaders were understandably angered, and the Labour party entered the campaign badly divided.

Because of the rift in the party, the 1,500 delegates who met at Scarborough on October 1 for the annual conference were generally gloomy and pessimistic. But Attlee busied himself with the work of reconciliation. A drafting committee, which included Bevan himself, produced an acceptable compromise that dealt with the tasks of securing peace, maintaining high production and full employment, reducing the cost of living, and building a just society. The influence of *One Way Only* was apparent in the argument. The imminence of the war peril was stressed less than the idea that war could and must be avoided. The assertion that the scale of rearmament accepted by the government was an irreducible minimum disappeared. The earlier passing reference to the danger from the hungry millions of Asia and Africa as potential communists was now played up as meriting equal treatment with rearmament. The former confident statement that the British economy could carry the arms burden at the level contemplated was absent.

While the manifesto was under discussion, balloting took place for seats on the national executive. The results in the section chosen by the constituency parties were startling: Bevan himself headed the poll, with three of his followers, Mrs. Barbara Castle, Thomas Driberg, and Ian Mikardo, in second, third, and fifth places. James Griffiths, Morrison, and Dalton held on with greatly reduced majorities, while Shinwell, Minister of Defence and a most outspoken anti-Bevanite, was crowded out. The outcome revealed the Bevanite strength in the "grass roots" constituency parties. They were still in a minority on the executive, however, because, with a total of 23, the other members, representing mainly the trade unions, the women's section, and the professional bodies, easily outnumbered them.

Attlee's conciliatory policy won general approval. It was widely regarded as political wisdom to retain the dissident minority and the powerful personality of Bevan. Although betting odds were against the party and a recent Gallup poll had revealed Labour as far as eleven points behind the Conservatives, the delegates scattered for the campaign with morale and confidence restored.

On the whole, domestic issues dominated the campaign, though few speakers devoted themselves to the basic problem of how fifty million people could make a good living on islands that of themselves could not provide it. Conservatives and Liberals had much to say about Labour's alleged obsession with socialist theory and their overcentralized "governess" state. They charged extravagance and waste; they dwelled upon the £36,000,000 lost in the groundnuts scheme in Tanganyika and the million and a half on eggs in Gambia. They asserted the responsibility of the government for the repeated exchange crises, the devaluation of the pound, the shortages of fuel and meat, the heightened taxation, and the dependence upon loans from abroad. A Labour victory, they claimed, would worsen what was already bad, especially because of the increasing influence of Bevan. This socialist leader was attracting audiences second in size only to those of Churchill. There were many predictions that, if Labour won, the moderate Attlee would be thrust aside by a determined and ruthless Bevan. Tories conjured up visions of "a policy of wild extremism" from this "Tito of Tonypandy." But as it became increasingly clear that heavy rearmament was plunging Britain into deeper difficulties, Bevan's prestige rose in spite of these attacks.

Labourites stressed their accomplishments. Notwithstanding all the shortages, bottlenecks, and losses in manpower, the volume of industrial production, compared with prewar, was up by over half, of agriculture by one-third, and of exports by three-fourths. They claimed credit for better industrial relations, which were exemplified by the loss of only 11,000,000 days in strikes in the five postwar years as compared with 178,000,000 in the comparable period after 1918. They spoke of their pride in the welfare state.

While the campaign was at its height, the results of Seebohm Rowntree's third survey of York appeared under the title of *Poverty and the Welfare State*. Like Booth's famous survey of London, Rowntree's first one in 1899 revealed that 2 persons out of every 7 lived under conditions so crowded and on incomes so low that they constituted abject poverty. The second survey in 1936 showed the proportion down to 2 out of 11, while the third in 1950 brought out the impressive fact that, in spite of postwar shortages, the proportion was now only 2 out of 118, and of this remnant of extreme poverty nine-tenths was due to old age and illness. The 1936 survey also adopted a second standard of measurement, namely, income sufficient to provide food and clothing, household sundries, and a small margin for recreation. By this standard, higher but still rigorous, 31.1 per cent were below the minimum; the 1950 survey showed an amazing drop to 2.77 per cent.

Rowntree also examined the relation of these facts to the welfare measures introduced or extended since 1936, e.g., food subsidies, family allowances, and school milk, and found that without them the number below the minimum would be not 2.77 per cent but 22.18 per cent. Had the national health service been taken into consideration, these figures would have been even more impressive. It was omitted from the study on the ground that no comparison was possible with the earlier survey, because at that time so many of the later beneficiaries would simply have gone without medical and dental help.

Both parties took cognizance of this convincing study, and each hastened to assume credit for the improvement. The Conservatives emphasized the names of their famous social reformers and the acts of the Churchill Coalition. Labour produced an election leaflet, *Ending Poverty*, to buttress its claim to be the party of social progress.

The loss of the great Abadan refineries and the Egyptian demands relative to Suez and the Sudan produced the bitterest exchanges of the campaign. The return of the last Britons from Abadan brought flamboyant headlines to the *Daily Mail* and other Conservative papers. Emotion was deeply stirred, so that Morrison's handling of the crisis became a point of attack. Neither Churchill nor Eden advocated a resort to force against Iran, but Labourites charged their opponents with bellicosity and untrustworthiness with weapons. A popular Labour paper, the *Daily Mirror*, produced a scarehead: "Whose finger do you want on the trigger?"

In an election poll of 82.6 per cent, Labour secured the largest total vote of 13,948,385. It was the largest the party had yet received, but because of a heavy concentration of the vote in some constituencies, the party elected only 295 members. The Conservatives with 13,724,418 votes returned 321 members. The Liberals with 730,551 votes elected only 6 members. The Communists lost over three-fourths of their 1950 poll and every election deposit. In percentages Labour had 48.77, Conservatives 47.98, Liberals 2.55, and others 0.7. Labour's defeat despite its huge total was due, in part, to the fact that the Liberal loss of 1,890,000 went more to the Conservatives, and, in part, to the concentration of the Labour vote; in 25 constituencies Labour captured over 75 per cent of the vote as compared with 8 such Conservative victories, and of seats held on minority votes only 13 were Labour while 24 were Conservative.

The number of seats that actually changed was very small. Labour had scattered losses in East Anglia, the North, and Scotland; they were just enough to turn its over-all majority of 6 into a Conservative majority of 17. But the result did not alter the appearance of the election map. The industrial and mining regions, together with working-class London, lower Thames-side, and scattered industrial towns in the South, showed Labour's red, while the rural areas, Ulster, and suburbia were Conservative blue. The result indicated a degree of correlation between social classes and voting practice, but the correlation was far from absolute. About three-eighths of the trade unionists did not pay the political levy, and about a quarter of them voted Conservative or Liberal. The very size of the Conservative vote indicated that much of it was working class. It was significant that some Labour politicians argued that the party's room for expansion lay in the still unconverted workers rather than among the middle classes.[5]

In the years following the defeat of 1951, the party was divided on policy and racked by dissension. There was uncertainty about the place of nationalization in the program, while the Bevanite dispute, patched up for the election, reappeared to rage more furiously than ever.

Although it had had to begin its nationalization program with some of the least promising industries, Labour could claim a measure of success in those nationalized. In the case of coal, unification made possible reorganization and mechanization, so that with a labor force three-fifths that of a generation earlier record quantities were produced. A 1957 report of the National Coal Board, *The First Ten Years*, noted the progress in investment and mechanization: the number of locomotives working underground, for example, had been increased from 28 to 700, and modern mine cars from 3,000 to 20,000. Although the coal was sold at a price that did not reflect its scarcity value, the mines were paying their way; at the same time the miners fared better in wages and welfare than ever before.

At present, this picture is less glowing. Although production per man hour is rising and is the highest in Europe and British coal is the cheapest in Europe, not all the fields are profitable. Most mines in South Wales, Scotland, Lancashire, and Durham are producing at a loss; they are kept in operation because to close them down would make whole areas derelict, confront the country with a vast unemployment problem, and create a dangerous social situation. Only under nationalization, Labour claims, can the human and economic problems of the industry be solved.[6]

The railways, operating at a loss before nationalization, for a time seemed to be on the road to recovery, but now are in the worst situation of any of the nationalized industries. Pressed by the competition of other means of transport, squeezed between rising costs and rate restrictions, and compelled to retain unremunerative lines as a public service, they are again in financial distress. The Beeching report (1963) shows that by ruthlessly eliminating unprofitable lines (5,000 miles out of a total of 18,000) and stations (2,000 out of 7,000), the railways could again pay their way. However, such a step would deprive of service large sections of Scotland, Wales, and rural England.

Road haulage, on the contrary, has always done well. Electricity is in the best condition of the nationalized industries and is rapidly expanding. In the first seven years consumption increased 76 per cent. The price of electricity rose only half that of the cost-of-living index, but there was a surplus for investment and, due to efficiency in fuel use, a saving of 17,000,000 tons of coal per year. The gas industry is doing satisfactorily, but the airlines have problems. Before the war they were subsidized; by 1954 both B.O.A.C. and British European Airways (B.E.A.) were expanding services and making profits. Then, saddled with uneconomic routes and the cost of expensive new aircraft, financial difficulties arose; although B.E.A. has continued to be profitable, B.O.A.C. has incurred some heavy deficits. Labourites note that the difficulties of railways and airlines are not confined to Britain, and complain that the successes of nationalization have been insufficiently publicized.[7]

The effect of nationalization on society has been disappointingly slight. In the giant public corporation the ordinary trade unionist felt little, if any, greater sense of partnership. The same gap existed between those who gave orders and those who took them, and there was a corresponding difference in income. When the railways were taken over, the men chalked "These are ours now" on the waggons (freight cars), but soon discovered they were as remote as ever from management. Workers had assumed that the problem of production was solved and that socialization would bring immediate tangible benefits, but amid the difficulties of postwar Britain what they got were appeals to work harder and produce more. Some renewed the demand for a voice in management, but the T.U.C. still opposed direct workers' representation on national boards for fear of compromising independence. Compensation to former owners involved a continued payment to the capitalist. To the workers the benefits from the welfare state were far more visible than those from the nationalization of industry.[8]

Some sections of the labor movement opposed the extension of great public corporations. Proponents of local government control were unfriendly to "administrative elephantiasis." They noted, for example, that the Labour government's acts included some gains for local authorities, but that on balance the authorities lost, because bus, gas, electricity, and other services were centralized under national boards. The cooperators, too, found some areas of conflict on both national and local levels. In Labour-controlled Sheffield, for example, a proposed municipal milk service was abandoned in face of the cooperators' opposition. The Cooperative party and the Cooperative Union then brought out a series of policy reports on their relations with Labour. *The People's Industry* (1952) accepted the idea of further nationalization, but claimed a large sector for cooperative action; consumers' cooperatives should control distribution, and, on the principle of self-supply, should have control, where they desired it, of the whole chain from raw materials to finished product. Generally, they argued, as long as voluntary organizations were ready to assume responsibilities and risks, a democratic government should encourage them. Labour publicists always accepted the theory of an important sector for the cooperators, but no policy statement sought to define it.[9]

In 1953 Labour's *Challenge to Britain,* prepared in anticipation of the next election, attempted to relate nationalization directly to the country's fundamental problems of higher productivity, the trade balance, and defense. Iron and steel, denationalized by the Conservative government, would be returned to public ownership, and beet sugar and water nationalized. In industries vital to the export and defense problems there would be a new line of advance: although there would be no complete nationalization, particular sections of essential industries would be taken over. Mentioned specifically were engineering, machine-tool making, mining machinery, aircraft manufacture, and chemicals. Land-reclamation schemes would become government owned, as would land not producing as it should. In the attack upon Britain's fundamental problems, government would cooperate with private enterprise, but, where the latter failed, government might enter the field or acquire an interest in existing concerns. Underlying such an approach to public ownership was an awareness that, in order to survive, Britain must continue to produce and export.[10]

Meanwhile, the personal and sectional feuds did not improve the party's image as an effective alternative government. The line between the Bevanites and the majority did not coincide with that between the constituency parties and the trade unions, but the Bevanites were strong in the constituency parties and were supported by some leftist unions such as the Electrical Trades and the Amalgamated Engineers. In the *Tribune,* the *New Statesman,* and *Reynolds',* the Bevanite journalists continued their attack on the right-wingers, and Michael Foot did the same on the radio.

The Bevanites won considerable support in both the annual conference and the parliamentary party. At the 1952 conference at Morecambe they captured six of the seven places in the constituency section of the executive; R. H. S. Crossman and Wilson defeated the veterans Dalton and Morrison. The Bevanites' attack on the scale of rearmament, stressing the inability of the British economy to stand it, lost by 3,644,000 to 2,288,000, but they won the support of some large unions, including the Electrical Trades, Amalgamated Engineers, Distributive and Allied Workers, and National Union of Railwaymen.[11]

In the years that followed, the proposed armament of Germany stirred deep feeling. Attlee carried the parliamentary party in favor of it, but in the minority along with the Bevanites were those who, like Dalton, could not forget their fears of a revival of Nazism. The 1954 T.U.C. supported the official policy by a vote of 4,077,000 to 3,622,000, but shortly afterward the Labour party conference at Scarborough gave it the slim majority of 3,270,000 to 3,022,000, and even that was achieved only when the Woodworkers' Union changed sides.[12]

In March 1955 Bevan and Attlee again clashed openly, this time over the question of British manufacture and use of the H-bomb. Bevan attacked his own front bench and interrupted his leader's speech, and some 57 Labour M.P.'s followed him in abstaining from voting for the official amendment. The parliamentary committee, or "shadow cabinet," thereupon recommended, and the parliamentary party majority agreed, to withdraw the whip from Bevan. But Attlee interceded for Bevan, so that by 14 to 13 the Labour executive decided to give him an opportunity to save himself with an apology. He did, and so remained a party member, although politicians like Morrison and trade-union rightists like Arthur Deakin, who now held Ernest Bevin's former position at the head of the Transport Workers, would have been happy at his expulsion.

Bevan also made his bid for leadership. Attlee was unassailable, but in 1952 and again in 1953 he challenged Morrison for the post of deputy leader; he lost by 194 to 182 and by 181 to 76, respectively. He did, however, win a place on the shadow cabinet. When Greenwood died in 1954, Bevan sought the party treasurership, but Gaitskell, with strong trade-union support, defeated him by a two to one vote in the first of a series of contests between them. In April 1954, following another open disagreement with Attlee in the Commons over the Southeast Asia Treaty Organization, he suddenly resigned from the shadow cabinet. Although Attlee strove to reconcile the factions, there was a good deal of truculence on both sides, because a number of right-wing trade-union leaders could be as pungent as Bevan. In view of an approaching election, however, the crack in the party structure was once more papered over.[13]

The general election of May 26, 1955, was called by Anthony Eden, who had become Prime Minister on April 5 when Churchill resigned. It appeared an opportune moment for the Conservative party to secure a comfortable working majority and a maximum term of office, because production was at record levels and Britain was prospering. The Conservatives were united behind a Prime Minister whose rating in opinion polls topped even that of the great war leader, while Labour, as its astute political manager, Morrison, complained, was divided and unready.

Labour's campaign manifesto, *Forward with Labour,* was based on the 1953 policy statement, *Challenge to Britain.* It gave primacy to the problem of peace and the menace of the hydrogen bomb; it warned that the time in which to decide between world cooperation and annihilation was short. Its practical suggestions included support of "high-level talks," cessation of H-bomb tests, cooperation in disarmament, another effort to reunite Germany through free elections, admission of Communist China to the United Nations, neutralization of Formosa, evacuation of the Chinese offshore islands, and aid to the peasant millions of Asia and Africa. It recognized, however, that in a troubled world the democratic powers must remain strong; it cited the Labour government's record on Korea as evidence that it would not shirk responsibility. In the Empire it would continue constitutional progress toward the Commonwealth ideal, attack the problem of poverty, and eliminate racial discrimination.

The greater part of *Forward with Labour* was devoted to domestic matters. The high cost of living was attributed to the Tories, who assertedly favored business and finance, while prosperity was credited not to Tory wisdom but to the recently favorable terms of trade. Labour's positive program to lower prices involved long-term agreements with Commonwealth countries, action against monopolies, and controls where necessary; that implementing the program would involve a return to rationing was flatly called "a deliberate Tory lie." A proposal for a Consumers' Advisory Service and the enforcement of quality standards was designed to appeal to the millions of cooperators and to consumers generally.

The manifesto promised to foster the welfare state, to further the housing program, and to abolish all health-service charges. Education would be radically reformed; in the interest of equality Labour would encourage comprehensive secondary schools instead of the existing grammar, technical, and modern schools, to which children were assigned on the basis of an examination taken in their twelfth year.

Labour rightly emphasized that the welfare program would have to be paid for by increased production, while more capital would have to be plowed back into industry. Nationalization was not stressed, but steel and road haulage, which had been denationalized by the Conservatives, would be renationalized, and water supply added to the list. Elsewhere Fabian caution asserted itself; not whole industries but sections of chemicals and machine tools would be nationalized, and the state would start new industries if necessary. Nothing was said about taking over the beet-sugar industry, or portions of mining machinery, engineering, and aircraft production, all of which had been mentioned in *Challenge to Britain*; the proposals were avowedly limited to what might be accomplished in the lifetime of one Parliament.

On industrial relations there was a vague promise to encourage schemes of industrial democracy. For agriculture there would be a return to a system of fixed guarantees and attention to the injustices connected with the tied cottage system. Attention was promised the local needs of Wales, Scotland, and Northern Ireland.

The Conservatives had by far the better organization for the campaign. Labour lacked the means to pay many full-time agents, to nurse marginal constituencies between elections, and to provide as many cars for polling day as could their opponents. It did, however, employ the traditional means of leaflets and meetings and the newer ones of radio and television, where the time was fairly shared among the parties. Bevan conducted his own campaign; he neither offered his services to the Transport House headquarters nor was invited to appear on Labour's radio and television series. Conservatives exploited the rift; their *Campaign Guide* contained more entries under Bevan's name than under Attlee's or Eden's. The Tory popular press caricatured Attlee as Bevan's tool. The electorate showed much interest in him. Only he and Churchill, the two outstanding orators, could be counted on to fill a hall. Bevan's sponsors could even charge a fee.

The campaign was quiet, even apathetic. Conservative speakers sought to link Labour with shortages and austerity, while Labourites harked back to prewar unemployment. But a new generation that knew only full employment and the benefits of the welfare state had grown up; canvassers were soon reporting that younger voters no longer responded to allusions to the "bad old Tory days."

The social services were frequently mentioned, but the measure of agreement was greater than that of difference. Conservatives attacked the nationalization proposals, and sought to create the image of a Labour party bent upon bureaucratic centralization. Most Labourites stressed the need for planning, but not the specific measures of socialization. Some socialists like Morrison stated the general principle that where the public interest would best be served, industries should be publicly owned, but anything more precise was left for an empirical future.

Gaitskell did suggest a new approach to nationalization: he proposed that the state accept industrial shares as part of inheritance taxes and thereby secure dividends for the public welfare, reap capital gains for the community, and gradually modify the unequal distribution of wealth. Labour speakers paid more attention to the accomplishment in industries already nationalized. The specific new proposals had no mass appeal; it was impossible to coin a popular slogan about acquiring a third of an industry or establishing something resembling a pilot plant.

Even though circumstances had combined to produce similar attitudes toward the United Nations, close cooperation with the United States, and "summit conferences" to secure peace, foreign affairs received unusual attention. The debate on summit conferences finally simmered down to the question of whether Eden or Attlee could better represent Britain. There was a difference on atomic weapons; Labourites supported stockpiling but, because of the danger of atmospheric pollution, opposed further experimental explosions. Sir Richard Acland, who had represented Gravesend as a Labourite since 1947, resigned from the party and stood as an independent solely on the issue of opposition to Britain's manufacture of the H-bomb. He was supported by Lord Bertrand Russell. The Bevanites demanded that under no circumstances would Britain resort to the bomb before an aggressor used it. The Communists plugged away steadily at the line of "ban the bomb." Attlee answered that because the most effective weapon at hand would always be employed in a life-and-death struggle, attempts to ban particular weapons were futile; disarmament would have to cover conventional weapons and forces as well.

The campaign reached no peak of excitement. The apathy was ominous for Labour. The percentage of the electorate that voted, 76.8, was a drop from the previous elections. The Conservatives received 13,311,938 votes and elected 345 members; the Labourites 12,-405,246 and 277; the Liberals 722,395 and 6. The Communists polled only 33,144. As compared with 1951, the Conservative vote declined by 412,480, but Labour with a loss of 1,543,139 suffered most from indifference and abstention. Actual changes in unaltered seats were few; Conservatives captured ten from Labour and one from Irish Labour, while Labour took one from the Conservatives. The changes did not affect the election map; Labour held its areas of strength. In the Commons it was still an effective Opposition. The left wing fared no better than the rest of the party; two prominent Bevanites were defeated, and some others barely survived. Its fortunes would not seem to support a theory that Labour lost from lack of a more vigorous socialist policy. The Liberals' hopes were dashed. Only the Conservatives had reason for satisfaction. The popular association of Tory rule with a low standard of living and mass unemployment was fading. For the first time since 1865, a government increased its majority in a general election; its over-all margin of 59 assured the possibility of the maximum life of five years.[14]

The decisive defeat led to some soul-searching on the part of the Labour party. An investigating committee under Harold Wilson pointed to its organizational weaknesses and its financial poverty. It had failed to get out the vote; one and one-half million adherents simply had not troubled to go to the polls. The committee recommended that a special subcommittee of the national executive be set up to head the electoral organization, that more full-time agents be secured, and, because most minds were made up before a campaign officially opened, that party activity be continuous. It discouraged giving undue attention to hopeless constituencies and advised concentrating on marginal ones that held the balance. It also urged greater attention to absentee voters, who had given the more diligent Conservatives their victory in 21 constituencies. The party built up an election fund; thanks to the trade unions, which provided 96 per cent of it, the fund amounted to £345,678 in 1959, as compared with £104,880 in 1951.[15]

Changes in the party leadership ensured that Labour would fight the next election with a much younger team. Since it was manifest that Attlee would soon retire, there was a good deal of jockeying for position with an eye to the succession. Competition for the treasurership had begun in 1953, when pressure to resign was put on the aging Greenwood. Morrison accepted the urging of some right-wing trade-union leaders to stand, but the party rather sentimentally rallied behind Greenwood. Morrison agreed to a compromise whereby, as deputy leader, he would be given a post ex officio in the executive. Greenwood died in 1954, but in his present position Morrison was ineligible for the treasurership. Many constituency parties and five unions, including the Railwaymen and the Electrical Trades Union, then nominated Bevan. But most of the unions, including Bevan's own Mineworkers, together with a minority of the constituency parties, supported Gaitskell. In a contest that all knew involved the possible succession to the leadership, Gaitskell won by a margin of more than two to one. In 1955 the contest was repeated. But because Bevan's noncooperative and insubordinate conduct in the interval had again nearly brought about his expulsion from the party, he lost most of his trade-union support and suffered a worse defeat. Not until 1956, after he had made his peace and the leadership had been settled, did he win the treasurership. Even then his margin over George Brown, a right-winger, was only 274,000 votes.[16]

Meanwhile, Dalton hastened the retirement of several veterans in order to make room for younger men. After complaining to Attlee that nine of the fifteen members of the shadow cabinet were over sixty-five, he set the example by resigning. He was followed—more or less graciously—by Shinwell, Ede, and others, and the average age was soon brought down from sixty to fifty-two.

In the interest of party unity, Dalton urged Attlee to continue; what he had in mind was the advancement of Gaitskell, his former right-hand man in the Ministry of Economic Warfare. Although Dalton had formerly supported Morrison, Morrison's age was now held against him. His standing in the party was generally lower, too, than it had been before the war, and his reputation had never recovered from the decline it suffered during his brief tenure at the Foreign Office. When Attlee finally resigned on December 7, 1955, the parliamentary party gave Gaitskell 157 votes, Bevan 70, and Morrison 40. It was a bitter blow to Morrison, so long the second man in the party; he refused to continue as deputy leader. Attlee accepted an earldom. In 1959 Morrison followed him to the Lords as a life peer, an unusual position for one born the son of a London policeman.

The Gaitskell-Bevan feud was closed at the end of 1956, when Gaitskell invited Bevan to be his shadow foreign secretary. Most of the Bevanites made their peace, so that when Gaitskell and Bevan stood side by side at the Brighton conference of 1957, Labour appeared to be enjoying greater solidarity than at any time since the war. It had a new leader, a former economics lecturer still under fifty, who, like Attlee, but unlike Hardie, Henderson, MacDonald, and Bevan, had come from the comfortable classes. Nevertheless, he had become a socialist because of his compassion for the less fortunate and his hatred of social injustice.[17]

The Suez crisis of 1956 helped to bring Gaitskell and Bevan together and to solidify the leadership. Although in the Commons' first major debate on the issue on August 2 Gaitskell and other Labourites were sharply critical of Nasser and in broad support of a policy of firmness, they soon took alarm at the government's military preparations. The shadow cabinet urged the government to make it clear that no action inconsistent with the United Nations Charter was intended. The T.U.C. resolved unanimously to oppose force exercised without reference to the United Nations or without its consent. Upon the Anglo-French ultimatum to Egypt, Gaitskell urged the government to make no irrevocable decisions until the United Nations' policy was known. The first bombing on October 31 brought a Labour motion of censure which, after considerable uproar, was defeated. In the country the National Council of Labour launched a "Law, not War" campaign; the first protest meeting of November 4 was one of the largest assemblages seen in London for some years.

Labour's official record was one of consistent opposition to the resort to force. Yet there was a strong rank-and-file sympathy for the government, particularly after British troops went into action. Morrison, conscious of his own feelings about Abadan and ideas of justice for large nations as well as small, charged the leadership with giving the impression of having greater consideration for Nasser's Egypt than for Britain. A private poll at North Lewisham during a by-election shortly afterwards revealed such sympathy with the government's action that the Suez issue was soft-pedaled. That this nationalist feeling, though strong, left no trace in resolutions made at trade-union or Labour party conferences, was an example of the relative silence of right-wing deviation.[18]

The Labour-Communist feud continued unabated. It flared at a dinner given by the parliamentary party in April 1956, for Khrushchev and Bulganin, at which it appeared that "left could speak to left" only in the most acrimonious terms. Russian interference in Polish politics and the Red Army's harsh suppression of the Hungarian uprising isolated the British Communists, weakened their position in some trade unions where they had been strong, and brought a decline in the party membership. The fuller revelation of the sanguinary nature of the Stalinist regime caused that party to fall further into disrepute, though its hard core faithfully followed the Moscow line.

Along with the improvement of the Labour party machinery there was a reconsideration of the program. Much had been written about the goals and tools of socialism, including a volume of *New Fabian Essays* (1952). Common ownership was not enough; it confused means and ends, while the specific proposals recently advanced had been no vote-getters. Nor was statism necessarily good. Russia allegedly sacrificed the individual and in the fifties produced a society of greater extremes than contemporary Britain. British Labour, ran the contrast, with its ideals rooted in Benthamite radicalism and Christian socialism, valued the individual. Shortly after Labour's defeat in 1955, Gaitskell voiced the party's need to restate its aims in phrases designed to impress the rising generation.[19]

During the 1955 campaign Gaitskell had suggested another approach to nationalization by proposing that the state accept in inheritance taxes not only cash but also land, securities, and other property. Dalton had advanced the idea in *Practical Socialism for Great Britain* (1935), and, when Chancellor of the Exchequer, had applied it on occasion to land. Gaitskell now envisioned a government investment corporation with a large portfolio of stock that might be increased by the judicious investment of pension funds and budget surpluses. Under his leadership the party appointed a committee, which included Bevan as well as moderates, to prepare a policy statement for the guidance of the next Labour government.

The committee's report, *Industry and Society* (1957), accepted Gaitskell's proposals. After a general statement on the merits of public ownership, it proceeded to a lengthy analysis of trends in industry that indicated the changed socialist concept of the relation between ownership and power. It found that in the approximately five hundred large firms in Britain power rested with the professional managers, while ownership was vested in nearly functionless stockholders. It was into the coffers of the stockholders, however, that dividends and capital gains flowed. Through Gaitskell's plan of acquiring equity shares, the community would participate in the gains of industry.

Except for reversing the Conservative action on iron and steel and on road haulage, the committee made no other proposals concerning large industries, though it approved the principle of acquiring parts of them. With respect to the thousands of small businesses in which the capitalist was still important in that he provided risk capital and served as owner-director, the state should give encouragement and permit large rewards.

This report was submitted to the 1957 party conference. To some life-long socialists it was a shock. J. Campbell of the Railwaymen led the assault upon it and called for injecting into it "the rich red blood of Socialist objective." He was supported not only by many from the constituency parties but also by veterans like Morrison and Shinwell. Shinwell called the leadership "a set of reformed characters," and likened a future party conference to one of shareholders with the directors on the platform. Others predicted that the "shareholder state" would tie Labour to the capitalist system and kill the labor movement, but the report was approved by 5,309,000 votes to 1,276,000. A year later, at Scarborough, its proposals were reaffirmed and the Gaitskell leadership strengthened.[20]

When Harold Macmillan, Eden's successor as Prime Minister, set October 8, 1959, as the date of the next general election, Labour felt ready with its new leadership, improved organization, and revised program. It planned to contest all 630 seats except 9 hopeless ones in Northern Ireland. Of its 621 candidates, 129 were sponsored by trade unions, but the great majority were such middle-class men as educators, lawyers, and journalists. A few company directors, landowners, farmers, and members of the armed services were also included, but these elements were far more numerous among their Conservative opponents. The Conservatives, very dejected after the Suez fiasco but now cheerful over the renewed prosperity at home and a momentary relaxation of world tensions, went to the country with the slogan, "You never had it so good." The Liberals hoped for a stronger group in the Commons, while small Celtic nationalist parties hoped to take votes from both major ones.

Labour's campaign manifesto, *Britain Belongs to You* (1959), was based on a longer policy statement, *The Future Labour Offers You* (1958). It denied the Conservative thesis of one happy and prosperous nation; such complacency disregarded the four hundred thousand unemployed, the million on national assistance, and the very low rate of increase in production. For all have-nots there was generous concern. The manifesto gave priority to the plight of the aged with an emergency plan to raise pensions at once by ten shillings a week

($1.40); a long-term contributory scheme for employees would provide them with approximately half pay upon retirement.

For education, "an investment in the future," the aim was to improve school plants, reduce the size of classes, and extend technical and higher education; in the interest of equality of opportunity and of social "integration," Labour would end the system that channeled children into three types of schools and, instead, develop comprehensive schools similar to the public schools in the United States, and open grammar-school education to all who could benefit by it.

Whereas on housing the Conservatives boasted of their building record, Labour pointed to the seven million households still without baths and the more than three million sharing or without a water closet. Private building would be encouraged, but, because landlords were slow to modernize old houses, local councils should assume that task. For the national health service there was a promise of more of almost everything, especially hospital building; a policy report, *Members One of Another* (1959), advocated the abolition of all charges on teeth, spectacles, prescriptions, and artificial limbs. In an age of greater leisure, government should do more to encourage the arts and provide for recreation.

Such an extensive program of social services would require funds, but they would come mainly from a policy of planned economic expansion. Further sums could be obtained by instituting a capital gains tax and stopping leaks such as existed in expense-account abuse and the avoidance of death duties and surtax. Public ownership was not stressed, but steel and road haulage would be renationalized and water supply reorganized under public ownership. "We have no other plans for further nationalization," was the categorical statement, but, where necessary, part or all of any industry "failing the nation" might be nationalized. Public investment agencies might also invest in equity shares—the Gaitskell plan to enable the community to participate in profits and capital gains.

Turning to foreign affairs, the manifesto argued that Labour's loyalty to the United Nations and the rule of law, in contrast to Tory cynicism revealed by "the Suez gamble," gave it the better right to speak for Britain at a summit conference. Labour would strive to end the atomic weapons race, and in the meantime would permit no weakening of Britain's alliances. The manifesto would end nuclear tests. It advocated a comprehensive disarmament treaty, disengagement in Central Europe, and, in order to prevent the spread of nuclear weapons, the formation of a "non-nuclear club" of nations, which Britain would join. It took pride in Labour's part in the evolution of the Commonwealth and pledged an annual sum equal to 1 per cent of Britain's national income to help the underdeveloped countries.

Although Conservative strategy contemplated a quiet campaign that would not arouse potential Labour voters, the Labour party launched a vigorous attack. Its organization was still inferior to that of its wealthier rival, but for this election it produced an innovation in the form of a special committee, including such able publicists as Richard Crossman and Thomas Driberg, which held daily sessions to control its direction and emphasis. The daily press conferences of Morgan Phillips, the party secretary, set a pace and standard that the Conservative Central Office sought to emulate. The Labour television programs, it was generally conceded, were the most original, imaginative, and entertaining of all, and, somewhat to the viewers' surprise, in this medium Gaitskell was more effective than the Prime Minister.

Labour chose as its first point of attack the pensioners' predicament, admittedly serious, and unemployment. Gaitskell's opening broadcast denied the Conservative claim of universal prosperity and progress, citing the low rate of increase in productivity and the pockets of unemployment in Scotland, Wales, Northern Ireland, and the Lancashire cotton belt. The social services were much discussed, but the differences were not over principle but on which party would best administer them.

Nationalization received greater attention from Conservatives and Liberals who wanted no more of it than from Labourites who generally wanted some but not a great deal more. The Labour policy statement *Steel and the Nation* and the weekly *Tribune* stated the case for renationalizing iron and steel, but speakers seldom discussed it. Gaitskell and some of his colleagues did treat the place of a public sector in a mixed economy, but many Labour candidates shied away from the issue or even gave assurances that particular industries, such as a local branch of Imperial Chemicals, would not be touched.

On the whole, nationalization was something of a handicap to Labour in this "prosperity" election. The Conservative Central Office, the Institute of Directors, the Iron and Steel Federation, the Aims of Industry, and other hostile organizations had successfully instilled an image of Labour as a party bent upon creating giant bureaucratic state monopolies. When Conservatives featured the alleged high cost of the Labour program, Gaitskell answered frankly that the cost depended upon industrial expansion; if British industry could be expanded, the necessary revenue would flow in without resort to heavier taxation. Douglas Jay, also an economist, said that surely something was wrong if Britain, relatively so prosperous, could not achieve old-age pensions like the Germans, housing standards like the Scandinavians, and educational expenditure like the Russians.

Current Commonwealth problems received attention, but there was no dispute over ultimate goals. There were very real differences, however, over what steps should be taken next. Conservatives emphasized caution and safeguards, reminding the voters of the bloodshed and displacement that had affected millions during the withdrawal from India. Labourites urged a speedier tempo in the evolution of the Commonwealth, denounced racial discrimination, and blamed the government for the troubles in Cyprus and Africa.

Foreign affairs generally attracted less attention than domestic. Both major parties supported N.A.T.O. and the Anglo-American alliance, but the Labour left still distrusted American leadership and policy. Liberals and Labourites alike passionately denounced the government's Egyptian policy, which Conservatives as ardently defended. Both major parties accepted nuclear weapons as basic to N.A.T.O. defensive strategy, though on the Labour left voices for unilateral renunciation were strong. The party majority, however, was unwilling to stake all upon one single dramatic gesture that would leave a Labour government with no basis for negotiation. In *Disarmament and Nuclear War: The Next Step* (1959), Labour suggested that, if all nations except the United States and the Soviet Union would agree not to make, possess, or test nuclear weapons, and to submit to controls and inspection, Britain would cease to manufacture them and dispose of existing stocks. Finally, it was debated which leader could better represent Britain at the proposed summit conference, which had now become a symbol of hope.

In a 78.7 per cent poll on October 8, Conservatives received 13,750,-965 votes and elected 365 members; for Labour the figures were 12,-216,166 and 258, and for the Liberals 1,640,761 and 6. An independent Conservative won in Caithness and Sutherland, but no minor party came near success anywhere. The Conservatives' over-all majority of 100 was greater than any expert had predicted. Their total vote was up by 439,027 over 1955, while Labour's was down by 189,-080; the Liberals' was up by 918,366. The Communists' vote, with 30,-897, was down by 2,247. In percentages Conservatives had 49.4, Labour 43.8, Liberals 5.9, and all others 0.9; Labour's percentage loss since 1955 was 2.5. Labour lost 8 seats in the London area, 10 in the Midlands, and a scattered 10 elsewhere, but suffered only a slight loss of votes in Wales. In Lancashire and Scotland, it actually increased its total and captured 5 seats from the Conservatives. The changes were not sufficient to alter the general appearance of the election map; again the industrial and mining areas of South Wales, south Lancashire, the Midlands—though less solidly—the West Riding with a strip south to Leicester, Durham and Tyneside, and central Scotland, together with working-class London, voted Labour.

The Labourites were sadly disappointed that in spite of improved organization, able leadership, and a well-planned campaign they had not only lost three times in a row but also had seen their high poll of 1951 steadily decline. That they gained only in areas of distress and discontent was an ominous sign. They had not captured one of the new towns settled so largely from former crowded Labour strongholds; many of those former underprivileged workers, and more of their wives, now comfortably housed and owning television sets and even a car, quietly changed sides to help return Tories. The Labourites felt threatened by the success of their own welfare policies; if Labour could win only in times of adversity and then be associated with necessary but unpopular policies, the political future was bleak.

Trade-union–sponsored candidates had fared well; of 129 so supported, 92 were elected, including all 31 Miners, 14 of 19 Transport Workers, and 8 of 15 Engineers. But these successes reflected the unions' tendency to contest only safe seats and nominate their veteran servants, which unfortunately deprived the parliamentary party and the House of Commons of the services of promising young men. Yet the defeat, though serious, was not overwhelming. Next time a swing of four, or even three, votes in a hundred could give victory.

This third successive defeat produced a spate of analyses and reappraisals. Many leaders, including Gaitskell, found the adverse trend rooted in economic and social factors. Prosperity had reduced unemployment to a point where 2 per cent was considered high, while better distribution, due in large part to the social services, had abolished abject poverty. Even more significant was the changing character of the labor force. There were fewer manual workers and more clerical, administrative, and technical ones; the typical factory worker was more likely to be a skilled man in a new modern plant than an underpaid cotton operative in a dark, obsolete cotton mill.[21] Class lines were becoming blurred. Workers were better paid; many were buying homes and cars; some paid income tax; they considered themselves middle class. Scholarships enabled their sons to attend the universities and enter the professions. Surveys indicated that children of Labour fathers were more apt to go over to the other party than were those of Conservative ones. It behooved Labour, reasoned some leaders, to adjust its outlook to the changing times, for the Britain of the 1960's was vastly different from the Britain of Keir Hardie.[22]

In order to "modernize" the party and destroy the image of Labour as doctrinaire and a trade-union tool, some right-wingers proposed severing the link with the unions, making a pact or fusing with the Liberals, or changing the party's name to "Labour and Radical" or "Labour and Reform." Gaitskell, however, rejected all such proposals, and concentrated upon revising Clause 4 of the 1918 constitution, which stated that one party object was "to secure for the producers by hand or by brain the full fruits of their industry, and the most equitable distribution thereof that may be possible, upon the basis of the common ownership of the means of production."

To the makers of that constitution "common ownership" was clearly a means to an end, but in the popular mind, Gaitskell contended, there had arisen such confusion of means and ends that socialism and nationalization were regarded as synonymous, a belief that was a barrier to party success. At the annual party conference of November 28–29, 1959, he proposed to amend Clause 4 in order to emphasize alternative roads to socialism and that the party objectives were much broader than common ownership. He immediately stirred up a conflict with the perfervid idealists who had fought under the banner of nationalization, regarded the suggestion as a desertion, and preferred a lifetime of opposition to a surrender of principle. The keynote speech of the chairman, Mrs. Barbara Castle, a former Bevanite, stressed the theme of working to make more socialists. Other "fundamentalists" like Michael Foot spoke with blazing conviction of the need to continue the socialist crusade. One militant was ready to read Gaitskell out of the party. Gaitskell's supporters, like Denis Healey, rallied to him and were blunt about the growing gap between the party and the voters, and most of the trade-union leaders except Frank Cousins of the Transport Workers stood with him. Bevan attempted a conciliatory speech, but left no doubt that he upheld nationalization.[23]

In succeeding months the dispute raged so violently that the Labour executive sought a compromise. Clause 4 stood unamended, but the executive proposed a supplementary declaration of party objectives and the means of obtaining them that included much of what Gaitskell had asked. Among the proposals were statements on social justice, the classless society, democracy in industry, support of the

United Nations, and the end of racial discrimination. As to common ownership, there would be an expansion sufficient to give the community power over "the commanding heights of the economy"—Bevan's phrase—but Gaitskell got something in that common ownership was now defined to include public participation in private concerns along with state ownership, municipal ownership, and producer and consumer cooperation. In spite of fundamentalist objections to tampering with the creed, the executive's proposal was accepted by a vote of 4,304,000 to 2,226,000 at the Scarborough conference of October 1960.[24]

No precise blueprint of the party's nationalization plans exists as yet. A militant minority calls for more and rapid nationalization. Labourites agree that the total nationalization should be somewhat greater than at present, but the party, democratic and parliamentary, will move no faster than the electorate will follow. The voluntary principle is backed by millions of cooperators, and Labourites agree that local authorities and private enterprise will have important sectors in the future mixed economy. In 1937 Attlee wrote, "They [British socialists] have never accepted the beehive or the ants' nest as an ideal. . . . On the contrary, they appreciate that the wealth of a society is in its variety, not its uniformity."[25] The moderate majority would accept Crosland's restatement: "The ideal . . . is a society in which ownership is thoroughly mixed up—a society with a diverse, diffused, pluralist, and heterogeneous pattern of ownership, with the State, the nationalized industries, the Cooperatives, the Unions, Government financial institutions, pension funds, foundations, and millions of private families all participating."[26]

More serious than the strife over Clause 4 was that over nuclear weapons, since it became a moral issue that could not be settled by compromise or majority votes. For years the party's official position had been that disarmament must follow political understanding, and that it must be multilateral. From 1955 onward the party divided on the H-bomb issue, although in that year passionate emotion was not yet roused and a resolution to oppose its manufacture and use was defeated by a five-to-one vote.

In 1957 the question was whether Britain should unilaterally refuse to make, test, or use nuclear weapons. Few would have expected Bevan to agree with Gaitskell on this issue, but at the conference of reconciliation at Brighton he said that a British Foreign Secretary must not be sent "naked into the conference chamber." Unilateralism lost by 5,836,000 to 781,000.[27] In 1958 three resolutions on the question met the same fate.[28] At these annual party conferences trade-union support for unilateralism was slight, because few had confidence in the efficacy of the one grand moral gesture that would deprive British diplomacy of further bargaining power. Their big battalions gave the executive its decisive majorities.

But there was a growing uneasiness and much discussion about the horrific results to Britain in the event of nuclear war. American bases in Britain and bomber patrols incurred greater danger from retaliation than ever, while even testing involved threats to the present and future generations. At the end of the decade a vigorous Campaign for Nuclear Disarmament gathered strength. Well-known persons such as Lord Bertrand Russell and Canon Collins supported it, and much money, publicity, and organizing effort went into it. The campaign drew support from a circle far wider than that of the Christian pacifists, left-wingers, fellow-travelers, and Communists that had provided the drive for minority movements in the past. It appealed particularly to idealistic youth. Eventually, it broke up the trade-union combination that so often gave the Labour executive its majority. As the campaign developed strength, it appeared that the decision in the 1960 Labour conference would be very close.

In July 1960, in view of the collapse of the Big Four summit conference two months earlier, the Labour executive and the T.U.C. general council issued a statement calling for support of N.A.T.O., arms control in Central Europe as a step toward disengagement, and an agreement to end nuclear tests. It opposed an independent nuclear weapon for Britain. It would reduce N.A.T.O.'s dependence on nuclear weapons, state that Britain would never be the first to use the H-bomb, avoid the spread of nuclear weapons to other powers, and not provide them to Germany.

In presenting the statement to the Scarborough conference, Gaitskell put the case against neutralism and for the need and positive value of a deterrent. In the vote, however, the executive policy was opposed not only by Communist-controlled unions, such as the Electrical Trades Union, but also by several of the Big Six, including Cousins' Transport and General Workers Union (T.G.W.U.). The policy was defeated, though narrowly, by 3,339,000 to 3,042,000. An Amalgamated Engineering Union motion for the unilateral renunciation of manufacturing, stockpiling, and basing of nuclear weapons in Britain was carried by 3,303,000 to 2,896,000. A T.G.W.U. resolution by Cousins that a Labour government would reject any defense policy based on nuclear weapons, halt their manufacture, and put an end to patrols carrying them from British bases passed narrowly by 3,282,000 to 3,239,000. Everywhere the left was triumphant.[29]

The alignment of the conference on one side of a major issue and the leader and parliamentary party majority on the other precipitated another crisis. Gaitskell was confirmed in the leadership when he won by 166 to 81 over Harold Wilson, an advocate of compromise with the unilateralists, and Gaitskell's supporter, George Brown, was elected deputy leader to succeed the recently deceased Bevan. Gaitskell proclaimed his determination to "fight and fight and fight again" to reverse the Scarborough decision, whereupon his opponents denounced him as unfaithful to the party constitution.

The constitutional issue arose out of a provision of the document of 1918 stating that the parliamentary party should "give effect as far as may be practicable to the principles from time to time approved by the party conference."[30] Soon two interpretations of this provision appeared. One held that the parliamentary party was the creature of the conference, the other that the clause about practicability in effect left it free. In 1920 Shinwell, not yet an M.P., had asserted that the parliamentary party was the property of the Labour movement, but Clynes had promptly answered that it was autonomous.[31] In 1937 Attlee had written that conference instructions must be carried out by the party's representatives in Parliament, but in his 1945 interchanges with Churchill he had insisted that a Labour government would be under no extraconstitutional control.[32] In the 1950's, official party literature was specific on the parliamentary party's independence.

For forty years the question was academic; the parliamentary party conducted itself as though autonomous, but although it was agreed that a conference of 1,100 could not foresee the circumstances under which the M.P.'s would have to act, its resolutions were valued, and even sought, as expressions of party and public opinion. Moreover, the political and trade-union leaders understood one another and cooperated so closely that the political leaders ordinarily got their conference majorities. In practice, the parliamentary party enjoyed an autonomy in accord with the doctrine that M.P.'s were representatives of their constituencies and not delegates from a particular organization.[33]

Gaitskell had reason to believe that he could secure a reversal of the Scarborough decision. The activity of the sincere, zealous, sometimes single-minded left groups has often been noted. The votes of many constituency parties and trade unionists had been determined by a minority of such enthusiasts who attended meetings and worded the resolutions sent to the conference. Although trade unions had democratic constitutions, their block votes were usually determined by the minority, often 10 per cent or less, who troubled to participate. It was to the potentially democratic character of their movement that Gaitskell appealed.

The party executive and T.U.C. general council prepared a new statement, *Policy for Peace* (1961). It emphasized the urgency of disarmament with a ban upon nuclear tests and weapons, but accepted the present need of nuclear power by the West, though the West should never be the first to use it. Britain, which should cease the attempt to be a nuclear power, should permit the American bases to remain, but must be free to decide whether a particular project would be accepted and under what conditions. The statement expressed hope in ultimate world government.

Meanwhile, Gaitskell was gradually rallying the party to his views. A group of younger members initiated a Campaign for Democratic Socialism, which showed that youth was not all with the extremists. Trade unionists had second thoughts; the Railwaymen's executive recommended a change in their vote and the Shop, Distributive, and Allied workers with 300,000 votes did likewise. Others fell into line, so that when the conference assembled at Blackpool on October 2, 1961, it was apparent that Gaitskell would win.

At Blackpool the official position was put by Brown, the new deputy leader: unilateralism would serve only to disturb the balance that, though precarious, had held through the dangerous years; it would increase fear, and force the United States to augment its armaments to compensate for the weakening of the West; the gesture would reduce British influence. In spite of the attitude of Cousins, who opposed any defense based upon nuclear weapons, the conference emphatically rejected unilateralism and approved the official policy by a vote of 4,526,000 to 1,756,000. By 5,476,000 to 846,000 it overwhelmed a resolution favoring neutralism. But the conference defeated the platform on two issues: it condemned the government by 3,519,000 to 2,733,000 for allowing Germany to use British territory to train German troops, and disapproved by 3,611,000 to 2,739,000 the establishment of a Polaris base in Holy Loch, near Glasgow, because of the danger of accidental disaster, accidental war, and enemy retaliation.[34]

Gaitskell's triumph spiked the theory that the parliamentary party was a tool of the conference. He received tribute for his courage, integrity, and leadership in securing the rejection of unilateralism. But the defeated minority, convinced that nuclear war meant gain for none and possibly death for all, fought on for the cause it believed moral and necessary. At times the tactics of its members degenerated to the point where Gaitskell's public meetings were marred by rowdy demonstrations. Meanwhile, the Electrical Trades Union and some other left unions fell more into line by ridding themselves of their Communist officials.

The Labour majority also followed Gaitskell on the question of the European Economic Community. One wing of the party, led by Roy Jenkins and John Diamond, who were both Fabians and M.P.'s, actively supported Britain's entry. Another, including Douglas Jay and Mrs. Barbara Castle, were definitely opposed. Gaitskell took a middle ground. He expressed hope that Britain could join, but also a fundamental objection to entry into any union operated in a restrictive, inward-looking manner and not regarded as a step toward a free world-trading community. He stipulated that Britain must retain the right to plan its own economy, control its own foreign policy, and safeguard its agriculture. He would ensure the vital interests of the Commonwealth and of the members of the European Free Trade Association—the counterorganization of Britain, the Scandinavian countries, Austria, Switzerland, Portugal, and Finland.

Since there was little expectation that Gaitskell's terms could be obtained, they looked like a rejection. Whatever chance of consideration existed disappeared in January 1963 with the French veto of the British application, and the Labour party was saved the pain of attempting to reconcile the differences among its members. To the nationalist sentiment that took pride in "the thousand years of British history" and had rallied the party to the national defense in two world wars, it was not without relief that even a remote possibility of absorption in a greater European union was averted; in spite of its internationalism, the British Labour party is British.

Gaitskell's views on domestic policy were incorporated in *Signposts for the Sixties,* a statement adopted by the annual conference at Blackpool (1961) as the program to be followed should Labour regain power. Basic in it is a plan for economic growth, upon the success of which depend all plans for improved social services and bettered living conditions. In order to stimulate British industry, which is relatively lagging and in some instances dangerously behind its competitors, a Labour government would create a National Industrial Planning Board to ensure speedy and purposeful investment in both the public and the private sectors. It would reconstruct the National Research Development Corporation and authorize it to engage in production either directly or jointly with private companies, sponsor research, and modernize backward industries. Nationalization would have a place: steel and road haulage would be renationalized, but no other whole industries were specifically mentioned. Other possible forms of nationalization would be the establishment of competitive public enterprises where present results are unsatisfactory, and state and private partnerships where subsidies and loans are necessary or where industries, e.g., aircraft and pharmaceutical, produce mainly for the public services.

In the interest of social equality, a Labour Chancellor of the Exchequer would use the tax weapon to narrow the gap between the extremes of wealth and poverty. Specifically mentioned are the taxation of capital gains and closure of the loopholes of tax avoidance. To halt the uncontrolled rise in land values, facilitate effective town and country planning, encourage local authorities to build houses, and make it easier for people to buy their own homes, Labour proposes to transfer to public ownership the freehold of land needed for public use or for building. Agricultural land and the freehold of existing houses would be unaffected, but a land commission is proposed which would purchase the freehold of land upon which new building is authorized. The commission would lease the site on terms that would ensure for the community the benefits of any future increase in the value of the land.

Once the necessary industrial expansion is obtained, it will be possible to improve the system of social security, the social services, and education. Labour envisages a completely free health service, a national superannuation plan that will recast the level of contributions and benefits in a way that will ensure at least half pay on retirement, and better provision for widows, the sick, and the redundant workers.

The statement on education proposes improvement on all levels, with smaller classes in the primary grades, an end to the much criticized eleven-plus examination and the reorganization of secondary schools on comprehensive lines, a great expansion of higher and technical education, and the abolition of fee-paying in the universities. The public schools, criticized for their "contribution to unequal opportunities and to social inequality," would be integrated with the system, but the decision on method is left for the future.

The theme of equality runs throughout this document and appears in much Labour writing.[35] There is much overlap in the programs of the British parties, but this emphasis on equality is uniquely Labour's. To equality before the law, achieved long ago, and to the more recently won political and religious equality, Labour would add equality of opportunity and social equality. No regimented uniformity is contemplated, but Labour wishes to abolish special privilege, class distinctions, and great inequality of wealth. The practical goal is a broad and genuine equality with a degree of difference not so great that it would prevent the achievement of a spirit of fraternity in the nation and the possibility of fellowship among its people.

Gaitskell strove valiantly to reconcile the factions in the party and to heal its wounds. Even those who had differed with him recognized his brilliance, honesty, and integrity. Aided by the party's usual tendency to minimize feuds and present a common front in face of a general election, his efforts were successful. Labour appeared united as it had not been in years when on January 18, 1963, at the height of his influence, Gaitskell suddenly died, leaving a sense of tragic loss shared by political opponents and followers alike.

The succession to the leadership was contested by George Brown, the deputy leader, who had right-wing and some trade-union support; Harold Wilson; and James Callaghan, the shadow chancellor. On the first ballot the parliamentary party gave Brown 88 votes, Wilson 115, and Callaghan 41. Since no candidate had a majority, a second ballot was necessary. When Callaghan dropped out, Wilson with 144 votes against Brown's 103 was the winner. Brown remained as deputy leader.

Harold Wilson was born in 1915 in Huddersfield, Yorkshire, the son of an industrial chemist. Unlike Attlee and Gaitskell, who had been educated at select public schools, he attended a grammar school and retained a north country accent. He studied at Jesus College, Oxford, and at 21 became a lecturer in economics at New College, Oxford. During the war Dalton brought him into public service, and he remained to make politics his profession. At 31 he was the youngest member of the Attlee government. Independent in thought, he belonged to no section of the party, though his views placed him left of center. He was often associated with opposition to official policy. In 1951 he resigned on principle with Bevan and later stood against Gaitskell for the leadership. But in the interest of party unity, he strove to heal the breach he had helped to create and in the shadow cabinet cooperated faithfully with Gaitskell, thus manifesting the independence and flexibility that have laid him open to charges of political opportunism. After election to the leadership, he stressed the idea of continuity; he would devote himself to the preservation of party unity on the principles associated with Gaitskell and of *Signposts for the Sixties*.

Labour's defense policy, as stated by Wilson, Patrick Gordon Walker, shadow foreign secretary, and other spokesmen, is essentially that of Gaitskell.[36] The party pledges firm support to the United Nations and N.A.T.O. It would keep the United States' bases in Britain including Holy Loch, although ideally it would prefer to have them under United Nations auspices. It officially accepts the West's need of a nuclear deterrent, but opposes an independent British one. The failure of the costly Blue Streak missile, it holds, showed that Britain cannot afford both the deterrent and conventional weapons. It denies that the Nassau arrangement of December 1962, whereby Britain could purchase Polaris missiles, added anything to the strength of the West; it would renegotiate that agreement, and unless proof of necessity were forthcoming, would cancel it.

Labour would prevent the proliferation of nuclear powers. It believes a multilateral mix-manned nuclear force is politically undesirable. Because it fears that all hope of an agreement with the Soviet Union would be ended if Germany should get nuclear power, Labour wants no German hands on "the bomb," and would accept the proposed multilateral force only as a last resort to prevent the development of another independent nuclear power. The policy is essentially that of Gaitskell's non-nuclear club and confinement of nuclear striking force to the two great powers.

Accordingly, Britain's effort should be directed not toward prestige symbols but toward strengthening efficient mobile conventional forces, including the navy, where British tradition is great. They would be made available through N.A.T.O. to put out "brush fires" that otherwise might flare into world crises. The crises in Cyprus and Malaysia have shown the existence of this danger and need. These forces would be of particular use at Aden and Singapore, where bases should be kept and adequately garrisoned.

Wilson, who looks with even less favor than Gaitskell on entry into the European Economic Community, would strengthen ties with the United States and the Commonwealth. He holds that Labour's policy toward the United Nations is closer to that of the United States than is the Conservatives', and cites opposing views on Katanga separatism as a case in point. Unlike the United States, however, Wilson and Labour advocate admitting China to the United Nations in the belief that no other course will induce China to behave more like a member of the family of nations. Labour regards the Commonwealth as the greatest experiment in multiracial association that mankind has known, and one that might set an example in a world where race relations are a central problem. In Central Europe Labour would like to see a nuclear free zone to include at least Germany, Poland,

and Czechoslovakia, and regards the free zone as a concept that might be extended to Latin America, the Far East, and the Middle East.

Wilson and his party hold that the Labour program is not outdated merely because the worst abuses and inequalities of the nineteenth century have been alleviated and all parties accept, in principle, the welfare state. Not only is much still undone, but the automation revolution is now widely replacing the human mind as the earlier industrial revolution replaced human muscle. Although this development presents the possibility of unrivaled prosperity for all, it may, unless properly guided, result in benefits to the few and misery for the many. Labour is convinced that its socialism is relevant to this tremendous challenge.

Wilson's domestic policy continues that outlined by Gaitskell and *Signposts for the Sixties.* He is concerned with the slow pace of many British industries, the low rate of expansion, and the failure of some industries to keep up with rapidly changing techniques. A Labour government should plan for the further "rationalization" of industry in a way that would recapture its dynamism. It would tolerate no inefficiency. It would increase investments, encourage expanding firms, and stimulate efforts. Not doctrinaire on forms of organization, it would have industry carried on by private firms, by joint participation of government and private capital, and by publicly owned industry. But where the community shared in the venture, it would share in the profits. Above all, it would be the task of government to link the scientific revolution to socialism. Such a task would involve a great expansion of secondary and university education to train scientists, the mobilization of scientific research, and the application of science to industry. Once the industrial expansion is obtained, it would make possible the solution of such problems as full employment, housing, health, and retirement, and through national and local government aid to the arts and recreation make provision for a better use of leisure time.[37]

Such is the role of socialism in modern Britain as seen by the Labour leadership today. In that party, however, a wide range of ideas is still found. It contains members who, had they lived in the 1880's, would have followed Henry Hyndman or William Morris, and others who would have been content with limited trade-union objectives on hours and wages. Most Labourites, however, hold views that come closer to those of the Fabians with their ideas of gradualism, a mixed economy, and a socialism based upon parliamentary democracy and human freedom.

Notes

Notes

Chapter One

1. *Manchester Guardian Weekly,* Oct. 5, 1961.
2. Henry Pelling, Ed., *The Challenge of Socialism* (London, 1954), p. 175.
3. I.L.P., *Report of the First General Conference* (1893).
4. I.L.P., *Report* (1900), p. 5.
5. T.U.C., *Report* (1899), pp. 64–65.
6. Quoted by Philip P. Poirier, *The Advent of the British Labour Party* (New York, 1958), p. 82.
7. I.L.P., *Report* (1900), p. 6.
8. *The Clarion,* Mar. 10, 1900.

For fuller accounts of Labour party origins see Henry Pelling, *The Origins of the Labour Party, 1880–1900* (London, 1954); J. H. Stewart Reid, *The Origins of the British Labour Party* (Minneapolis, 1955); Philip P. Poirier, *The Advent of the British Labour Party* (New York, 1958); G. D. H. Cole, *British Working Class Politics, 1832–1914* (London, 1941); Godfrey Elton, *'England Arise!' A Study of the Pioneering Days of the Labour Movement* (London, 1931); Francis Williams, *Fifty Years March* (London, 1949); Max Beer, *A History of British Socialism,* Vol. II (London, 1921).

Among the many works dealing with special aspects of Labour party history are Edward R. Pease, *A History of the Fabian Society* (London, 1916); Margaret Cole, *The Story of Fabian Socialism* (London, 1961); H. M. Hyndman, *The Record of an Adventurous Life* (New York, 1911); C. Tsuzuki, *H. M. Hyndman and British Socialism* (New York, 1961); William Stewart, *J. Keir Hardie* (London, 1921).

Chapter Two

1. Frank Bealey and Henry Pelling, *Labour and Politics, 1900–1906* (London, 1958), pp. 32–58.
2. Pease, *History of the Fabian Society,* pp. 128–38; Stewart, *J. Keir Hardie,* pp. 143–52; M. Cole, *Fabian Socialism,* pp. 95–102.

3. Poirier, *Advent of the British Labour Party*, pp. 118–35.

4. Sidney and Beatrice Webb, *The History of Trade Unionism, 1666–1920* (London, 1919), pp. 600–604; Bealey and Pelling, *Labour and Politics*, pp. 55–72.

5. J. R. MacDonald, *Socialism and Society* (London, 1905), p. 154.

6. Stewart, *J. Keir Hardie*, pp. 85–104.

7. Bealey and Pelling, *Labour and Politics*, pp. 125–59, 298–99.

8. For a tabulation of the returns, see G. D. H. Cole, *British Working-Class Politics*, pp. 283–86; see also Bealey and Pelling, *Labour and Politics*, pp. 256–81, 290–92.

9. Philip Snowden, *An Autobiography* (2 vols., London, 1934), I, 121ff.

10. Labour party, *Report* (1907), pp. 3, 68–71; Mary Agnes Hamilton, *Arthur Henderson* (London, 1938), pp. 46–64.

11. Fenner Brockway, *Socialism over Sixty Years: The Life of Jowett of Bradford* (London, 1946), pp. 78–87; Reid, *Origins of the British Labour Party*, pp. 136–39.

12. Labour party, *Report* (1908), pp. 92–98; *ibid.* (1909), p. 81; Reid, *Origins of the British Labour Party*, pp. 145–56.

13. Labour party, *Report* (1909), p. 14.

14. I.L.P., *Report* (1909), pp. 35–40.

15. Pease, *History of the Fabian Society*, pp. 163–84.

16. M. Cole, *Fabian Socialism*, pp. 117–24, 146–55.

17. Stewart, *J. Keir Hardie*, pp. 260–75, 298–302; Brockway, *Socialism over Sixty Years*, pp. 110–29; Benjamin Sacks, *J. Ramsay MacDonald in Thought and Action* (Albuquerque, N. Mex., 1952), pp. 470–79.

18. Labour party, *Report* (1910), pp. 101–10; Webb and Webb, *History of Trade Unionism*, pp. 608–34.

19. Labour party, *Report* (1912), pp. 96–98.

20. *Ibid.* (1914), p. 137.

21. Raymond Postgate, *The Life of George Lansbury* (London, 1951), pp. 134–51.

22. G. D. H. Cole, *A Short History of the British Working-Class Movement* (3 vols., London, 1927), III, 70–113; Herbert Tracey, Ed., *The Book of the Labour Party* (3 vols., London, 1925), I, 191–201.

Chapter Three

1. *Labour Leader*, Aug. 6, 1918; *Socialist Review*, XII (Oct.-Dec. 1914), 312–14.

2. Labour party, *Report* (1916), p. 4.

3. *Labour Leader*, Aug. 13, 1914.

4. Labour party, *Report* (1916), p. 31; *Clarion*, Feb. 26, 1915; *Forward*, Jan. 23–30, 1915. For a fuller account of the war aims and peace programs of British Labour, see the author's *British Labour's Rise to Power: Eight Studies* (Stanford, 1941), pp. 55–120.

5. Labour party, *Report* (1916), p. 5; *Manchester Guardian,* May 20, 1915. For a fuller account of this subject, see the author's *British Labour's Rise to Power,* pp. 28–54.

6. *Manchester Guardian,* May 21, 1915.

7. *Forward,* May 29–June 12, 1915; *The Call,* May 18, Aug. 17, 1916.

8. David Kirkwood, *My Life of Revolt* (London, 1935), pp. 93–162; G. D. H. Cole, *A History of the Labour Party from 1914* (London, 1948), pp. 23–39.

9. *The Times,* Jan. 7, 1916; *New Statesman,* Jan. 15, 1916.

10. Labour party, *Report* (1916), pp. 8, 57, 105, 124–28.

11. *Labour Leader,* July 15, 1915; H. M. Swanwick, *Builders of Peace, Being Ten Years History of the Union of Democratic Control* (London, 1924), pp. 39–40, 51–53; Catharine Ann Cline, *Recruits to Labour: The British Labour Party, 1914–1931* (Syracuse, N.Y., 1963), p. 42.

12. T.U.C., *Report* (1915), pp. 327–28.

13. *Clarion,* May 14, 21, 1915, Mar. 17, 1916; *The Call,* Mar. 23, May 4, 1916.

14. I.L.P., *Report* (1916), pp. 10–11. For a fuller account of British Labour and the International during the war, see the author's *British Labour's Rise to Power,* pp. 165–98.

15. *Labour Leader,* Apr. 20–27, 1916; *The Call,* Apr. 20, June 8, 1916.

16. Labour party, *Report* (1916), p. 136; *ibid.* (1917), pp. 98, 125–29; I.L.P., *Report* (1916), pp. 32–33; *ibid.* (1917), pp. 29–31.

17. *The Times,* Dec. 2, 1916.

18. Snowden in the *Labour Leader,* Dec. 14, 1916.

19. *British Citizen and Empire Worker,* Dec. 2–9, 1916.

20. *The Times,* Dec. 8, 1916; Labour party, *Report* (1917), pp. 3, 43.

21. *Manchester Guardian,* Dec. 9, 1916; *Forward,* Dec. 16, 1916; *The Call,* Dec. 14, 1916.

22. Labour party, *Report* (1917), pp. 82–96.

Chapter Four

1. *Forward,* Oct. 3, 1914.

2. 93 H. C. Deb., cols. 1665–79. All references to the *Parliamentary Debates* are to the Fifth Series.

3. *Herald,* June 9, 1917; *Labour Leader,* June 7, 1917.

4. I.L.P., *Report* (1918), p. 8; Mrs. Philip Snowden, *A Political Pilgrim in Europe* (New York, 1921), p. xi.

5. Labour party, *Report* (1918), pp. 3–4; I.L.P., *Report* (1918), pp. 9–10; *Labour Leader,* May 17–July 19, 1917; Arno J. Mayer, *Political Origins of the New Diplomacy, 1917–1918* (New Haven, 1959), pp. 215–16.

6. Labour party, *Report* (1918), pp. 4, 45; *Labour Leader,* July 26–Aug. 16, 1917; Hamilton, *Arthur Henderson,* pp. 120ff.

7. Labour party, *Report* (1918), pp. 4–6, 47–51; files for Aug. 1917 of the *New Statesman, Clarion, Labour Leader, Forward, Bradford Pioneer.*

8. 97 H. C. Deb., cols. 909–23; 1510.

9. Lloyd George's version of the Henderson resignation is given in his *War Memoirs* (London, 1934), IV, 1881ff. For a criticism of it see Hamilton, *Arthur Henderson*, pp. 158–62.

10. Labour party, *Report* (1918), pp. 6–8; Miners Federation of Great Britain, *Report of the Special Conference Held at the Westminster Hall, London, August 20, 1917.*

11. Labour party, *Report* (1918), pp. 8–12; *Labour Leader,* Sept. 6, 1917.

12. Texts published in the *Herald,* May 11, 1918.

13. *New Statesman,* Jan. 5, 1918; *Herald,* Jan. 5, 1918.

14. Published in the *New Statesman,* July 10, 17, 1915.

15. *Labour Leader,* Jan. 3, 10, 1918; *Herald,* Jan. 12, 1918.

16. For a fuller account see the author's *British Labour's Rise to Power,* pp. 121–49.

17. Henry J. Winkler, *The League of Nations Movement in Great Britain, 1914–1919* (New Brunswick, N.J., 1952), pp. 167–98.

18. Labour party, *Report* (1918), pp. 7–8; *Socialist Review,* XV (Apr.-June, 1918), 98–108.

19. Labour party, *Report* (1918), pp. 8–10; *ibid.,* (1919), pp. 3–11; Labour party, *The Replies of the Socialist Parties of the Central Powers to the Memorandum on War Aims* (1918).

20. The constitution of 1918 is reprinted in G. D. H. Cole, *History of the Labour Party from 1914,* pp. 71–81.

21. Resolution XIV.

22. *Labour and the New Social Order: A Report on Reconstruction* (London, June 1918).

23. *The Times,* Nov. 16, 1918; *Labour Leader,* Nov. 21, 1918.

24. Labour party, *Report* (1919), pp. 28–30, 187–95.

Chapter Five

1. William P. Maddox, *Foreign Relations in British Labour Politics* (Cambridge, Mass., 1934), pp. 86ff.

2. For a fuller account see the author's *British Labour's Rise to Power,* pp. 150–64.

3. Labour party, *Report* (1919), p. 216.

4. *Daily Herald,* May 8, 1919. The *Herald* had become a daily on March 31.

5. I.L.P., *Report* (1920), pp. 9–10.

6. Quoted by Swanwick, *Builders of Peace,* p. 121.

7. *New Statesman,* May 17, 1919.

8. Labour party, *Report* (1919), pp. 139–42, 217.

9. E.g., Hamilton, *Remembering My Good Friends* (London, 1944), p. 106.

10. Sec. 3(g).

11. I.L.P., *Report* (1920), p. 53.

12. Arthur Henderson, *Labour and Foreign Affairs* (London, 1922); Winkler, "The Emergence of a Labor Foreign Policy in Great Britain, 1918–1929," *The Journal of Modern History*, XXVIII, (September 1956), pp. 247–58.

13. T.U.C., *Report* (1921), pp. 278, 281.

14. Labour party, *Report* (1923), p. 263.

15. J. R. MacDonald, *The Foreign Policy of the Labour Party* (Oxford, 1923), p. 17.

16. F. H. Rose, M.P., *Sword Blades or Ploughshares* (London, 1922), p. 2.

17. T.U.C, *Report* (1921), pp. 294–306.

18. Labour party policy report, *Control of Foreign Policy: Labour's Programme* (1919); Henderson, *Labour and Foreign Affairs*.

19. Labour party pamphlet, *Labour Policy and the Famine* (1919).

20. Labour party, *Report* (1920), p. 202.

21. *Ibid.* (1921), pp. 177–81; *ibid.* (1922), pp. 27–29, 193, 247–51; T.U.C., *Report* (1922), pp. 78–85; Henderson, *Labour and Foreign Affairs*.

22. *Beatrice Webb's Diaries, 1912–1924* (M. Cole, Ed.), pp. 144, 221, 252.

23. Hamilton, *Remembering My Good Friends,* pp. 101–2.

24. Labour party, *Report* (1921), p. 201.

25. *Ibid.* (1922), pp. 188–93.

26. Labour party pamphlet, *Labour and the Ruhr* (1923).

27. Labour party, *Report* (1923), pp. 2–8, 20–39, 52–58, 104–6; I.L.P., *Report* (1923), pp. 46–55, 86–98; T.U.C., *Report* (1923), pp. 417–19.

28. Sacks, *Ramsay MacDonald,* pp. 521ff., gives collected utterances.

29. Labour party, *The White Terror in Hungary* (1920); Josiah C. Wedgwood, *Memoirs of a Fighting Life* (London, 1940), pp. 159–60.

30. Henderson, *Labour and Foreign Affairs,* pp. 5–8.

31. Labour party, *Report* (1923), p. 19.

32. T.U.C., *Report* (1923), pp. 311–15.

33. *Labour's Russian Policy: Peace with Soviet Russia* (Jan. 1920), p. 9.

34. Labour party, *Report* (1919), pp. 113–23.

35. *Ibid.* (1920), pp. 4, 133–36; Margaret Bondfield, *A Life's Work* (London, 1948), pp. 189–205.

36. *Daily Herald,* Mar. 27, Apr. 12, July 31, 1920; Postgate, *Life of George Lansbury,* pp. 201–15.

37. Labour party, *Report* (1921), pp. 11–18; Alan Bullock, *The Life and Times of Ernest Bevin* (London, 1960), I, 133–42.

38. Snowden, *Autobiography,* II, 562.

39. Labour party, *Report* (1922), pp. 36–37, 193–96.

40. Labour party, *Labour's Russian Policy,* p. 6.

Chapter Six

1. For unemployment statistics and for an excellent survey of the interwar period see C. L. Mowat, *Britain Between the Wars* (Chicago, 1955), p. 76.

2. Bullock, *Life of Bevin,* I, 143–49.

3. For a fuller discussion of Labour-Communist relations, see the author's *British Labour's Rise to Power,* pp. 232–86.

4. *Workers' Dreadnaught* (organ of the Workers Socialist Federation), Feb. 21–May 15, 1920.

5. *Ibid.,* June 26, July 3, 1920.

6. Manifesto printed in Tom Bell, *The British Communist Party* (London, 1937), pp. 53–55.

7. *Daily Herald,* Aug. 2, 1920; *Labour Leader,* Aug. 5, 1920.

8. V. I. Lenin, *"Left Wing" Communism, an Infantile Disorder* (rev. trans., London, 1934), pp. 36–77.

9. *Ibid.,* p. 68.

10. *Report of the Second Congress of the Communist International* (Moscow, 1920), pp. 70–71, 409–13.

11. *The Communist,* Feb. 5, 1921.

12. *Ibid.,* Sept. 16, 1920, commented on this reply, "To be quite frank, we never supposed they were. Our worst enemy will not accuse us of ever pretending they were."

13. See Labour party, *Report* (1921), pp. 18–22 for the correspondence between MacManus and Henderson.

14. Lansbury was of a different mind after he saw the hard conditions laid down for the French party for entry into the Third International (see *Daily Herald,* Sept. 11, 1920). In November he could write that all who were against Bolshevik methods should come together to prove that parliamentary methods were better machinery for accomplishing social salvation than the dictatorship of the proletariat (*Labour Leader,* Nov. 18, 1920).

15. *Daily Herald,* June 22, 1920.

16. I.L.P. pamphlet, *The I.L.P. and the Third International* (London, 1920), p. 37.

17. *New Statesman,* June 19, 1920.

18. *The Communist,* Feb. 10, Mar. 5, 1921.

19. Labour party, *Report* (1921), pp. 158–66; I.L.P., *Report* (1921), p. 124.

20. Labour party, *Report* (1922), pp. 76–80, 177–79, 193–99; *New Statesman,* July 1, 8, 1922.

21. Labour party, *Report* (1923), pp. 85, 101, 181–92.

22. For a fuller discussion of Labour party-Communist relations on the international front see the author's *British Labour's Rise to Power,* pp. 199–231.

23. Labour party, *Report* (1921), p. 227; International Labour Organization, Studies and Reports, Series A, No. 6, *The Congress of the Labour and Socialist International,* pp. 5–6.

24. I.L.P., *Report* (1921), pp. 113–24, 134.

25. Labour party, *Report,* (1922), pp. 16–24; *Daily Herald,* Apr.–June, 1922, *passim.*

26. Labour party, *Report* (1923), pp. 7–18.

27. *Communist Review,* IV, 114–20 (July, 1923).

28. Tables of election results in G. D. H. Cole, *History of the Labour Party from 1914,* p. 131.

Chapter Seven

1. Labour party, *Report* (1924), pp. 192–93.
2. *Labour Monthly,* V (Dec. 1923), 315ff.; *Communist Review,* IV (Dec. 1923), 346ff.
3. Labour party, *Report* (1924), pp. 11–37.
4. *Beatrice Webb's Diaries, 1912–1924,* pp. 255–56.
5. S. Webb, "The First Labour Government," *The Political Quarterly,* XXXII (Jan.–Mar., 1961), 9–18.
6. Richard W. Lyman's *The First Labour Government, 1924* (London, 1957), is a sound analytical study.
7. See Marian Bowley, *Housing and the State, 1919–1944* ([London, 1945], p. 271) for statistics on houses built in England and Wales.
8. Lyman, *The First Labour Government,* p. 128.
9. Frederick D. Schneider, "The First British Labour Government" (Unpublished Ph.D. thesis, Stanford University, 1950).
10. Postgate, *Life of Lansbury,* pp. 216–25; Lyman, *The First Labour Government,* pp. 133–34.
11. Snowden, *Autobiography,* II, 638–59.
12. Bevin later developed a broader view of politics than he had in 1924. See Bullock, *Life of Bevin,* I, 245.
13. Emanuel Shinwell, *Conflict Without Malice* (London, 1955), pp. 92–93.
14. 171 H. C. Deb., col. 319.
15. Lyman, *The First Labour Government,* p. 213.
16. *The Times,* Jan. 30, 1924.
17. Schneider, "The First British Labour Government," pp. 126–46.
18. E.g., Labour party, *Report* (1920), pp. 156–59.
19. *The Times,* Jan. 26, 1924. For collected utterances of MacDonald on India see Sacks, *Ramsay MacDonald,* pp. 389–424.
20. Paul L. Hanna, "The Mosul Question" (unpublished M.A. thesis, Stanford University, 1936).
21. Labour party, *Report* (1921), pp. 159ff.
22. Schneider, "The First British Labour Government," pp. 163–79.
23. *Forward,* July 26, 1924; Lyman, *The First Labour Government,* pp. 216–17.
24. *The Times,* Feb. 4, Mar. 3, 1924.
25. Snowden, *Autobiography,* II, 665–79; Viscount D'Abernon, *An Ambassador of Peace* (3 vols., London, 1930), III, 32, 70–73, 88–100.
26. Labour party, *Report* (1925), pp. 177, 252; T.U.C., *Report* (1925), pp. 542–46.
27. Schneider, "The First British Labour Government," pp. 107–13.

28. The speech was circulated as a Labour party pamphlet, *The Way to Peace.*

29. Hamilton, *Arthur Henderson,* p. 248.

30. Mowat (*Britain Between the Wars,* p. 181) says that Labour had every intention of ratifying. Cf. Winkler, *Journal of Modern History,* XXVIII (1956), 257; Lyman, *The First Labour Government,* pp. 176–81.

31. Wedgwood, *Memoirs of a Fighting Life,* p. 184.

32. E.g., in a Labour party pamphlet, *Protocol or Pact* (1925), p. 2.

33. S. Webb, *The Political Quarterly,* XXXII (Jan.–Mar. 1961), 27.

34. Harold Nicolson, *King George the Fifth* (London, 1952), p. 397.

35. Snowden, *Autobiography,* II, 680–86; Lyman, *The First Labour Government,* pp. 184–207; S. R. Graubard, *British Labour and the Russian Revolution, 1917–1924* (Cambridge, Mass., 1956), pp. 260–65.

36. *The New Leader,* Aug. 15, 1924.

37. *The Observer,* Aug. 10, 1924.

38. 177 H. C. Deb., col. 700; Sir Patrick Hastings, *Autobiography* (London, 1948), pp. 246–47; S. Webb, *The Political Quarterly,* XXXII (Jan.–Mar. 1961), 28–31.

39. Labour party, *Report* (1924), pp. 194–95.

40. *Ibid.* (1924), p. 131.

41. J. H. Thomas, *My Story* (London, 1937), p. 78.

42. Robert D. Warth, "The Mystery of the Zinoviev Letter," *South Atlantic Quarterly,* XLIX (Oct. 1950), 441ff.; Lyman, *The First Labour Government,* pp. 286–88.

43. Labour party, *Report* (1925), pp. 3–9.

Chapter Eight

1. Hamilton, *Arthur Henderson,* p. 72.

2. Labour party, *Report* (1925), pp. 244–52.

3. Brockway, *Socialism over Sixty Years,* pp. 224–31.

4. T.U.C., *Report* (1925), pp. 154–70, 289–93.

5. *Ibid.* (1927), pp. 369–70.

6. Bullock, *Life of Bevin,* I, 248–78.

7. Pelling, *The British Communist Party: A Historical Profile* (London, 1958), p. 34.

8. Mowat, *Britain Between the Wars,* pp. 309–10; Bullock, *Life of Bevin,* I, 321.

9. *Ibid.,* p. 286.

10. W. H. Crook, *The General Strike* (Chapel Hill, N.C., 1931). For a shorter account see Mowat, *Britain Between the Wars,* pp. 294–338.

11. 181 H. C. Deb., cols. 839–41.

12. Duff Cooper, *Old Men Forget* (London, 1953), p. 143.

13. Martin Harrison, *Trade Unions and the Labour Party* (Detroit, 1960), pp. 21–108.

14. 202 H. C. Deb., cols. 666–67.

15. Labour party, *Report* (1925), p. 189.

16. *Ibid.* (1928), pp. 23, 162–67.

17. *International Press Correspondence,* Eng. ed., May 13, 1926, p. 650.

18. Communist Party of Great Britain, *Report* (1925), p. 138.

19. Labour party, *Report* (1930), pp. 31–34.

20. *The Communist,* III (Mar. 1928), 141–43 (Apr. 1928), 193–210 (Dec. 1928), 717–24; Bell, *The British Communist Party,* p. 128.

21. 188 H. C. Deb., col. 443; Henderson, *Labour and the Geneva Protocol* (1925).

22. Labour party, *Report* (1926), p. 84.

23. *Ibid.* (1925), pp. 61, 94, 174, 253–59; *ibid.* (1926), pp. 253–54; *ibid.* (1927), pp. 235–44; Labour party pamphlet, *Arbitrate! Arbitrate! Arbitrate!* (1926).

24. Labour party, *Report* (1925), p. 98.

25. 210 H. C. Deb., col. 2095; *ibid.,* 213, col. 18.

26. Labour party, *Report* (1928), p. 266.

27. MacDonald, 217 H. C. Deb., cols. 433–35, 445–46.

28. Labour party, *Report* (1928), p. 43.

29. *Ibid.,* p. 184.

30. *Labour and the Nation* (1928), pp. 41–49.

31. Labour party, *Report* (1926), pp. 256–57.

32. I.L.P., *Report* (1928), pp. 76–78.

33. *Ibid.* (1929), pp. 86–90.

34. T.U.C., *Report* (1925), pp. 553–55.

35. *Ibid.* (1927), pp. 391–95.

36. Labour party, *Report* (1925), pp. 63, 260–62; *ibid.* (1926), pp. 255–56; *ibid.* (1927), pp. 56–59, 205–8, 255–56; I.L.P., *Report* (1928), pp. 31–36, 74–75.

37. Bullock, *Life of Bevin,* I, 392ff.

38. *The Times, House of Commons, 1929.*

39. G. D. H. Cole, *History of the Labour Party from 1914,* pp. 222–23.

Chapter Nine

1. Snowden, *Autobiography,* II, 759–64.

2. Cf. Hamilton, *Arthur Henderson,* pp. 283ff., and Bondfield, *A Life's Work,* p. 316, with D. C. Somervell, *British Politics Since 1900* (New York, 1950), pp. 170, 210. For a balanced view, see Winkler, "Arthur Henderson," in Gordon A. Craig and Felix Gilbert, Eds., *The Diplomats, 1919–1939* (Princeton, N.J., 1953), pp. 311ff.

3. Snowden, *Autobiography,* II, 778–825; Hamilton, *Arthur Henderson,* pp. 313–18.

4. 250 H. C. Deb., col. 718; Winkler in Craig and Gilbert, *The Diplomats,* pp. 338–39.

5. 229 H. C. Deb., cols. 465–66.

6. D. N. Lammers, "British Foreign Policy, 1929–1934: The Problem of Soviet Russia" (unpublished Ph.D. thesis, Stanford University, 1960), pp. 75–117; Labour party, *Notes for Speakers*, Nov. 8, 1929; W. N. Medlicott, *British Foreign Policy Since Versailles* (London, 1940), pp. 108–13.

7. Lammers, "British Foreign Policy," pp. 122–32; W. P. Coates, *Religion in Tsarist and Soviet Russia* (London, 1930).

8. Lammers, "British Foreign Policy," pp. 141–51.

9. Labour party, *Report* (1929), pp. 208–9; Henderson, *Labour's Foreign Policy* (1933); Labour party pamphlet, *The Record of the Second Labour Government* (1935); Hamilton, *Arthur Henderson*, pp. 319–55.

10. Apr. 23, 1930.

11. Conyers Read, "Recent United States and British Government Publications on the London Naval Conference of 1930," *American Historical Review*, LIV (1949), 307–14; Labour party, *Report* (1929), pp. 210–15, 306–19; *ibid.* (1930), pp. 53–56, 80–93; *ibid.* (1931), pp. 53–58; Labour party, *Notes for Speakers*, Nov. 29, 1929; Jan. 31, Apr. 25, 1930; Labour party pamphlet, *The Freedom of the Seas* (1929).

12. Oct. 9, 1930.

13. T.U.C., *Report* (1930), pp. 208–11, 257–87; Bullock, *Life of Bevin*, I, 439–44.

14. Rixford K. Snyder, "The Second British Labour Government and the General Election of 1931" (unpublished M.A. thesis, Stanford University, 1934), p. 57.

15. *Ibid.*, pp. 35–37; *New Statesman*, Aug. 3, 1929; *Manchester Guardian Weekly*, May 9, 1930; *The Times*, Mar. 4, 1931.

16. Snyder, "The Second British Labour Government," pp. 35–39.

17. Labour party, *Report* (1930), pp. 220–22; *ibid.* (1931), pp. 198–99.

18. *New Statesman*, Sept. 7, 1929.

19. 237 H. C. Deb., col. 1466.

20. *The Times*, Feb. 14, 1931.

21. Paul L. Hanna, *British Policy in Palestine* (Washington, 1942), pp. 87–108; Sacks, *Ramsay MacDonald*, pp. 452–58.

22. Hamilton, *Arthur Henderson*, pp. 295–308; Nicolson, *King George the Fifth*, pp. 441–44.

23. C. R. Attlee, *The Labour Party in Perspective* (London, 1937), pp. 245–47.

24. Attlee, *As It Happened* (New York, 1954), p. 76.

25. 229 H. C. Deb., cols. 64–65.

26. *The Labour Magazine*, Dec. 1929, p. 339.

27. *Spectator*, Nov. 2, 1929; Postgate, *Life of Lansbury*, pp. 254–56.

28. Bullock, *Life of Bevin*, I, 437.

29. G. D. H. Cole, *History of the British Labour Party from 1914*, p. 237; Postgate, *Life of Lansbury*, pp. 252–57.

30. Labour party, *Report* (1930), pp. 200–204, 229; Michael Foot, *Aneurin*

Bevan, A Biography (London, 1962), pp. 126–27; Mowat, *Britain Between the Wars,* pp. 359–61.

31. *New Statesman,* Feb. 21, 1931; Snyder, "The Second British Labour Government," p. 121.

32. *Manchester Guardian Weekly,* Mar. 6, 1931.

33. Mowat, *Britain Between the Wars,* p. 364; Snyder, "The Second British Labour Government," pp. 91–100.

34. D. E. Butler, *Electoral System in Britain* (Oxford, 1953), pp. 58ff.

35. Herbert Morrison, *Socialisation and Transport* (London, 1933); Lincoln Gordon, *The Public Corporation in Great Britain* (London, 1938), pp. 245ff.

36. Snowden, *Autobiography,* II, 853–73.

37. Aug. 8, 1931.

38. Keith Feiling, *The Life of Neville Chamberlain* (London, 1946), pp. 190–91.

39. Bullock, *Life of Bevin,* I, 479–91.

40. For the fall of the Labour government there is a detailed and documented account, too favorable to MacDonald, in R. Bassett, *Nineteen Thirty-One: Political Crisis* (London, 1958). A shorter account is given in Mowat, *Britain Between the Wars,* pp. 379–93. Snowden, *Autobiography,* II, 929ff., is the principal source. Other useful contributions are made in Nicolson, *King George the Fifth,* pp. 453–69, and Feiling, *Neville Chamberlain,* pp. 189–93. For a critique of the "plot theory," i.e., that the replacement of Labour by a National Government was a long-planned and deliberately contrived scheme of MacDonald, see Bassett, *Nineteen Thirty-One,* pp. 408–21.

Accounts of the final Cabinet meeting, some melodramatic, disagree. Most were written later or at second hand. Perhaps the most reliable version was that written by Webb immediately after the Cabinet dispersed (Bassett, *Nineteen Thirty-One,* p. 160).

Chapter Ten

1. Attlee, *As It Happened,* p. 107.

2. Hugh Dalton, *Call Back Yesterday* (London, 1953), pp. 277–79.

3. *Manchester Guardian Weekly,* Oct. 2, 1931.

4. The broadcast is reproduced in Bassett, *Nineteen Thirty-One,* pp. 444–49.

5. G. D. H. Cole, *History of the Labour Party from 1914,* pp. 262–67; Bassett, *Nineteen Thirty-One,* pp. 329–37; Dalton, *Call Back Yesterday,* pp. 293–98.

6. *Daily Herald,* Oct. 17, 1931; *New Statesman,* Oct. 24, 1931.

7. Bullock, *Life of Bevin,* I, 511–12; Pelling, *A Short History of the Labour Party* (London, 1961), p. 77.

8. Brockway, *Inside the Left* (London, 1942), pp. 237–47.

9. G. D. H. Cole, *History of the Labour Party Since 1914,* pp. 282–84.

10. Communist Party of Great Britain, *Resolutions of the Eleventh Congress* (1929), p. 44.

11. T.U.C., *Report* (1929), pp. 168–82, 394–412; Labour party, *Report* (1930), pp. 27–33, 166–68.

12. Labour party, *Report* (1933), pp. 18, 30, 143–45.

13. T.U.C., *Report* (1935), pp. 110–12, 260–74.

14. Labour party, *Report* (1934), p. 141.

15. Pelling, *The British Communist Party*, pp. 67–68.

16. *Labour Monthly*, *XV* (Apr. 1933), 211.

17. Labour party, *Report* (1933), pp. 220–21; Postgate (an ex-Communist), "A Critique of Communist Tactics," *American Mercury*, **XXXII** (July 1934), 281–89.

18. Labour party, *Report* (1935), pp. 312–18; *ibid.* (1936), pp. 77–78, 301–2; Brockway, *Inside the Left*, pp. 248–63; Allen Hutt, *The Post-War History of the British Working Class* (London, 1937), pp. 244–73.

19. H. J. Laski, *Democracy in Crisis* (London, 1933); John Strachey, *The Coming Struggle for Power* (London, 1932).

20. Dalton, *The Fateful Years* (London, 1957), p. 46.

21. Webb and Webb, *Soviet Communism, a New Civilisation?* (London, 1935).

22. Labour party, *Report* (1932), pp. 182–94.

23. Morrison, *Socialism and Transport*, p. 149.

24. Dalton, *Practical Socialism for Great Britain* (London, 1935), p. 94.

25. Labour party, *Report* (1932), pp. 211–25; Dalton, *The Fateful Years*, p. 30; Morrison, *Autobiography*, pp. 120–21.

26. Labour party, *Report* (1933), pp. 204–10.

27. *Ibid.*, pp. 159–66.

28. *For Socialism and Peace*, p. 32.

29. Labour party, *Report* (1934), pp. 148–51, 261–63.

30. *Ibid.* (1933), p. 134.

31. *Ibid.* (1932), p. 68; Labour party, *Notes for Speakers*, Feb. 26, 1932.

32. Labour party, *Report* (1933), p. 51; Henderson, *Labour's Foreign Policy* (1933), pp. 26–27; Henderson, *Labour's Way to Peace* (1934), pp. 64–71.

33. T.U.C., *Report* (1932), pp. 358–68.

34. Labour party, *Report* (1935), p. 132; Bassett, *Democracy and Foreign Policy, a Case History: The Sino-Japanese Dispute, 1931–33* (London, 1952), pp. 551–56.

35. Labour party, *Report* (1934), p. 128.

36. *Ibid.* (1933), p. 281; *Labour Monthly*, XV (Apr. 1933), 267–69, (July 1933), 458–60.

37. Labour party, *Report* (1933), pp. 224–25, 277; Labour party, *Notes for Speakers*, Mar. 31, 1933.

38. T.U.C., *Report* (1933), pp. 134, 318, 325–40, 425–35; *ibid.* (1934), p. 249; Ralph Milibank, *Parliamentary Socialism, a Study in the Politics of Labour* (London, 1961), pp. 216ff.

39. Cooperative Congress, *Report* (1933), pp. 470–71; *ibid.* (1934), p. 435.

40. "Fascism at Home and Abroad," Labour party, *Report* (1934), pp. 305–8; Labour party, *Notes for Speakers,* Feb. 2, 1934.

41. Labour party, *Report* (1934), pp. 128, 299–304.

42. T.U.C., *Report* (1933), pp. 296–304.

43. Labour party, *Report* (1933), pp. 185–92; Dalton, *The Fateful Years,* pp. 44–45.

44. Labour party, *Report* (1934), p. 17.

45. *Ibid.,* p. 244.

46. *Ibid.,* p. 245.

47. T.U.C., *Report* (1934), pp. 318–39.

48. Labour party, *Report* (1934), pp. 152–78.

49. Cf. Winston Churchill, *While England Slept* (New York, 1938), p. 133; G. M. Young, *Stanley Baldwin* (London, 1952), p. 177.

50. Labour party, *Report* (1934), p. 15.

51. Churchill, *The Gathering Storm* (London, 1948), p. 117.

52. Labour party, *Report* (1935), p. 15.

53. T.U.C., *Report* (1935), pp. 12, 63–67, 345–68; Labour party, *Report* (1935), pp. 10–11, 179.

54. *Ibid.,* p. 132.

55. *Ibid.,* p. 153.

56. *Ibid.,* pp. 132–33, 153–93; Francis Williams, *Ernest Bevin: Portrait of a Great Englishman* (London, 1952), pp. 190–97; Eric Estorick, *Stafford Cripps: Prophetic Rebel* (New York, 1941), pp. 87–92; George Lansbury, *My Quest for Peace* (London, 1938), pp. 17–21.

57. *Daily Herald,* Oct. 16, 1935.

58. *Ibid.,* Oct. 21, 28, Nov. 4, 1935.

59. *New Leader,* Oct. 11, 1935.

60. Peter D. P. Scott, "The British General Election of 1935" (unpublished M.A. thesis, Stanford University, 1948).

61. *New Statesman and Nation,* Nov. 30, 1935.

Chapter Eleven

1. Morrison, *Autobiography,* p. 164.

2. Dean E. McHenry, *His Majesty's Opposition, 1931–1938* (Berkeley, Calif., 1940), pp. 35–41, 60–62; G. D. H. Cole, *History of the Labour Party from 1914,* pp. 338, 480.

3. Labour party, *Report* (1936), pp. 50–51.

4. G. D. H. Cole, "A British People's Front: Why and How?" *Political Quarterly,* VII (Oct.–Dec. 1936), 490–98.

5. T.U.C., *Report* (1936), p. 428.

6. Dalton, "The 'Popular Front,' " *Political Quarterly,* VII (Oct.–Dec., 1936), 481–89.

7. Labour party, *Report* (1936), p. 300.

8. *Ibid.*, pp. 207–11, 250–57; Laski, "British Labor and the World Crisis," *Nation* (New York), Oct. 31, 1936, pp. 515–17.

9. Laski, *Communism* (New York, 1927), pp. 210–11; *ibid.*, in the *Labour Monthly,* XIX (Mar. 1937), 142.

10. J. R. Campbell in the *Labour Monthly,* XIX (May, 1937), 304–6.

11. Brockway, *Workers' Front* (London, 1938), p. 183.

12. Labour party, *Report* (1937), pp. 25–28, 158–64, 181, 247, 268–70.

13. *Manchester Guardian Weekly,* Apr. 22, 1938.

14. *Ibid.,* May 27, 1938.

15. *Labour Monthly,* XX (June 1938), 346. Italics in the original.

16. *Manchester Guardian Weekly,* Jan. 20, 27, Feb. 10, Mar. 10, 1939; *Daily Herald,* May 30–June 2, 1939; Labour party, *Report* (1939), pp. 43ff., 291ff; Foot, *Aneurin Bevan,* I, pp. 287–92.

17. Labour party, *Report* (1936), pp. 32–33, 77–78, 107; Roy Jenkins, *Mr. Attlee* (London, 1948), pp. 172–73; Mowat, *Britain Between the Wars,* pp. 556–62.

18. Labour party, *Report* (1936), pp. 33–34, 108, 182–84; *Daily Herald,* May 4, 1936.

19. Swanwick, *Collective Insecurity* (London, 1937).

20. Labour party, *Report* (1936), pp. 34, 79, 302–3; T.U.C., *Report* (1936), pp. 180–82; Dalton, *The Fateful Years,* pp. 88–90.

21. T.U.C., *Report* (1936), pp. 362–90; K. W. Watkins, *Britain Divided: The Effect of the Spanish Civil War on British Opinion* (London, 1963), pp. 150–63.

22. Labour party, *Report* (1936), p. 171.

23. *Ibid.,* pp. 28–32, 169–81, 212–15, 258–62; Dalton, *The Fateful Years,* pp. 95–100; Jennie Lee (Mrs. Aneurin Bevan), *This Great Journey* (New York, 1942), pp. 171–81; Eric Estorick, *Stafford Cripps,* pp. 115–21.

24. Labour party, *Report* (1937), pp. 8–14, 82–87, 212–15; Labour party, *Notes for Speakers,* July 2, 23, Sept. 24, Dec. 17, 1937; T.U.C., *Report* (1937), pp. 177, 260–63.

25. Jennie Lee, *This Great Journey,* p. 181.

26. Attlee, *As It Happened,* p. 133; Brockway, *Inside the Left,* pp. 298–318, 339; Douglas Hyde, *I Believed* (New York, 1950), pp. 63–64; Hugh Thomas, *The Spanish Civil War* (London, 1961), pp. 634–43.

27. T.U.C., *Report* (1938), pp. 183–89; Labour party, *Notes for Speakers,* Mar. 18, 25, 1938.

28. Labour party pamphlet, *Hitler's Threat to Czech Democracy* (June 1938).

29. Labour party, *Report* (1939), p. 28; Adolf Sturmthal, *The Tragedy of European Labour, 1919–1939* (New York, 1943), p. 309.

30. Stanford Shapiro, "The British Labour Party and the Munich Crisis" (unpublished M.A. thesis, Stanford University, 1952), pp. 43–61. Kingsley Martin, Ed., *New Statesman* (e.g., Mar. 19, July 9, 23, Aug. 27, 1938), supported a minority view that Czechoslovakia would be better off without its Germans.

31. Charles Madge and Tom Harrison, *Britain by Mass-Observation* (Harmondsworth, Middlesex, 1939), pp. 217–18.

32. Labour party, *Report* (1939), pp. 13–14.

33. T.U.C., *Report* (1938), pp. 371–86.

34. *Daily Herald*, Sept. 20, 1938.

35. Dalton, *The Fateful Years*, pp. 188–89.

36. Labour party, *Report* (1939), p. 15; Madge and Harrison, *Britain by Mass-Observation*, pp. 40–70.

37. Labour party, *Report* (1939), p. 16.

38. *Daily Herald*, Sept. 23, 1938.

39. *Ibid.*, Sept. 26, 1938.

40. Labour party, *Report* (1939), p. 17.

41. 339 H. C. Deb., col. 26 (Sept. 28, 1938); Attlee, *As It Happened*, pp. 145–46.

42. Labour party, *Report* (1939), p. 18.

43. 339 H. C. Deb., col. 52 (Oct. 3, 1938).

44. *Daily Herald*, Oct. 4, 1938.

45. Labour party, *Report* (1936), pp. 202–4.

46. *Ibid.*, pp. 182–206.

47. Dalton, *The Fateful Years*, pp. 132–38; Attlee, *As It Happened*, pp. 139–40.

48. Labour party, *Report* (1937), p. 279.

49. T.U.C., *Report* (1937), pp. 402–26.

50. Labour party, *Report* (1937), pp. 138, 195–212; Dalton, *The Fateful Years*, pp. 141–46.

51. Labour party, *Report* (1939), pp. 139, 160; *ibid., Notes for Speakers*, June 3, 1938.

52. T.U.C., *Report* (1938), pp. 226–32, 295–310; Herbert Tracey, *Trade Unions Fight—For What?* (London, 1940), pp. 104–40.

53. In retrospect this position appeared mistaken. (Attlee, *As It Happened*, p. 148; Dalton, *The Fateful Years*, p. 250.)

54. Labour party, *Report* (1939), pp. 70–71, 274–89, 306–9; Churchill, *Step by Step* (New York, 1939), pp. 218, 269.

55. 345 H. C. Deb., col. 535.

56. T.U.C., *Report* (1939), p. 207.

57. Labour party, *Report* (1939), p. 163; Dalton, *The Fateful Years*, pp. 242–43.

58. Labour party, *Notes for Speakers*, July 14, 1939.

59. Labour party, *Report* (1939), pp. 242, 252.

60. *Daily Herald*, Apr. 13, 1939; T.U.C., *Report* (1939), pp. 208, 334; Dalton, *The Fateful Years*, pp. 249–50.

61. Labour party, *Report* (1940), pp. 6–7.

62. *Ibid.*, pp. 8, 67; *Daily Herald*, Aug. 29, 1939.

63. Labour party, *Report* (1940), p. 10; T.U.C., *Report* (1939), p. 290.

64. 351 H. C. Deb., cols. 282–83; *The Times* (London), Sept. 4, 1939.

65. T.U.C., *Report* (1939), pp. 306, 337–38.

Chapter Twelve

1. Labour party, *Report* (1940), pp. 19, 22–23; G. D. H. Cole, *History of the Labour Party from 1914*, pp. 398, 413.
2. Labour party, *Labour's Home Front* (1940).
3. *Ibid., Report* (1940), pp. 80–82; Irvin M. Roth, "The Labour Party in the Second World War" (unpublished Ph.D. thesis, Stanford University, 1957), pp. 13–27.
4. Attlee, *Labour's Peace Aims* (London, 1940).
5. Labour party, *Report* (1940), pp. 135–37, 188–90.
6. *Ibid.*, pp. 13–14, 83; Dalton, *The Fateful Years*, p. 293.
7. I.L.P., *The Independent Labour Party 1893–1943, Jubilee Souvenir* (London, 1943), p. 3; Labour party, *Report* (1941), pp. 65, 111.
8. *Ibid.* (1940), p. 27; *ibid., The Communist Party and the War* (London, 1943); Hyde, *I Believed*, p. 76; A. P. Donoghue, "History of the Communist Party of Great Britain, 1939–1946" (unpublished Ph.D. thesis, Stanford University, 1953), pp. 147–201.
9. 390 H. C. Deb., col. 1094; L. S. Amery, *The Unforgiving Years, 1929–1940* (London, 1955), pp. 360–65.
10. Labour party, *Report* (1940), pp. 123–34; Francis Williams, *A Prime Minister Remembers* (London, 1961), pp. 22–38; Churchill, *The Gathering Storm* (London, 1948), pp. 658–67.
11. Attlee, *As It Happened*, pp. 162–63.
12. Labour party, *Report* (1941), p. 3; *ibid.* (1942), p. 104.
13. E. Bevin, *The War and the Workers* (London, 1940); Roth, "The Labour Party in the Second World War," p. 136.
14. Labour party, *Report* (1944), p. 70.
15. *Ibid.* (1942), p. 137; *ibid.* (1944), pp. 59, 75; *ibid.* (1945), p. 40.
16. *Ibid.* (1943), pp. 143–46; *ibid.* (1944), pp. 154–56; *ibid.* (1945), pp. 138–49; *ibid., National Service for Health* (London, 1943).
17. *Ibid., Report* (1943), pp. 5, 84, 136, 142; Churchill, *The Hinge of Fate* (London, 1951), p. 862.
18. Labour party, *Report* (1943), p. 202; *ibid.* (1944), pp. 118–19.
19. *Ibid.* (1942), pp. 140–45; *ibid.* (1943), p. 44; *ibid.* (1944), pp. 61, 67, 185.
20. 380 H. C. Deb., cols. 1347–50
21. T.U.C., *Interim Report on Post-War Reconstruction* (1944).
22. Labour party, *Report* (1943), pp. 152–53; *ibid.* (1946), p. 14.
23. *Ibid.* (1941), p. 21; Hyde, *I Believed*, p. 95.
24. Labour party, *Report* (1942), p. 160; Morrison, *Autobiography*, p. 225.
25. Labour party, *Report* (1942), pp. 7, 158; *ibid.* (1943), pp. 9–18, 159–68; Donoghue, "History of the Communist Party of Great Britain, 1939–1946," pp. 229–324.
26. Labour party, *Report* (1941), p. 110; ibid. (1942), pp. 22, 93, 154.
27. *Ibid.*, pp. 6, 11, 95, 164; *ibid.* (1945), p. 44; *Daily Herald*, Feb. 13, 1945.
28. 406 H. C. Deb., cols. 907–1014; 407 *ibid.*, cols. 515–611; Labour party,

Report (1944), pp. 143–51; Sir Llewellyn Woodward, *British Foreign Policy in the Second World War* (London, 1962), pp. 358, 402.

29. Labour party, *Report* (1944), pp. 4–9, 131–33; *Ibid.* (1945), pp. 107–8; Labour party, *The Old World and the New Society* (London, 1942), *ibid.*, *The International Post-War Settlement* (London, 1944); Dalton, *The Fateful Years*, pp. 424–27, 431–33.

30. Labour party, *Report* (1945), pp. 12–15.

31. *Ibid.* (1943), pp. 171–73; *ibid.* (1944), pp. 37, 110, 117.

32. *Ibid.* (1945), pp. 86–88; Attlee, *As It Happened*, pp. 185–94; Dalton, *The Fateful Years*, pp. 458–63; Roth, "The Labour Party in the Second World War," pp. 184–200.

33. Churchill, *Triumph and Tragedy* (London, 1954), p. 508.

34. R. B. McCallum and Alison Readman, *The British General Election of 1945* (London, 1947), pp. 142–44, 175.

35. *Ibid.*, p. 242; W. T. Morgan, "The British General Election of 1945," in R. L. Schuyler and H. Ausubel, Eds., *The Making of English History* (New York, 1952), p. 660.

36. McCallum and Readman, *The British General Election of 1945*, pp. 247–65, 273; G. D. H. Cole, *History of the Labour Party from 1914*, p. 441.

Chapter Thirteen

1. John Wheeler-Bennett, *King George VI: His Life and Reign* (London, 1958), pp. 636–38.

2. Attlee in *The Observer*, Aug. 23, 1959; Dalton, *High Tide and After* (London, 1962), pp. 8–14; Morrison, *Autobiography*, pp. 245–49.

3. Williams, *A Prime Minister Remembers* (London, 1961), pp. 150, 224–25; Dalton, *High Tide and After*, pp. 236–47.

4. Williams, *A Prime Minister Remembers*, pp. 129–30.

5. Dalton, *High Tide and After*, pp. 220–22.

6. *Ibid.*, pp. 24–31, 109–20, 225–35.

7. *Ibid.*, pp. 257–75.

8. Dalton, *The Fateful Years*, pp. 480–81; Dalton, *High Tide and After*, pp. 33–49.

9. British Information Services, *Nationalization in Britain* (London, 1949), pp. 7, 13; Shinwell, *Conflict Without Malice*, pp. 172–75; Miliband, *Parliamentary Socialism*, p. 288.

10. B.I.S., *Nationalization in Britain*, pp. 10–11, 14.

11. *Ibid.*, pp. 8–10, 13–15; Herbert E. Weiner, *British Labor and Public Ownership* (Washington, D.C., 1960), pp. 55–59.

12. G. D. H. Cole, *Why Nationalize Steel?* (London, 1948).

13. Dalton, *High Tide and After*, pp. 135–40, 248–53, 308–12; Morrison, *Autobiography*, p. 296; A. A. Rogow, *The Labour Government and British Industry* (Oxford, 1955), pp. 158–71.

14. Williams, *Socialist Britain* (New York, 1949), pp. 116–18; John Parker, *Labour Marches On* (Harmondsworth, Middlesex, 1947), pp. 88–90.

15. Ernest Watkins, *The Cautious Revolution* (London, 1950), pp. 175–204; Williams, *Socialist Britain*, pp. 122–29.

16. *The National Health Service Act in Great Britain: A Review of the First Year's Working*, published by *The Practitioner* (London, 1949); Watkins, *The Cautious Revolution*, pp. 204–25.

17. Martin Harrison, *Trade Unions and the Labour Party Since 1945* (Detroit, 1960), pp. 28–29, 62, 64.

18. Attlee, *As It Happened*, pp. 253–66; Williams, *A Prime Minister Remembers*, pp. 202–19.

19. Frederick D. Schneider, "The Fabian Society and the British Empire" (unpublished M.A. thesis, Stanford University, 1947), pp. 63ff.

20. F. M. Bourret, *The Gold Coast* (Stanford, Calif., 1952), pp. 165–212.

21. 423 H. C. Deb., cols. 779–90.

22. Williams, *A Prime Minister Remembers*, pp. 175–78; Douglas Aitken, "The Suez Canal in Anglo-Egyptian Relations" (unpublished M.A. thesis, Stanford University, 1955), pp. 36–80.

23. D. R. Shibley, "Ernest Bevin and the Arab League" (unpublished M.A. thesis, Stanford University, 1957), pp. 21–46.

24. Dalton, *The Fateful Years*, pp. 423–27; Dalton, *High Tide and After*, pp. 146–49.

25. Williams, *A Prime Minister Remembers*, pp. 180–201; Shibley, "Ernest Bevin and the Arab League," pp. 80–117; M. A. Fitzsimons, *The Foreign Policy of the British Labour Government, 1945–1951* (Notre Dame, Ind., 1951), pp. 80–83.

26. Williams, *A Prime Minister Remembers*, pp. 153–72.

27. Dalton, *High Tide and After*, pp. 206–9.

28. Williams, *A Prime Minister Remembers*, pp. 95–119.

29. *Ibid.*, pp. 153–59; Fitzsimons, *The Foreign Policy of the British Labour Government*, pp. 30–48, 101–4.

30. Labour party, *Report* (1948), p. 23.

31. Shinwell, *Conflict Without Malice*, pp. 196–223; Fitzsimons, *The Foreign Policy of the British Labour Government*, pp. 98–108.

32. Dalton, *High Tide and After*, pp. 313–36; Fitzsimons, *The Foreign Policy of the British Labour Government*, pp. 107–43.

33. *Ibid.*, pp. 61, 130–36.

34. Williams, *A Prime Minister Remembers*, p. 169.

35. Eugene J. Meehan, *The British Left Wing and Foreign Policy* (New Brunswick, N.J., 1960), pp. 66–171.

36. The author gives a fuller account, "The British General Election of 1950," based on party literature, in the *South Atlantic Quarterly*, L (Oct. 1951), 478–98.

Chapter Fourteen

1. Dalton, *High Tide and After*, pp. 362–74; Shinwell, *Conflict Without Malice*, pp. 224–25.

2. Williams, *A Prime Minister Remembers,* pp. 230–40.

3. *New Statesman and Nation,* Feb. 3, 24, 1951; Meehan, *The British Left Wing and Foreign Policy,* pp. 156–68.

4. Morrison, *Autobiography,* pp. 281–82; Williams, *A Prime Minister Remembers,* pp. 243–55.

5. The author gives a fuller account of this election, based on party materials, newspapers, and periodicals, in the *South Atlantic Quarterly,* LII (Jan. 1953), 29–53.

6. *Manchester Guardian Weekly,* Jan. 11, 1962; *The Times,* Apr. 30, 1962.

7. Labour party, *Report* (1954), pp. 173–74; *ibid.,* "The Nationalized Industries" in *Campaign Notes,* May 17, 1955; Roy Jenkins, *Pursuit of Progress* (London, 1953), pp. 87–90.

8. R. H. S. Crossman in the *New Statesman,* Aug. 14, 1954; Socialist Union, *Twentieth Century Socialism* (Harmondsworth, Middlesex, 1956), pp. 62, 124–25, 146; C. A. R. Crosland, *The Future of Socialism* (London, 1956), pp. 172–73, 474–75.

9. W. A. Robson, "Labour and Local Government" in the *Political Quarterly* (Special Number, Jan.–Mar. 1953), pp. 39–55; Cooperative Union, *Social Ownership and Consumer Problems* (London, 1952).

10. For a brief survey of Labour's postwar attitude toward public ownership, see the author's "The British Labour Party and Nationalization" in the *South Atlantic Quarterly,* LXVIII (Spring 1959), 153–66.

11. Labour party, *Report* (1952), pp. 142–54.

12. *Ibid.* (1954), pp. 92–108.

13. Dalton, *High Tide and After,* pp. 384–93, 408–10; Harrison, *Trade Unions and the Labour Party Since 1945,* pp. 224–32.

14. The author gives a fuller account, "The British General Election of 1955," in the *South Atlantic Quarterly,* LV (July 1956), 289–312.

15. Labour party, *Report* (1955), pp. 63–92; Harrison, *Trade Unions and the Labour Party Since 1945,* pp. 66–67.

16. *Ibid.,* pp. 315–19; Leslie Hunter, *The Road to Brighton Pier* (London, 1959), p. 274.

17. Dalton, *High Tide and After,* pp. 413–23, 444; Morrison, *Autobiography,* pp. 292–94; Hunter, *The Road to Brighton Pier,* pp. 213–24.

18. *Manchester Guardian* pamphlet, *The Record on Suez* (Nov. 1956), pp. 6–16; Morrison, *Autobiography,* p. 328; Harrison, *Trade Unions and the Labour Party Since 1945,* p. 122.

19. *Manchester Guardian,* June 3, 1955.

20. Labour party, *Report* (1957), pp. 128–61; *ibid.* (1958), pp. 167–73; *The Times,* July 18, 29, Oct. 3, 1957.

21. Gaitskell at Blackpool, Labour party, *Report* (1959), p. 107.

22. *Socialist Commentary* (May 1962), pp. 3–5, 10–14; Leon D. Epstein, "British Class Consciousness and the Labour Party" in *The Journal of British Studies,* (May 1962), pp. 136–50.

23. Labour party, *Report* (1959), pp. 83–86, 112–55; *Tribune,* Dec. 5, 1959.

24. Labour party, *Report* (1960), pp. 207–21.

25. Attlee, *The Labour Party in Perspective,* p. 139.

26. Crosland, *The Future of Socialism,* p. 496.

27. Labour party, *Report* (1957), pp. 179–83.

28. *Ibid.* (1958), pp. 191–224.

29. *Ibid.* (1960), pp. 13–16, 176–202.

30. Section 3(c).

31. Labour party, *Report* (1920), pp. 147–53.

32. Attlee, *The Labour Party in Perspective,* p. 93.

33. R. T. McKenzie, *British Political Parties* (London, 1955), pp. 385–411, 452–56.

34. Labour party, *Report* (1961), pp. 7–8, 178–94.

35. E.g., Labour party, *Towards Equality* (London, 1956).

36. E.g., *The Times,* March 4, 9, 10, 19, 1964; Harold S. Wilson, "The Relevance of British Social Democracy," in *Britannica Book of the Year, 1964* (Chicago, 1964), pp. 36–40.

37. *Ibid.,* pp. 16–43.

Bibliographical Note

Bibliographical Note

This book, especially for the period since 1914, is based primarily upon a collection of British labor materials made over a period of years and deposited in the Hoover Institution on War, Revolution, and Peace at Stanford University, California. The collection includes the annual *Reports* of the Labour party, the Independent Labour party, the Trades Union Congress, and the Cooperative Congress, together with special policy reports, pamphlets, leaflets, and election materials. It contains files or long runs of a number of newspapers and periodicals, including the *Clarion,* the *Labour Leader, Forward,* the *Bradford Pioneer,* the *Herald,* the *Call,* the *New Leader,* the *New Statesman,* the *New Age,* the *Tribune,* and the *Socialist Review.* This list, including the *Herald* under George Lansbury until 1922, exemplifies the great activity of the socialist left in the British labor movement.

For official views the researcher has to rely more upon speeches given by recognized leaders at party and trade-union conferences and in Parliament and upon authorized pamphlets and pronouncements. In 1922 the T.U.C. general council and the Labour party executive took over the ownership of the *Herald,* though its editor was often in dissent from majority views; after 1929 its political policy was that of the Labour party conference and its industrial policy that of the T.U.C.

The Hoover Institution collection includes some trade-union journals and a considerable body of Communist party materials. For this study, *The Times,* the *Manchester Guardian,* the *Observer,* the *Spectator,* the *Nation,* and the *Economist* were consulted. For the *Parliamentary Debates* all references are to the Fifth Series.

Unpublished theses of graduate students that have been found useful are cited in the footnotes, as are relevant articles by the author previously published in the *American Historical Review,* the *Journal of Modern History,* the *Pacific Historical Review,* and the *South Atlantic Quarterly.*

This select bibliography lists only the works of greater significance for the history of the Labour party. Others will be found in the appropriate foot-notes. Unless otherwise noted, the place of publication is London.

Among the more valuable memoirs and autobiographies are those of Bea-trice Webb, *Our Partnership,* edited by Barbara Drake and Margaret I. Cole (New York, 1948), and *Beatrice Webb's Diaries, 1912–1924* (1952), and *1924–1932* (1956), edited by M. I. Cole; Philip Snowden, *An Autobiography,* 2 vols. (1934); and the three volumes by Hugh Dalton, *Call Back Yesterday: Memoirs, 1887–1931* (1953), *The Fateful Years: Memoirs, 1931–1945* (1957), and *High Tide and After: Memoirs, 1945–1960* (1962), which provide a sur-vey of Labour politics over a period of four decades as seen by a leading par-ticipant. C. R. Attlee's *As It Happened* (New York, 1954) is disappointing, but Francis Williams, *A Prime Minister Remembers* (1961), reveals some of the history of the third Labour government.

Other useful volumes are H. M. Hyndman, *The Record of an Adventur-ous Life* (New York, 1911); G. N. Barnes, *From Workshop to War Cabinet* (New York, 1924); R. B. Haldane, *An Autobiography* (1929); David Kirk-wood, *My Life of Revolt* (1935); George Lansbury, *My Life* (1928); Lord Snell, *Men, Movements, and Myself* (1936); Josiah C. Wedgwood, *Memoirs of a Fighting Life* (1940); F. W. Pethick-Lawrence, *Fate Has Been Kind* (1943); Margaret Bondfield, *A Life's Work* (1948); Mary Agnes Hamilton, *Remembering My Good Friends* (1944); Fenner Brockway, *Inside the Left* (1942); Emanuel Shinwell, *Conflict Without Malice* (1955); and Lord Morri-son of Lambeth, *Herbert Morrison: An Autobiography* (1960). The memoirs of J. H. Thomas, *My Life Story* (1937), and J. R. Clynes, *Memoirs,* 2 vols. (1937), contain less than one would expect from such key figures.

Good biographies are those by William Stewart, *J. Keir Hardie* (1921); Mary Agnes Hamilton, *Arthur Henderson* (1938); Lord Elton, *The Life of James Ramsay MacDonald, 1866–1919* (1939); Fenner Brockway, *Socialism over Sixty Years: The Life of Jowett of Bradford* (1946); Raymond Postgate, *The Life of George Lansbury* (1951); and Alan Bullock, *The Life and Times of Ernest Bevin,* Vol. I (1960). A good study of Arthur Henderson as Foreign Secretary can be found in Henry R. Winkler's "Arthur Henderson" in Gor-don A. Craig and Felix Gilbert, Eds., *The Diplomats, 1919–1939* (Princeton, 1953). Michael Foot, *Aneurin Bevan, a Biography,* Vol. I: 1897–1945 (1962), is an account by a sympathetic left-winger.

Of the general works on the Labour party, the two volumes of the Fabian and guild socialist G. D. H. Cole, *British Working Class Politics, 1832–1914* (1941) and *A History of the Labour Party from 1914* (1948), still present the most complete survey of the subject down to the Attlee government. Henry Pelling's *A Short History of the Labour Party* (1961) is brief. For the origins and early years there are excellent studies: Henry Pelling, *The Origins of the Labour Party, 1880–1900* (1954); Frank Bealey and Henry Pelling, *La-bour and Politics, 1900–1906* (1958); and Philip P. Poirier, *The Advent of the Labour Party* (1958).

Other general accounts are Francis Williams, *Fifty Years March* (1949);

J. H. Stewart Reid, *The Origins of the British Labour Party* (Minneapolis, 1955); Godfrey Elton, *'England Arise!' A Study of the Pioneering Days of the Labour Movement* (1931); Max Beer, *A History of British Socialism,* Vol. II (1921); and Herbert Tracey, Ed., *The Book of the Labour Party,* 3 vols. (1925). Charles Loch Mowat's *Britain Between the Wars* (Chicago, 1955) also contains much material on the Labour party.

Among the more specialized studies are *The History of the Fabian Society* (1916) by Edward R. Pease, long its secretary, and Margaret I. Cole, *The Story of Fabian Socialism* (1961). Paul U. Kellogg's and Arthur Gleason's *British Labor and the War* (New York, 1919) is an account by two American observers. Richard Lyman's *First Labour Government, 1924* (1957) is an excellent study. Stephen R. Graubard, *British Labour and the Russian Revolution, 1917–1924* (Cambridge, Mass., 1956) deals with both the foreign policy of Labour and the internal struggle with the Communist party.

R. Bassett's *Nineteen Thirty-One: Political Crisis* (1958) is strongly pro-MacDonald. Francis Williams' *Socialist Britain* (New York, 1949) and Ernest Watkins' *The Cautious Revolution* (1951) are contemporary accounts of the Attlee government. Leslie Hunter's *The Road to Brighton Pier* (1959) deals with the dissensions of the fifties. A. A. Rogow's *The Labour Government and British Industry* (Oxford, 1955) and Herbert E. Weiner's *British Labour and Public Ownership* (Washington, D.C., 1960) are good studies of nationalization.

Foreign policy is discussed in William P. Maddox, *Foreign Relations in British Labour Politics* (Cambridge, Mass., 1934); M. A. Fitzsimons, *The Foreign Policy of the British Labour Government, 1945–1951* (Notre Dame, Ind., 1951); Elaine Windrich, *British Labour's Foreign Policy* (Stanford, Calif., 1952); and Eugene J. Meehan, *The British Left and Foreign Policy* (New Brunswick, N.J., 1960).

Ralph Miliband, *Parliamentary Socialism, A Study in the Politics of Labour* (1961), attacks the revisionist leadership as being concerned with humanizing a capitalist society rather than with creating a socialist one. Catharine Ann Cline, *Recruits to Labour, The British Labour Party, 1914–1931* (Syracuse, N.Y., 1963), examines the impact of the recruits from Liberalism upon Labour's development.

The best analytical study of the Labour party is that of R. T. McKenzie, *British Political Parties* (1955). Earlier studies were those of Dean E. McHenry, *His Majesty's Opposition, 1931–1938* (Berkeley, Calif., 1940), and C. R. Attlee, *The Labour Party in Perspective* (1937).

Trade union-Labour party relations are discussed in Sidney and Beatrice Webb, *The History of Trade Unionism, 1666–1920* (1920 ed.); N. Barou, *British Trade Unions* (1947); V. L. Allen, *Trade Unions and the Government* (1960). An especially good account is given in Martin Harrison, *Trade Unions and the Labour Party Since 1945* (Detroit, 1960).

Index